Law and Economics of International
Telecommunications

Under the Auspices of the
Max Planck Institute for Foreign and
International Private Law
edited by Prof. Ernst-Joachim Mestmäcker

Volume 8

Verena A.-M. Wiedemann

Law of International Telecommunications in the United Kingdom

Regulation of Electronic Media

Nomos Verlagsgesellschaft
Baden-Baden

CIP-Titelaufnahme der Deutschen Bibliothek

Wiedemann, Verena A.-M.:
Law of International Telecommunications in the United Kingdom: Regulation of
Electronic Media / Verena A.-M. Wiedemann. – 1. Aufl. – Baden-Baden: Nomos
Verl.-Ges., 1989
(Law and Economics of International Telecommunications; Vol. 8)
ISBN 3-7890-1649-7
NE: GT

1. Auflage 1989
© Nomos Verlagsgesellschaft, Baden-Baden 1989. Printed in Germany. Alle
Rechte, auch die des Nachdrucks von Auszügen, der photomechanischen Wieder-
gabe und der Übersetzung vorbehalten.

For my parents

Editor's Preface

This book on the »Law of International Telecommunications in the United Kingdom: Regulation of Electronic Media« is part of an ongoing research project on the international communications system undertaken at the Max Planck Institute for Foreign and International Private Law in Hamburg. Like similar reports on other countries, this report is based upon questionnaires prepared at the Institute and reproduced at the end of the volume. In contrast to other reports in this series, the present study takes up audiovisual media and their interrelation with telephone services and data processing. To this extent, only Part 3 of the questionnaire is relevant here. The questionnaires are identical for all countries in order to facilitate comparative evaluations of the national reports. They serve as guidelines without, however, interfering with the authors' individual judgment in adapting their presentation to the special national situation. The project will include comparative analysis of key problem areas and the examination of the role of international organizations, the task of which is the facilitation of international communications.

Dr. *Verena A.-M. Wiedemann* has been a research associate at the Max Planck Institute since 1985. Following completion of her legal studies and practical training in Hamburg in 1983, she spent one year at the University of California, Berkeley, receiving her Master of Laws degree in 1984. In February 1988, Dr. Wiedemann was awarded a Ph.D. in Law from the University of Hamburg.

We gratefully acknowledge a grant from the Volkswagen Foundation, which made this Report possible. We also extend thanks to Paul Aliferis, J. D., for his editorial assistance.

Hamburg, September 1988

Ernst-Joachim Mestmäcker

Preface

The report on the Regulation of Electronic Media in the United Kingdom is set in the greater framework of the rapid and fundamental developments in international telecommunications, both in terms of new technologies and with regard to innovative legal reforms that attempt to meet these challenges. The report thus deals with those legal rules that today determine the structure of the British media and that have arisen from the traditions and history of British society and English law. However, international law, in responding to the growing significance and interdependence of international media markets, has increasingly tended to have an impact on the British media law system. This international legal and economic framework is paving the way for the future of British broadcasting. The Council of Europe's contemplated convention on transborder broadcasting serves as only one example. For these reasons, the study has attempted to treat equally the international legal regime, to the extent of its relevance for the British regulations. Part I deals with the principle of freedom of information as recognized by English law and as providing the basis for the law on the electronic media. Part II addresses the traditional British public-service broadcasting system and the fundamental changes it is presently facing as a result of new technologies and new legal concepts. Part III looks at the legal framework dealing with video and satellite broadcasting. Part IV analyses the legal problems that result from the growing convergence of conduit and content in cable television. Part V examines the impact of competition and antitrust laws, including EC law. The study concludes with a look at the international legal order and its influences on British technical standard setting, transborder broadcasting and programme exchange.

The study was accepted by the University of Hamburg, Faculty of Law, as my doctoral thesis. Although the report was completed in the summer of 1987, I have attempted to update it as far as possible.

I wish to express my deep gratitude to my »Doktorvater,« Prof. Ernst-Joachim Mestmäcker, for entrusting me with this part of the Max Planck Institute's project. His support and advice were invaluable to me in preparing this study as a staff member of the Max Planck Institute.

I would also like to thank a number of people in Great Britain who were so generous with their time in relating their experiences with the British media during two extended research stays of mine in London. For their freely provided views and suggestions, I am most indebted to Kenneth W. Blyth, Jon Davey, Chris Daubney, Tim Heath, Elisabeth Hiester, Anthony Jennings, Prof. Ian M. Kennedy, Ken R. Penry, N.C. Sanderson, Prof. Lewis Schnurr, David Sibbick, Ivor Stolliday, Michael Storey, S.R. Temple, Jane Vizard, A.C. Warlow, and David Williams.

Finally, I would like to thank Ingeborg Stahl at the Max Planck Institute for her enormous efforts in preparing the manuscript and Paul Aliferis for his editorial help and assistance.

Hamburg, August 1988   Verena A.-M. Wiedemann

Table of Contents

12

ABBREVIATIONS

A.C.	Law Reports. Appeal Cases, House of Lords
All E.R.	All England Law Reports
ASA	Advertising Standards Authority
BABT	British Approvals Board for Telecommunications
BACT	Advisory Committee on Telecommunications for Small Businesses
BBC	British Broadcasting Corporation
BBFC	British Board of Film Classification
BCC	Broadcasting Complaints Commission
BCS	British Cable Services (U.K. company)
BEC	British Electrotechnical Committee
BSB	British Satellite Broadcasting (U.K. company)
BSC	Broadcasting Standards Council
BSI	British Standards Institution
BT	British Telecom (U.K. company)
Bus.L.Rev.	Business Law Review
c.	chapter
CCIR	International Radio Consultative Committee
CCITT	International Consultative Committee on Telegraph and Telephone
CCTV	China Central Television
CEN	European Committee for Standardization
CENELEC	European Committee for Electrotechnical Standardization
CEPT	Conference of European Posts and Telecommunications Administrations
C.I.A.	U.S. Central Intelligence Agency
C.J.	Chief Justice
C.M.L.R.	Common Market Law Reports
Cmnd.	Command
COCOM	Coordinating Committee for Export to Communist Area(s)
Coll. Dec.	Council of Europe, European Commission of Human Rights: Collection of Decisions
Com.	Commission
CUG	closed user group
DBS	direct broadcasting by satellite
Dec.Ad.Com.Ap.	Decision of the European Commission of Human Rights as to the Admissability of Application
DIEL	Advisory Committee on Telecommunciations for Disabled and Elderly People
D–Notice	Defence Notice
DR	Council of Europe, European Commission of Human Rights: Decisions and Reports
DTI	Department of Trade and Industry
EBU	European Broadcasting Union
EC	European Community
ECLR	European Competition Law Review
ECS	European Communication Satellite
ed.	editor
EEC	European Economic Community
e.g.	for example
E.G.	Employment Gazette
E.H.R.R.	European Human Rights Reports

Eliz. 2	Queen Elizabeth II
ELT	East London Telecommunications (U.K. company)
ESA	European Space Agency
et al.	and others
et seq.	and sequence
EUCJ	European Court of Justice
EUCT	European Court of Human Rights
EUCM	European Commission of Human Rights
Eur.GrundRZ	Europäische Grundrechte Zeitschrift
EUTELSAT	European Telecommunications Satellite Organization
Fin.	Financial
FM	frequency modulation
FPO	Frequency Planning Organization
F.S.R.	Fleet Street Patent Law Reports
FSS	fixed service satellites
GATT	General Agreement on Tariffs and Trade
Geo. 6	King George VI
GRUR/Int.	Gewerblicher Rechtsschutz und Urheberrecht, Internationaler Teil (law journal)
H.C.	House of Commons
HDTV	high definition television
H.L.	House of Lords
HVC	Home Video Channel
IBA	Independent Broadcasting Authority
ICPR	International Covenant on Civil and Political Rights
i.e.	that means
ILR	Independent Local Radio
Inc.	Incorporated
INTELSAT	International Telecommunications Satellite Consortium
IRA	Irish Republican Army
IRLR	Industrial Relations Law Journal
ISDN	integrated services digital network
ISO	International Organization for Standardization
ITAP	Information Technology Advisory Panel
ITCA	Independent Companies Trade Association
ITN	Independent Television News (U.K. company)
ITU	International Telecommunications Union
ITV	Independent Television
J(J).	Judge(s)
J. Media L. & Prac.	Journal of Media Law & Practice
J.P.	Justice of the Peace Reports
J. World Trade L.	Journal of World Trade Law
Judg. Dec.	Council of Europe, European Court of Human Rights: Judgements and Decisions
K.B.	Law Reports, King's Bench Division
L.J.	Lord Justice, i.e. judge of the Court of Appeal, England and Wales
L.N.T.S.	League of Nations Treaty Series
LS Gaz.	Law Society's Gazette
Ltd.	Limited
LWT	London Weekend Television (U.K. company)
MAC	multiplexed analogue components
MATV	master antenna television system
MGM	Metro Goldwyn Mayer (U.S. company)
MMC	Monopolies and Mergers Commission
MMDS	multi-microwave distribution system

16

M.R.	Master of the Rolls, England and Wales
n.	note
N.L.J.	New Law Journal
No.	number
NJW	Neue Juristische Wochenschrift
OECD	Organization for Economic Cooperation and Development
OFT	Office of Fair Trading
OFTEL	Office of Telecommunications
O.J.	Official Journal
p(p).	page(s)
para(s).	paragraph(s)
PATAC	Posts and Telecommunications Advisory Committee
PBS	Public Broadcasting System (U.S.)
PTO	public telecommunications operator
PTT	Post, Telephone and Telegraph Administration
Pub. Court A	Publications of the European Court of Human Rights, Series A: Judgements and Decisions
Pub. Court B	Publications of the European Court of Human Rights, Series B: Pleadings, Oral Arguments and Documents
Q.B.	Law Reports, Queen's Bench Division
R.	Regina
RabelsZ	Rabels Zeitschrift
RDS	Radio Data System
RRD	Radio Regulatory Division
S 4 C	Welsh Fourth Channel
S.C.	Session Cases, Court of Session, Scotland
SES	Société Européen des Satellites (Luxembourg company)
S.I.	statutory instrument
S.J.	Solicitor's Journal
SMATV	satellite master antenna television
TAB	tree-and-branch system
T.S.	Treaty Series
tv	television
TV-am	ITV breakfast-time television (U.K. company)
TVRO	television receive-only earth station
UA	United Artists (U.S. company)
UDHR	Universal Declaration on Human Rights
UIR	Union International de Radiodiffusion
U.K.	United Kingdom
UN	United Nations
UNISAT	United Satellites Ltd. (U.K. company)
UNTS	United Nations Treaty Series
U.S.A.	United States of America
v.	versus
VANS	value added network services
V–C	Vice Chancellor
VCR	video cassette recorder
VHF	very high frequency
Vol.	Volume
WARC-BS	World Administrative Radio Conference on Broadcasting Satellites
WLR	Weekly Law Reports
YB	Yearbook

Introduction

The legal order governing the British media system had for many decades remained stable and appeared almost to be unchangeable and unchallengeable. The structure of the broadcasting system reflected the common consensus of society about the role of the public broadcasting authorities in administering as trustees of the public interest the limited resource of the radio spectrum. The task of the public broadcasting organizations was identified as a duty to educate, inform and entertain the British public in conformity with the ethical and political value system of a democratic society.

Under conditions of spectrum scarcity, the right of freedom of expression as recognized in the contexts of individual speech and of the press could not extend to the broadcast media. The reflection of the plurality of public opinion in radio and television had to be safeguarded by detailed programme-content requirements and by the representation of the various political, religious and cultural social groups in internal bodies of the broadcasting organizations. With the advent of the new media – cable and satellite television – new horizons for public communications were opened: they multiplied the number of technical facilities available for the communication of ideas and opinions to the public by means of electronic media.

In the early 1980s, the United Kingdom opened the way for the general introduction of the new media with the passage of necessary legislation. These developments resulted in strong repercussions for the traditional broadcasting structure. The public-service concept of broadcasting was just as affected by the factual and legal changes as was the role of the broadcasting organizations themselves. They began increasingly to experiment with data transmission and similar services not directly related to their traditional tasks. At the same time established network providers, who thus far had been solely engaged in the technical operation of communication systems, entered the programme-supply side and with it the broadcasting domain. Their activities greatly contributed to the growing tendencies toward a convergence of conduit and content in telecommunications.

Yet the deep-rooted changes forecast by the new media have only just begun noticeably to affect the British media structure. Many problems arising from the introduction of the electronic media still need to be properly identified and addressed. The restructuring of the British audiovisual media system that took place in the early 1980s does not represent the end, but instead marks only the beginning, of the new broadcasting era.

Since explicit recognition of freedom of communication is not found in any English legal statute, article 10 of the European Convention on Human Rights, which guarantees freedom of information, has gained particular significance for the regulation of communications in the United Kingdom. In certain instances, the U.K. government was obliged to change a statutory- or common-law rule in order to make it consistent with the standard of freedom of information as applied by the European Court of Human Rights; in other cases, the English courts have fallen back on article 10 of the Convention for an interpretation of an English rule of law.

Historically, most case law on freedom of information has been connected with issues of freedom of speech and freedom of the press, because these were the traditional domains of individual communication. This case law laid the foundation for a definition of freedom of information, which was held to include both communication by traditional methods of speech and print and communication by electromagnatic waves. During this period, however, the broadcasting sector was governed by a totally different legal regime, under which it was subjected to regulatory control and a public-service obligation. Gradually, though, the established principles defining the scope of freedom of speech and the press began as well to gain significance in the context of broadcasting. This is due to the diminishing technical and legal distinctions between the characteristics of the broadcasting media and those of other forms of public communication resulting from the multiplication of the methods of conveying messages to the public via electromagnetic means.

Because of this inseparable interrelation between freedom of speech and the press and freedom of broadcasting, the first chapter will treat these legal principles as one complex in order to attempt to define the status of the present freedoms relating to the British information order. It will also focus on the British legal regime governing freedom of information; this forms the basis of the individual's right to participate in the public exchange of opinions independent of the technical means of communication used. The changing structure of the public broadcasting system brought about by the challenge of the new media will be the subject of the second chapter, to be followed by a discussion of the concepts and regulatory mechanisms that apply to the new media. The third chapter will focus on the convergence in cable television of conduit and content, i.e., cable television brought about the transition from network providers to information providers and vice versa. Individual participation in the rapidly growing electronic media market to a great extent depends on market structures; their regulation by the competition and antitrust laws, to be analyzed in the fourth chapter, determines the relationship between the various media markets and the private power over public opinion that can be gained in individual cases. National media markets are increasingly shaped as well by the international legal order, which regulates such diverse subjects as technical standards and broadcast-content requirements. The impact of international law on the British media system will be the subject of the final chapter.

I. *General Framework of the British Media: The Principle of Freedom of Information*

A. *Freedom of Information Under English and International Law*

Freedom of information is one of the key elements in the free and dignified development of the human personality. Free communication between individuals means the uninhibited exchange of ideas, facts and opinions. Such communication is the prerequisite for self-determination and has the quality of a fundamental human right. At the same time, freedom of expression is the foundation of a free and democratic society. For these reasons, every state is obliged to respect this principle and may not unduly encroach on it through any legislative, administrative or judicial act. In order to safeguard fundamental human rights, many countries have embodied them in a written constitution that guarantees their supremacy over any governmental act. The United Kingdom[1] has never had such a constitutional document. The following sections will therefore look at the way English law[2] safeguards these freedoms absent any formal bill of rights.

1. *Civil Liberties in the Absence of a Constitution*

In England, there exist a number of constitutional documents, such as the Magna Carta (1215) and the Bill of Rights, signed in 1689. But the constitutional law, which broadly deals with the institutions of government,

---

1 The United Kingdom consists of Great Britain and Northern Ireland. Great Britain in turn is composed of England, Scotland and Wales.

2 The whole treatise will focus on English law, i.e., the law of England as opposed to the laws of Wales, Scotland, Northern Ireland, the Channel Islands and the Isle of Man. For historical reasons the laws of England and Wales are mostly identical. But in particular the common laws of England, Scotland and Northern Ireland differ considerably. In the Treaty of Union with England, ratified by both the English and the Scottish Parliaments in 1707, Scotland retained its own legal system (subject to the modification that legislative authority was transferred to some extent to the new Parliament of Great Britain at Westminster). Northern Ireland, on the other hand, unlike England, Scotland and Wales, has a written constitution that includes a reference to human rights albeit restricted to freedom of religion and the freedom to hold political opinions (*see* Northern Ireland Constitution Act 1973, secs. 17-23 (c.36)). Finally, the Isle of Man and the Channel Islands are separate dependencies of the British Crown and have retained their own unique bodies of law. *See, e.g.,* D.C.M. YARDLEY, INTRODUCTION TO BRITISH CONSTITUTIONAL LAW 80-87 (6th ed. 1984).

23

i.e., the monarchy, the legislature, the executive and the judiciary, was never entirely written down. The Bill of Rights of 1689, which sets the principle rights gained by Parliament and the nation from the monarchy, contains no human-rights charter. In England, civil rights are instead part of the ordinary law of the land.

While civil rights for the most part are not positively prescribed by law,[3] it is a fundamental principle of English law that they are protected, to the extent that they are not restricted by any rule of law. Such restrictions may stem from parliamentary enactments or judge-made law. Acts of Parliament play a particularly important role in the context of civil rights because of the overriding principle of parliamentary sovereignty. According to this principle, Parliament has the authority to abridge at its discretion any individual right, no matter how fundamental it may be, provided that it passes a formal statute.[4] A court of law in Great Britain cannot then declare such an ordinary statute invalid by testing it against any human-rights principle. Only Parliament itself can reinstate the status quo ante. Equally important as the principle of sovereignty of Parliament, however, is the deep-rooted respect for civil rights evidenced in the long history of Parliament. For this reason the calls for the passage of a formal bill of rights – which would contain an explicit human-rights charter and at the same time would curtail Parliament's sovereign power to abridge those freedoms – have often been rejected on the ground that such a measure would be unnecessary: Human rights in the United Kingdom are thought to be already properly safeguarded by the consciousness and sensitivity of the members of Parliament relating to the inviolability of the essence of civil rights, the role of tradition, custom and usage, and last an alert sense for political expediency.

The courts have traditionally played an important role in the protection of individual human rights in England. While they cannot declare any parliamentary enactment void, they have often interpreted acts of Parliament in the most restrictive way possible so as to limit the encroaching effect of these statutes on individual freedoms.[5] Still, the political struggle for an

---

3 An exception are the Habeas Corpus Acts of 1679 and 1816.

4 It may be interesting to note in this context that the above-mentioned differences (*see supra* note 2) in the laws of England and Scotland may be substantial. In MacCormick v. Lord Advocate, 1953 S.C. 396, the Lord President Cooper argued that in contrast to English law, Scottish constitutional law recognized no principle of unlimited sovereignty of Parliament.

5 Lord Wilberforce, Die bürgerlichen Grundrechte des Einzelnen, Speech held before the Juristische Studiengesellschaft in Karlsruhe, Apr. 4, 1966, Juristische Studiengesellschaft Karlsruhe, Schriftenreihe No. 74 (1966) 9.

enactment of a formal bill of rights has been going on for a fairly long time and has only recently received new impulses.[6] Such a bill of rights, so the arguments go, would give a firm backing to civil rights and protect them against any involuntary or purposeful infringements.[7] If such a bill of rights were passed by a qualified majority in both Houses of Parliament, it could only be altered by the same majority. While this legislative method would preserve parliamentary sovereignty, it would establish a control of and restriction on ordinary legislation passed by simple majorities and geared to the satisfaction of group interests and expediencies of the day; it would in addition enable courts to review any doubtful administrative actions.[8] But until and unless the endeavours to pass a bill of rights succeed, freedom of expression in England can only be defined in a negative way: Citizens are free to express any views so long as they contravene no law restricting the expression of ideas and opinions. In general, then, the existing scope and contents of civil rights in the United Kingdom is what remains of them once all the rules of law restricting them have been subtracted.[9]

Because no remedy against an unduly encroaching rule of law is available in an English court, the human-rights guarantees and procedural mechanisms of the European Convention on Human Rights[10] have become increasingly important for British subjects trying to remedy an injustice suffered. The

---

6 For an overview of the public debate, see A. DRZEMCZEWSKI, EUROPEAN HUMAN RIGHTS CONVENTION IN DOMESTIC LAW 186 and n. 66 (1983). *See also* B. SCHMID, RANG UND GELTUNG DER EUROPÄISCHEN KONVENTION ZUM SCHUTZE DER MENSCHENRECHTE UND GRUNDFREIHEITEN VOM 3. NOVEMBER 1950 IN DEN VERTRAGSSTAATEN 56-57 (1984); B. SIGEL, ÜBER DIE GRUNDRECHTE, INSBESONDERE DIE PRESSEFREIHEIT, IN DER SCHWEIZ UND IN GROSSBRITANNIEN, ZÜRICHER STUDIEN ZUM ÖFFENTLICHEN RECHT 106-109 (1981). Even the United Nations Human Rights Committee pressed the British government to enact a bill of rights. *See* 135 NEW LAW JOURNAL 841 (1985). *See also* the latest public campaign for a bill of rights following the »Spycatcher« episode, The Times, Sept. 14, 1987.

7 von Simson, *Towards a Bill of Rights in Great Britain*, in GRUNDRECHTSSCHUTZ IM NATIONALEN UND INTERNATIONALEN RECHT, WERNER VON SIMSON ZUM 75. GEBURTSTAG 177, 186 (J. Schwarze and W. Graf Vitzthum ed. 1983). M. SUPPERSTONE, BROWNLIE'S LAW OF PUBLIC ORDER AND NATIONAL SECURITY 338 (2nd ed. 1981).

8 *See* von Simson, *supra* note 7, at 183.

9 *See, e.g.* P. O'HIGGINS, CASES AND MATERIALS ON CIVIL LIBERTIES 149-338 (1980); B. SIGEL, *supra* note 6, at 96-198, and in particular 104-106.

10 Convention for the Protection of Human Rights and Fundamental Freedoms, *signed* in Rome, Nov. 4, 1950, *ratified by* the United Kingdom Mar. 8, 1951, U.K.T.S. 71/1953, Cmnd. 8969. *See also* Protocol to the Convention for the Protection of Human Rights and Fundamental Freedoms, *signed* in Paris, Mar. 20, 1952, *ratified by* the United Kingdom Nov. 3, 1952, U.K.T.S. 46/1954, Cmnd. 9221; Second Protocol *signed* in Strasbourg, May 6, 1963, U.K.T.S. 104/1970, Cmnd. 4551; Third Protocol, *signed* in 1983, U.K.T.S. 106/1970, Cmnd. 4552.

role of the Convention in the context of freedom of information in the United Kingdom thus deserves closer scrutiny.

2. *The Impact of Article 10 of the European Human Rights Convention on Freedom of Information in the United Kingdom*

The United Kingdom was one of the original signatories to the European Human Rights Convention (EUHR). Article 10(1) grants everyone the »right to freedom of expression.« The Convention was concluded under the auspices of the Council of Europe and represented the first regional attempt to give effect to the principles embodied in the Universal Declaration on Human Rights (UDHR) adopted by the United Nations (UN) in 1948. Article 19 of the UDHR had already stated that the right to freedom of opinion and expression includes the »freedom to hold opinions without interference and to seek, receive and impart information and ideas through any media and regardless of frontiers.«[11]

Article 10(1) of the EUHR in turn provides that the right to freedom of expression »shall include freedom to hold opinions and to receive and impart information and ideas without interference by public authority and regardless of frontiers.«[12] The particular significance of the EUHR stems from its enforcement mechanism. It serves to transform otherwise abstract rules of law into justiciable contexts. The Convention establishes a Commission of Human Rights (EUCM) and a Court of Human Rights (EUCT) (article 19). Under article 24, state parties may refer to the Commission any alleged breach of the provisions of the Convention. More importantly, individuals may petition the EUCM directly, claiming to be the victim of a human-rights violation by a state party, if they have exhausted all domestic legal remedies. This procedural right of individuals presupposes that the country accused of the breach has recognized the Commission's com-

---

11 While at the time of its adoption the Universal Declaration on Human Rights (UDHR) was not intended to create legally binding obligations for the member states of the United Nations (UN), according to some legal writers its provisions have by now become customary international law. At the least, they have become binding on UN member states through explicit acceptance and reference. *See* P. SIEGHART, THE INTERNATIONAL LAW OF HUMAN RIGHTS para. 6.2.1 (1983).

12 Article 19 of the International Covenant on Civil and Political Rights (ICPR) contains a similar provision. The ICPR was adopted by the UN General Assembly in 1966, and came into force on Mar. 23, 1976. *Ratified by* the United Kingdom May 20, 1976, U.K.T.S. 6/1977, Cmnd. 6702. The United Kingdom did not become a party to the Optional Protocol, adopted by the UN General Assembly on Dec. 16, 1966, *entered into force* Mar. 23, 1976, U.K.T.S. 6/1977, Cmnd. 6702. The Optional Protocol allows individuals to petition the UN Human Rights Committee alleging breaches of the Covenant.

26

petence to receive such petitions (article 25(1)). After some hesitation, the United Kingdom in 1966 accepted both the competence of the Commission and the compulsory jurisdiction of the Court under article 46 of the Convention.[13] For British subjects, this procedural right creates the unique opportunity ultimately to bring a violation of their fundamental rights as embodied in the EUHR personally before a court of law. The EUCT is authorized to declare that a particular rule of British law contravenes the EUHR. Since the Convention itself has no direct legal effect in the United Kingdom, British courts are hindered in themselves applying its provisions.[14] The situation is further complicated by the fact that a finding by the EUCT, according to which a particular act violated the EUHR, is not directly enforceable in the United Kingdom. Such a holding creates an obligation for the U.K. government under international law to change the objectionable law and to remedy the complainant's grievance (article 53 EUHR). But as long as Parliament has taken no actions to this effect, British courts are prevented from applying the EUCT's holding in similar cases. This dilemma faced by the courts is well illustrated in Lord Scarman's dictum in *Attorney General v. BBC*:

> [N]either the Convention nor the European Court's decision in *The Sunday Times* case is part of our law. This House's decision, even though the European Court has held the rule it declares to be an infringement of the Convention, is the law. Our courts must continue to look not to the European Court's decision reported as *The Sunday Times v. United Kingdom*, (1979) 2 E.H.R.R. 245, but to the House of Lord's decision reported in *Attorney-General v. Times Newspapers Ltd.* [1974] A.C. 273 for the rule of English law. Yet there is a presumption, albeit rebuttable, that our municipal law will be consistent with our international obligations...[15]

The last sentence of the foregoing quote points to the method employed by the courts in taking account of the human-rights guarantees of the Convention. While acknowledging the overriding authority of acts of Parliament and judicial precedent, they have traditionally applied the rule that any legislative or common-law rule should be interpreted in a manner as to avoid inconsisten-

---

13 The last renewal of both recognitions was announced by the British government on Oct. 24, 1985 for a period of five years beginning in January 1986. *See* 129 S.I. 758 (1985).

14 In the United Kingdom, (ratified) international treaties do not form part of the law of the land unless they have been transformed into domestic law by an act of Parliament. *See* M. ROŠ, DIE UNMITTELBARE ANWENDBARKEIT DER EUROPÄISCHEN MENSCHENRECHTSKONVENTION. EIN BEITRAG ZUR LEHRE DER SELF-EXECUTING TREATIES (38 Schweizer Studien zum internationalen Recht) 66-67 and n. 5 (1984).

15 Attorney General v. BBC, [1980] 3 W.L.R. 109, 130. *See also, e.g.*, R. v. Home Secretary, ex parte Bhajan Singh, 1976 Q.B. 198.

cies with the United Kingdom's international treaty obligations.[16] In *Gleaves v. Deakin*,[17] for example, Lord Diplock explained the demands on domestic legislation imposed by article 10(2) of the Convention in the context of the criminal offence of defamatory libel. Stating that the English law in this respect was difficult to reconcile with the EUHR's provisions on freedom of expression, he suggested that the Attorney General adopt a new approach regarding prosecutions for criminal libel in order to »avoid the risk of our failure to comply with our international obligations under the European Convention.«[18]

On occasion, the British government has in the past voluntarily agreed to change internal laws so as to make them consistent with the provisions of the EUHR if a formal complaint by an individual had been lodged to the EUCM and the Commission had pressed for a settlement of the case.[19] If such a settlement fails and the Commission refers the case to the Court, even more time will pass until the complainant, who has already spent the time and money to fight his case through all instances of the domestic courts, eventually obtains justice. In the renowned *Sunday Times* case,[20] in which the newspaper had claimed that the English contempt of court law contravened article 10 of the EUHR, it took nine years from the time the conflict had first arisen until Parliament, complying with the judgment of the EUCT, changed the law by passing the Contempt of Court Act 1981.[21] This arduous and costly way to achieve the recognition of rights guaranteed under the Convention may cause numerous plaintiffs to refrain from appealing their cases to the EUCM at all.

In order to solve the problems stemming from the unenforceability of the EUHR in the United Kingdom, a private member introduced a bill in the House of Commons, demanding that the Convention be formally incorporated into British law.[22] The declared aim of the initiative was to ensure swifter jus-

---

16 *See* K. HOLLOWAY, MODERN TRENDS IN TREATY LAW 288-94 (1967); Duffy, *English Law and the European Convention on Human Rights*, 29 INT. & COMP. L.Q. 585-99 (1980); A. DRZEMCZEWSKI, *supra* note 6, at 314-22; B. SCHMID, *supra* note 6, at 52-56.

17 [1979] 2 All E.R. 497.

18 *Id.* at 498-99. *See also* R. v. Lemon, [1979] 1 All E.R. 898, 927 (per Lord Scarman justifying the Court's reasoning by referring to articles 9 and 10 of the Convention).

19 The case Home Office v. Harman, [1983] 1 A.C. 280, was brought to the EUCM, and the British government agreed to change the law of contempt of court in order to bring it in line with the Commission's legal views. *See* 130 S.I. 473 (1986).

20 The Sunday Times v. United Kingdom, [1979] 2 E.H.R.R. 245 = 1979 Eur.GrundRZ 386 = 22 YB Human Rights 402 (1979) (English and French language summaries). The case is dealt with in more detail in the context of the law of contempt. *See infra* at sec. B(2).

21 Contempt of Court Act 1981 (c.49).

22 Fin. Times, Nov. 21, 1986.

tice at lower costs to British citizens. If this bill had been passed, British courts could for the first time have heard a case claiming an infringement of human rights as embodied in the EUHR. But even today, the United Kingdom's ratification of the European Convention has already made an imprint on British media law. Just like its membership in the European Economic Community (EEC), membership in the EUHR serves to intertwine the developments of media law and policy in Britain with the major parallel developments in Western Europe.

The right to freedom of expression as guaranteed by the European Human Rights Convention is qualified in a number of ways. This takes account of the fact that the exercise of the right to free expression may collide with a number of other individual rights and state concerns worthy of protection. These recognized rights and objectives may justify or even require certain restrictions on the freedom of expression. Article 10(2) of the EUHR permits such restrictions if they are prescribed by law. They have to be:

> necessary in a democratic society, in the interest of national security, territorial integrity or public safety, for the prevention of disorder or crime, for the protection of health or morals, for the protection of the reputation or rights of others, for preventing the disclosure of information received in confidence, or for maintaining the authority and impartiality of the judiciary.

Each element listed constitutes an independent authorization for the legal restraint of freedom of expression,[23] provided that such a restraint is reasonable. British laws restricting freedom of information have numerous times been scrutinized by the EUCM and the EUCT and tested against the guarantee prescribed by article 10(1) of the EUHR. The following section will focus on the most important legal restrictions, with a particular view to their conformity with the European Human Rights Convention. From the viewpoint of the domestic English law, the legal restrictions serve to define the true extent of freedom of information in England, the latter emerging in a figurative sense, i.e., less all its restrictions.

23 U. HOFFMANN-REMY, DIE MÖGLICHKEITEN DER GRUNDRECHTSEINSCHRÄNKUNG NACH DEN ART. 8-11 ABS. 2 DER EUROPÄISCHEN MENSCHENRECHTSKONVENTION (49 Schriften zum Völkerrecht) 173 (1976).

B. *Freedom to Impart Information*

Freedom of information encompasses both the freedom to impart information and the freedom to receive information. The one can only be conceived of as a reflection of the other, because only together do they constitute the process of communication. The right to state one's opinion in public, be it orally or in a written or any other form, would be meaningless if others were prevented from listening to these manifestations of ideas and opinions. The freedom to impart information can also be referred to as the freedom of expression. Both terms make a general reference to the statement of opinion in public independent of the means of communication used. In contrast, freedom of speech and freedom of the press are more specific terms. The latter deals with the particular rights pertaining to the press, which has the institutionalized task of informing the public. The former expression is the general heading for the right of any individual to impart information. Both freedoms have many elements in common or can even be identical, but in a number of countries, like the United States and West Germany, for example, the press as an institution enjoys special legal protection. The following sections will pursue the questions of how the United Kingdom protects the freedom to impart information and whether it differentiates between the right to free speech and the right of the press. A third element of the freedom to impart information is the right to broadcast. This is indeed only a facet of freedom of speech and refers to the possibility of making use of this right by means of electromagnetic waves, be they in the form of radio or television. In the historical perspective, the availability of this form of communication is of rather recent vintage. In addition the unique technical features of electromagnetic communication have led to a different set of rules relating to the freedom to broadcast. This freedom is often dealt with under the – conceptually more restricted – heading of access to the broadcast media and will therefore be discussed separately. The following three sections will focus on freedom of speech and related matters, freedom of the press, and freedom to broadcast. These analyses will be followed by a discussion of the freedom to receive information.

1. *Freedom of Speech, of Correspondence and of Assembly*

The classical notion of free speech envisages the individual human being who imparts his ideas and opinions to his fellow men either orally or in written form. When this exchange of ideas occurs as a manifestation of opinions of a group of people in public, one also speaks of the freedoms of assembly and association. The regulation of all three elements is decisive for the extent of freedom of speech in any society.

Freedom of speech primarily deals with the right of individuals to state their ideas and opinions in public in order to participate in the general intellectual debates characterizing the society as a whole. But free communication between individuals also necessitates the protection of the privately spoken word against interference by and indiscretions of third parties or public authorities. Article 8 of the EUHR explicitly pronounces that everyone has the right to respect for his correspondence. The provision only permits interference with this right in accordance with the law and if this is necessary in a democratic society in the interests of national security, public safety or the economic well-being of the country, for the prevention of disorder or crime and similar matters.

In line with this provision, the Interception of Communications Act 1985[24] protects the secrecy of the mail and of telephone conversations. Section 1 makes it a criminal offence for a person intentionally to intercept a communication in the course of its transmission by mail or by means of a public telecommunications system. An interception of such a communication may only take place on the basis of a warrant issued by the Secretary of State. Under Section 2 of the Act, such a warrant may only be made if the Secretary considers it necessary (a) in the interest of national security; (b) for the purpose of preventing or detecting serious crimes; or (c) for the purpose of safeguarding the economic well-being of the United Kingdom. The provision repeats the formulation of article 8(2) of the EUHR but limits the authorization of the public authorities to only a few of the causes named in the EUHR. A specially appointed Commissioner has the task of keeping the Secretary of State's execution of these powers under constant review (section 8 of the Act).[25] Furthermore, any person who suspects that communications sent to or by him have been intercepted may apply to a tribunal specially provided for that purpose by the Act. The tribunal will investigate the complaint. If it finds that an illegal interception has taken place, it may quash the relevant warrant, direct the destruction of copies of the illegally obtained material and order the Secretary of State to compensate the applicant financially (section 7).

24 Interception of Communications Act 1985 (c.56).
25 The Commission issues an annual report. *See* the first Report of the Commissioner for 1986: Interception of Communications Act, 1985, Chapter 56, Cmnd. 108 (1987), holding that in all cases of warrants examined, the requirements of the Act had been fulfilled.

On the other hand, content restrictions also apply with regard to such communications. Thus, under section 11(1)(b) of the Post Office Act 1953,[26] the sending of indecent or obscene material through the mails constitutes a criminal offence. Similarly, vicious letters containing a threat to kill a person, or to damage property, violate section 16 of the Offences Against the Person Act 1861[27] and section 2 of the Criminal Damage Act.[28]

The right of prisoners to the secrecy of their correspondence may be considerably more restricted. The EUCT has on several occasions held that limitations of this right are an inherent feature of lawful imprisonment.[29] However, when a prisoner in a U.K. prison had been prevented from corresponding with his solicitor, the EUCT found that the prisoner's right under article 8 of the EUHR had been violated, because the restriction could not be justified as being »necessary in a democratic society.«[30]

English law further protects privately spoken words by granting a civil action for breach of confidence. The claim can be based in either equity or contract, if the information disclosed was of a confidential nature, had been imparted to a person under circumstances suggesting an obligation of confidence and was used without authorization to the disadvantage of the person who entrusted it.[31] The plaintiff may ask for an injunction against publication or may claim damages after the fact.

Originally, the law of breach of confidence was merely concerned with commercial secrets. In this context, liability often rests on the concept of a breach of a contractual obligation, but the action now extends to the matrimonial sphere and has furthermore been based on the broad principle of a »duty to be of good faith.«[32] In the *Argyll* case,[33] the Duchess of Argyll successfully prevented her former husband from publishing marital confidences obtained during their marriage. The duty to be in good faith,

---

26 Post Office Act 1953 (1 & 2 Eliz. 2, c.36).
27 Offences Against the Person Act 1861 (24 & 25 Vic., c.100).
28 Criminal Damage Act 1971 (c.48). *See also* sec. 43(1) of the Telecommunications Act 1984 (c.12), making it an offence for any person to send grossly offensive messages or messages of an indecent, obscene or menacing character by means of a public telecommunications system, such as the telephone.
29 Decision of July 13, 1970 (No. 4133/69), 36 COLL. DEC. 61, 64-65 (1971); Decision of July 8, 1974 (No. 5270/72), 46 COLL. DEC. 54, 60 (1974). *See also* Decision of July 7, 1977 (No. 7215/75), 11 DR 36, 45 (1978).
30 Judgment of Feb. 21, 1975 (»Golder«), 18 JUDG. DEC. 21-22.
31 *See* Coco v. Clark, 1969 R.P.C. 41, 47-48 (per Megarry J.).
32 Fraser v. Evans, [1969] 1 Q.B. 349, 361 (per Lord Denning M.R.).
33 Argyll (Duchess) v. Argyll (Duke), [1965] 1 All E.R. 611.

also referred to as the iniquity rule,[34] rests on the argument that »[n]o person is permitted to divulge to the world information which he had received in confidence unless he has just cause or excuse for doing so.«[35] A just cause exists if publication is in the public interest. This defence may be valid, for example, if a publication discloses a crime, a fraud or a misdeed already committed or in the planning process.[36] But the misdeed element does not necessarily need to be present. In the *Crossman Diaries* case, the Attorney General tried to obtain an injunction against the publication of a former cabinet minister's account of cabinet discussions. The Court concluded that such discussions were generally conducted in confidence but added that after some years (in this particular case, about ten), a higher public interest in publication existed.[37] On the other hand, when a senior employee at the U.K. Ministry of Defence, who had been convicted for publishing information obtained in the course of his employment by giving a television interview, complained of a violation of his rights under article 10 of the EUHR, the EUCM rejected the complaint. It held that restrictions against the publication of such information were justified under the Convention because they were necessary in a democratic society for the protection of the employer.[38]

An important restriction on the publication of books, magazines or other like works applies if they are likely to fall into the hands of children or young persons and consist »wholly or mainly of stories told in pictures (...), being stories portraying (a) the commission of crimes; or (b) acts of violence or cruelty; or (c) incidents of a repulsive or horrible nature; in such a way that the work as a whole would tend to corrupt a child or young person into whose hands it might fall.«[39] The printing, publication and selling of such a work constitutes a criminal offence under section 2 of the Act. The legislation is directed against horror comics and has practically eliminated them in the United Kingdom.

One of the most elementary restrictions on free speech stems from the prohibition to use defamatory words. The English tort law of libel and

34 *See* British Steel Corporation v. Granada Television Ltd., [1980] 3 W.L.R. 774, 822 (per Lord Wilberforce).
35 *Fraser*, [1969] 1 Q.B. at 361.
36 Initial Services Ltd v. Putterill, [1968] 1 Q.B. 396, 405 (per Lord Denning M.R.).
37 Attorney General v. Jonathan Cape Limited, 1976 Q.B. 752, 771 (per Lord Widgery C.J.). *See also* Woodward v. Hutchins, [1977] 1 W.L.R. 760. For an account of the public-interest defence, see Grant, *In the Public Interest? The Disclosure of Confidential Information*, 6 J. MEDIA L. & PRAC. 178 (1985). On cabinet secrets, see also H. STREET, FREEDOM, THE INDIVIDUAL AND THE LAW 232-35 (5th ed. 1982).
38 Application 10 293/83 v. United Kingdom (1985), 83 LS Gaz 965.
39 Children and Young Persons (Harmful Publications) Act 1955 (3 & 4 Eliz. 2, c.28), sec. 1.

slander, generally referred to as the law of defamation, provides a civil action for anyone affected by false statements that tend to lower him in the esteem of right-thinking members of the society or that are likely to make him the target of hatred, contempt or ridicule. The defamatory words must be published, i.e., they must have been conveyed to a third party.[40] If the words were communicated only to the offended person himself, the matter is not actionable, but it may under certain circumstances constitute criminal libel.[41] Defamatory statements made in some transitory form, at the instance of a conversation, for example, constitute slander. Libel is committed if the defamation is cast in some permanent form or broadcast by means of wireless telegraphy[42] or is incorporated into a theatre play. In libel cases, the law presumes that the plaintiff suffered damages, and proof of actual damages is unnecessary. In contrast, slander is actionable only to the extent that the plaintiff can show that he actually suffered damages, unless certain aggravating circumstances apply.[43] Defamatory words include »any reference to pictures, visual images, gestures and other methods of signifying meaning.«[44] The law establishes a presumption in favour of the plaintiff that the defamatory words used were untrue. If the defendant is unable to justify himself by proving that his words were true, he has the further defence that he made a fair and honest comment on a matter of public interest.[45] Other qualified privileges deal with comments made on the basis of a legal, social or moral duty,[46] as long as no abusive or malicious element is involved.[47] Finally, statements made during proceedings in Parliament and during judicial proceedings enjoy absolute privilege.[48]

Freedom of speech is further restricted if the words used are threatening,

---

40 P. LEWIS (ed.), GATLEY ON LIBEL AND SLANDER para. 221 (8th ed. 1981) (hereafter referred to as GATLEY ON LIBEL AND SLANDER).

41 *Id.* at para. 1594. However, hardly anyone has been prosecuted for criminal libel in the last two years. Between 1970 and 1983 only 5 persons were committed for trial, with three being committed. Robilliard, *Punish the Wicked Libellers?,* 7 J. MEDIA L. & PRAC. 11 (1986).

42 Defamation Act 1952 (15 & 16 Geo. 6 & 1 Eliz. 2, c.6) sec. 1.

43 *See* Defamation Act 1952, secs. 2 and 3; GATLEY ON LIBEL AND SLANDER, *supra* note 40, at para. 143.

44 Defamation Act 1952, sec. 16(1).

45 The defence of fair and honest comment presupposes that (a) the comment was in the pubic interest; (b) the basic facts on which the comment was based were correct; (c) the defendant honestly believed in his opinion, and (d) on the basis of these facts a fair-minded man might honestly have arrived at the defendant's opinion. London Artists Ltd. v. Littler, [1969] 2 Q.B. 375, 391-93 (per Lord Denning M.R.).

46 *See* Adam v. Ward, 1917 A.C. 309, 334.

47 *See* Horrocks v. Lowe, 1975 A.C. 135, 147-53 (per Lord Diplock).

48 GATLEY ON LIBEL AND SLANDER, *supra* note 40, at paras. 422, 383.

abusive or insulting and are intended to stir up racial hatred, or if racial hatred is likely to be stirred up thereby.[49] Any such behaviour, including the display, publication or distribution of any written material with such a content or the public performance of a play involving the use of such words, constitutes a criminal offence under the Public Order Act 1986. These provisions are designed for the protection of groups of persons in Great Britain that are defined by reference to colour, race, nationality or ethnic or national origin (section 17). Even the mere possession of racially inflammatory material, including recordings of sounds or visual images, may subject a person to criminal liability under certain circumstances (section 23). A court may order the forfeiture of the offensive material. Similarly, the publication of advertising that indicates an intention by a person to commit an act of discrimination prohibited by the Race Relations Act 1976[50] against someone for reasons of his colour, race, nationality or ethnic or national origin is unlawful under section 29 of that Act. Section 27(1) of the Public Order Act 1986 requires the Attorney General to give his consent to any prosecutions for the offence of racial hatred. This also applies with respect to offences committed in the context of broadcasting and cable television (section 22 of the Public Order Act 1986). However, section 22(7) exempts broadcasts by the British Broadcasting Corporation (BBC) and the Independent Broadcasting Authority (IBA) from the scope of the provision.

Other criminal offences relate to the attempt to cause disaffection among members of the police[51] and the attempt to seduce members of the armed forces from their duty of allegiance.[52] In a case in which a British citizen had been convicted under the Incitement of Disaffection Act 1934 for distributing leaflets to British soldiers that encouraged them to refuse to be posted in Northern Ireland, the EUCM held that the conviction was justified under article 10(2) of the EUHR in the interest of national security and the prevention of disorder within the army.[53] The Commission stated that even in peacetime, desertion of soldiers could cause serious problems for the national security, because it could impair the army's ability to protect a democratic society from internal and external threats.

Numerous enactments dealing with treason are further examples of restrictions on the permitted content of speech. These restrictions are

49 Public Order Act 1986 (c.64), sec. 18.
50 Race Relations Act 1976 (c.74).
51 Police Act 1964 (c.48), sec. 53.
52 Incitement of Disaffection Act 1934 (24 & 25 Geo. 5, c.56)
53 Opinion of Oct. 12, 1978 (»Arrowsmith«), 19 DR 5, 22-25 (1980).

universally accepted as being justified in the interest of national security.[54]

While the Public Order Act 1986 abolished the common-law offences of riot, rout, unlawful assembly and affray, it created new offences relating to public order. Under section 11 of the Act, the police station in the area concerned needs to be notified six days in advance of any procession in public, unless it is not reasonably practicable to give advance notice or unless the procession is one commonly or customarily held in that police area. The legality of a procession intended to demonstrate support for or opposition to the views of other persons, to publicize a cause, or to commemorate an event does not depend on any prior approval by a public authority. Section 11 thus manifests the right to freedom of assembly with the proviso of a notification specifying the date and time of the intended procession, its proposed route and the name and address of the persons organizing it. The senior police officer may impose certain conditions on the organizers, relating, for example, to the route to be taken by the procession. However, such directions may only be given if there is reasonable cause to believe that the public procession might result in serious public disorder, serious damage to property or serious disruption to the life of the community, or that the purpose of the procession is to intimidate others with the view to compelling them to any involuntary action (section 12(1)). An order totally prohibiting the proposed procession may only be issued as a matter of last resort if less severe directions appear insufficient to prevent serious public disorder (section 13(1)). Because the prohibition order represents the most drastic restriction on freedom of speech in this context, the Public Order Act 1986 requires that such an order only be given by the council of the district with the consent of the Secretary of State.

Assemblies require no prior notification and may not be prohibited in advance. Public assemblies, i.e., assemblies of twenty or more persons in a public place that is wholly or partly open to the air, may be subjected to certain directions if this appears necessary to prevent serious public disorder, serious damage to property, and the like (section 14(1) of the Public Order Act 1986). Such directions may regulate such conditions as the place of the assembly, its maximum duration, or the maximum number of people that may take part.

The exercise of the powers under sections 12 and 13 of the Public Order

---

54 This is also true for the offences of sedition and incitement to mutiny, for example. *See* G. ROBERTSON & A. NICOL, MEDIA LAW. THE RIGHTS OF JOURNALISTS AND BROADCASTERS 277-78 (1984).

Act 1986 have to conform with the requirements under article 11 of the EUHR. This provision grants everyone the right to freedom of peaceful assembly and the freedom of association with others. Article 11(2) of the EUHR permits restrictions on these rights only if they are necessary in a democratic society in the interests of national security or public safety, for the prevention of disorder and crime, for the protection of health and morals or for the protection of the rights and freedoms of others. In one case the EUCM held that a procession deserved the protection of article 11(1) of the EUHR even if the possibility of violent counter-demonstrations existed or if it appeared possible that violent extremists not associated with the organizers of the procession would join the demonstration.[55] In such a case, any restrictions imposed on the organizers still have to comply with the conditions set out in article 11(2) of the EUHR. However, if people assemble for the purpose of committing violence against persons or property, such assembly enjoys no protection under article 11 of the EUHR. According to sections 1-3 of the Public Order Act 1986, riot, violent disorder and affray are criminal offences. Similarly, a person who directs at another person threatening, abusive or insulting words or behaviour or who distributes or displays any writing or sign that is threatening, abusive or insulting is guilty of an offence under section 4 of the Act, if he acted with intent to cause that person to believe that immediate unlawful violence would be used against him or a third person. The use of threatening or insulting words or any behaviour to this effect is also punishable if it is done within the hearing or sight of a person likely to be caused harassment, alarm or distress thereby (section 5(1)).

Since the Theatres Act 1968,[56] all forms of theatre censorship formerly exercised by the Lord Chamberlain on such subjects as the royal family, public figures, religious themes, and the like[57] have ceased to exist. Theatres need a licence under section 12 of the Theatres Act for the use of the premises on which the performances will take place, but the licensing authority is expressly prohibited from imposing any conditions regarding the nature of the plays or the manner of performance.[58] The licensing authority may therefore only impose terms, conditions and restrictions necessary in the interests of physical safety, health or the control of

---

55 Decision of July 16, 1980 (»Christians against Racism and Fascism«), 21 DR 138, 148-49 (1981).
56 Theatres Act 1968 (c.54).
57 *See* the examples given for theatre censorship by H. STREET, *supra* note 37, at 72.
58 Theatres Act 1968, sec. 1(2).

demonstrations of hypnotism.[59] The sole responsibility for the granting of these licences lies with the local authorities. Appeal against the refusal of the grant or renewal of a licence or any conditions imposed on the licensee may be lodged with the magistrate courts; from there, a further appeal is possible to the Crown Court.[60] Public performances of plays without a licence under section 12 of the Theatres Act 1968 or in contravention of any conditions contained in a licence constitute a criminal offence punishable by a fine not exceeding £ 200 or imprisonment of not more than three months or both.[61]

While the general criminal laws are principally applicable to the theatre as well, the Theatres Act 1968 has created three special offences taking precedence over the corresponding offences specified by other enactments or the common law. These three newly created offences are the presentation of obscene performances of plays and incitement to racial hatred or the provocation of breach of the peace by means of the public performance of a play.[62] No intent on the part of the offender is necessary to commit the offence of obscenity under the Act.[63] However, a person charged with this offence has the »defence of public good,« if he can prove that the performance was justified »in the interests of drama, opera, ballet or any other art, or of literature or learning.«[64]

Freedom of association is granted to all persons, unless they associate to an illegal end. Under the Prevention of Terrorism (Temporary Provisions) Act 1984,[65] for example, membership in or the assistance of any terrorist organization constitutes a criminal offence. The same is true for any display of support in public for such organizations (section 2). Similar prohibitions apply to the membership in and support of terrorist organizations in Northern Ireland.[66]

In principle, all individuals residing in the United Kingdom enjoy the same human-rights guarantees, independent of whether they are U.K. nationals or aliens.[67] However, article 16 of the EUHR allows contracting states to

---

59 *Id.* at secs. 12, 1(2) and Schedule I.

60 *Id.* at sec. 14.

61 *Id.* at sec. 13.

62 *Id.* at secs. 2, 5, 6. Under certain circumstances, the Sexual Offences Act 1956 (c.69) may also be applicable to theatrical scenes. *See* the account of a 1981 case by J. SUTHERLAND, OFFENSIVE LITERATURE – DECENSORSHIP IN BRITAIN 1960-1982 180-87 (1982).

63 L. COTTERELL, PERFORMANCE 461 (2nd ed. 1984).

64 Theatres Act 1968, sec. 3(1).

65 Prevention of Terrorism (Temporary Provisions) Act 1984 (c.8).

66 *See* Northern Ireland (Emergency Provisions) Act 1978 (c.5), sec. 21.

67 COUNCIL OF EUROPE, DIRECTORATE OF HUMAN RIGHTS, HUMAN RIGHTS OF ALIENS IN EUROPE 393 (1985).

restrict the political activities of aliens. Under the law of the United Kingdom, an alien is prohibited from voting[68] and from sitting in the House of Commons.[69] In a case involving the United Kingdom, the EUCM held that the deportation of an alien journalist on security grounds as such did not amount to an interference with his rights under article 10 of the Convention; his right to freedom of expression was held to be independent of his right to stay in the country.[70]

2. *Freedom of the Press*

Ever since the abolition of the Cromwellian licensing system, everyone in Britain enjoys the right to publish newspapers, books or magazines without government authorization. No licence is needed to run a newspaper, and no statutory duty exists for the press to report political or other matters with impartiality. Any government representative wishing to prevent the publication of a newspaper article may attempt to do so by obtaining a court injunction, but he has no right directly to restrain the publication. The same is true for the publication of books, with the reservation that all present or former civil servants are required to have books that they have written about the government cleared before publication.[71]

One of the crucial legal safeguards of the freedom of the press is the rule against prior restraint. According to this principle, only after the publication of an article may a civil or criminal action be brought against a journalist on the allegation that the article is false or libellous. Journalists may not be prevented by means of a court injunction from publishing the contested matter before the end of the legal proceedings determining the legitimacy of the plaintiff's complaint. For centuries the rule against prior restraint has formed an integral part of the English law on the press. However, as one commentator put it, in the course of time this rule »has been badly eroded.«[72]

The common law has developed two partly conflicting concepts, according to which exceptions to the rule against prior restraint are permitted. Under

---

68 *See* Representation of the People Act 1983 (c.2), sec. 1(1). According to this provision, Commonwealth citizens and citizens of the Republic of Ireland may be entitled to vote in parliamentary elections if they are resident in the United Kingdom, are not subject to any legal incapacity to vote and are at least 18 years of age. Similar conditions apply with respect to local government elections (*see* Representation of the People Act 1983, sec. 2(1)).
69 Act of Settlement 1700 (12 & 13 Will. 3, c. 2) sec. 3.
70 Decision of Dec. 17, 1976 (»Agee«), 7 DR 164, 174 (1977).
71 H. STREET, *supra* note 37, at 230.
72 G. ROBERTSON & A. NICOL, *supra* note 54, at 13.

the less restrictive approach, a court should not issue an injunction prohibiting publication if a possible defence to the complaint exists.[73] The underlying rationale of the concept is that the public interest in receiving prompt and complete information usually outweighs the right of an individual to prevent any interference with his private rights. Thus, English courts have generally accepted this concept in cases where the plaintiff's claim was based on an allegation of libel, injurious falsehood or contempt of court, as long as the defendant publisher maintained that he told the truth or asserted the defence of fair comment.[74]

If a plaintiff seeks an interlocutory injunction restraining (further) publication on grounds of a libel action, for example, the raising of the defence of justification or privilege will have the result that a court »because of the value the court has placed upon freedom of speech and ... upon the freedom of the press« will refrain from granting the application, absent any strong evidence of malice on the part of the defendant.[75] The Defamation Act 1951 also contains a number of qualified privileges applying to newspaper articles, unless the publication is made with malice (section 7 and Schedule of the Act).[76]

The highest damage claim so far awarded by an English jury for libel amounted to £ 450,000. The judgment was passed on June 3, 1987 against a Greek daily newspaper and one of its Greek reporters and involved an article, written in Greek, containing allegations against the plaintiff, a former British naval intelligence agent in Greece during the days of dictatorship between 1967 and 1974.[77] The plaintiff had claimed that the article had severely lowered his reputation in Greece. The English court accepted jurisdiction on the ground that some 50 copies of the newspaper, which practically no English person had read, had been sold in England. Technically, the selling of newspapers in Great Britain constitutes a publication in that country. According to articles 2 and 5(3) of the 1968 Brussels Convention on Jurisdiction and the Enforcement of Judgments in Civil and Commercial Matters, which was incorporated into U.K. law by the Civil

---

73 Sun Printer Ltd. v. Westminster Press Ltd., 1982 IRLR 292; *Fraser*, [1969] 1 Q.B. at 360 (per Lord Denning M.R.).

74 G. ROBERTSON & A. NICOL, *supra* note 54, at 120 and n. 37, *citing, e.g.*, Trevor & Sons v. Solomon, 248 E.G. 779 (1978) (libel); Bestobell Paints Ltd. v. Bigg, 1975 F.S.R. 421 (injurious falsehood); Attorney General v. BBC, [1980] 3 All E.R. 161, 183 (contempt of court).

75 Herbage v. Pressdram Ltd, [1984] 1 W.L.R. 1160, 1162 (per Griffiths L.J.).

76 *See* Boston v. Bagshaw & Sons, [1966] 1 W.L.R. 1126, 1132 (per Lord Denning M.R.).

77 *See* Douzinas, McVeigh & Warrington, *It's all Greek to Me: Libel Law and the Freedom of the Press*, 137 N.L.J. 609 (1987).

Jurisdiction and Judgments Act 1982,[78] a person domiciled in an EC member state may, in a tort action, be sued in the member state in which the harmful event occurred as well as in the state of his domicile. In libel cases, the tort and the damage both occur in the place of publication. However, under these circumstances it was argued that bringing an action of the present kind for a tort committed in Greece before an English court could be said to be oppressive under English law, and that a Greek newspaper should only be answerable to Greek law instead of to the law of a jurisdiction where virtually no interest existed in the contents of the disputed article.[79] In addition, it was doubted that the judgment, the enforcement of which against the newspaper would force it into instant liquidation, would be enforced in Greece due to the violation by the English judgment of the Greek *ordre public*, which inter alia protects the constitutionally guaranteed freedom of the press.[80]

In a tort action for defamation, prima facie liability extends to everyone who has taken part in the publication process; in the case of books or newspapers, these are the journalist or writer, the editor, the printer, and the vendor.[81] Anyone who has played only a subordinate part in disseminating the libel, such as the distributor or the vendor, has a special defence, in which he needs to show that (a) he did not know that the book or paper contained the libel complained of and that the book or paper was of a character likely to contain a libel; and (b) such want of knowledge was not due to negligence on his part.[82]

In actions based on breach of confidence or copyright, the courts have occasionally favoured a second test to define the rule against prior restraint, based on »the balance of convenience.« According to this approach, courts may grant an injunction if the action is not frivolous and the plaintiff's damages could not be adequately compensated in a subsequent court proceeding.[83] The action of breach of confidence can only be invoked to prevent publication if the disputed information was revealed under circumstances creating a duty of confidentiality on the part of the party receiving the information. However, the existence of such a duty has been considered to be doubtful even in cases where documents destined for publication had been stolen. Even if a breach of confidence is

---

78 Civil Jurisdiction and Judgments Act 1982 (c.27).
79 Douzinas, McVeigh & Warrington, *supra* note 77, at 609.
80 *Id.* at 610.
81 GATLEY ON LIBEL AND SLANDER, *supra* note 40, at paras. 236-40.
82 *Id.* at para. 241.
83 *See, e.g.,* American Cyanamid Co. v. Ethicon Ltd., 1975 A.C. 396, 406 (per Lord Diplock).

clearly evident, a court will refrain from issuing an injunction if the story reveals a crime, misconduct, fraud, or gross hypocrisy.[84] In such a case, the public-interest element will prevail over the individual's interest in confidentiality. Also, no injunction against the publication of information obtained by means of lawful telephone tapping will be granted.[85]

A recent case that achieved international notoriety in the context of breach of confidence and prior restraint is the *Spycatcher* case. In 1985, Peter Wright, a retired member of the British Security Service MI5, wrote and published his memoires in Australia, alleging serious illegal actions by MI5 members during his time of service. The British Attorney General thereupon won interlocutory injunctions in the Australian Court of Appeal against Wright and his publisher, restraining publication pending full trial in Great Britain. In Britain, too, the affair became the subject of a number of lawsuits between the Crown and – in most cases – British newspapers with an interest in reporting both the Australian court proceedings and the allegations contained in the *Spycatcher* book. A number of the injunctions sought by the Attorney General against the author in Australia as well as those subsequently sought against several newspapers in Britain were based on the allegation of a breach of the duty of confidentiality said to exist between the Crown and its former civil servant and also extending to third parties such as the British press.

In the summer of 1986, the Attorney General won interlocutory injunctions in the British courts against *The Guardian* and *The Observer*, after both newspapers had published in the United Kingdom outlines of the allegations made in the book. These injunctions prevented the newspapers from disclosing or publishing any of the information contained in the book, with the exception of those materials that had been disclosed in open court before the Australian court and that were not subject to any prohibition from publication by the Australian judges. One year later, two other English newspapers published major summaries of Wright's allegations,[86] and *The Sunday Times*, having acquired the copyright for the serialization of the

---

84 G. ROBERTSON & A. NICOL, *supra* note 54, at 14, 113 and n. 3.
85 Malone v. Commissioner of Police of the Metropolis (No. 2), [1979] 2 All E.R. 620, 646 (per Sir Megarry V-C).
86 The Attorney General brought contempt procedures against these newspapers, arguing that the disregard for the injunctions against *The Guardian* and *The Observer* amounted to a criminal contempt of court. In Attorney General v. Newspaper Publishing plc, High Court judgment of June 3, 1987, the Court held for the defendants. On appeal, the Court of Appeal held for the plaintiff. *See* Attorney General v. Newspaper Publishing plc, [1987] 3 W.L.R. 942. Final judgment has not been passed in these matters.

book in Great Britain, published the first installment of extracts from the book on the same day on which it was published in the United States.[87] Thereupon, *The Guardian* and *The Observer*, arguing that a material change of circumstances had taken place since the original granting of the preliminary injunctions, sought the lifting of the original injunctions against them. This action was joined by *The Sunday Times*.

The central question, which occupied five courts in this matter in the following months, was whether preliminary and ultimately permanent injunctions should be issued against the newspapers in Britain in light of the publication of *Spycatcher* in the United States and elsewhere. The five ensuing judgments[88] give fascinating evidence of the difficulties the courts faced in trying to balance the interests of freedom of the press and freedom of information on the one hand and the interest of the government in securing vital state secrets on the other hand. The case also offers a striking example of the growing interdependence of the information markets around the world and the impossibility for a government in controlling the availability of information on its own territory once this information has been made public abroad.

With respect to the decisions emanating from the newspapers' applications to lift the injunctions, one has to distinguish between those court rulings that dealt with the upholding of the preliminary injunctions and those deciding about the legality of permanent injunctions against the press. As for the interlocutory proceedings, the High Court discharged the orders against the newspapers in the summer of 1987.[89] The Court considered that there had been a material change of circumstances since the orignal granting of the preliminary injunctions against *The Guardian* and *The Observer* one year earlier: In Great Britain, *The Independent* had meanwhile published an article on the matter, including some literal quotations from the book, and *The Sunday Times* had published the first part of its serialization. The allegations made in *Spycatcher* had been widely publicized in the foreign press, and, more importantly, the whole book had been published in the

---

87 With respect to U.S. law, the British Attorney General was advised that the rule against prior restraint as interpreted in the United States made injunction proceedings against the publishing company futile, so that the British government refrained from trying to suppress publication of the book in that country. In New Zealand and Hong Kong, however, injunction proceedings were brought against the publishers, as was done in Australia.

88 Attorney-General v. Guardian Newspapers Limited, [1987] 1 W.L.R. 1252; Attorney-General v. The Observer Limited; Attorney-General v. Times Newspapers Ltd., [1987] 1 W.L.R. 1271; [1987] 1 W.L.R. 1282; (No. 2) [1988] 2 W.L.R. 810; [1988] 2 W.L.R. 865.

89 [1987] 1 W.L.R. 1252 (per Sir Nicolas Browne-Wilkinson V-C).

United States. From there it had reached the United Kingdom mostly by way of British tourists taking the book back with them from the United States. Before this background, the Court concluded that the once-confidential information had gone into the public domain. Since the newspapers that were parties to the action had neither participated in the breach of duty of confidentiality committed by the author of the books nor participated in the revelation of the information to the public, Judge Browne-Wilkinson applied a »balance of convenience« test, weighing the interests of the government in preventing the further dissemination of the information against the interest of the press in freely reporting about the matter, and he decided in favour of the latter.

On appeal, both the Court of Appeal and the House of Lords in a 3:2 decision held for the government. There were some half-hearted and unconvincing arguments holding that with the exception of those matters that had been discussed in the Australian courts and in Parliament, the information concerned could not yet be said to be in the public domain. The main argument of both courts, however, rested on the overwhelming concern for the interests of the government in protecting the Security Service. While the government could no longer prevent foreign secret services or the public abroad from learning about the allegations, the courts were convinced that it could still shield the members of the British Security Service, who were legally unable to respond to any accusations of wrongdoing, from harassment in the British press:

> The publication in this country of *Spycatcher* will thus cause grievous harm to individuals and deal a blow to the morale of the Security Service. The British public will lose confidence in the Security Service. Our friends will be dismayed and our enemies will rejoice at the failure of the British to protect the Security Service from calumny reported in the British press.[90]

Yet again, these arguments lacked persuasive power, given the widespread knowledge about the allegations in Britain at the time of the Court of Appeal's decision and the damage to the reputation of the Security Service at home and abroad already done. However, an attentive reading of the decisions reveals the true underlying rationale guiding the British judges in their decisions, namely, a stunned disbelief and a sense of profound indignation over the realization that British law and the British courts could not effectively prevent the embarrassing consequences of a – virtually undisputed – flagrant breach of the English law of duty of confidence and

90 [1987] 1 W.L.R. 1282, 1298 (per Lord Templeman).

instead had helplessly to watch the »traitor« take full advantage of the foreign information channels to circumvent successfully English law. The rationale that the author of the book simply »should not get away« with his wrongdoing surfaces in several passages of the decision:

> [I]t would be *a denial of justice* to refuse to allow the injunction to be continued *until the action is heard*. ... It would be established without trial and for all time, that by the simple expedient of going abroad, arranging for publication in the press, in a country, such as the United States, where there is no remedy by way of injunction, the courts in this country then become incapable of exercising their well established jurisdiction. Your Lordships would have established a »Charter for Traitors« to publish on the most massive scale in England whatever they have managed to publish abroad. ...
>
> If the publication of this book in America is to have, for all practical purposes, the effect of nullifying the jurisdiction of the English courts to enforce compliance with the duty of confidence both by interlocutory and by permanent injunction, then, ..., English law would have surrendered to the American Constitution.[91]

In his dissenting opinion, Lord Bridge rejected the majority's reasoning arguing that in light of the free availability of the information to the general public, freedom of the press weighed much more heavily than the government's interest in maintaining the injunctions. The judge found unusually strong words for stressing his point:

> We have not adopted as part of our law the European Convention for the Protection of Human Rights and Fundamental Freedoms to which this country is a signatory. Many think that we should. I have hitherto not been of that persuasion, in large part because I have had confidence in the capacity of the common law to safeguard the fundamental freedoms essential to a free society including the right to freedom of speech which is specifically safeguarded by article 10 of the Convention. My confidence is seriously undermined by your Lordships' decision. ... If the Government are determined to fight to maintain the ban to the end, they will face inevitable condemnation and humiliation by the European Court of Human Rights in Strasbourg. Long before that they will have been condemned at the bar of public opinion in the free world.[92]

---

91 [1987] 1 W.L.R. 1282, 1305, 1306 (per Lord Ackner).
92 *Id.* at 1286 (per Lord Bridge of Harwich).

As a more appropriate remedy against the author of the book and its publishers, Lord Bridge identified the action for an account of profits, stripping those responsible for the breach of confidence of its financial awards.

In the following proceedings the government sought permanent injunctions against the newspapers and claimed against *The Sunday Times* an account of profits for the publication of the first part of the serialization of the book. The Attorney General's legal argument was that third parties were generally under the same duty of confidentiality as the original confident, in this case, the author of the book, and that confidential information disclosed to third parties did not thereby lose its confidential character, provided that the third parties knew that the disclosure had been made in breach of a duty of confidence.

After the High Court had discharged the injunctions, but had held *The Sunday Times* liable for account of profits,[93] the Court of Appeal decided that the injunctions should be discharged but would continue pending appeal to the House of Lords.[94] Both courts agreed in principle with the Attorney General that the duty of confidence that bound a former Secret Service agent vis-à-vis the government also extended to third parties, such as newspapers coming into possession of this information and knowing about its confidential character.[95] However, the courts identified three main exceptions to this rule, namely, if (1) the confider of the information had given his consent; or (2) the information had become available to the general public; or (3) the disclosure could be said to be in the public interest, because, e.g., there was evidence of serious iniquity committed. In all cases it was up to the Crown to establish before the courts that publication constituted a breach of confidence requiring a restraining order in the public interest.

This said, both courts took recourse to article 10 of the European Convention of Human Rights, applying the balancing-of-interests test contained therein. While recognizing that the Convention was not directly binding upon them, the judges concurred that there existed no significant difference between article 10 of the Convention and the English law on freedom of speech.[96] The test applied accordingly was whether there ex-

93 Attorney-General v. Guardian Newspapers Limited (No. 2); Attorney-General v. Observer Limited; Attorney-General v. Times Newspapers Limited, [1988] 2 W.L.R. 812 (per Scott J.).
94 Attorney-General v. Guardian Newspapers Limited (No. 2); Attorney-General v. Observer Limited; Attorney-General v. Times Newspapers Limited, [1988] 2 W.L.R. 865. The appeal to the House of Lords is presently pending.
95 This argument formed the basis for the Court's decision holding *The Sunday Times* liable for an account of profits for the first installment of the serialization of the book.
96 [1988] 2 W.L.R. 812, 848-51; 865, 869, 892, 897, 907-09.

isted a »pressing social need« for the maintenance of confidentiality »proportionate to the legitimite aim pursued.« Considering that the publication of the book in the United States had destroyed all secrecy as to its contents and that copies of the book could be obtained by every citizen in the United Kingdom wishing to get them, the balancing of the public interest in freedom of speech and the right to receive information against the government's legitimate – and in cases such as this, generally compelling – interest in national security came out in favour of the former: the injunctions were held to be no longer necessary.

It has been deplored that the restrictions imposed in particular by the law of defamation on free press reporting seems to have the tendency to suppress the publication of press investigations on such matters as government corruption, poor performance of public work contracts, the aptness of public figures for office, their connection with criminals, and the like.[97] Munro cites several incidents relating to television journalism that suggest that similar tendencies inhibiting the reporting of matters of public concern exist in the broadcast media.[98]

The rule against prior restraint would seem to make a corresponding right of reply pertaining to individual citizens all the more necessary. The right of reply allows an individual to state his case and to deny publicly any demeaning statements of facts about him in the same newspaper that printed the allegations. However, such a right of reply, which is a recognized elementary legal principle in many other countries, is nonexistent in England. Individuals may turn to the Press Council, alleging the use of unethical methods of information gathering or an unethical standard of reporting. The Press Council, set up in 1953, is a voluntary body independent of the government and made up of representatives of the press and laymen. It is concerned with the observance by the press of ethical standards and, most importantly, with the adjudication of private complaints against press organs. The complaints procedure is a voluntary one on the part of the Council, the complainant and the newspaper, which agrees to adhere to any decision by the Council. If a complaint raises legal issues, such as libel, that could also be the subject of a court action, the Press Council assumes jurisdiction only on condition that the complainant sign a waiver releasing all legal claims arising out of the complaint.[99]

Anyone, personally aggrieved or not, may complain to the Council. The editor of the newspaper or magazine responsible then has the opportunity

97 *See* C. WINTOUR, PRESSURES ON THE PRESS 111 (1972).
98 C. MUNRO, TELEVISION, CENSORSHIP AND THE LAW 79-80 (1979).
99 G. ROBERTSON & A. NICOL, *supra* note 54, at 342.

to contact directly the complainant and to settle amicably the matter. If the complainant gets no redress within a reasonable period of time, he must then file a formal written complaint with the Council, stating the facts and saying what he thinks was improper on the part of the newspaper, periodical or journal.[100]

The Council has thus far failed to issue a code of press conduct. Thus, a complainant is almost without formal guidelines to argue a breach of ethical standards,[101] especially in view of the fact that until the mid-1980s, the Council formally adjudicated an average of only fifty cases per year.[102] It also usually took several months before it released a final decision, and therefore the criticism expressed by the Royal Commission on the Press seemed well-founded. The Commission disapproved, i.a., of the lack of public confidence in the work of the Council, of the quality of the Council's decisions, and of its lack of enforcement powers.[103] In response, the Press Council has tried to improve both its procedures and the promptness of its decision making; the number of decisions has as well increased.[104]

Apart from times of war, when military censorship was regularly imposed on the British press,[105] no censorship laws are in force in England.[106]

In principle, journalists are free to write about any subject, unless they contravene some common-law or statutory provision restricting freedom of speech in general. Nevertheless, although »Fleetstreet newspapers« have a worldwide reputation for good journalism, few people outside Britain are aware of the numerous legal restrictions applying to the press in England. Although freedom of the press is a recognized fundamental principle of English law, the right often is justified only with the necessity and the

---

100 Guidance on Procedure for Complainants, Press Council Leaflet 109 (revised Jan. 1984).

101 G. ROBERTSON & A. NICOL, *supra* note 54, at 342.

102 This figure was calculated by the author on the basis of the statistics given by G. ROBERTSON & A. NICOL, *supra* note 54, at 341. In 1984 the number of complaints rose by 31 per cent. Of the total of 1,193 complaints received by the Council, 113 were fully adjudicated. Of these, 72 complaints were upheld and the rest were rejected. *See* 7 J. MEDIA L. & PRAC. 17 (1986).

103 Royal Commission on the Press, Final Report 1977, Cmnd. 6810 (1977).

104 *See, e.g.,* The Press Council, The Press and the People, 33rd Annual Report 1986, 11-12; The Press Council, Guidance on Procedure for Complainants, *supra* note 100.

105 During the Falkland crisis, for example, reports from journalists on the military conflict were censored at least twice: first at their source, and once again by the Ministry of Defence in London. *See* Defence Committee, First Report, Session 1982-83, The Handling of Press and Public Information During the Falklands Conflict, Vol. I, Report and Minutes of Proceedings, H.C. 17 I, paras. 44-80, 125 (1982).

106 The Northern Ireland (Emergency Provisions) Act 1978 (c.5) applies only to Northern Ireland. Section 22 prohibits the collecting, recording and publishing of information relating to the activities of the army, the police, the courts, court officers or prison officers, if the information is likely to be useful for terrorists.

extent of the advancement of the public good by the press. This view denies that freedom of the press is an aim in itself. An illustrative example of this conceptual approach is the following passage cited from the 1977 Final Report of the Royal Commission on the Press:

> [P]roprietors, contributors and editors must accept the limits to free expression set by the need to reconcile claims which may often conflict. The public, too, asserts a right to accurate information and fair comment which, in turn, has to be balanced against the claims both of national security and of individuals to safeguards for their reputation and privacy except when these are overridden by the public interest. But the public interest does not reside in whatever the public may happen to find interesting, and the press must be careful not to perpetrate abuses and call them freedom. Freedom of the press cannot be absolute. There must be boundaries to it and realistic discussion concerns where those boundaries ought to be set.

> We define freedom of the press as that degree of freedom from restraint which is essential to enable proprietors, editors and journalists to advance the public interest by publishing the facts and opinions without which a democratic electorate cannot make responsible judgments...[107]

In this definition, freedom of the press – in the sense of a personal right of individual journalists, editors and publishers – appears to take second place. The approach suggests that the journalist's right to free reporting depends upon his advancement of the public interest. Public interest in turn is defined as the interest in that kind of information essential to make »responsible« political judgments. Under this definition, only the reporting of information of a political nature appears to be protected, while »non-political« information falls outside the definition. Also, the term »responsible« judgments used in connection with the term »democratic electorate« comes dangerously close to suggesting that the expression of any views inconsistent with the incumbent political system deserves no legal protection. While this last impression does not properly reflect the English concept of freedom of the press (press publications advancing communist views, for example, enjoy the same legal protection as views supporting one of the political parties represented in Parliament), the cautious approach of the Royal Commission to the kernel of guaranteed press freedom is symptomatic of a broad consensus within British society on the role of the print media. According to this commonly shared view, the press bears a special responsibility for balancing the interest of the public in proper information and the interests of the state. These state interests, often summarized under the heading of security interests, encompass much more than secret information vital to the military and general security of the country. Often, reference to these security interests serves to protect the tem-

---

107 Royal Commission on the Press, *supra* note 103, at paras. 2.2, 2.3.

porary political conveniences of the governments of the day. This effect stems from the operation of an intricate system of – more or less – voluntary self-censorship practised by the press, as well as such stringent laws as the Official Secrets Act 1911.[108] While criminal convictions under this particular act take place only on rare occasions, its »chilling« effect appears to be significant.

A central feature of the system of voluntary self-restraint are the secret Defence Notices (so-called D-Notices). A committee consisting of high-ranking members of the armed forces and representatives of the newspaper and television media regularly issue the D-Notices. These non-public notices directed at journalists, editors, publishers and broadcasters list such matters as »[s]ecret intelligence or counter-intelligence methods and activities in or outside the UK,« »[a]ny information from which the number, duties or type of the staff or other details of the organization of MI5 could be ascertained«[109] and similar subjects about which journalists are asked not to write. The wording of the notices appears to be broad and general. The D-Notice cited above covers almost anything perceivably pertaining to the Secret Service, its staff and activities. Although these notices have no legal effect, the media usually respect them and refrain from reporting about anything covered by the notices. On rare occasions, a newspaper disregards the guidelines and publishes a story. In these cases, the publisher acts on the conviction that the public interest in the information outweighs the government's interest in secrecy or that the observance of the notice in the particular case would only serve the convenience of the government instead of the country's security.

In certain instances, such a transgression of the unwritten rules may constitute a criminal offence under the Official Secrets Act 1911, although prosecution will not necessarily follow. The most effective way to discipline a difficult journalist is the refusal of any future access to secret Whitehall information, a practice government representatives generously apply.[110]

---

108 Official Secrets Act 1911 (1 & 2 Geo. 5, c.28).
109 Extracts from the wording of a D-Notice published disobediently by *The Spectator* in 1964 and reprinted in C. MUNRO, *supra* note 98, at 71.
110 *See* C. MUNRO, *supra* note 98, at 71-73.

As Hewitt has rightfully pointed out,[111] »the Government and major commercial interests protect themselves by suppressing information: keeping secrets has taken over from punishing sedition.«

Off-the-record talks with journalists are the service in return provided by the government for the press. It thus came as no surprise that a 1980 House of Commons Committee report denounced the system as being based on the theory, if not the practice, of covert censorship.[112]

In 1986, two newspapers, *The Independent* and *The Guardian*, challenged the shadowy business of these off-the-record government briefings. They announced that they would stop attending such unofficial meetings held by the press secretary to the prime minister twice a day. They also declared that they would report what was said and – contrary to established practice – would quote the names of those government officials mentioned by the press secretary. While other newspapers admitted that the system was wide open to abuse and that the public might be better served if British journalists were to employ American methods of investigative journalism to bring government activities to light, these newspapers decided to maintain the »lobby system,« for fear that government briefings might otherwise not take place at all.[113] The two newspapers that had broken rank were excluded from future government briefings.

While the system of D-Notices and the »lobby system« go a long way to protecting government secrecy, the Official Secrets Act 1911 is the central legislative feature that has caused Whitehall, the seat of the British government, to be called »the citadel of the Monte Cassino of excessive secrecy in the Western World.«[114] The Official Secrets Act 1911 is the primary statute restricting freedom of information about government activities. While the Act applies to private individuals to the same extent as to the press, its restrictions are most severely felt by journalists. Section 2 of the Act creates over 2,300 different offences, amounting to the most serious limitation on freedom of the press in the United Kingdom. The provision makes it a criminal offence punishable by two years in prison to

---

111 P. HEWITT, THE ABUSE OF POWER – CIVIL LIBERTIES IN THE UNITED KINGDOM 81 (1982).

112 House of Commons Defense Committee 3rd Report, 1979-80, »The D-Notice System«, H.C. 773, para. 24.

113 The Economist, Oct. 25, 1986. *See also* J. MICHAEL, THE POLITICS OF SECRECY – CONFIDENTIAL GOVERNMENT AND THE PUBLIC RIGHT TO KNOW 84 (1982). The author reports an incident in June 1975 when Prime Minister Harold Wilson's press secretary terminated briefings for a while, because the press had gone »too far« in its reporting.

114 Hennessy, *Public Watchdogs and Executive Poodles*, in INSIDE INFORMATION: BRITISH GOVERNMENT AND THE MEDIA 89 (A. May and K. Rowan ed. 1982).

communicate unauthorized information to third parties. Third persons, including journalists, who receive the illegal information also violate the Act. Even if the journalist has no intention to publish the material, he commits an offence under section 2 if he knowingly receives the information. However, in view of the fact that this provision has long not been invoked against members of the press, it seems unlikely that a journalist would be prosecuted under these circumstances.[115]

The scope of the Act is so broad as to protect not only matters of national security; it also covers anything related to government activities in general, as, for example, the number of chairs around the table at a cabinet meeting. The Attorney General must authorize every prosecution under the Act, a circumstance adding to the highly political nature and application of the statute. Since 1945, the Act has only been invoked about once a year. But its most effective bearing lies in the fact that it has a long history of being used by the governments of the day as a welcomed instrument to intimidate journalists. This practice is an excellent tool for the suppression of unwelcomed publications critical of or embarrassing to the incumbent administration.[116]

A public-interest defence exists against section 2 of the Act if the unauthorized communication was in the interest of the state.[117] The Official Secrets Act 1911 explains why the »lobby system« of informal government briefings could survive for such a long time: It represents one of the few ways to receive information about the government and to publish it without fear of violating the Act. Newspapers that contest the system run the risk of prosecution if they employ methods of investigative journalism to gather and to publish inside information about the government.

Another piece of legislation that is universally applicable but has a particularly restrictive impact on press freedom is the Contempt of Court Act 1981. The law of contempt of court is concerned with the prevention of serious risks that might substantially impede or prejudice the course of justice in particular proceedings. It applies equally to criminal and civil proceedings. Prior to 1981, when Parliament passed the Contempt of Court Act as the result of the ruling of the European Court of Human Rights in *The Sunday Times* case,[118] contempt was a common-law offence only. In *The*

---

115 G. ROBERTSON & A. NICOL, *supra* note 54, at 265-66.
116 *See* the examples given by J. AITKEN, OFFICIALLY SECRET ch. 3 (1971). *See also*, C. MUNRO, *supra* note 98, at 70-71; H. STREET, *supra* note 37, at 219.
117 *See* G. ROBERTSON & A. NICOL, *supra* note 54, at 264.
118 The Sunday Times v. United Kingdom, [1979] 2 E.H.R.R. 245 = 1979 Eur.GrundRZ 386-93 = 22 YB. Human Rights 402-09 (1979).

Sunday Times case, the newspaper had published an article in 1972 dealing with the fact that between 1959 and 1962 a number of British children had been born deformed. Allegedly, this was the result of the drug »Thalidomide,« which the mothers had taken during pregnancy. The newspaper had announced its intention to publish another article on the manufacture and testing history of the drug. When the first article appeared, the manufacturer of the drug and the parents of the victims were still negotiating a settlement of the case; the court had suspended the proceedings subject to the outcome of the settlement negotiations. The manufacturer applied for an injunction to restrain publication of the second article on the ground that this publication would, in view of the litigation still outstanding, constitute contempt of court. The High Court granted the injunction, and the House of Lords ultimately upheld this decision.[119] The European Court of Human Rights concluded that the restriction imposed on the applicant's right to freedom of expression was in breach of article 10(1) of the EUHR.[120] The EUCT placed great weight on the fact that the Thalidomide disaster had victimized numerous children, many of whose families were unaware of the legal difficulties involved. The Court stated that the families had a legitimite interest in getting complete information about all the underlying facts and implications of the case. A restriction on their right to receive this information under these circumstances would only be justified, the Court reasoned, if the publication would otherwise have presented a threat to the »authority of the judiciary.« Clearly, the Court relied heavily on the public's freedom to receive information about a tragedy of such extensive proportions. Since the case arose because *The Sunday Times* had claimed an unjustified restriction on its freedom to publish information, the EUCT's reasoning is a well-illustrated example of the dual character of the right to freedom of information under the European Convention.

The Contempt of Court Act 1981 now imposes strict liability on anyone responsible for a publication in connection with judicial proceedings, if the published material created a serious risk of substantially impeding or prejudicing an »active« case.[121] Under the »strict liability« concept, liability occurs regardless of intention on the part of the person responsible for

---

119 Attorney-General v. Times Newspapers Ltd., 1974 A.C. 273.

120 *See also* VAN DIJK & VAN HOOF, THEORY AND PRACTICE OF THE EUROPEAN CONVENTION ON HUMAN RIGHTS 317-18 (1984).

121 Contempt of Court Act 1981, secs. 1, 2(3),(4) and Schedule I. Independent of whether a case is still active, section 8 of the Act prohibits the publication of any particulars disclosing what happened during jury deliberations.

the offence. As a general rule, a criminal case is »active« when a person has been arrested. In civil cases the decisive moment is the setting down of the case for trial. These events cause a break, after which contempt of court[122] will almost certainly result from subsequent publications revealing the defendant's previous convictions or his previous lifestyle, for example, or reports predicting the outcome of the trial, anticipating the jury verdict, or, in civil litigation, articles revealing a »payment into court.«[123] Criteria limiting liability require that the risk of a *substantial* prejudice be *serious*. The latter requirement was not met in a case in which the British Broadcasting Corporation (BBC) had broadcast a programme only for the region of the southwest of England, while the trial in question had been held in London. The court argued that jury members must have to have had a reasonable chance to view the programme or read the article in order realistically to threaten their objectivity.[124]

Certain defences are available against the rule of strict liability. Section 5 of the Contempt of Court Act 1981 provides for a public-interest defence, if the revelations about an active case are made in good faith for the benefit of a discussion of matters of general public interest. In such a case, the risk of impeding or prejudicing the proceedings must be merely incidental to the discussion. In one case, a »Pro-Life« candidate had written an article during an election campaign for the *Daily Mail* with reference to a doctor charged with the death of a handicapped child. The article was generally concerned with the allegedly widespread practice by hospital personnel of letting deformed children die. Here, the reference to the case on trial was considered a bona fide discussion of an issue of serious public concern.[125] Section 5 of the Contempt of Court Act 1981 acknowledges that in certain cases a superiour public interest in a comprehensive public discussion of critical issues may outweigh the judiciary's interest in preventing any interference with pending criminal trials and the litigant's interest in avoiding any prejudice to his causes.

The absence of any clear-cut rules defining what may safely be published has rightfully been criticized as a drawback to these provisions. This criticism also applies to the lack of publicity given to cases that may have

---

122 *See* G. ROBERTSON & A. NICOL, *supra* note 54, at 164-73.
123 A »payment into court« is a measure employed by defendants wishing to make a formal offer to settle for the paid-in sum. Such payments may not be publicly revealed, not even to the judge.
124 Blackburn v. BBC, The Times, Dec. 15, 1976, *cited in* G. ROBERTSON & A. NICOL, *supra* note 54, at 164 and n. 7.
125 Attorney-General v. English, [1982] 2 All E.R. 903, 920 (per Lord Diplock).

possible disadvantages for defendants and could sometimes result in arbitrary enforcement.[126]

Section 4 of the Contempt of Court Act 1981 additionally exempts from the strict-liability rule any person making a »fair and accurate report of legal proceedings held in public, published contemporaneously and in good faith.« The rationale for this provision is that the general public may be told what has already been made public in official proceedings. The report needs to be accurate in the sense that essentials are correctly but not necessarily literally stated; the report is contemporaneous if it is published as soon as practically possible. In the majority of cases, this will probably be within a day or two of the proceedings, in any event within the time period that is reasonably necessary to prepare and print or broadcast the report. In certain cases, the court has the power to order the postponement of the publication, if it appears necessary in the interest of the administration of justice.[127]

In June 1986, the U.K. government, following discussions with the EUCM, agreed to change the law of contempt of court to allow journalists to use information that had previously been read into open court. This concession came about after all instances of the English courts had upheld the conviction of a person for contempt of court for having shown to a reporter confidential documents that the Home Office had released for court proceedings and that had then been read out publicly during the court proceedings. When it became clear to the government that the EUCM would give priority to the right of freedom of expression over copyright or confidentiality, it forestalled a ruling by the EUCT and agreed to change the law by means of a statutory instrument altering the court rules.[128]

A provision safeguarding the freedom of the press is section 10 of the Contempt of Court Act 1981. Under this provision, a journalist may not be forced by a court to disclose his source of information for an article, unless the disclosure »is necessary in the interests of justice or national security or for

---

126 Cooke, *Contempt and the Media*, 7 J. MEDIA L. & PRAC. 2, 4 (1986).

127 Contempt of Court Act 1981, sec. 4(2). This provision is being challenged before the European Commission of Human Rights as violating article 13 of the European Convention on Human Rights, because the Act provides no effective remedy against a court order of this provision. *See* Decision of Mar. 9, 1987, 11553/85, G.M.T. Hodgson et al. v. U.K.; 11658/85, Channel Four Television Co. Ltd. v. UK, *reported in* 8 J. MEDIA L. & PRAC. 70 (1987). In the same decision, the EUCM rejected the applicants' complaint under article 10 of the Convention. The applicants had argued that the order by the court, prohibiting them from broadcasting a programme on English court proceedings on every evening of the trial by using actors to read the edited court transcripts, violated article 10. They had been free, however, to cover the trial by way of using experienced newsreaders instead of actors.

128 *See* 7 J. MEDIA L. & PRAC. 101 (1986).

the prevention of disorder or crime.« The exception referred to by the term »in the interest of justice« has been interpreted rather narrowly by the courts to further the protection of secret sources of press information.[129]

The strict-liability rule applies only with regard to publications. The term »publication« as used in section 2(1) »includes any speech, writing, broadcast or other communication in whatever form, which is addressed to the public at large or any section of the public.« Anyone in the chain of distribution may be liable, i.e., the publisher, the editor, the journalist, the printer, the importer or the newsvendor.[130] With regard to television, the broadcasting company, the producer and director, and the cable television operator distributing the programme to the subscribers may be held liable. However, under section 3 of the Act, a publisher may defend himself by proving that at the time of publication (having taken all reasonable care), he did not know and had no reason to suspect that the proceedings were active. This is a very narrow defence. If a suspect is being questioned by the police, for example, a journalist may already have reason to suspect that an arrest might be imminent and could occur before the time of publication of the article.

In the *Griffiths* case,[131] the court found the British distributors of the U.S. magazine *Newsweek* guilty of contempt of court. The defendants had had no knowledge of the contested article in one of *Newsweek*'s issues, which dealt with the trial of a medical practitioner conducted in England at the time of distribution of the magazine. The article had been written in the United States, and the magazine had been printed entirely in the Netherlands. Later it had been flown to London for distribution in the United Kingdom. *Newsweek* had maintained an office with a correspondent in London, but the court acquitted the correspondent on the ground that he had nothing to do with the writing, printing or distribution of the article in Britain.[132] The British distributors, on

---

129 *See, e.g.*, Maxwell v. Pressdram Ltd. (1986), The Times, Nov. 12, 1986 (Court of Appeal, Kerr and Parker, L.J.J.); Secretary of Defence v. Guardian Newspapers Ltd., [1984] 3 All E.R. 601.

130 G. ROBERTSON & A. NICOL, *supra* note 54. at 174.

131 R. v. Griffiths, [1957] 2 Q.B. 192.

132 *Id.* at 200-02 (per Lord Goddard C.J.). In 1987 the High Court, in yet another decision dealing with the consequences of the publication of the book *Spycatcher* by a former member of the British Security Service, imposed a ban on a public library in Derbyshire, holding that making available to members of the public copies of the book would amount to contempt of court as an interference with the due administration of justice, in light of the preliminary injunction against publication imposed on several British newspapers. However, the court held that the library authority was generally not obliged to examine foreign

the other hand, had done everything possible to stop the circulation of the magazine once the offending article had been brought to their attention. They claimed the defence of innocent dissemination, on the basis that they had distributed the magazine for twenty years without receiving any complaints about its content and had at the outset examined three consecutive issues of *Newsweek* to ensure that objectionable material would not be included. Nonetheless, the court imposed a fine on the distributors, stating its regret that it could not deal with the truly responsible people – namely, the publisher in New York and the printer in Amsterdam – because they were outside its jurisdiction.[133]

According to section 3(2) of the Contempt of Court Act 1981, distributors may advance the defence that at the time of distribution (having taken all reasonable care), they did not know that the publication contained any offensive material and had no reason to suspect that this was likely. In order to comply with the standard of reasonable care, distributors sometimes require magazines to enclose lawyers' opinions stating that the publication contains no offensive matters.[134] Like the publishers, the distributors carry the burden of proof to establish their defence (section 3(3) of the Act). Even so, it has been argued that in a case with facts similar to the *Griffiths* case, distributors might still be held in contempt of court.[135] This precedent therefore still represents a potential threat to the distribution and sale of a broad variety of foreign periodicals in the United Kingdom.

Another aspect of English contempt law, although with somewhat less factual significance for freedom of the press, is contempt of Parliament. This is an offence that rests neither in statutory nor in case law. The law and custom of Parliament are independent sources of English law binding on members of Parliament and on ordinary citizens alike. This law grants many privileges to the individual members of Parliament as well as to Parliament as an institution. Thus, a member of the press who reports parliamentary proceedings may be held in contempt of Parliament unless he

---

newspapers and periodicals that it made available to the public to see whether they contained, directly or indirectly, any information obtained by the book's author. Attorney-General v. The Observer Ltd.; Attorney-General v. Guardian Newspapers Ltd.; In re application by Derbyshire County Council, High Court (Chancery Division), judgment of Oct. 20. 1987, Fin. Times, Oct. 20, 1987 (per Knox J.).

133 *Griffiths,* [1957] 2 Q. B. at 204-05.
134 G. ROBERTSON & A. NICOL, *supra* note 54, at 174.
135 H. STREET, *supra* note 37, at 158.

acted in good faith and issued a fair report.[136] Also, if Parliament feels that a criticism directed at its character is capable of diminishing the respect due to the House, it may convict the perpetrator under its own law of contempt.[137] The editor of the *Sunday Express* was held in contempt of Parliament because an article in his newspaper had suggested that during the petrol rationing following the Suez Crisis in 1956, members of Parliament had unduly favoured themselves in the apportionment of petrol.[138]

The disciplinary means available to both Houses of Parliament in cases of contempt are most severe. Parliament sits as a judge in its own cases. It may convict a person without granting him a hearing if it feels that the breach of privilege is obvious. It may issue warrants for the arrest of the offender without giving him any reasons for the arrest and cross-examine him with the help of several Queen's Counsel without allowing the accused either to be represented as well by counsel or to cross-examine the witnesses. Parliament may send the convict to prison, impose fines, or, in less severe cases, admonish or reprimand the offender.[139] It seems only all too obvious that these procedural rights retained by Parliament contravene in more than one aspect the principles of the European Convention on Human Rights. But it seems also probable that Parliament would find it difficult to curtail its own rights that have existed since time immemorial.

The obscenity laws further restrict the freedom of the press. They are applicable to private citizens as well as to newspaper publishers, publishing companies, distributors, printers and similar persons. The cardinal statute dealing with obscenity is the Obscene Publications Act 1959.[140] Before considering the Act in detail, however, it seems appropriate to cite from the 1979 report of the Williams Committee on obscenity and film cen-

---

136 *Id.* at 170. Contempt of Parliament may also be involved if a newspaper publishes a report of one of the committee meetings of either House on the basis of information obtained through a breach of parliamentary privilege. *Id.* at 171-72. (*citing* three such cases from the years 1968, 1975, and 1978 respectively). When in 1986 the House of Commons Committee found that a journalist of *The Times* had published a report that constituted a serious contempt of Parliament, it recommended barring the reporter from Parliament for six months and withdrawing permanently one accredited place of *The Times*. However, the majority of the House of Commons voted against the imposition of any of these sanctions. *See* 7 J. MEDIA L. & PRAC. 104 (1986).

137 *See* Hansard, 5th. series, H.C. Vol. 443, col. 1100 et seq.

138 2nd Report from the Committee of Privileges 1956-1957, Feb. 5, 1957.

139 H. STREET, *supra* note 37, at 173-76.

140 Obscene Publications Act 1959 (7 & 8 Eliz. 2, c.66), as amended by the Obscene Publications Act 1964 (c.74). *See also* the Indecent Displays (Control) Act 1981 (c.42), prohibiting the public display of indecent matter.

sorship, which has the following to say about the English law on obscenity and related matters:

> The law is scattered among so many statutes, and these so often overlap with each other and with the various common law offences and powers which still exist in this field, that it is a complicated task even to piece together a statement of what the law is, let alone to attempt to wrestle with or resolve the inconsistencies and anomalies to which it gives rise. ... The law, in short, is a mess.[141]

In the time since this statement was made, the situation has remained unchanged. Section 2 makes the publishing of an obscene article or the possession of an obscene article for publication for gain an offence punishable by a maximum of three years in prison or an unlimited fine. An article is deemed to be obscene if its effect tends to deprave and corrupt persons likely to read, see or hear the matter contained in it (section 1(1) of the Act). A person publishes an article when he »(a) distributes, circulates, sells, lets on hire, gives, or lends it, or who offers it for sale or for letting on hire; or (b) in the case of an article containing or embodying matter to be looked at or a record, shows, plays or projects it.«[142] The Act explicitly denies the applicability of alternative (b) to anything done in the course of television or sound broadcasting (section 1(3) of the Act). This is because the BBC and the IBA are already under an obligation imposed by charter and statute, respectively, not to broadcast anything indecent.[143] On the other hand, sound recordings, cinematograph films and video recordings are covered by the Act.

It is a defence under the Act to prove that the person charged with the offence had not examined the article and had no reason to suspect that it was obscene (section 2(5) of the Act). Additionally, the defendant may successfully claim that publication was for the public good, if it was »in the

---

141 Home Office, Report of the Committee on Obscenity and Film Censorship, Cmnd. 7772, para 2.29 (1979, reprinted 1981) (hereafter cited as 1979 Report of the Williams Committee).

142 Obscene Publications Act 1959, sec. 1(3); *see also* Obscene Publications Act 1964, sec. 2.

143 *See infra* at chapter II(B). In April 1986, a bill introduced by several Conservative members of Parliament to extend the Obscene Publications Acts to broadcasting failed to gain the necessary support in Parliament (*see* Obscene Publications (Protection of Children) (Amendment) Bill). Its supporters had claimed that the guidelines under which the BBC and the IBA operate were ineffective. Fin. Times, Apr. 26, 1986. Less than a year later, another attempt to subject the broadcasters to the obscenity laws was made. *See* The Times, Feb. 17, 1987. The Conservative government has announced that it intends to subject broadcasting to the general obscenity laws as part of the proposed media law reform to be carried through in autumn of 1988; *see* Fin. Times, June 24, 1987.

interests of science, literature, art or learning, or of other objects of general concern« (section 4(1) of the Act). In order to establish the defence of public good, justices may hear expert witnesses on the literary and other merits of the publication, although they are free to reject favourable testimony advanced by such experts.[144] In determining the literary merits, a book is considered as a whole and attention is paid to the general message the author intended to convey.[145] The provisions of the Obscene Publications Act 1959 may also extend to matters outside the sexual context. In 1965, despite unanimous testimonies by expert witnesses to the contrary, a book was held to be obscene on the ground that it advocated drug taking.[146]

In the *Handyside* case,[147] the EUCT had to reach a verdict on the consistency of the Obscene Publications Act 1959 with article 10 of the EUHR. The publisher of the *The Little Red Schoolbook* had complained that the seizure of the book, his conviction and the subsequent forfeiture and destruction of numerous copies of the book as provided for under section 3 of the Act[148] had not been »necessary in a democratic society« in the interest of the protection of morals. The English court had inter alia held that the anti-authoritarian passages of the book, which was specifically directed at children, could undermine the children's respect for parents, teachers, the church and similar institutions; this could aggravate the tendencies to »deprave and corrupt« that resulted from other parts of the book. The EUCM, stressing that freedom of expression was a crucial prerequisite to a pluralistic, open and tolerant society, noted in the same case that such a society

> [o]f necessity... involves a delicate balance between the wishes of the individual and the utilitarian »greater good of the majority.« But democratic societies approach the problem from the standpoint of the importance of the individual and the undesirability of restricting the individual's freedom.
>
> The Commission accepts, however, that, in striking the balance, certain controls on the individual's freedom of expression may, in appropriate circumstances, be acceptable in order to respect the sensibilities of others. It notes, in this context, that »freedom of expression is commonly subject in a democratic society« to laws importing restrictions considered »necessary to prevent sedicious, libellous, blasphemous and obscene publications« (De Becker case, Application No 214/56).

---

144 John Calder (Publications) Ltd. v. Powell, [1965] 1 Q.B. 509.
145 *See* H. STREET, *supra* note 37, at 128; P. MACMILLAN, CENSORSHIP AND PUBLIC MORALITY 17-30 (1983).
146 *John Calder (Publications) Ltd.*, [1965] 1 Q.B. at 515 (per Lord Parker C.J.).
147 Judgment of Dec. 7, 1976 (»Handyside«), 24 JUDG. DEC. (Series A).
148 The Obscene Publications Act 1959, sec. 3, does not create a criminal offence. A person whose property is forfeited under this section is not for this reason alone guilty of a criminal offence.

60

The Commission therefore acknowledges the necessity of certain restrictions on obscene publications for the protection of the morals of that society, particularly the morals of young people and children.[149]

Against this background the Court examined the question whether the particular actions taken against Handyside and the book conformed with the standards of the Convention. The applicant asserted that translations of the book had freely circulated in other member states to the Convention. The Court rejected the implication of this argument, reasoning that the aim of the Convention had not been to establish a uniform standard of morality throughout the member states. Instead, an examination of the lawfulness of a state's actions would have to take place on the basis of the moral standards prevailing in that country.[150] The EUCT argued that the standard set out in article 10(2) of the EUHR for the restriction of freedom of expression opened for the legislative, administrative and judicial bodies of each state a margin of appreciation; the EUCT could not therefore simply replace the decisions of the domestic courts with its own judgment. It could only review their decisions under the aspect of whether they had acted properly within their margin of appreciation. The Court concluded that provisions of the Obscene Publications Act 1959 as well as the measures taken in this individual case had been compatible with article 10(2) of the EUHR, particularly in light of the fact that the protection of children necessitated special safeguards.

In the United Kingdom, the Obscene Publications Act 1959 also applies with respect to magazines, books, etc. intended for export. In the *Gold Star* case,[151] the House of Lords affirmed the decision of a lower court ordering the forfeiture of magazines that had been stored in an English warehouse to await their export to countries in Europe, Asia, Africa and America. Gold Star had claimed that the extension of the Act to goods destined for publication abroad constituted an extraterritorial application of U.K. law and that there was no evidence that the articles would tend »to deprave and corrupt« the ultimate foreign reader. The court found that it had jurisdiction because the magazines had been located in England and the seizure had also taken place within its jurisdiction.[152] In addition,

---

149 Opinion of Sept. 30, 1975 (»Handyside«), 22 JUDG. DEC. (Series B) 8, 45.
150 *Handyside, supra* note 147, at p. 22.
151 Gold Star Publications Ltd. v. Director of Public Prosecutions, [1981] 2 All E.R. 257.
152 *Id.* at 265 (per Lord Roskill).

the court held, the magazines had been kept for publication for gain; the fact that the publication had been planned to take place abroad made no difference to the court. It agreed with the defendant that the question whether the articles were obscene depended on an evaluation of their impact on the ultimate foreign readers. Citing the *Handyside* case, the court then admitted that the standard of morality was a relative one and could differ considerably from one country to the next; thus for an English court to decide whether certain articles would tend to deprave and corrupt the ultimate foreign readership was a very difficult task.[153] Nonetheless, the court held that in judging the standard of obscenity, an English court could always fall back on the standard of »ordinary human nature,« according to which certain articles would »clearly« be obscene.[154] In effect, the House of Lords pronounced that the standard of morality applied to publications destined for the English market could be more strict than the one an English court might apply to articles solely intended for export.

One judge, Lord Simon of Glaisdale, dissented, arguing that had Parliament wanted to extend the Obscene Publications Act 1959 to export goods, it would have said so explicitly.[155] However, such a holding leading to the inapplicability of the Act to articles destined for export would have contravened the United Kingdom's international obligations under the International Convention for the Suppression of the Circulation of and Traffic in Obscene Publications.[156] Under article 1(2) of this Convention, the contracting states agreed to take all measures to discover, prosecute and punish any person who imports, conveys or exports or causes to be imported, conveyed or exported any obscene matters.[157] While these treaty provisions form no part of English law, the courts traditionally have interpreted where possible the domestic law in a way to make it consistent with the United Kingdom's treaty obligations. Although the *Gold Star* decision made no mention of the Convention, the House of Lords' holding in effect gave recognition to these international obligations.

---

153 *Id.* at 259 (per Lord Wilberforce).
154 *Id.*
155 *Id.* at 260-62.
156 *Concluded* in Geneva, Sept. 12, 1923, *ratified by* the United Kingdom on Dec. 11, 1925, Cmnd. 2575, U.K.T.S. 1/1926 = 27 L.N.T.S. 213; and 1947 Protocol, Cmnd. 8438, U.K.T.S. 2/1952 = 46 U.N.T.S. 169. The acceptance of this Convention entails the acceptance of the Agreement for the Suppression of Obscene Publications, *concluded* in Paris, May 4, 1910, *ratified by* the United Kingdom on Mar. 15, 1911, Cmnd. 5657, U.K.T.S. 11/1911 = 11 L.N.T.S. 438; and 1949 Protocol, Cmnd. 8152, U.K.T.S. 13/1951 = 30 U.N.T.S. 3.
157 The Convention refrains from defining the term obscenity and leaves this task to the contracting states.

Finally, the export of security-sensitive material is controlled under the Import, Export and Custom Powers (Defence) Act 1939.[158] While this Act mainly deals with export controls of such goods as arms and other military appliances, atomic energy materials and high-technology articles, the export of any drawings, designs, descriptions and similar matter relating to these articles is also prohibited unless a proper export licence is obtained.[159] Under this statute the United Kingdom can also give effect to the restrictions imposed on the export of certain sensitive items defined as such by the Coordinating Committee (COCOM).

In summary, it may be said that freedom of the press, while a recognized principle of English law, is restricted in numerous ways, not least of which through a system of voluntary self-censorship. As long as no constitutional rights guarantee press freedom in England, article 10 of the European Convention on Human Rights will maintain considerable importance as the only legal instrument that may help to fend off stifling restrictions on the freedom of the press. However, only few cases are ever decided by the Commission, and even fewer reach the EUCT. The arduous and expensive route that this system entails for individual plaintiffs has already been documented in the context of freedom of speech. As things stand now, press freedom in England faces strong adverse currents and could well use more explicit protection.

3. *Freedom to Broadcast*

The dissemination of ideas via electromagnetic waves can take place either in the form of terrestrial broadcasting, via satellite, or through cable systems. The latter two communications facilities have only in recent years gained considerable importance in the context of freedom of information, because of the revolutionary developments in telecommunications technology. While the individual right to freedom of broadcasting is relevant in respect of all three communications technologies, it may be helpful first to look at the way access to terrestrial broadcasting has been regulated in the United Kingdom.

From 1927, when the BBC in its present legal form was first established by Royal Charter, until 1954, when the Independent Television Authority (ITA) and with it commercial television were created, terrestrial broadcasting in the United Kingdom was solely a public monopoly. No private in-

---

158 Import, Export and Custom Powers (Defence) Act 1939 (2 & 3 Geo. 6, c.69).
159 *See* The Export of Goods (Control) Order 1978, 1978 S.I. No. 796 and Schedule 1.

dividual was able to broadcast his own radio or television programmes. The Television Act 1954[160] changed this, such that the ITA as a public authority with supervisory functions received the power to grant regional licences for the provision of television programmes to private individuals or private enterprises. The fourteen television licence areas franchised by the IBA together cover the whole territory of the United Kingdom. Each licence guarantees a monopoly position for the provision of programmes on one channel in the respective licence areas. Radio broadcasting remained a BBC monopoly until 1973, when the ITA, then renamed the Independent Broadcasting Authority (IBA), was enshrined with the additional task of granting local radio licences to private applicants. These commercial stations in turn have so far faced no competition in their service areas from other commercial radio stations.

The introduction of commercial television in the United Kingdom thus only created the possibility for some fourteen[161] licensees to make use of their right to freedom of expression via television, while all other potentially interested persons remained excluded. Also, non-EC nationals have been totally ineligible for a broadcasting licence.[162] Independent Television (ITV), as the commercial television system came to be called, therefore did not acknowledge or even create a true individual freedom to broadcast that would have opened up a broadcasting opportunity to any interested party. This situation remained unchanged with the introduction of Independent Local Radio (ILR). Although this gave a greater number of individuals the chance to disseminate their ideas by means of terrestrial broadcasting, the radio licences were granted local monopolies, thus preventing others from also broadcasting in the same locality. At the same time, the BBC continued to preserve its monopoly position with regard to national television services[163] and regional and national radio broadcasting services. As a result, despite the existence of commercial broadcasting in the United Kingdom, the right to freedom of (terrestrial) broadcasting did not become a recognized legal principle.

The reasons for the initial establishment of a purely public broadcasting monopoly and the later introduction of a severely restricted commercial

---

160 Television Act 1954 (2 & 3 Eliz. 2, c.55).

161 In reality, the total number of ITV licensees is 16, because two licences have been awarded for the London area, and all ITV companies jointly operate Independent Television News (ITN), the contractor responsible for the provision of news programmes.

162 *See* Broadcasting Act 1981 (c. 68), sec. 20(6).

163 An exception to some extent is Channel 4. The special legal regime that applies to this service permits its being left outside the present analysis. For more details on Channel 4, see *infra* at chapter II(B)(2).

64

broadcasting system have been twofold. The reason most often advanced first is spectrum scarcity. As a matter of physics, broadcasting frequencies are limited in number. Their use must be regulated and assigned to certain specified users, if a chaos of mutually disturbing transmissions is to be avoided. In a situation of unregulated use of radio frequencies, public reception of broadcasts would be greatly impeded, if not completely frustrated. In the United Kingdom, the concern for a proper administration of the radio spectrum has caused the use of the broadcasting frequencies to be entrusted entirely to the two public broadcasting organizations BBC and IBA. While the BBC is responsible for its own transmissions, the IBA has exclusive control over the technical facilities, i.e., transmitters and similar equipment, needed for the transmission of the regional ITV television programmes. Spectrum scarcity thus leads to a natural limitation of the number of people who are able to run their own television stations.

Spectrum scarcity cannot explain, however, why in the early days of broadcasting a *public* monopoly was established or why the commercial television system was later heavily regulated with regard to programme content. The answer is one of media policy. The 1923 Report of the Sykes Committee gave the key to the understanding of the future structure of the broadcasting system, a regulatory framework that in essence has been preserved up to this day. The Committee, referring to the broadcast media, stated that »the control of such a potential power over public opinion and the life of the nation ought to remain with the State and that the operation of so important a national service ought not to be allowed to become an unrestricted commercial monopoly.«[164] The presumption of the Committee was that since frequencies were very sparse, the only alternative to a public broadcasting monopoly would have been a private broadcasting monopoly. This situation would have operated against the public interest of ensuring that the single source of information be unbiased and informative. In the Sykes Committee's line of argument, considerations of spectrum scarcity and media policy were still intricately intertwined.

However, with the setting up of the BBC, the public-interest concept was transformed and carried beyond the initial idea that a public monopoly was merely necessary to prevent the creation of a privately controlled propaganda machine. The new impetus was represented and forcefully carried through by the first BBC Director General John Reith, later Lord

---

164 The Broadcasting Committee: Report, Cmnd. 1951 (1923) (hereafter cited as 1923 Sykes Report).

Reith. His declared policy was to »[g]ive the public something slightly better than it now thinks it likes.«[165] Another passage quoted from Lord Reith is even more telling: »In earliest years accused of setting out to give the public not what it wanted but what the BBC thought it should have, the answer was that few knew what they wanted, fewer what they needed.«[166] The aim of the public broadcasting monopoly then became to educate and inform the public in order »to help them become better citizens.« Some forty years later, the BBC, looking back at its early days, itself declared that its programme policy had been »imperial, patrician, and Christian.«[167] This special zeal to educate the nation and to control firmly all broadcasting programmes to which British citizens could turn to for a number of years remained the ultimate reason for the public broadcasting monopoly. The argument of spectrum scarcity played a subordinate role. When in the 1920s private companies began to transmit radio programmes over wire, particularly to areas with poor off-air signal reception, they used the technical opportunities of these cable transmissions also to relay foreign, particularly commercial, radio programmes over their wires.[168] The foreign radio programmes enjoyed great popularity, but the BBC strongly opposed these services.[169] It feared not only for its broadcast monopoly if relay companies were able to transmit their own programmes. More than anything else, the BBC worried that its programme policy would be undermined by the common practice of relay operators replacing parts of BBC programmes with foreign material while retaining other parts. This changed BBC programme balance and programme mixture.[170]

By 1937 the strong lobbying of BBC supporters showed signs of success: relay services were more and more heavily regulated, »must-carry« rules for BBC (and later IBA) services were introduced, and – most importantly – a strict prohibition of programmes originated by the relay operators applied.[171] Even then the BBC continued to oppose the practice of many relay operators offering one foreign sound programme channel, like Radio

165 B. PAULU, TELEVISION AND RADIO IN THE UNITED KINGDOM 154 and n. 5 (1981), *citing* Lord Reith in *BBC Handbook* 71 (1928).
166 *Id.*, *citing* Lord Reith's book, *Into the Wind*, at p. 101 (no date).
167 B. PAULU, *supra* note 165, at 156 and n. 13, *citing BBC Memorandum, The BBC's Programme Policy* paras. 22, 25 (1974).
168 *See* the detailed account given by T. HOLLINS, BEYOND BROADCASTING: INTO THE CABLE AGE 39-40 (1984).
169 *Id.* at 39.
170 B. PAULU, *supra* note 165, at 20-21 and n. 56, *citing BBC Yearbook 1933*.
171 *Id.* at 21.

Luxembourg, or a mixture from Continental stations to their sub-scribers.[172]

These early programme-policy conflicts have also been cited as evidence that the widespread explanation given for the public broadcasting monopoly as a historical necessity due to spectrum scarcity is a myth:[173] When some 60 years ago a recognized demand for and the – though limited – technical feasibility of privately originated cable programmes existed, this potential development of complementary media programmes was stifled for media-policy reasons.

The paternalistic approach of British media policy began to change in the 1940s and particularly in the 1950s with the emergence of a competing commercial broadcasting system. More room was generally given to entertainment. But the active conveyance of ideas and attitudes reflecting much of Reith's ethical and political value system is still enshrined in today's broadcasting regulations. The principle tasks of both the BBC and the IBA are to inform, educate and entertain, in this order.[174] Fur-thermore, stringent programme-content regulations and a system of programme review designed to implement these content standards are in operation for both broadcasting systems.[175] These rules heavily restrict the freedom of expression of broadcasting journalists, television film directors, and similar persons. For example, under section 4(1)(f) of the Broadcasting Act 1981, persons providing the programmes have to preserve »due impartiality« as regards matters of political or industrial controversy or relating to current public policy. Also, on all of these subjects (with the exception of issues having to do with broadcasting), the ITV licensee himself is prohibited from expressing his own opinion (section 4(2)). This provision deprives the ITV contractor's freedom to broadcast of its essence, i.e., the right to express freely his own ideas by means of broadcasting. What is left is merely the shell of the right to broadcast: it is the right to run a television company.

A first move towards the opening of the broadcasting system to third par-ties was made with the establishment in 1980 of Channel 4, a television channel under the control of the IBA.[176] Channel 4's programme policy is

---

172 Report of the Committee on Broadcasting, 1960, Cmnd. 1753, para. 944 (1962) (hereafter cited as 1960 Pilkington Committee Report).
173 R. COASE, BRITISH BROADCASTING. A STUDY IN MONOPOLY 84 (1950). *See also* H.-P. REITER, DIE STRUKTUR DES BRITISCHEN RUNDFUNKS – FOLGERUNGEN FÜR DIE MEDIENLANDSCHAFT DER BUNDESREPUBLIK DEUTSCHLAND 316-17 (1986).
174 *See* Broadcasting Act 1981, sec. 2(2)(a).
175 For more details on BBC and IBA content control, see *infra* at chapter II(C).
176 For more details on Channel 4, see *infra* at chapter II(B)(2).

characterized by the commission of programmes from third parties, such as the ITV contractors. However, from the beginning it was also anticipated to commission programmes from independent (British) producers. This independent broadcasting production sector was virtually nonexistent in 1980 but began to boom soon after access to the new channel was made available.

As a result of the government's more recent commitment to the introduction of increased competition in broadcasting, the so-called independents have even gained its support for access to both the BBC television channels as well as the ITV system. Thus, in 1987, as a result of sustained political pressure to make 25 per cent of total broadcasting time available to the independents over a period of four to five years, the BBC announced a £ 4 million package of independently produced programmes. After negotiations between the ITV companies and the independent production sector over specific terms of the contracts for commissioned programmes had broken down, the IBA announced in early 1988 that it would work out a binding framework for production fees, i.e., in essence, the profits of independent producers and the exploitation rights for the sale of the programmes abroad.[177] Earlier, the ITV companies had announced their willingness to commission £ 42 million worth of programmes from the independents.[178]

The government's policy of supporting an independent production sector is of vital significance for the recognition of third-party access rights to the broadcasting system. The government has made it clear that it would introduce a 25-percent quota by legislation in favour of the independents unless the broadcasters voluntarily agreed to provide such access to their systems. While a more pluralistic broadcasting system is thus well underway, some important restrictions still remain. Starting with the maximum of a 25-percent share of total broadcasting hours, the independents moreover are subject to the same programme content restrictions as the traditional broadcasters. Just like in the case of the latter, their freedom of expression remains regulated by the standards characterizing the public broadcasting system.

The right of political candidates to make their views known via the broadcast media has also been curtailed. In the 1940s, British candidates had availed themselves of the opportunity to advertise on foreign radio stations, a possibility that did not exist in Britain. The Representation of

177 Fin. Times, Jan. 15, 1988.
178 Fin. Times, Dec. 4, 1987.

the People Act 1949[179] therefore expressly prohibited the use of foreign broadcasting stations for this purpose in parliamentary elections (section 80(1)). An amendment to this section in 1969 also interdicted the practice of political advertisements on »pirate« stations during local elections.[180] These provisions were consolidated in the Representation of the People Act 1983[181] and are now encompassed in section 92 of that Act. Since the scope of the provision expressly extends to »any television or other wireless transmitting station outside the United Kingdom for the transmission of any matter having reference to the election otherwise than in pursuance of arrangements made with« the BBC or the IBA, it also encompasses satellite transmissions of television programmes, an application certainly unforeseen when the provision was first drafted.

The two-tiered basis of the broadcasting structure in the United Kingdom, namely, media policy and the proper administration of the radio spectrum ensuring the provision of high-quality television for the whole population, is generally referred to as the public-service concept of broadcasting. This concept is the key to the understanding of the British broadcasting system.

The broadcasting duopoly and the limitations on a third-party right of access makes a right of reply or some other measure of defence against unjust and unfair treatment in a programme all the more necessary. However, just as in the context of press publications the rights of individuals to look after their interests vis-à-vis the broadcasters have found only weak legal considerations. The Broadcasting Complaints Commission (BCC) is a rough parallel to the Press Council, with the important difference that – unlike the latter – it is a statutory body with effective enforcement powers. It was set up in 1980[182] with the task of considering and adjudicating complaints of (a) unjust or unfair treatment in sound or television programmes actually broadcast,[183] or (b) unwarranted infringements of privacy in the acquisition of material included in such programmes (section 54(1) of the Broadcasting Act 1981).

Originally, the BCC was only responsible for the adjudication of complaints directed against programmes broadcast by the BBC or the IBA. With the Cable and Broadcasting Act 1984, its jurisdiction was extended to

---

179 Representation of the People Act 1949 (12, 13 & 14 Geo. 6, c.68).
180 Representation of the People Act 1969 (c.15), sec. 9(5).
181 Representation of the People Act 1983 (c.2.).
182 Broadcasting Act 1980 (c. 64), sec. 17.
183 »>[U]njust or unfair treatment‹ includes treatment which is unjust or unfair because of the way in which material included in a programme has been selected or arranged.« *See* Broadcasting Act 1981, sec. 54(3).

programmes included in a cable television service (section 29 of the Cable and Broadcasting Act 1984). The Commission consists of a minimum of three members appointed by the Home Secretary. While they hold office they may not be in any way affiliated with either the IBA, the BBC or the Cable Authority or any television or radio programme contractor or cable television service provider. Unlike the Press Council, the BCC only considers complaints of persons who were personally affected by the treatment complained of or who have at least a direct interest in the subject matter (sections 55(2), 54(3) of the Broadcasting Act 1981). The Commission lacks jurisdiction over complaints about bad taste, offensiveness or indecency and may not concern itself with programmes already recorded but not yet broadcast (section 54(1),(2) of the Broadcasting Act 1981). Its jurisdiction is further limited by the provision that it may not proceed with the complaint if the unjust or unfair treatment or unwarranted infringement of privacy is the subject of legal proceedings in a U.K. court of law or if the person affected has a legal remedy in a court of law and it is not appropriate for the Commission to consider the complaint in the particular circumstances. In a case where the complainant had a remedy in libel against the BBC and where the libel action was only a possibility and not all of the aspects complained of could have been made the subject of a court action, the Court of Appeal refused to prohibit the Commission from adjudicating the complaint.[184] In another case, however, where a libel action was already pending, the Commission was effectively barred from adjudicating the complaint.[185]

One of the outstanding features of the Commission is its extremely wide statutory discretion to entertain or dismiss complaints. In light of the fact that English law acknowledges no individual right of reply, the Commission's broad discretion is only minimally counterbalanced by the individual's right to appeal a BCC decision to the courts. In the *Owen* case,[186] the Court upheld the exercise of this wide discretion where the Commission had refused to review a complaint by David Owen, the leader of the Social Democratic Party (SDP), who presented strong evidence that suggested that his party had been unfairly treated in comparison with the Labour Party in the amount of the BBC's political coverage. The Court

---

184 R. v. Broadcasting Complaints Commission, ex parte BBC, The Times, May 17, 1984. A summary of the case is contained in 5 J. MEDIA L. & PRAC. 308 (1984).

185 R. v. Broadcasting Complaints Commission, ex parte Thames Television, The Times, Oct. 8, 1982. A summary of the case is contained in G. ROBERTSON & A. NICOL, *supra* note 54, at 358.

186 R. v. Broadcasting Complaints Commission, ex parte Owen, [1985] 2 W.L.R. 1025.

pointed to the statutory language of section 55(4) of the Broadcasting Act 1981. The provision first states four specific reasons for the refusal to consider a complaint and then provides that the BCC may also deny relief »if it appears to them for any other reason inappropriate for them to entertain, or proceed with the consideration of, the complaint.«[187] The Commission had turned down the complaint, holding, inter alia, that an inquiry would be especially burdensome and might require extra staff. The Court rejected this reasoning as a basis for the Commission's decision but held that where a statutory body could have reached the same decision on valid grounds, a court would not reverse the disputed decision. A reason to uphold the decision in the present case, the Court argued, could be seen in the fact that (1) Parliament had intended to make the complaints procedure available only to limited personal complaints about specific programmes, while David Owen had complained about the *policy* of the broadcasting organization, a matter which should get a full public hearing with representations from all political parties; (2) the Commission could not grant the relief sought, namely, a change in the BBC's editorial policy; and (3) there would be more appropriate alternative channels to launch a complaint, namely, under sections 2(2)(b) and 4(1) of the Broadcasting Act 1981 to the IBA and under the appendix to article 13(7) of the BBC Licence and Agreement. The third reason given by the Court appears to be rather odd, considering that the cited provisions of the Broadcasting Act 1981 say nothing about an individual's right to complain of an infringement of a personal right but rather contain only general statements about the programme standards to be maintained by the IBA. The Court's ruling implies that in certain cases an individual should complain directly to the IBA or the BBC. This advice serves to reestablish the situation that existed before the establishment of the BCC, when both broadcasting authorities had their own inhouse tribunals to consider complaints. Because of the lack of independence of these tribunals, the public's very limited aquaintance with their existence, and the ineffective publication of their adjudications, Parliament had created the BCC to remedy this unsatisfactory situation.[188]

The Court's holding in the *Owen* case makes it clear that the law reform has not resulted in the provision of truly effective means to safeguard the

---

187 Other grounds for the refusal to consider a complaint are, e.g., that the complaint is frivolous (Broadcasting Act 1981, sec. 55(4)(d)) or that the Commission is of the opinion that the complaint has not been made within a reasonable time after the broadcast (sec. 55(5)).

188 *See* G. ROBERTSON & A. NICOL, *supra* note 54, at 354.

interests of private individuals against the broadcasting media in cases of unjust or unfair treatment. The Commission's jurisdiction is on the one hand too limited, and on the other hand its broad and unaccounted-for discretion can easily amount to the total refusal of a legal remedy.

During the year April 1986 to March 1987, the Commission received 222 complaints, of which 174 were rejected as falling outside the Commission's jurisdiction.[189] The Commission adjudicated 53 complaints, of which 21 were subjected to a full hearing.[190] 12 complaints were upheld (9 in part only) and 9 were rejected. The figures evidence how slight the chances are for any complainant to be even fully heard by the Commission, not to mention the chances to have a complaint upheld. In most cases of the formal findings, the BCC directs the BBC to publish a summary of the adjudication in its publication *Radio Times*, sometimes supplemented by a full publication of the decision in *The Listener*. Decisions against the IBA usually have to be published in *TV Times*.[191] While in the beginning the BCC only on rare occasions made use of its powers to order the broadcasting authorities to broadcast a summary of its findings (section 57(1) of the Broadcasting Act 1981),[192] this practice has since changed, making the means to satisfy the interests of the persons aggrieved more effective. Of the 21 complaints adjudicated in 1986 to 1987, 19 decisions along with brief summaries were broadcast on the radio or television channel that had originally broadcast the controversial programme. In one case concerning Channel 4, only publication of the adjudication in *TV Times* was required; the second decision involving BBC 1 refrained from giving any direction to publish or broadcast the finding. In both these exceptional cases, the Commission had rejected the complaints.

The days of the BCC's existence may be limited. The setting up of the Broadcasting Standards Council (BSC) in early 1988 may have the consequence that the BCC will have to merge into the BSC, following the new legislation on broadcasting that is being prepared by the government.[193] Among the tasks, the BSC is to receive and decide upon complaints from individuals and organizations on the showing of sex and violence on terrestrial, satellite and cable television as well as on video.

---

189 Report of the Broadcasting Complaints Commission 1987, para. 9 (July 1987).
190 Together with the 28 complaints that had been before the Commission as of Mar. 31, 1986, a total of 76 complaints fell under the Commission's jurisdiction during the period. *Id*.
191 G. ROBERTSON & A. NICOL, *supra* note 54, at 359.
192 *See id.* at 360.
193 *See* Fin. Times, Apr. 13, 1988.

Unlike the present BCC, the BSC is not dealing with factual complaints but with programme standards.[194]

The duopoly of the BBC and ITV systems and their heavy content restrictions raise the question of the compatibility of these regulations with the principle of freedom of expression as guaranteed by article 10 of the EUHR. Twice, in 1968 and 1972, the EUCM decided on the applications of individuals who had claimed that a public monopoly on broadcasting violated article 10 of the EUHR. In its decisions, the Commission relied on article 10(1) of the EUHR. The third sentence of this provision reads: »This Article shall not prevent States from requiring the licensing of broadcasting, television or cinema enterprises.« The Commission, pointing to the widespread and long-standing practice of public broadcasting monopolies in many Convention member states, interpreted this clause as permitting such monopolies.[195] This reasoning made article 10(2) of the EUHR inapplicable. According to the Commission's view, a public broadcasting monopoly constituted an interference with the applicants' freedom of expression; but the monopoly needed no justification under article 10(2).

These holdings have been widely criticized. One of the arguments advanced against them is that the broadcasting clause, if interpreted as an exception clause, would allow states to structure their broadcasting systems arbitrarily, even to the point of establishing a state-controlled propaganda machine.[196] A narrow interpretation of the broadcasting clause has therefore been recommended: a public broadcasting monopoly is permissible if its specific regulation can be justified under article 10(2) of the EUHR.[197] The EUCM, too, has hinted at its readiness to modify its adjudication in future cases.[198] With regard to the British broadcasting system, one could argue that if a public monopoly could be justified under the broadcasting clause of article 10(1) of the EUHR, a duopoly system like the British that permits commercial broadcasting side by side with a public broadcasting organization should be all the more compatible with the Convention. But if one agrees that a public monopoly needs to be justified under the public-interest elements of article 10(2) of the EUHR,

194 For more details on the Broadcasting Standards Council, see *infra* at chapter II(C)(1).
195 Decision of Feb. 7, 1968 (No. 3071/67), 26 COLL. DEC. 71, 75 (1968); Decison of Mar. 20, 1972 (No. 4750/71), 40 COLL. DEC. 29, 30 (1972).
196 Engel, *Constitutional and International Guarantees of Freedom of Speech: The Position of Public Monopolies on Broadcasting Under the European Convention on Human Rights*, in THE LAW AND ECONOMICS OF TRANSBORDER TELECOMMUNCIATIONS: A SYMPOSIUM 55, 58 (E.-J. Mestmäcker ed. 1987).
197 *Id.* at 58-59.
198 Decision of Mar. 12, 1976 (»Sacchi«), 5 DR 43, 50 (1975-76).

restrictions on the freedom of private broadcasters also have to meet these tests. The first crucial legal problem in this context is that the commercial broadcasting system is itself structured as a monopoly system in which licensees enjoy regional (in the case of television) and local (in the case of radio) broadcasting monopolies, thus excluding other persons. In this respect, the need to administer properly the few available frequencies for terrestrial broadcasting provides a sufficient justification under article 10(2) of the EUHR. The private monopolies serve to protect the guarantee of freedom of reception, which may be subsumed under the »rights of others« as set out in subsection 2. They also ensure the availability of frequencies needed for public services, such as official notices, traffic announcements and similar matters necessary in the interest of »public safety.«[199]

A second and more complicated question is whether the heavy content regulations applying to ITV can be justified under article 10(2) of the EUHR. Content standards imposed on the programme makers and relating to the showing of violence or of explicitly sexual matters can be justified with the need to protect young persons; they fall under the clause of the »protection of health or morals.« Also, the application of the Official Secrets Act 1911 and the Contempt of Court Act 1981 – as well as the laws on defamation and breach of confidence, etc. – to broadcasting may be justified »in the interests of national security,« »for the protection of the reputation of others,« »for preventing the disclosure of information received in confidence,« and »for maintaining the authority and impartiality of the judiciary.«

However, a particular difficulty arises with respect to the obligation to maintain impartiality on all matters of public policy or to refrain even from expressing personal opinions on any such subject matters. The question has been posed whether the aim of media policy to ensure the presentation of a spectrum of the views and opinions held by different groups of the society that is as broad as possible can be justified under the clause of »rights of others.«[200] The freedom of reception as guaranteed by article 10(1) cannot serve as an argument in this context. This right is concerned with the freedom to receive what *is* available or could be available if all broadcasting frequencies were used; it does not grant the right to demand a certain content in programmes.[201] However, the individual's freedom to broadcast could serve as a justification. If for technical reasons this right has to be curtailed to the point that only one or at least a severely limited

199 *See* Engel, *supra* note 196, at 60.
200 *Id.* at 64-65.
201 *Id.* at 64.

number of private individual(s) may receive a broadcasting licence to the exclusion of all others, a licensee's obligation to give proper consideration to the views of these others represents a compromise between the »all or nothing« approach of a system in which only one person can get a licence to the detriment of the rest of the population. Clearly, not everybody's views on every subject matter – particularly the opinion of a miniscule minority – could be represented. Some views would always remain excluded. But since this would for practical reasons be the case under any broadcasting system (including one with an unlimited number of frequencies), the argument cannot serve as a justification to exclude all but the opinion of one person, i.e., the broadcast licence holder, from the programmes. A private monopoly on broadcasting without obligations to represent properly the views and opinions of the whole spectrum of public opinion would lead to the emergence of a powerful political propaganda apparatus threatening the very foundations of a democratic society. A rule requiring impartiality on all political matters, therefore, lies within the margin of appreciation granted to member states. Such a rule permits the presentation of specific opinions with the only proviso that opposite opinions be given equal recognition.

An impartiality rule under conditions of spectrum scarcity is also both sensible and reasonable, particularly in light of the fact that a private individual or organization cannot claim a right of access to the broadcasting media under article 10 of the EUHR. According to the EUCM, the provision contains no general right granting an individual access to broadcasting time in order to make his opinions personally known to the public.[202]

However, the rule that the ITV contractors may not at all express their own views on matters of current public-policy issues goes beyond the margin of appreciation afforded to member states. Like the impartiality rule, this regulation is designed to prevent the monopolization of public opinion by an ITV contractor. But it finds no justification in any of the criteria of article 10(2) of the EUHR. The freedom to broadcast may justify an impartiality rule requiring that differering opinions on public-policy matters be presented equally in programmes. But the freedom to broadcast

---

202 Judgment of July 12, 1971 (No. 4515/70, X and Association of Z. v. UK), 38 COLL. DEC. 86. In this case, the BBC had refused to allow an association access to broadcasting time. In obiter dictum, the EUCM held that unlike in the case before the Commission, an issue under article 10 alone or in conjunction with article 14 might »in principle, arise, for instance, if one political party was excluded from broadcasting facilities at election time while other parties were given broadcasting time.« *Id.* at 88.

is a *positive* right to make one's views known over the broadcast media; it cannot serve as an argument to suppress the expression of opinion of any particular individual. Besides, a possible monopolization of public opinion is already counteracted by the impartiality rule.

All in all, therefore, the British broadcasting monopoly complies in all but one aspect with article 10 of the EUHR: Any prohibition directed at ITV contractors not to express their personal opinions on their own stations is unjustified under the Convention.

Considerations similar to those presented above and relating to arguments of spectrum scarcity and the prevention of monopolization of public opinions apply in the context of direct broadcasting by satellite (DBS). For the use of this new broadcasting technique, only five satellite channels, i.e., the frequencies necessary for their operation, are available to the United Kingdom.[203] The U.K. government has granted three of the five channels to a private consortium following the public tender of the franchise. For a certain number of years (at present, plans are for the first five years) until the allotment of the last two DBS channels, the consortium will have a monopoly on British DBS broadcasting services.[204] As in the context of terrestrial broadcasting, the programmes have to comply with certain programme standards, although these standards are less restrictive and detailed. Again, these restrictions lie within the margin of appreciation afforded to member states under article 10 of the EUHR. However, since section 4(2) of the Broadcasting Act 1981 – prohibiting the statement of personal political opinions by the ITV contractor – also applies to the DBS contractor,[205] the current DBS regulation unduly infringes upon the DBS contractor's right to freedom of expression under article 10(1) of the EUHR.

A different regulatory regime applies to the dissemination of television and radio programmes over communication or fixed-service satellites (FSS). Because of the weakness of the signal transmissions from these satellites, the programmes cannot be normally received by individual households. The signals have to be rebroadcast either by means of terrestrial transmitters or via cable networks. Because of the need for these intermediary technical systems, the United Kingdom takes the position that the original satellite transmissions do not constitute »broadcasting,« because the signals

---

203 For more details on direct broadcasting by satellite (DBS), see *infra* at chapter III(B).
204 The DBS satellite consortium will also spur the growth of the independent-production sector in Great Britain. Thus, the consortium plans to commission a considerable number of programmes from the independents. Fin. Times, Jan. 9, 1988.
205 *Compare* sec. 37(2) of the Cable and Broadcasting Act 1984 (c.46).

are not »aimed at the general public.« Independent of the legal qualification of satellite transmissions as broadcasts, however, individuals making use of the technical possibility to distribute their programmes to cable systems via FSS exercise their right to freedom of expression as specified in article 10 of the EUHR.

In the United Kingdom no legal regime applies to the dissemination of programmes via FSS. A company that manages to enter into a commercial agreement with British Telecom (BT) or Mercury Communications, the companies with common-carrier status for the technical provision of satellite transmissions,[206] can disseminate its programmes to all countries covered by the footprint of the satellite. However, since British law regulates the programme content of all programmes distributed via U.K. cable systems,[207] the reception of those programmes by the U.K. public is restricted. Only those satellite programmes that comply with the requirements of the Cable and Broadcasting Act 1984 may reach the ultimate audience. This regulatory structure evidences that the freedom to impart information is only the other side of the coin of the freedom to receive information: the total liberalization of the one right is meaningless without the simultaneous possibility to exercise the other. In principle, it may be said that, as in the context of terrestrial broadcasting and DBS, the imposition of content restrictions in the interest of the »rights of others« is justified under article 10(2) of the EUHR.

However, a special problem arises from the announcement by the British government that it would »use its own powers over the use of the frequency spectrum to ensure that no television service or part of a service shall be transmitted by satellite if the Cable Authority certifies that it would be unsuitable for distribution by a cable operator in this country.«[208] The reason for this announcement rests in considerations of international law and policy.[209] At present, the important question is whether the government's approach meets the requirements of article 10 of the EUHR. This is doubtful because article 10(2) permits restrictions on the freedom of expression only as »prescribed by law.« The allocation of frequencies takes

206 For more details on British Telecom's (BT) and Mercury Communications' role in this context, see *infra* at chapter IV(C)(1); BT and Mercury hold monopolies on satellite uplink transmissions.
207 Satellite Master Antenna Television (SMATV) has been exluded. For more details, see *infra* at chapter IV(B)(2).
208 Home Office/Department of Industry, The Development of Cable Systems and Services, Cmnd. 8866, para. 162 (1983) (hereafter cited as 1983 White Paper on Cable Systems).
209 Fore more details on these international law and policy aspects, see *infra* at chapter VI(B)(3).

place on the basis of the Wireless Telegraphy Act 1949.[210] This enactment does not authorize a decision to be taken on the ground of programme content in the way the government insinuated it would proceed. The Cable Authority, on the other hand, as the public authority responsible for the licensing and programme supervision of cable television, has no jurisdiction over satellite-television companies. The dependence of the allocation of satellite frequencies on the Cable Authority's certification is thus not »prescribed by law,« as required by article 10(2) of the EUHR. In order to ensure compliance with the European Convention, Parliament would need to pass a statute subjecting the provision of FSS programme services to a specific legal regime.

Freedom of broadcasting in the area of cable television is regulated by the Cable and Broadcasting Act 1984. Anyone wishing to provide cable television needs a licence from the Cable Authority under section 4 of the Act. Anybody who is either an EC national or a resident of the United Kingdom, the Isle of Man or the Channel Islands may apply for a cable licence.[211] The cable licences impose certain content restrictions on the operators that are less severe than those applying to ITV programme channels. An applicant is expected himself to choose the franchise area for which he would like to receive the cable television licence. Although a few limitations apply with respect to the possible size of the franchise area, it may be said that – aside from satellite television – the individual's freedom to broadcast is most developed in the area of cable television. The number of potential franchise areas in the United Kingdom is very large in comparison with the fourteen regional franchises available for ITV contractors. Their number is limited only by economic restraints: franchise areas must provide the prospect of profitability at least in the long run in order to present viable options.

However, one other serious limitation on the freedom to provide cable services applies. The cable franchisee is to enjoy a monopoly on these services in his franchise area. This is not a legal requirement. The Cable and Broadcasting Act 1984 is silent on the possible number of cable systems in a single area. But as a matter of industrial and media policy with a view to providing additional financial incentives to potential cable operators, the Cable Authority has announced that it »does not envisage in

210 Wireless Telegraphy Act 1949 (12, 13 & 14 Geo. 6, c.54).
211 Cable and Broadcasting Act 1984, sec. 8(1)(a). The section further restricts the group of eligible applicants and lists a number of individuals and entities that may not hold a licence. Most of these restrictions apply in the interest of preventing media-market distortions. For more details, see *infra* at chapter V(B)(2),(3).

the foreseeable future granting a licence to more than one operator in the same area.«[212] This policy excludes all other potential candidates from also laying cables and providing cable-television services in already franchised areas. The compatibility of this policy with article 10(2) of the EUHR appears doubtful. If a cable-franchise application were denied solely on the ground that another cable licence had already been granted for the same area, the restriction on the applicant's freedom of expression would not be »prescribed by law.« Even if a statutory monopoly on cable systems applied, it could hardly be justified as being »necessary in a democratic society,« unless the cable operator acted as a common carrier and third parties had a right of access to the system. At present, however, third-party access rights to the local cable monopolies are nonexistent.[213] This rule applies even in cases in which the cable operator has a large number of idle cable channels at his disposal. A cable operator may volunteer to produce access programmes, granting individual members of the community an opportunity to take active part in the making of a programme or at least to contribute ideas. A variety of such programmes have already been produced for the BBC, ITV and ILR channels. But since there exists no right of access, the decision-making power on whether to include such programmes at all and whom to grant the opportunity to participate rests entirely with the professional broadcasters.[214]

This regulation of cable television represents an extension of the rules that apply to the commercial television system ITV. The cable operator receives the monopoly on programme distribution subject to more or less detailed content regulations. The persons providing the service are also prohibited from expressing their own views and opinions on religious matters or on matters relating to political or industrial controversy or current public policy.[215]

The (in many respects) identical regulation of terrestrial and cable television overlooks the totally different natures of these two broadcasting media. Modern technologies, particularly fibre-optic cable, have created a new dimension for the dissemination of ideas. The new era of communication is characterized by the feasibility of an unlimited number of channels that could be used by an equally unlimited number of people to disseminate

---

212 Cable Authority, Guidance to Franchise Applicants, para. 16 (March 1985).
213 An exception is the »must-carry« rule, according to which the cable operator has to carry all BBC programmes plus the two IBA channels that are aimed at the audience in the cable franchise area.
214 *See* J. HEYN, PARTIZIPATION UND LOKALKOMMUNIKATION IN GROSSBRITANNIEN. VIDEO, FERNSEHEN, HÖRFUNK UND DAS PROBLEM DER DEMOKRATISIERUNG KOMMUNALER KOMMUNIKATION 270-90 (1979).
215 Cable and Broadcasting Act 1984, sec. 11(3)(b).

their opinions to the public. Thus the evolution of modern cable technology has resulted in an increasing similarity between broadcasting via cable and traditional paper publishing. Just like the latter, cable technology provides the possibility for an »electronic publishing market« characterized by a great diversity of different publishers and individual consumer choice. These developments and their potential significance for the total broadcasting system were explicitly recognized in 1986 by the Peacock Committee, which had been set up by the government one year earlier to prepare a report on the future of broadcasting.[216] The Committee recognized that the new technologies give rise to the emergence of a »full broadcasting market« analogous to the already existing publishing market, thereby making it possible to extend the principle of freedom of information to the broadcasting sector. For want of a corresponding provision under domestic law, the Committee took recourse to the First Amendment of the U.S. Constitution guaranteeing freedom of speech and of the press. It referred to the First Amendment in order to stress the overriding importance of these principles for a free and democratic society.[217] The reason why the Committee did not turn to article 10 of the EUHR for guidance may be evidence of the general lack of public awareness of the implications of the European Convention in this context.

From a technical perspective, the Committee visualized that a national grid of optic-fibre cables could offer the adequate means for such a unified information market. The national grid would be operated by a public or private common carrier, who would be under an obligation to grant access to the system to anybody willing to pay the user fees. Not only would an infinite number of channels on the grid be used for broadcasting services of all kinds, an almost unlimited number of channels would equally be available for any other sort of information services, including data-processing services. As a second prerequisite of the new system, the Committee identified the viewers' possibility to express their preferences by direct subscription payment. Occasionally, the Committee referred to the aggregate of these different services as »electronic publishing.« The choice of this term is by no means accidental: It is the direct reflection of the Committee's conviction that the future information market should parallel the publication market of the printed word, the only difference being the medium for the transportation of the information would not be paper but electronic signals carried on a national grid.

216 Home Office, Report of the Committee on Financing the BBC, Cmnd. 9824 (1986) (hereafter cited as 1986 Peacock Report).
217 *Id.* at para. 548.

The availability of the technology alone, however, would not be enough to guarantee freedom of communication. The Committee defined a number of conditions that the legal system would in addition need to set up to meet this aim. Free access to the grid and free consumer choice would have to be safeguarded. Also, under the new legal regime, programme censorship would ultimately be abolished. Clearly, the Committee regarded the heavy government regulation and inhouse censorship practices of the broadcasting authorities not as an aim in itself but as an historical necessity due to existing spectrum scarcities; with increasing channel capacity the justification for government interference and censorship diminishes, ultimately to be totally abrogated and replaced by a system of true consumer sovereignty and unrestricted access of programme makers to an uncensored broadcasting market.[218] Any information carried on the grid, whether in the form of television or sound programmes, teletext services or the like, would only be subject to the general laws of the land dealing with defamation, obscenity, confidentiality, and the like.[219] No special content requirements as now imposed on traditional broadcasters, cable operators and a future DBS service would apply. »The end of all censorship arrangements would be a sign that broadcasting had come to age... .«[220]

The realization that the increase of the number of programme providers carries with it a diminuation of any justification for the content regulations of broadcast speech appears to also take place within the government itself. The 1987 Home Office Green Paper on Radio[221] acknowledged that due to international agreements and a number of reallocations of user groups of the radio spectrum, the 1990s would see a great increase in radio frequencies. Before this background of diminishing spectrum shortage, the government agreed with the Peacock Committee that the detailed content obligations presently imposed on ILR are no longer suitable for radio. As long as the BBC provided public-service programmes, there would be no need for other radio stations to bear the full weight of the obligations to inform, educate and entertain.[222] While the government did not go so far as to advocate the abolition of all content-related restrictions for commercial radio and refrained from supporting the idea that these radio stations – like the printing press – should only be subject to the laws of

218 *Id.* at paras. 479-80, 586.
219 *Id.* at para. 594.
220 *Id.* at para. 696.
221 Home Office, Radio: Choices und Opportunities, Cmnd. 92 (1987) (hereafter cited as 1987 Green Paper on Radio).
222 *Id.* at para. 4.1.

the land, the recommendations, if adopted, would mark a milestone for freedom of broadcasting in the United Kingdom.

The implementation of these recommendations had been made dependent on the reelection of the Conservative government in the parliamentary elections of June 1987. With the Thatcher government once again in power, the legal changes now are imminent. The requirements contained in article 10(2) of the EUHR would be satisfied: While under this provision member states may regulate programme content if a monopolization of opinion in the broadcast media would otherwise be likely, it equally requires states to ease their regulatory regime on content if broadcasting monopolies are no longer unavoidable for technical reasons.

C. *Freedom to Receive Information*

1. *General Framework, Including EC Law*

Article 10(1) of the EUHR guarantees the »freedom to receive information and ideas without interference by public authority and regardless of frontiers.« The right is the mirror image of the freedom to impart information. Thus, laws safeguarding the latter, like the Interception of Communications Act 1985, or laws protecting (peaceful) assemblies, or the rule against prior restraint, for example, also serve to shield the individual's right to obtain information.

A very interesting piece of legislation in the context of the freedom to receive information is the Local Government (Access to Information) Act 1985.[223] Its aim is to provide greater public access to local meetings, reports and documents.[224] To a certain, although limited, extent the new legislation counteracts the Official Secrets Act 1911 and evidences a cautious move towards greater freedom of information in the United Kingdom. The 1985 Act establishes that meetings of local government councils be held in public, unless the disclosure of confidential information as

223 Local Government (Access to Information) Act 1985 (c.43). The Act was incorporated into the Local Government Act 1972 (c.70). It came into force on Apr. 1, 1986.
224 The Access to Personal Files Act 1987 (c.37) has a similar aim. It grants a right of access to individual citizens to manual files relating to housing and social work records. A complaint against the United Kingdom brought before the EUCM concerning the refusal to allow the complainant access to the files held by a local authority and relating to the time when he was in its care has been declared admissible. Application No. 10454/83, Council of Europe Press Release, Jan. 24, 1986.

defined by the Act warrants the exclusion of the public from the meeting (section 100 A). The right of access to the official information is further safeguarded by the provision that public notice of a meeting has to be given at least three days in advance. While the meeting is open to the public, a council may not exclude any particular person from the meeting for any reason other than disorderly conduct. The press enjoys a number of additional rights. Duly accredited newspaper journalists attending a meeting »shall, so far as practicable, be afforded reasonable facilities for taking their report and, ... for telephoning the report at their own expense« (section 100 A(6)(c)). Also, on request of any newspaper and on payment of postage, copies of the agenda for a meeting, the reports for the meeting and similar documents necessary to indicate the nature of the items included in the agenda have to be sent to the newspaper. Members of the public have the right to look at the documents at the offices of the council. After the meeting, copies of the minutes have to be opened for inspection by the public for six years (four years for background papers). All these documents have to be accessible at all reasonable hours and generally without payment. Copies of the documents may be made upon payment of a reasonable fee. The person who has custody of any such document and who without reasonable excuse intentionally obstructs any person from making use of his right of access to the information commits a statutory offence punishable on summary conviction by a fine (section 100 H(4)).

The Local Government (Access to Information) Act 1985, by granting the right of access to specific documents, goes further than article 10 of the EUHR. In a complaint to the EUCM against the United Kingdom, an applicant had alleged a violation of his right to receive information because the authorities had refused to show him a post-mortem report on his murdered wife. The Commission held that the complaint under article 10 was inadmissible because the provision did not entitle any person to receive information in any particular form. In consideration of the information that had been supplied to the husband, the EUCM rejected the allegation of any interference with the man's right to receive information. [225]

Apart from article 10 of the EUHR, the United Kingdom's EC membership has also had a liberalizing impact on the free flow of information across U.K. frontiers, due to the effects of the principles of free movement of goods and services between member states. Section 42 of the Customs Consolidation Act 1876 [226] and section 304 of the Customs and Excise Act

225 EUCM, Application No. 11516/85, 83 LS Gaz. 2319 (1986).
226 Customs Consolidation Act 1876 (39 & 40 Vict., c.36).

1952[227] have twice been scrutinized by the European Court of Justice (EUCJ) for their compatibility with these EC law principles. According to the British customs provisions, indecent and obscene articles, including books and magazines, are liable for forfeiture and destruction upon their importation into the United Kingdom, and anyone fraudulently importing such goods is guilty of an offence.[228] Unlike the Obscene Publications Act 1959, which subjects »obscene« articles to the test of whether they »tend to deprave and corrupt,« the customs provisions have been held to apply a lower standard according to the ordinary or dictionary meaning of the terms »indecent« and »obscene.«[229]

In the case of *Henn and Darby*,[230] the EUCJ upheld the conviction of the two appellants for the importation of films and magazines of a sexually explicit nature. The trade in such publications is unlawful in England and Wales under the Obscene Publications Acts 1959 und 1964; and specific legislation in the other parts of the United Kingdom also prohibits such activities. The appellants had claimed that the customs provisions were incompatible with articles 30 and 36 of the EEC Treaty. Article 30 prohibits quantitative restrictions on imports and all measures with equivalent effects, while article 36 provides that prohibitions on the importation of goods may be justified inter alia »on grounds of public morality.« The appellants pointed to the fact that the laws on obscenity varied in the different parts of the United Kingdom and argued that clearly defined rules on public morality that alone could justify import restrictions under article 36 were missing. The Court agreed that a ban on the importation of pornographic articles constituted a quantitative restriction on imports within the meaning of article 30, but it concluded that the first sentence of article 36 permitted member states to prohibit the importation of obscene matters »as understood by its domestic laws and that such prohibitions may lawfully be implied to the whole of its national territory even if, in regard to the field in question, variations exist between the laws in force and the different constituent parts of the Member States concerned.«[231] While this first judgment confirmed the United Kingdom's rigorous restrictions on the importation of obscene publications, the *Conegate* case[232] established the criteria limiting an EC member state's freedom to impose such restrictions. The case was concerned not with the

227 Customs and Excise Act 1952 (15 & 16 Geo. 6 & 1 Eliz. 2, c.44).
228 *See* Customs and Excise Management Act 1979 (c.2), secs. 49, 50, 170.
229 *See* R. v. Anderson, [1971] 3 All E.R. 1152, 1158.
230 R. v. Henn and Darby (case 34/79), 1979 E.C.R. 3795, [1980] 1 C.M.L.R. 246.
231 1979 E.C.R. at 3817.
232 Conegate Ltd. v. Her Majesty's Customs and Excise (case 121/85), [1986] 1 C.M.L.R. 739.

84

importation of printed material or films but with that of inflatable dolls and similar articles of a sexual nature. In England, Wales and Northern Ireland, the manufacture of such erotic articles is legal, and restrictions apply only with respect to their transmission by post, their public display, and with regard to the places where these articles can lawfully be sold to the public. The U.K. government had argued that since the manufacture and distribution of the goods were totally prohibited under the laws of the Isle of Man, a member state like the United Kingdom, comprised of various constituent parts with differing laws but with a common customs regime, should be allowed to bring its customs laws in line with the most rigorous internal rules. The Court was unconvinced of this argument. It looked at the entirety of the obscenity laws in the United Kingdom and stated:

> Although it is not necessary, ..., that the manufacture and marketing of the products whose importation has been prohibited should be prohibited in the territory of all constituent parts, it must at least be possible to conclude from the applicable rules, taken as a whole, that their purpose is, in substance, to prohibit the manufacture and marketing of those products.[233]

Since this was not the case in the United Kingdom, the Court concluded that, on the grounds of public morality, the import restrictions constituted an infringement of article 30 if a different standard of morality was applied to domestic and imported goods. It is this last criterion – the missing, unified condemnation of the behaviour objected to – that distinguishes *Henn and Darby* from *Conegate*.[234]

The EUCJ also briefly dealt with another argument put forward in support of the U.K. government's position, namely, that the absolute ban on the importation of obscene publications was required in order to comply with the United Kingdom's obligations under international treaty law. As has been noted above,[235] article 1(2) of the 1923 International Convention for the Suppression of the Circulation of and Traffic in Obscene Publications requires contracting states to take all measures to prevent inter alia the importation of obscene matters. A similar obligation arises under the Universal Postal Convention.[236] Section 11 of the Post Office Act 1953[237] creates a criminal offence for the sending of any indecent or

---

233 *Id.* at 753-54.
234 *See also* Millett, *Free Movement of Goods and Public Morality*, 137 N.L.J. 39, 40. (1987).
235 *See supra* at chapter I(B)(2).
236 *See* art. 33(2) of the Universal Postal Convention, *concluded on* July 5, 1974, *ratified by* the United Kingdom, Feb. 23, 1976, U.K.T.S. 57/1976, Cmnd. 5988.
237 Post Office Act 1953 (1 & 2 Eliz. 2, c.36). *See also* P. MACMILLAN, *supra* note 145, at 145-49.

obscene print, cinematograph film, book and similar matters by mail. However, the provision applies only to mail posted within the United Kingdom. Mail containing indecent articles and posted from overseas can be detained and disposed of under the Overseas Letter Post Scheme 1971.[238] Yet in 1978 the Post Office discontinued seizing such imported material on the ground that it lacked the competence to do so, and the customs authorities, which had since then only controlled large commercial consignments, also took over the task of forfeiting obscene material posted in small quantities.[239]

In the *Conegate* case, the United Kingdom government had relied on article 234(1) of the EC Treaty, which provides that rights and duties resulting from international treaties that had been concluded before the ratification of the EEC Treaty and that had existed between EC member states and third countries will not be affected by the EEC Treaty. The Court stated that article 234 applied only with respect to obligations between member states and non-member countries and could not justify restrictions on trade between EC member states. While the United Kingdom's complete ban on the importation of obscene articles from non-EC countries thus remained valid, Customs and Excise in 1986 dropped charges under section 42 of the Customs Consolidation Act 1876 against the directors and a staff member of a British bookshop and its American supplier for having imported books with gay and lesbian content, including works from Allen Ginsburg and Tennessee Williams. The EUCJ's holding in the *Conegate* case had pursuaded the authorities that they could not apply to imported books and other printed material tests of obscenity and indecency that were stricter or different than those applied to books of British origin and that »it would be inequitable not to apply the same standards to all imports,« including those from non-EC countries.[240]

Copyright laws can also severely limit the free flow of information across national frontiers because of the right of the copyright holder to restrict the reproduction, distribution or other use of his work to the territory of one country. Here again the EEC Treaty provides the principles governing the regulation of copyright works that may be imported into or exported from the United Kingdom.

---

238 Made under section 28 of the Post Office Act 1969 (c.48). Schemes are made by the Post Office and do not constitute statutory instruments. All schemes are published in the London, Edinburgh and Belfast Gazettes.

239 *See* 1979 Report of the Williams Committee, *supra* note 141, at para. 2.26.

240 *See* 7 J. MEDIA L. & PRAC 101 (1986).

The EEC Treaty nowhere mentions the term copyright. The EUCJ has taken the position that copyright works, to the extent that they are embodied in some material form, such as books, discs, tapes or cassettes, are subject to article 30 of the Treaty.[241] Article 36 allows quantitative restrictions on imports, if they are necessary for the protection of industrial property rights. The Court of Justice clarified that industrial property rights within the meaning of article 36 not only encompass trademarks and patents but also copyrights to the extent of their commercial use.[242] But the Court also stated that this provision did not justify the artificial partitioning of the Common Market through the exercise of copyright with regard to the importation of copyright works embodied in material objects, if these objects had lawfully been marketed in one member state.[243] In these cases the principle of the free flow of goods within the Common Market prevails.

A different set of rules applies to the exercise of copyrights, if they are concerned with »the category of literary and artistic works made available to the public by performances which may be infinitely repeated.«[244] Such public performances – like television broadcasts[245] and the transmission of signals by cable television[246] – are considered services within the meaning of articles 59 ff. of the EEC Treaty. In contrast to the rules on the free flow of goods, these provisions contain no explicit acknowledgement of permissible restrictions on the free flow of services in the interest of industrial property rights. Nonetheless, the EUCJ held that article 59 did not limit »the exercise of certain economic activities which have their origin in the application of national legislation for the protection of intellectual property, save where such application constitutes a means of arbitrary

---

241 *See* Musik-Vertrieb membran GmbH and K-Tel Int. v. GEMA (joined cases 55 and 57/80), 1981 E.C.R. 147, 161, [1981] 2 C.M.L.R. 44.
242 A number of academic writers had previously denied the applicability of article 36 to copyright works. *See, e.g.*, the review given by A. DIETZ, COPYRIGHT LAW IN THE EUROPEAN COMMUNITY paras. 27-31 (1978).
243 *See* a similar holding with regard to the marketing of products protected by trademarks: Terrapin v. Terranova (case 119/75), 1976 E.C.R. 1039, 1061; and the preliminary ruling in Centrafarm B.V. v. Winthrop B.V. (case 16/74), 1974 E.C.R. 1183, [1974] 2 C.M.L.R. 480. For a case dealing with patents, see Centrafarm B.V. v. Sterling Drug Inc. (case 15/74), 1974 E.C.R. 1147, [1974] 2 C.M.L.R. 480.
244 S.A. Compagnie Générale pour la Diffusion de la Télévision, Coditel v. S.A. Ciné Vog Films (case 62/79), 1980 E.C.R. 881, 902, [1981] 2 C.M.L.R. 362. (hereafter cited as *Coditel I*).
245 *See* Sacchi (case 155/73), 1974 E.C.R. 409, 427, [1974] 2 C.M.L.R. 177.
246 Procureur du Roi v. Marc J.V.C. Debauve (case 52/79), 1980 E.C.R. 833, 855, [1981] 2 C.M.L.R. 362.

discrimination or disguised restriction on trade between Member States.«[247] As a result, the owner of the copyright may effectively restrict a licence for the performance of a work in the form of broadcasting, cable distribution or the like to a certain territory, which may coincide with the territory of a member state.

Furthermore, the EUCJ has asserted jurisdiction under EC competition and antitrust laws over licence and similar agreements dealing with copyright and related rights[248] and entered into on one side by national collecting organizations. Thus, the conduct of collecting organizations, such as the British Performing Rights Society Ltd. or Phonographic Performance Ltd., has to conform with articles 85 and 86 of the EEC Treaty.[249] Also, while copyright as such is not subject to the prohibitions set out in articles 85 and 86 of the EEC Treaty, its exercise may come within the scope of the provisions where it has the effect of restricting a certain activity to an appreciable degree or of distorting competition on the relevant market.[250] This distinction has itself been criticized as being impractical in the area of EC competition law.[251]

This short overview of the EEC Treaty's application to the flow of information in and out of the United Kingdom demonstrates the strong dependency of U.K. domestic laws on the supranational EC law, a body of law effectively restricting British parliamentary sovereignty. Similar observations apply with respect to the European Convention on Human

---

247 *Coditel I, supra* note 244, at 903.
248 *See* preliminary ruling in Deutsche Grammophon GmbH v. Metro-SB-Großmärkte GmbH & Co. K.G. (case 78/70), 1971 E.C.R. 487, 1971 C.M.L.R. 631 The case established that it is unlawful under Community law for a manufacturer of sound recordings to prohibit the distribution of articles placed by him or with his consent on the market of one member state on the market of another member state even if he holds a licence for exclusive distribution of the article under the laws of the latter state.
249 *See* first and second judgments of the European Court of Justice in Belgische Radio en Télévisie v. SABAM and NV Fonior (case 127/73), 1974 E.C.R. 51 and 313, [1974] 2 C.M.L.R. 238.
250 Preliminary ruling in Coditel SA v. Ciné Vog Films SA (No. 2) (case 262/81) (*Coditel II*), 1982 E.C.R. 3381, [1983] 1 C.M.L.R. 49. The distinction between the existence of an industrial property right and its exercise was first drawn by the Court in Consten & Grundig v. Commission (joined cases 56 and 58/64), 1966 E.C.R. 299, 1966 C.M.L.R. 418. *See also* Sirena v. Eda (case 40/70), 1971 E.C.R. 69, 1971 C.M.L.R. 260. In this case, the Court established that the rules governing competition to a certain degree take precedence over the exercise of industrial property rights. For a discussion of the conflict between English copyright and competition law, see *infra* at chapter V(A)(1).
251 *See* Mestmäcker, *Copyright in Community Law*, 10 JOURNAL OF WORLD TRADE L. 24 (Special Supplement No. 3) (1976).

Rights. These bodies of law set the parameters of the British information order.

2. *Freedom to Receive Broadcasts*

The public broadcasting authorities BBC and IBA are under an obligation to provide broadcasting services »of high quality (both as to the transmission and as to the matter transmitted), for so much of the United Kingdom, the Isle of Man and the Channel Islands as may from time to time be reasonably practicable.«[252] Both authorities have in the past undertaken great efforts to ensure the nationwide coverage of their transmissions. As of Dec. 31, 1984, for example, the IBA's coverage for UHF television transmitters reached more than 99 per cent of the population.[253]

In principle, the use of any apparatus for the reception of signals of wireless telegraphy is subject to a licence requirement under section 1(1) of the Wireless Telegraphy Act 1949. In the case of radio broadcasts, the Minister of Posts and Telecommunications in 1971 exempted from this licence requirement the installation and use of apparatus for the reception of sound broadcasts transmitted by authorized broadcasting stations and broadcasting for general reception; apparatus used for the reception of messages sent by telephony or telegraphy from licensed amateur stations were also exempted.[254] An authorized broadcasting station under this regulation means a station duly authorized to conduct a broadcasting service pursuant to the Radio Regulations published by the General Secretariat of the International Telecommunication Union (ITU).[255] The definition includes duly authorized foreign stations and thus comprises foreign broadcasts. Since the exemption applies only to the reception of broadcasts intended *for general reception*, the unauthorized interception of radio communications not intended for the general public by means of such radio apparatus constitutes a criminal offence under section 1(1) of the Wireless

252 Broadcasting Act 1981, sec. 2(1). *See also* the similar provision in article 3(a) of the Royal Charter for the continuance of the British Broadcasting Corporation (1981) (hereafter referred to as 1981 BBC Royal Charter).

253 Independent Broadcasting Authority, The IBA Annual Report & Accounts 1984-85 52 (1985) (hereafter cited as 1985 IBA Annual Report).

254 *See* Wireless Telegraphy Act 1949, sec. 1(1) and the Wireless Telegraphy (Broadcast Licence Charges and Exemption) Regulations 1984, 1984 S.I. No. 1053, revoking and consolidating all previous relevant orders. Up until 1971, owners of a radio set had to pay a licence fee to finance the BBC radio services. Since then, the BBC has financed its sound broadcasting services with a portion of the fees paid for the television licences.

255 Regulation 2 of the Wireless Telegraphy (Broadcasting Licence Charges and Exemption) Regulations 1984.

Telegraphy Act 1949. This statutory provision pays due regard to the United Kingdom's international obligation under article 23 of the ITU Radio Regulations 1979, requiring member states to prohibit the unauthorized interception of non-public radio communications. The wording of the British statutory provision would seem also to prohibit the reception of broadcasts for general reception transmitted by *unauthorized* stations. These so-called »pirate« stations often broadcast from the high seas and thereby avoid the licensing procedures of any country. They transmit on frequencies not assigned for this purpose by the ITU.[256] However, there appears to have been no incident when British listeners were charged with tuning in to the programmes broadcast by the often very popular pirate stations operating off the British coast, a circumstance that may in no small part be due to the difficulties in proving intentional wrongdoing on the part of the listener.

This liberal attitude towards the reception of foreign broadcasts has a long history in the United Kingdom. During World War II, when the countries at war with the United Kingdom, in particular Germany, heavily broadcast political propaganda to the United Kingdom, British citizens were free to listen to these programmes. The British government did not even take the pain to jam any of these transmissions.[257]

The reception of domestic and non-domestic sound broadcasts is thus generally exempted from any licence requirement, provided, however, that the radio apparatus does not cause undue interference with any wireless telegraphy.[258]

The reception of television broadcasts depends upon the payment of a yearly licence fee, presently £ 18 for a monochrome and £ 58 for a colour television licence per household. Any violation of the licence requirement constitutes a criminal offence punishable by a fine of up to £ 400. For the offence to be committed, it suffices that the set is available for use at any time, even if its owner had no intention and did not use it.[259] The licence fee is collected by the Post Office and serves to finance the BBC's services. In order to improve the collection of the licence fee and the registration of television owners, the Wireless Telegraphy Act 1967[260]

---

256 For more details on the British regulation of »pirate« stations, see *infra* at chapter VI(B)(2).
257 B. PAULU, *supra* note 165, at 389.
258 Regulation 3(2) of the Wireless Telegraphy (Broadcast Licence Charges and Exemption) Regulations 1984.
259 D (A Minor) v. Yates, 148 J.P. 455, 458 (Queen's Bench Division) (1984).
260 Wireless Telegraphy Act 1967 (c.72).

imposes a notification requirement on dealers of television sets. Under section 1 of the Act, television dealers have to register with the government. They are then required to give notice of any sale or hire of a television set, including the name and address of the buyer or hirer.[261]

Cable-television network operators are under a statutory obligation to connect interested users to their systems in places where the cable network has already been installed.[262] This regulation safeguards the individual's right to receive information by way of cable technology. But the reception of such cable programme services does not grant users any influence on the kinds of programmes transmitted via the system. Free choice among the various satellite-television programmes technically receivable on British territory would only be possible if individuals could themselves establish the necessary satellite receiving equipment.

Since 1985 British citizens for the first time enjoy the right to set up television receive-only satellite receiving equipment (TVRO).[263] These systems, because of their large dish antennae, can receive programmes transmitted from low-power satellites. TVROs were exempted from the cumbersome licence requirements under the Cable and Broadcasting Act 1984 and the Telecommunications Act 1984. Viewers pay a one-time licence fee of £ 10 to the Department of Trade and Industry (DTI), which grants the TVRO licenses. By mid-1987 an estimated 2,500 licences had been granted. The licences permit the reception of television or sound programmes »forming part of a programme service, intended for *ultimate* reception by members of the public or by any restricted group or audience.«[264] Thus the private interception of individual programme transmissions between different broadcasting organizations, for example, is prohibited. The government's main interest in permitting TVROs lay in stimulating the manufacturing industry for satellite dishes and ancillary equipment. A second but subordinate policy goal was to boost the potential audience for satellite television programmes. Thus industrial-policy concerns rather than media-policy considerations lead to a greater freedom to receive information.

261 Section 2 and Part I of the Schedule of the Wireless Telegraphy Act 1967.
262 *See* Telecommunications Act 1984, sec. 8(1)(b).
263 Department of Trade and Industry, Radio Regulatory Division, Annual Report 1985/86 18-19 (1986) (hereafter cited as 1986 Annual Report of the Radio Regulatory Division).
264 *Id.* at 19 (emphasis added).

II. *The BBC and the IBA: The Changing Structure of the Public Broadcasting System*

The public-service broadcasting concept has for the last sixty years been the foundation of the broadcasting structure in Britain. It rests on the presumption that the ultimate control over the broadcast media, with their »potential power over public opinion and the life of the nation,«[265] should remain with the government, which in turn is answerable to Parliament. A second element of this public-service concept is the independence of the public broadcasting organizations from the government in their day-to-day operation. Instead of a system of direct supervision, the general activities and programme policies of the broadcasting organizations have to follow the detailed principles set out in legislative and charter obligations.

This system for a long time ensured that the television programme diet of British citizens consisted of what Parliament had once broadly determined it should be, namely, a mix of information, education and entertainment. Yet the »comfortable duopoly« of the BBC and the IBA is rapidly coming to an end.[266] This is largely due to the new media – cable and satellite broadcasting. The widespread use in video recorders and the thriving business of video cassette rentals have also contributed considerably to greater consumer choice and a diminishing control of the public broad-casters over »the life of the nation.« But the broadcasters have shown no willingness simply to leave the new media to third parties; instead, they have themselves ventured into this area and have successfully tried at least partly to extend their broadcasting monopolies to some new media tech-nologies. The expanding activities have changed the nature of the broadcasting duopoly, while the regulation of the new media in turn has been strongly influenced by the concept and structure of the traditional public broadcasting system. The era of the new media in Britain only began in the 1980s, and the transformation of the old »closed shop« broadcasting system into a diversified audio-visual media market stands in its infancy. This is why the structure of the traditional broadcasting duopoly

---

265 1923 Sykes Report, *supra* note 164, at para. 4.4.
266 For an account of the various aspects of the traditional broadcasting duopoly, see, e.g., J. BAKEWELL & N. GARNHAM, THE NEW PRIESTHOOD – BRITISH TELEVISION TODAY (1970); N. GARNHAM, STRUCTURES OF TELEVISION (rev. ed. 1978, reprinted 1980); S. HOOD, A SURVEY OF TELEVISION (1967); A. QUICKE, TOMORROW'S TELEVISION (1976); M. SHULMAN, THE LEAST WORST TELEVISION IN THE WORLD (1973); H. THOMAS, THE TRUTH ABOUT TELEVISION (1962); E.G. WEDELL, BROADCASTING AND PUBLIC POLICY (1968).

still evidences the paramount importance of detailed content control. At the system's highest level, the government has retained a number of important powers that enable it to make direct use of the broadcasting facilities for its own purposes.

A. Government Control of the Public Broadcasting Authorities

In the case of commercial television, it is the IBA that regulates the programmes of the ITV contractors in accordance with the provisions of the Broadcasting Act 1981.[267] The government can only indirectly influence the IBA's programme policy through the appointment and dismissal of the members of the Authority. In the case of the BBC, the appointment of the members of the Board of Governors by the government serves a similar aim.

However, under section 29(3) of the Broadcasting Act 1981, the government has the additional right to order via a written notice the IBA to refrain from broadcasting any matter or classes of matters. In such a case the IBA may – but does not have to – broadcast an announcement of the notice. This measure, if applied, could potentially be embarrassing for the government, and thus it may be expected that a liberal use of the government's veto power is unlikely. The licence under which the BBC operates provides for the same governmental power and right of response on the part of the BBC.[268]

The government has indeed only on rare occasions exercised its veto power. The 1977 Annan Committee Report[269] and the 1978 Government White Paper on Broadcasting[270] observed that the government had never prohibited the broadcasting of a particular programme or a series of programmes, but on five occasions it had intervened to prevent the broadcasting of particular classes of programmes. Thus, in 1955 both the BBC and the IBA were directed not to anticipate parliamentary debates by broadcasting statements or discussions on issues scheduled to be debated in

267 For more details on IBA programme censorship, see *infra* at chapter II(C)(1).
268 Clause 13(4) of the Licence and Agreement Dated the 2nd Day of April 1981 Between Her Majesty's Secretary of State for the Home Department and the British Broadcasting Corporation (hereafter cited as BBC Licence and Agreement 1981).
269 Report of the Committee of the Future of Broadcasting, Cmnd. 6753, para. 5.10 (1977) (hereafter cited as 1977 Annan Report).
270 Broadcasting. Presented to Parliament by the Secretary of State for the Home Department by Command of Her Majesty July 1978, Cmnd. 7294, para 96 (1978) (hereafter cited as 1978 White Paper on Broadcasting).

Parliament within the coming fortnight (the »14-day Rule«). The directive was only withdrawn after both broadcasting organizations had assured the government that they would not »derogate from the primacy of Parliament as the forum for debating the affairs of the nation.«[271] Another directive in existence from 1955 to 1965 prohibited the BBC from broadcasting any »controversial party political broadcasts other than those arranged in agreement with the leading political parties for broadcasting throughout the United Kingdom.«[272] Now, a so-called Aide Mémoire regulates party political broadcasts in detail.[273]

These examples evidence the enormous potential for direct government censorship in the area of broadcasting. The fact that the government has so far not interfered with the broadcasting of individual programmes by issuing formal directives may perhaps be partially explained by the censorship that the IBA in particular itself exercises with regard to the ITV programmes. The IBA heavily intermeddles with the production of programmes by private television companies, often exercising pre-censorship, particularly with regard to current-affairs programmes.[274] Three events may serve to illustrate the functioning of indirect government censorship of the broadcast media. In early 1985, the IBA refused to allow the broadcasting of a documentary made for Channel 4 by one of the ITV companies. The programme contained allegations that telephones of numerous Union members and other people had been illegally tapped by the British intelligence service. The IBA, concerned about a possible violation of the Official Secrets Act 1911 if it allowed the broadcasting of the film, turned to the government for advice. Channel 4 officials arranged for the showing of the film to a group of Members of the House of Commons, and only after the Attorney General had announced that no one would be prosecuted did the broadcast take place. The incident attracted wide attention and criticism for setting a dangerous precedent of a supposedly independent authority leaving to the government the decision about the showing of a controversial and embarrassing programme.[275]

The BBC, on the other hand, has traditionally enjoyed a reputation of great independence from the government. The year 1985, however, saw the BBC in a deep crisis. The weekly newspaper *The Observer* revealed

---

271 1977 Annan Report, *supra* note 269, at para. 5.10.
272 *Id.*
273 The Aide Mémoire is reprinted in BBC, Annual Report and Handbook 1987 240 (1986) (hereafter cited as BBC Handbook 1987). For more details, see *infra* at chapter II(C)(1).
274 *See, e.g.*, the examples given by G. ROBERTSON & A. NICOL, *supra* note 54, at 276.
275 *TV Censorship – The IBA's Decision to ban »MI5's Official Secrets«*, 6 J. MEDIA L. & PRAC. 205-06 (1985).

that since 1937 BBC staff members before being hired had been systematically screened by the intelligence service for their political views; it also uncovered that an intelligence-service officer had a permanent office in the BBC headquarters and was regularly informing the management about any radical groups detectable within the organization.[276]

In July 1985, the Home Secretary told the BBC that he considered the intended showing of a film featuring an interview with one of the alleged heads of the Irish Republican Army (IRA) to be »contrary to the national interest.« The BBC Board of Governors, giving in to political pressure, prohibited the broadcasting of the documentary, bypassing the competence of the Director General. The ensuing public outrage over the government's interference with the freedom of the BBC was so serious that the Home Secretary gave the public assurance that the independence of the BBC was »unchallenged and unchallengable.«[277] The Board of Governors finally reversed its decision after minor changes in the programme had been made, and the documentary was shown on British television about two months later.

Another example of governmental pressure are the warnings made by the British Home Secretary in 1985 and directed at television journalists. He admonished them to practice self-restraint with regard to the showing of sex and crime on television unless they wanted to risk government action.[278]

The incidents show that it is politically infeasible for a British government openly to exercise censorship over BBC programmes. In the case of the IRA documentary, the Home Secretary apparently did not avail himself of his right to give a direct prohibition order under clause 13(4) of the BBC Licence and Agreement, thus refraining from breaking a long-standing tradition. But political pressures and such tacit arrangements as that with the intelligence service go a long way to ensuring compliance by the broadcast media with the policies of the government of the day.

Under the Broadcasting Act 1981, the government has additional powers to give directions as to the maximum and minimum television time per day and week and to the hours of the day in which broadcasts may take place

---

276 *See, e.g.*, Frankfurter Rundschau, Aug. 28, 1985. In April 1986, the BBC agreed in principle to end security vetting of existing staff and job applicants for editorial purposes with the exception of the staff members of the BBC's External Services and a limited number of staff outside the news department. Fin. Times, Apr. 16, 1986.

277 Fin. Times, Aug. 8, 1985.

278 Frankfurter Allgemeine Zeitung, Dec. 11, 1985.

(section 28(1) of the Broadcasting Act 1981); any Minister of the Crown may also, if it appears to him to be necessary or expedient to do so in connection with his functions, require the Authority by written notice to broadcast any announcement at any time (section 29(1) of the Broadcasting Act 1981). These statutory governmental powers are paralleled in the BBC Licence. In the unlikely case that the IBA would refuse to comply with a government directive, the Home Secretary could ask the courts for an order of mandamus requiring the IBA to comply. Unlike in the case of the BBC, where the Licence expressly links compliance with the directive with the right to broadcast, the government could not threaten the IBA in such an instance with the withdrawal of the right to broadcast.[279] However, it could dismiss the majority or even all the members of the Authority and replace them with members showing a greater willingness to implement governmental orders.

In consideration of the far-reaching powers of censorship connected with the right to veto programmes, the government has voluntarily expressed its intention to submit every exercise of this power to public scrutiny by presenting a copy of every directive before each House of Parliament.[280] However, this nonbinding statement of intent represents no obligation effectively preventing an over-anxious future government from massively interfering with the broadcasters' freedom of expression and the individual's right to information. Indeed, considering the ease with which the government could issue restrictive directives beyond the restrictions already imposed on the broadcasters by statute or, in the case of the BBC, through the licence provisions, the principle of freedom of broadcasting is hardly reflected in the written law. In practice, however, particularly the BBC enjoys the reputation of an independent institution guaranteeing free, uncensored and high-quality journalism; no government can attempt to curtail these rights without risking serious political embarrassment. In this sense the broadcasting system as a whole may be characterized as a system of self-restraint: The government voluntarily refrains from exercising its rights vis-à-vis the broadcasting organizations to the limit.

The following sections will attempt to present a more detailed examination of the legal rules regulating the two public broadcasting authorities BBC and IBA and the commercial broadcasting system controlled by the latter.

279 H. STREET, *supra* note 37, at 89.
280 1978 White Paper on Broadcasting, *supra* note 270, at para. 96.

B. The Organizational Structure of Television Broadcasting

1. The British Broadcasting Corporation (BBC)

The BBC is incorporated by letters patent under a Royal Charter. The first Royal Charter was issued in 1926.[281] The present and sixth Charter, granted in April 1981, runs until December 31, 1996. It confers upon the Corporation the right and duty to provide, as public services, broadcasting services of wireless telegraphy in the form of radio and television. Those broadcasting services for reception in the United Kingdom, Northern Ireland, the Channel Islands and the Isle of Man are called the Home Services; broadcasting services for reception outside the United Kingdom in Commonwealth and other overseas countries are referred to as External Services. Special rules apply to the latter services and will be the subject of a later chapter.[282]

In case of the BBC's non-compliance with the conditions imposed on it by its Royal Charter, the Secretary of State may require the corporation to remedy the situation within a certain period of time. If the BBC then fails to comply with the order, the Charter may be revoked (article 20(2) of the BBC Royal Charter 1981). As an expression of the concept of broadcasting as a public service, certain organizational structures of the broadcasting organizations were felt to be particularly suited to meeting the needs both of editorial independence from the government and of public accountability. Within the hierarchy of the BBC, the crystallizing point for these dual objectives is the Board of Governors.

The BBC is governed by twelve Governors, including the Chairman, the Vice-Chairman and three so-called National Governors – one each for Scotland, Wales and Northern Ireland (article 5 of the BBC Royal Charter 1981). They are appointed upon the recommendation of the Prime Minister by the Queen in Council for five-year terms and may be dismissed at will. During the term of office, a Governor may not hold any other office in which his interest could conflict with any interest of the BBC; if he is a member of the House of Commons, for example, he must first resign his

---

281 The present Royal Charter as well as the 1981 Licence and Agreement is printed in BBC Handbook 1987, *supra* note 273, at 222-39. For more details on the history of the BBC, see, e.g., A. BRIGGS, THE HISTORY OF BROADCASTING IN THE UNITED KINGDOM: (Vol. I) THE BIRTH OF BROADCASTING (1961); (Vol. II) THE GOLDEN AGE OF WIRELESS (1965); (Vol. III) THE WAR OF WORDS (1970); (Vol. IV) SOUND AND VISION (1979); *see also* G. ROSS, TELEVISION JUBILEE – THE STORY OF 25 YEARS OF BBC TELEVISION (1961).
282 *See infra* at chapter VI(B)(1).

seat in Parliament. The Board decides by majority vote, with the Chairman having the deciding vote in case of a tie. The Chairman and the Vice-Chairman are usually the only Governors working full-time on the Board. While this body is only to a very limited extent subject to government orders, its members are responsible to the government for the lawful execution of the organization's functions. The Governors determine the overall policies and objectives of the BBC but leave the day-to-day operation and individual programme decisions to the Director General and his staff of editors and journalists. The Governors have to »ensure that services are conducted in the general public interest and are in accordance with the requirements and objectives which Parliament places on that Authority.«[283] The Annan Committee defined the public-interest function of the Governors in the following way:

> They must candidly tell the professional broadcasters why they agree with certain public criticisms. At the same time, they have to defend the broadcasters from pressure groups who want to use the BBC services to further their own aims and to tell the public, and indeed the Government, why they are not prepared to interfere with the editorial independence of the broadcasters or admonish them when they have been exercising their editorial freedom responsibly. There can therefore be no doubt who takes the strategic decisions on the BBC's policies. The buck stops at the Governors.[284]

The BBC Governors are almost exclusively appointed from outside the broadcasting area on the ground of their individual merits and are personally responsible to the government. In this respect, their position is one of trustee of the public interest. To the extent that they identify with the needs and objectives of the broadcasters, particularly with their editorial independence, and set the overall objectives of the organization, they are an integral part of the organizational broadcasting structure and prone to defend the organization against governmental interference. Understandably, the institutionalized tension between these conflicting functions in the form of a dual responsibility has often caused concern, because the Board carries the ultimate responsibility for the Corporation's management.[285] At times, the Governors found themselves criticised by the government for defending the broadcasters against outside pressures. On other occasions, they were disliked by the broadcasters for an allegedly

283 1977 Annan Report, *supra* note 269, at para. 7.12.
284 *Id.* at para. 9.64.
285 *Id.* at paras. 9.60-9.71. *See also* A. BRIGGS, GOVERNING THE BBC 49-143 (1979). *See also* B. PAULU, *supra* note 165, at 133.

too close affiliation with the government and/or disregard for the needs of media professionals.[286] On occasion, the relationship between the Board and the broadcasters was even called »appalling.«[287]

In contrast to a number of foreign public broadcasting organizations, the BBC's constitution does not provide for the balancing of representatives of political parties on the Board. Still, the appointment of a new Governor, particularly of the Chairman of the Board, is a highly political matter. When the Conservative government appointed Mr Marmaduke Hussey to the post of BBC Chairman in late 1986, the decision sparked a heated political row, with opposition Labour MPs attacking the choice as »provocative.«[288] Only a few months later, however, the same Chairman sided with the BBC and protested vigorously when the Special Branch of the British intelligence service raided the BBC's Scottish headquarters and seized programme material on the Zircon satellite, a secret satellite project designed by the British government to monitor the Soviet Union.[289]

Instead of proportional representation of political parties, adequate representation of the population in the various countries of the United Kingdom received prominence within the organizational structure of the Corporation. This represents an acknowledgment of the great cultural differences within Britain. At the top of this hierarchy are the National Governors of Scotland, Wales and Northern Ireland. Under the BBC Royal Charter 1981, a National Governor is elected »by virtue of his knowledge of the culture, characteristics and affairs of Our People in the country ... and his close touch with opinion in that country« (article 5(3)). Each National Governor also serves as Chairman of the three National Broadcasting Councils, namely, the Broadcasting Councils for Scotland, Wales and Northern Ireland (article 10). The General Advisory Council selects the members of these councils after consultation with representatives of cultural, religious and other bodies in Scotland, Wales and Northern Ireland »with the view to securing a proper balance of representation on each Council« (article 10(2)(b)). Each National Council is required to discharge its functions »with full regard to the distinctive culture, language, interests and tastes« of the people in the country for which it is established. It controls the policy and content of those programmes that the BBC provides primarily for the general reception in that country and gives advice to the Corporation with respect to other

---

286 *See, e.g.*, Fin. Times, Aug. 8, 1985.
287 *See* Fin. Times, Sept. 2, 1986.
288 Fin. Times, Oct. 2, 1986.
289 *See* Fin. Times, Feb. 3, 1987.

broadcasting services affecting the interests of its people. Thus, the National Broadcasting Councils have a large degree of control over their regional programmes,[290] subject only to the Corporation's right to make reservations and to give directions in the interest of securing the transmission of broadcasting by the Queen, ministers of the government, party political broadcasts and broadcasts of national importance or interest throughout the United Kingdom. The Corporation may further restrict the powers of the Councils for reasons of finance or in order to ensure proper coordination and coherent administration of the BBC's affairs. Finally, the Home Secretary may suspend the Councils' functions if in his opinion an emergency has arisen and the measure appears expedient in the public interest (article 10(5)). The Regional Advisory Councils, on the other hand, and the Local Radio Advisory Councils have only advisory functions with regard to programme matters affecting the interests of the people in the various regions (article 11). Proper representation of the different countries in the United Kingdom is finally safeguarded also by means of the Governors' duty in addition to meeting in England to hold meetings in Scotland, Wales and Northern Ireland in such intervals as they consider appropriate with regard to their respective functions (article 7(3)(a)).

The highest-ranking advisory council is the General Advisory Council, to be appointed by the Board »for the purpose of advising the Corporation on all matters which may be of concern to the Corporation or to bodies or persons interested in the broadcasting services of the Corporation« (article 8(1)). The fifty to sixty members of the General Advisory Council have backgrounds in the humanities, science, religion, politics, industry, education, and the like.[291] They are usually figures of public standing, adding prestige to the Corporation and ensuring a link with the major British social currents. They meet about four times a year and raise all subjects of concern, including general programme policy, violence in broadcasting, news, election coverage, etc.[292] Although they cannot enforce their recommendations, their political influence on BBC policy matters is probably significant.

In addition to the various advisory councils that the BBC is under an obligation to establish, the Corporation is authorized to appoint persons or committees giving advice on certain specified matters relating to the

---

290 See B. PAULU, supra note 165, at 140. See also the Annual Reports of the National Broadcasting Councils for Scotland, Wales and Northern Ireland, in BBC Handbook 1987, supra note 273, at 71-90.
291 B. PAULU, supra note 165, at 139.
292 Id. at 139-40.

broadcasting services, its business, operation and its general affairs (article 9 of the BBC Royal Charter 1981). These committees are comprised of experts in their fields. The members meet with the heads of the relevant programme departments and help to determine programme guidelines, for example, in the area of religious or school programmes.[293] All of these advisory councils combined ensure that the Corporation's internal structure is pluralistic and democratic, a crucial safeguard to preserving some form of freedom of information in a monopolistic broadcasting system.

Public accountability also encompasses the duty of the broadcasting organizations themselves to discover how the public reacts to programmes and to learn from these feedbacks. In practice this is partly done through regular audience research.[294]

The Board of Governors appoints the Director General, who is both Editor-in-Chief and Chief Executive. He is the Chairman of the Board of Management, consisting of the three Managing Directors for television, radio and the External Services and four Central Directors for engineering, public affairs, finance and personnel, as well as the Chief Assistant to the Director General, who represents the latter in his absence.[295] The post of Director General is very powerful and influential. It is he who in practice decides on important matters of day-to-day operation, the broadcasting of controversial subjects and the like, while the Board of Management plays only an advisory role. Ultimately, however, he is dependent on the goodwill of the Board of Governors. This was demonstrated in early 1987, when the Board of Governors forced BBC Director General Alisdair Milne to resign his post and thereafter appointed a new candidate to this position.[296]

With regard to the lower-level staff, the BBC has about 25,000 full-time employees, making it the second largest broadcasting organization in the world after that of the Soviet Union.[297] The labour unions represent a powerful force within the BBC. Their presence there is safeguarded by article 13 of the BBC Royal Charter 1981, which requires the Corporation to negotiate with the appropriate organizations as to terms and conditions of employment and other matters of mutual interest, such as health and safety.

---

293 *Id.* at 141.
294 *See, e.g.*, British Broadcasting Corporation, Annual Review of BBC Broadcasting Research Findings, No. 8, 13-54 (1981/82); BBC Handbook 1987, *supra* note 273, at 91-93. *See also* R. SILVEY, WHO'S LISTENING? THE STORY OF THE BBC AUDIENCE RESEARCH (1974).
295 1977 Annan Report, *supra* note 269, at para. 9.58.
296 Fin. Times, Jan. 30, 1987; Jan. 31, 1987; Feb. 24, 1987.
297 B. PAULU, *supra* note 165, at 128.

The BBC's actual right to broadcast, i.e., to install and to make use of the necessary technical equipment, depends upon a licence granted in addition to the Charter by the Home Secretary under section 1 of the Wireless Telegraphy Act 1949.[298] This Licence and Agreement also contains a number of – albeit vague – programme-content regulations. The BBC is thus responsible for the determination of programme content and the production of the programmes as well as for their transmission. It operates the stations and transmitters and installs and maintains the necessary apparatus and equipment pursuant to the licence under the Wireless Telegraphy Act 1949.

Under its charter obligation to provide broadcasting services for the Home Services, the BBC currently broadcasts two television programmes, BBC 1 and BBC 2, and four national, four regional and about 30 local radio programmes. The two television networks are set up to complement each other, in that BBC 1 offers a general service while BBC 2 programmes are aimed particularly at minorities and are generally more experimental in nature. All BBC 2 programmes and many BBC 1 programmes are broadcast simultaneously throughout the United Kingdom. Following the introduction of a breakfast-time television service on BBC 1, the programme service has been extended in 1987 to broadcast throughout the day, in order to serve housewives and shift workers. Under the supervision of the National Advisory Councils, BBC regional production facilities also provide regional programmes on BBC 1 transmitted during opt-out periods and aimed at the special interests of the people in Scotland, Northern Ireland and Wales.[299] A number of Welsh programmes are produced in the Welsh language. The BBC also broadcasts Open University programmes via its radio and television networks. The Open University is an educational institution founded by charter in 1969. It designs educational programmes to be produced by the BBC and broadcast over BBC stations in the very early mornings and early evenings. The programmes are aimed at working adults who want to prepare themselves for a baccalaureate or post-graduate degree.[300]

The Home Services are financed through the licence fees paid annually by

298 The licence currently in force was granted in April 1981 and expires on Dec. 31, 1996. *See* BBC Licence and Agreement 1981, *supra* note 268, at clause 3.
299 *See also* B. PAULU, *supra* note 165, at 167-68.
300 The courses are very popular. In 1980 over 70,000 students were enrolled in the Open University, and some 21,000 had already graduated. B. PAULU, *supra* note 165, at 269. *See also* Educational Broadcasting and the Future, Speech given by George Howard at Leeds Polytechnic, Mar. 3, 1981 (published by the BBC).

102

television viewers. The fees are collected by the Post Office. The Home Secretary then pays to the Corporation a sum equal to the whole of the net licence revenues, i.e., the amount remaining after expenses incurred in the collection of the television fees are substracted (clause 16 of the Licence and Agreement 1981). In contrast to a number of other European public broadcasting organizations, the BBC is financed almost wholly through the licence-fee system and may not derive any income from advertising or sponsorship without the consent of the Home Secretary (clause 12 of the Licence and Agreement 1981).

In March 1985, the British Home Secretary announced that a committee chaired by Professor of Economics Alan Peacock would be set up to report on the advantages of alternative methods of financing the BBC and the replacement of the licence-fee system with advertising, sponsorship or subscription. Much to the relief of the BBC, the Committee ultimately spoke out in favour of the maintenance of the present system, although the report's long-term implications questioned the very assumptions on which the British broadcasting system is based.[301]

2. The Independent Broadcasting Authority (IBA)

The creation of the Independent Television Authority (ITA) in 1954 brought the BBC's television broadcasting monopoly to an end. In 1972 the ITA was also entrusted with the right to provide radio broadcasting. It consequently changed its name to Independent Broadcasting Authority (IBA).[302]

The IBA is a body corporate and owes its existence to a statute. The latest enactment regulating the structure and organization of the Authority is the Broadcasting Act 1981. It consolidates the Independent Broadcasting Authority Acts 1973, 1974 and 1978 and the Broadcasting Act 1980 and extends the existence of the Authority to December 31, 2005. The IBA is legally identical with its members, whose status and functions are very similar to those of the BBC Governors. The members are appointed by the Secretary of State for the Home Department for five-year terms and may be dismissed by him at will (section 1(4) and Schedule I of the

---

301 See *infra* at chapters II(E), VII.
302 For a general account of the independent television sector in the United Kingdom, see, e.g., B. SENDALL, INDEPENDENT TELEVISION IN BRITAIN: (Vol. 1) ORIGIN AND FOUNDATION 1946-62 (1982); ARBEITSGEMEINSCHAFT FÜR KOMMUNIKATIONS-FORSCHUNG E.V. (ed.), KOMMERZIELLES FERNSEHEN IN DER MEDIENKONKURRENZ: (Vol. I) W. MAHLE, GROSSBRITANNIEN – EIN MODELL FÜR DIE BUNDESREPUBLIK? (1984).

Broadcasting Act 1981). An IBA member may not at the same time hold the office of BBC Governor and may have no financial or other interests that might prejudice the objective discharge of his functions. Similar to the respective Charter provisions governing the structure of the BBC's Board of Governors, three members represent the interests of Scotland, Wales and Northern Ireland.[303]

The IBA's statutory obligation is to provide television and local sound broadcasting services as a public service for disseminating information, education and entertainment (section 2(2)(a)). The Broadcasting Act 1981 sets out a detailed number of programme standards to be observed by the Authority. However, it is not the IBA itself that produces the programmes broadcast by it. This is done by so-called programme contractors, upon which the IBA confers the right and duty to provide programmes under a contract with the Authority and subject to the provisions of the Broadcasting Act 1981 (section 2(3)). A number of advisory councils and committees, which the IBA is under an obligation to appoint or, in some cases, may appoint at its will, give advice to the Authority and the programme contractors on matters specified in the Broadcasting Act and on matters determined by the IBA itself (sections 16-18). The senior advisory body is the General Advisory Council. Its members represent a wide cross-section of the public. Other committees are the National Advisory Committees, i.e., the Advisory Committees for Northern Ireland, Scotland and Wales respectively, the Advertising Advisory Committee, the Advertising Liaison Committee, the Medical Advisory Panel, the Educational Advisory Council, three Appeals Advisory Committees, the Central Religious Advisory Committee, the Central, Scottish and Northern Ireland Appeals Advisory Committees and 45 Local Advisory Committees for Independent Local Radio.[304]

Apart from the setting and enforcement of programme standards and the approval of programme schedules, the IBA has the task of operating the technical facilities needed for the transmission of the programmes (section

303 They shall be »persons who appear to the Secretary of State to be suited to make the interests of Scotland, Wales and Northern Ireland, respectively, their special care.« Broadcasting Act 1981, sec. 1(4) and Schedule I(1).
304 See Independent Broadcasting Authority, The IBA Annual Report and Accounts 1985-86 Appendix IV (1986) (hereafter cited as 1986 IBA Annual Report). The councils, committees and panels together have more than 700 members. Independent Broadcasting Authority, Independent Television and Radio – A Pocket-Guide 2 (1985) (hereafter cited as IBA, Pocket-Guide). The Advertising Liaison Committee differs from the other committees, because it does not directly advise the IBA but rather discusses general problems regarding the commercial relationships between ITV companies and the advertising industry. 1985 IBA Annual Report, *supra* note 253, at 9.

3(1)). Both the IBA and BBC are licensed under section 1 of the Wireless Telegraphy Act 1949 for the operation of their transmitter stations and the installation and use of any apparatus for wireless telegraphy.[305] The broadcasting authorities have just one omnibus licence respectively, which makes an individual grant of a section 1 licence in each case of the setting up of a new station unnecessary. After consultation with the authorities, the Secretary of State of Trade and Industry from time to time effects the assignment of the actual frequencies under these licences.[306] The BBC Licence and Agreement 1981 also empowers the government to give directions to the BBC regarding the height and power of the aerials used, the characteristics of the modulating signals, the use or disuse of any stations, and the like (clause 5 of the BBC Licence and Agreement 1981). Under the Licence and Agreement, the Secretary of State may also order the BBC to cooperate with the IBA in the use of broadcasting installations (clause 6 of the BBC Licence and Agreement 1981). The IBA's corresponding obligation is set out in section 31 of the Broadcasting Act 1981. The 1981 Act precludes the IBA from carrying on any business as seller of or engage in the manufacture of any apparatus for wireless telegraphy or any other telegraphy equipment (section 3(4) of the Broadcasting Act 1981).

The IBA's Engineering Division is responsible for the operation, maintenance, design and construction of the IBA transmitter system,[307] experimental and development work, network planning, and the like. This division is the largest of the seven divisions in which the IBA staff of about 1,500 is organized.[308] For example, IBA engineers developed a standard for high-definition television (HDTV), called Enhanced C-Mac, for use with

305 See Broadcasting Act 1981, sec. 3(7). The BBC Licence and Agreement 1981 was granted by the Home Secretary in exercise of his then existing power under section 1 of the Wireless Telegraphy Act 1949. See BBC Licence and Agreement 1981, supra note 268, at clause 3.

306 A diagram on the U.K. spectrum occupancy by television and sound broadcasting between 30-960 MHz is contained in the Report of the Independent Review of the Radio Spectrum (30-960 MHz), Presented to Parliament by the Secretary of State for Trade and Industry by Command of Her Majesty, Cmnd. 9000, Annex H (July 1983) (hereafter cited as 1983 Report of the Radio Spectrum).

307 The ITV television coverage provides UHF colour/black-and-white on 625 lines from about 700 transmitters reaching over 99 % of the population. IBA, Pocket-Guide, supra note 304, at 21.

308 The Television and Radio Divisions are responsible for the independent television and radio programme output; the Advertising Control Division surveys the spot advertisements on television and radio; the Finance Division collects, inter alia, the Exchequer Levy to be paid by the programme contractors to the government; the Information Division concerns itself with public relations and related matters; and the Administrative Division handles legal and personnel affairs and the like. See 1985 IBA Annual Report, supra note 263, at 9.

DBS satellites.[309] The wide-screen picture that the system offers is entirely compatible (using an adapter) with the 625-line format of the existing receivers. The so-called D-Mac transmission standard is identical with C-Mac in terms of the total information handled, with the difference that it is not the optimal way to use satellite transmission capacity. But because D-Mac needs less complicated and thus less expensive technology on the receiver end, the United Kingdom eventually opted for the D-Mac standard as its future DBS transmission standard.[310]

The transmission of the IBA's first television channel (ITV) and the IBA's general administrative costs are financed through rentals paid by the ITV programme contractors to the IBA (section 32 of the Broadcasting Act 1981). The ITV contractors in turn earn their income from selling advertising time on the channel to the industry.

The IBA provides two television channels, ITV and Channel 4. The two channels operate under the same legal regime, but their programme mix is complementary. Programmes for ITV are for the most part provided by regional television programme contractors who have the contractual right to provide exclusively the programming in their respective franchise areas, subject only to certain modifications and restrictions specified in the contract with the IBA. The five largest ITV companies work as network operators. They distribute these programmes through the IBA network, thus supplementing the more limited programme output of the smaller ITV stations.

The network schedule is devised by a group of programme controllers that, until recently, consisted only of representatives of the five major companies. The schedules are then submitted for prior approval by the IBA on a quarterly basis. According to a 1986 figure, about 45 per cent of all programmes shown on ITV were provided by the network companies, while only about nine per cent of programmes produced by the other regional companies were shown nationwide.[311] The network operators have traditionally enjoyed a right to veto the acceptance of such programmes for nationwide distribution. On occasion, the smaller companies have thus felt at a disadvantage and have tried to place themselves in a better position vis-à-vis the five major companies.[312] In October 1987, their struggle was

309 Independent Broadcasting Authority, Enhanced C-Mac – Satellite Television with the Future in Mind (1983).
310 Information provided to the author by Mr Chris Daubney, Head of Engineering Secretariat, IBA.
311 1986 IBA Annual Report, *supra* note 304, at 32.
312 *See* Fin. Times, Nov. 28, 1986, reporting about Television South's attempt to join the five network companies.

crowned with success. Agreement was reached among all ITV companies to enlarge the group of programme controllers by two, who are now representing the interests of the ten regional companies. In addition, the total network hours of the »Big Five« were reduced from 42 hours to 35 hours a week, making more hours for network programming available to the regional companies.[313]

For the purpose of granting regional broadcasting contracts, the IBA has divided the British territory into 14 separate regions.[314] The IBA publicly advertises the contract for each of these regions. At the same time, the public in that particular area has the opportunity to comment and to make suggestions about the services proposed by the Authority (section 19(3) of the Broadcasting Act 1981). The contract is then concluded for a maximum of eight years, after which a new tender round commences (section 19(1), (2),(5)). During the last franchising round in 1980, the IBA removed two of the 15 ITV contractors and granted those franchises to other applicants. Because the IBA's explanation of its decisions was very short, there were only speculations as to why the two contractors had lost their franchises.[315] Part of the explanation may probably be found in the IBA's insistence during the process of readvertising that certain regional companies should substantially expand their production facilities in order to produce more regional programmes for all parts of their geographical service areas.

With the exception of the London area, where two contractors share the right to provide the programming in that region (one contractor provides the programming from Monday to Friday, the other on weekends), all regional contracts have each been granted to a single television company. The ITV companies have joined together to form a company providing ITV's breakfast-time television, TV-am, in all parts of the United Kingdom.[316] They also carry out their obligation to provide news programmes through a separate company, Independent Television News

313 Fin. Times, Oct. 31, 1987.
314 These regions are: North Scotland; Central Scotland; The Border; Northern Ireland; North-East England; Yorkshire, North-West England; East and West Midlands; East of England; Wales and West of England; London; Channel Islands, South-West England; South and South-East England.
315 *See* J. TUNSTALL, THE MEDIA IN BRITAIN 209-10 (1983).
316 The ITV companies also have joined together in a trade organization, the Independent Television Companies Trade Association (ITCA), which provides common services for all contractors.

(ITN).[317] Also, in 1987 some ITV companies were allowed to broadcast limited night-time television services. The two London contractors now provide a 24-hour programme for the London area, while three other ITV companies are planning to launch their own combined night-time service.[318]

The television programme contractors fund their programme production from income earned from the sale of advertising time to advertisers. They may include these advertisements in the programmes, provided that there are no more than seven minutes of advertising in any one hour. The advertising can be inserted in »natural breaks« in the programme's continuity or at the beginning or end of a programme.

The government has severely curtailed the profits of the ITV companies. In addition to normal taxation, such as corporation tax, the television contractors pay a 45-percent levy to the government on all domestic profits above £ 650,000 or 2.8 per cent of profits, whichever is the greater, and a levy of 22.5 per cent on profits from overseas sales (export levy).[319]

Channel 4 was set up by the Broadcasting Act 1980. It owes its existence to a number of considerations, the most prominent being a desire to create a channel with a distinctive character that would »provide a market for ›freelance‹ authors whose work was not necessarily compatible with the existing institutions.«[320] It was to encourage innovative and experimental programmes and cater particularly to the tastes of substantial groups not sufficiently represented in the already existing ITV broadcast channel.[321] Section 10(1) of the Broadcasting Act 1981 empowers the IBA to offer a second television service to be operated by the Authority itself. Consequently, the task of obtaining and assembling the necessary programme material and related activities are carried out through an IBA subsidiary, the Channel Four Television Company Limited (section 12(2)). The IBA appoints the Channel's board members, sets up the annual budget and

---

317 The ITV companies' shareholdings in ITN roughly reflect the companies' advertising revenues, with Thames Television, Central Television and Granada Television holding the largest single shares. In 1988 a staff of 1,067 produced 1,221 minutes of programming per week, while ITN's budget amounted to some £ 60 million per year. The Times, May 18, 1988.

318 Fin. Times, Jan. 13, 1988. Possibly, six further ITV companies will broadcast this combined service in their respective franchise areas, thus enlarging the service's potential audience.

319 See Broadcasting Act 1981, secs. 32-35. In early 1986 the government announced that it would reduce the levy on domestic profits from 66.7 per cent to 45 per cent but would impose a new export levy on the profits earned from the sale of television programmes abroad, 1986 IBA Annual Report, *supra* note 304, at 8.

320 S. LAMBERT, CHANNEL FOUR 47 (1982).

321 See Broadcasting Act 1981, sec. 11, imposing special content requirements on the Channel 4 service.

approves the programme schedules. As with ITV, the IBA also carries out Channel 4's technical operations. Within these structural confines, Channel 4's board members and its commissioning editors, who decide upon the realization of programme ideas submitted to them, have been said to be more independent in their decision-making processes than the ITV companies.[322] Since there is no franchise system in place for Channel 4, the only sanction the Authority has in cases of disapproval with the programme policy, apart from budget shortenings, is the replacement of the members of the board of directors.

Channel 4 has only negligible production facilities of its own, i.e., only one studio for programme continuity productions. Programmes stem mainly from the British market. Anyone may submit proposals for programmes to be included in the Channel 4 programme schedule. If the commissioning editors approve the idea, the Channel 4 Television Company will either partly or wholly finance the production of the programmes. Channel 4 has thus commissioned a large number of programmes from independent producers, who are granted control over their budgets and who also share some of the financial risks of production.[323] In the financial year to March 31, 1987, Channel 4 financed 360 independent productions (1986: 332 independents; 1985: 313 independents).[324] ITV and ITN together contributed 30 per cent to Channel 4's total programming time of about 80 hours per week, while the independent producers supplied a remarkable 25 per cent.[325]

ITV companies also sell programmes produced by them to Channel 4, but section 12(3) of the Broadcasting Act 1981 demands that a »substantial proportion« of Channel 4 programmes be supplied by persons other than ITV programme contractors or companies under the latter's control. This requirement has spurred the evolution of a lively independent television production sector in Britain, a basically new phenomenon.[326] Channel 4 has also sponsored numerous international coproduction agreements, while a small proportion of the 60 hours of weekly broadcasts on the Channel consists of foreign programme material, with an emphasis on »art house« films.[327]

Channel 4 is financed through subscription fees paid by the ITV contractors to the IBA. The ITV companies in turn have the exclusive right to

322 S. LAMBERT, *supra* note 320, at 161.
323 *Id.* at 152.
324 Channel Four Television Company Limited, Report and Accounts for the Year Ended 31st March 1987 11 (hereafter cited as 1987 Channel 4 Annual Report).
325 *Id.* at 8.
326 S. LAMBERT, *supra* note 320, at 154.
327 *Id.* at 140-41.

sell advertising time on Channel 4 in their respective regions (section 13 of the Broadcasting Act 1981). This arrangement disregards the complaints and concerns directed by the advertising industry during the 1970s at the adverse effects of the ITV companies' monopoly with respect to the purchase and placement of advertisements. This monopoly situation had led, the advertisers argued, to an increasing number of restrictive policies and selling practices employed by the television contractors.[328] Strongly favouring the introduction of a fourth television channel, the advertising industry had urged that control over advertisements on this new channel should be given to a body independent of the ITV companies. But the widespread belief that competition for advertising revenue would be contrary to the public interest because it would concentrate efforts on the winning of large audiences rather than on the maintenance of good broadcasting standards prevented the legislators from taking note of the advertisers' objections.[329]

For several years, the ITV companies complained about the financial burden placed upon them by the obligation to fund Channel 4. Subscriptions presently amount to 17 per cent of the ITV contractors' net advertising revenues. In the financial year to March 31, 1987, the total income from the sale of advertising on Channel 4 for the first time surpassed the total subscription fees paid to the IBA.[330]

Channel 4 is aimed at reception in all parts of the United Kingdom except Wales, where a separate broadcasting authority, the Welsh Fourth Channel Authority, is solely responsible for the provision of programmes in that area on the Welsh Fourth Channel (»S 4 C«).[331] The five members of the Welsh authority are appointed by the Home Secretary for five-year terms (section 46 and Schedule 5 of the Broadcasting Act 1981). Like the IBA, they are assisted by a number of advisory bodies (section 51) and financed through sums paid to them by the IBA (section 52). With regard to the character, quality and balance of its programmes, the Welsh Authority is under the same obligations as imposed upon the IBA, with the modification that a substantial proportion of the programmes on the Fourth Channel in Wales be in the Welsh language (section 47(3)). The ar-

---

328 *Id.* at 52-53.
329 *Id.* at 53.
330 In 1987 the net advertising revenue on Channel 4 amounted to £ 155.2 million (1986: £ 112.6; 1985: £ 75.2), while the total subscription fee was £ 135.9 (1986: £ 129.1; 1985: £ 111.0). *See* 1987 Channel 4 Annual Report, *supra* note 324, at 10. The ITV companies generally earn no profits from the sale of their programmes to Channel 4, because the companies are under a contractual obligation with the IBA to sell programmes to the Channel, and Channel 4 has consistently refused to pay anything above the direct costs of production. S. LAMBERT, *supra* note 320, at 131.
331 Broadcasting Act 1981, secs. 46, 47.

rangement for a separate channel in Wales came about as a result of the strong support for the preservation and fostering of the Welsh language as a cornerstone of Welsh culture.[332] The Welsh-language programmes are partly produced by the BBC and partly by the ITV regional programme contractor for Wales, both of which are under a corresponding statutory obligation.[333] The ITV programme contractor for Wales sells its programmes to the Welsh Authority on commercial terms and may also sell advertising time on the Welsh Channel.

Though for the longest time having prevented the emergence of a broadcasting market for the supply of programmes from pluralistic sources, the public broadcasting duopoly has internalized pluralistic structures through the institutionalization of a great variety of advisory councils. One of their most remarkable features is the fact that their composition is not based on concerns for a proportional representation of the dominant political forces, as is the case in the Federal Republic of Germany, for example. Instead, the regional ethical and linguistic particularities of the people in England, Scotland, Wales and Northern Ireland have most strongly influenced the make-up of the councils.

The pluralistic internal organizational structure forms just one tier of a public-service concept designed to reflect the variety of the society's cultures.[334] The second tier consists of detailed programme obligations and an intricate system of programme regulation ensuring the enforcement of these standards.

C. Content Control Mechanisms

1. Programme-Content Controls

The BBC Charter contains a single reference to programme content: Article 3(a) in connection with the Charter's preamble imposes upon the BBC an obligation to provide broadcasting services for the dissemination of information, education and entertainment. The Licence and Agreement is more specific on programme content. Clause 13(2) and (3) requires the Corporation to broadcast an impartial, day-by-day account of the proceedings of both Houses of Parliament and also to broadcast ministerial announcements whenever so requested by the government. As has been

---

332 The Welsh language is spoken by over half a million people, amounting to about 20 per cent of the Welsh population. S. LAMBERT, *supra* note 320, at 51.
333 Broadcasting Act 1981, sec. 48(3). The Welsh Authority may also obtain Welsh-language programmes from other sources.
334 *See* 1977 Annan Report, *supra* note 269, at para. 4.5.

noted above, thus far all governments have refrained from using their veto power under clause 13 for the purpose of prohibiting the BBC from showing specific programmes, although informal government pressures short of explicit orders have been numerous in this respect.[335] But the government has used its authority under clause 13 of the Licence for a number of so-called ministerial prescriptions prohibiting the BBC from broadcasting certain classes of programmes. These prescriptions have now been formally incorporated into the 1981 Licence and Agreement. Under clause 13(6), the Corporation may not include any subliminal images in its programmes. More importantly, »[t]he Corporation shall at all times refrain from sending any broadcast matter expressing the opinion of the Corporation on current affairs or on matters of public policy, other than broadcasting and matter contained in programmes which consist only of proceedings in either House of Parliament or proceedings of a local authority... .«[336] The BBC has also imposed a number of additional programme-standard obligations upon itself in a letter of BBC Chairman Lord Normanbrook to the Post Master General in 1964.[337] The assurances given in this letter have the status of quasi-ministerial prescriptions because of their formal acknowledgment and subsequent reaffirmations by consecutive governments.[338] These BBC programme-content obligations taken together amount in substance to the ,same programme standards imposed on the IBA by way of the Broadcasting Act 1981. Unlike in the case of the IBA, however, the Attorney General cannot enforce the BBC's self-imposed programme standards in court.[339] Lord Normanbrook's letter specifies, i.a., that BBC programmes have to maintain a high general standard, in particular as respects their quality and content, and a proper balance and wide range of subject matter, having regard to the programmes as a whole and to the days on which, and times at which, programmes are broadcast. It also states that the BBC must ensure that, as far as possible, nothing is included in the programmes that offends good taste or decency or is likely to encourage or incite to crime or lead to disorder or to be offensive to public feeling. The letter's most important passage requires the Corporation to ensure that, as far as possible, due impartiality is preserved in news programmes dealing with matters of public policy and controversial subjects generally.

335 See H. STREET, supra note 37, at 96, giving an instructive account of some of these instances of governmental interference.
336 BBC Licence and Agreement 1981, supra note 268, at clause 13(7).
337 The letter is reprinted in large part in C. MUNRO, supra note 98, at 10-11.
338 See 1978 White Paper on Broadcasting, supra note 270, at para. 101.
339 G. ROBERTSON & A. NICOL, supra note 54, at 376; C. MUNRO, supra note 98, at 11. See also Attorney General ex rel. McWhirter v. IBA, 1973 Q.B. 629, holding that a member of the public could not himself complain to the courts that a programme infringed one of the IBA's statutory content obligations. Only the Attorney General as the representative of the public interest had this right.

The BBC also regularly issues internal directives and guidelines further specifying standards, particularly with regard to the portrayal of sex and violence in programmes, and determining what »impartiality« in news programmes should look like.[340] Normally, editorial responsibility lies with the producer of a programme. In cases posing difficult ethical or legal questions, however, he must ascend the BBC hierarchy – all the way, if need be, to the Director General – in order to get a decision, a system called »reference-up.«[341]

Since the BBC provides national services, it is particularly vulnerable to the risks inherent in the differing statutory and common-law rules in England, Scotland and Northern Ireland relating to such matters as defamation, obscenity and the like. In borderline cases, the showing of a film may be lawful in England but constitute a criminal offence in Scotland under the Scottish law of contempt of court, for example. In critical cases, a broadcasting organization with national services is thus prone to refrain from showing a certain programme or particular aspects of certain programmes altogether simply because it may be worried about violating the law in one part of the country.[342]

Two more areas of content regulations deserve attention. The first concerns so-called party political broadcasts. According to a 1969 aide-mémoire (the latest in a number of such agreements going back to 1948) between the government and the major political parties, broadcasts by party spokesmen between elections (party political broadcasts) will only take place after the Committee on Party Political Broadcasting has decided upon the allocation of broadcasting time for these programmes. The Committee consists of two representatives each from the BBC, the IBA and the three major parties. The broadcasting time for each party is calculated on the basis of the party's polls

---

340 G. ROBERTSON & A. NICOL, *supra* note 54, at 377-78. Apparently, there also exist a number of unwritten traditions that are binding on the BBC in its day-to-day operation »as if they were law properly so-called.« Lincoln, *Landesbericht Großbritannien*, in RUNDFUNK-ORGANISATION UND KOMMUNIKATIONSFREIHEIT 125 (M. Bullinger and F. Kübler ed. 1979). For a critical assessment of BBC and ITV news programmes, see THE GLASGOW UNIVERSITY MEDIA GROUP, BAD NEWS (Vol. I) (1976); MORE BAD NEWS (Vol. II) (1980); *see also* M. HARRISON, TV NEWS: WHOSE BIAS? (1985); P. SCHLESINGER, PUTTING »REALITY« TOGETHER – BBC NEWS (1978). On programme content generally, see, e.g., P. HUGHES, BRITISH BROADCASTING: PROGRAMMES AND POWER (1981).
341 G. ROBERTSON & A. NICOL, *supra* note 54, at 376.
342 Opinion provided to the author by Prof. Ian Kennedy, King's College, London. Prof. Kennedy argued that this legal situation encourages stricter-than-necessary self-censoring tendencies among BBC television producers.

at the last general election.[343] This system ensures that the main political parties have control over the airing of their spokesmen's statements on television and radio. Both the BBC and the IBA are effectively prevented from inviting on their own account one or more party spokesmen to speak on television on current political affairs.

The Committee on Party Political Broadcasting also arranges party election broadcasts in accordance with a classified document, the content of which is so secret that it is not even revealed to the producers of these television programmes.[344] The Committee has in the past banned programmes in which the audience could question the politicians and programmes confronting opponents and evaluating party speeches by political commentators. Street summarizes the effect of these arrangements as follows: »In short everything the viewing and listening public wanted was denied them by the politicians, and what they abhorred was foisted on them.«[345] Another limitation on editorial freedom during elections is imposed on the broadcasters by virtue of section 93 of the Representation of the People Act 1983.[346] They may not broadcast the campaigning of a candidate in his electoral area, unless this candidate and all other candidates in this area have given their consent to the programme. The statutory wording has been interpreted to mean that the candidates' consent is needed for all programmes in which they »actively participate,« as is the case, for example, in a panel discussion. The television authorities are not prevented, however, from filming a candidate while he is merely walking through his electoral area; they may include this scene in an election programme without his consent, as long as they observe due impartiality in the programme.[347]

In addition to the interests of the government, political parties and the general public generally to ensure high ethical programme standards and due impartiality and objectivity on certain specified programme matters, there exists within the BBC itself a strong sense of responsibility towards the public and the determination to further public information, education and entertainment within the borderlines of generally acceptable principles of morality, decency and fairness. The BBC's inherent sense of responsibility and its attitude to play a sort of model role in society is well evidenced by

343 See H. STREET, supra note 37, at 92-93; G. ROBERTSON & A. NICOL, supra note 54, at 250-52; see also G. WYNDHAM GOLDIE, FACING THE NATION – TELEVISION AND POLITICS 1936-1976 92-103, 115-44 (1977).
344 H. STREET, supra note 37, at 93-94.
345 Id. at 94.
346 Representation of the People Act 1983 (c.2).
347 Marshall v. BBC, [1979] 1 W.L.R 1071, 1073 (per Lord Denning M.R.).

Lord Normanbrook's letter and goes even further back to the days of the BBC's first Director General, Lord Reith.

In the case of the IBA, the central statutory provision dealing with programme content is section 4 of the Broadcasting Act 1981. Its first part, a comprehensive clause, reads: »(1) It shall be the duty of the Authority to satisfy themselves that, so far as possible, the programmes broadcast by the Authority comply with the following requirements, that is to say (a) that nothing is included in the programmes which offends against good taste or decency or is likely to encourage or incite to crime or to lead to disorder or to be offensive to public feeling.« The section further specifies duties relating to accurate and impartial news programmes, impartiality in the presentation of political and industrial controversies and current policy issues, special obligations with regard to religious services, parliamentary proceedings or proceedings of local authorities, and the like. Subsection 3 prohibits the inclusion of »any technical device which, by using images of very brief duration or by any other means, exploits the possibility of conveying a message to, or otherwise influencing the minds of, members of an audience without their being aware, or fully aware, of what has been done.«

In 1986 the Court of Appeal held that a breach by the IBA of its duty to prevent the showing of subliminal images under this section did not constitute a criminal offence; in case of non-compliance it would be up to the Attorney General to apply for an order of mandamus, commanding the Authority to omit the subliminal image from the programme.[348]

Section 5 of the Broadcasting Act 1981 further obliges the IBA to draw up codes on programme standards as guidelines for the programme contractors. These guidelines deal with general programme matters and practices and, for example, with the showing of violence and children's programmes. Also, the programme contractors have to submit regularly their programme schedules to the IBA for prior approval.[349] The schedules are submitted in quarterly intervals to the IBA. They give a very detailed, minute-by-minute account of the proposed programmes. The Authority has broad discretion to require changes and give directions as it thinks fit. It will call for those programmes that it deems ought to be watched in

---

348 R. v. Horseferry Road Justices ex parte IBA, 1987 Q.B. 54.
349 Broadcasting Act 1981, sec. 6; and Schedule 2 of the Television Contract. A model »Agreement for Appointment of Television Programme Contractor« between the IBA and Ulster Television Limited (dated Dec. 31, 1981) was provided to the author by Mr Kenneth Blyth, Chief Assistant to the IBA Director General. Throughout this treatise, citations to a »Television Contract« will refer to the above-mentioned document.

advance. This system of reviews, the vetting system, is both reactive, if the IBA responds to programmes already produced, and innovative in those cases in which companies request the IBA to vet programme scripts in advance.

Several difficult legal issues have arisen in the past in connection with the Authority's duties laid down in the comprehensive clause of section 4(1)(a) Broadcasting Act 1981: (1) What procedures must the IBA adopt in order to discharge properly its duties relating to programme-content control, in particular, do the IBA members themselves have to screen controversial programmes before a decision on their showing can lawfully be reached? (2) To what extent can the courts review a programme decision that is within the discretion of the Authority? (3) Who is authorized to bring an action enjoining the IBA from broadcasting a certain programme, in particular, does a member of the general public have the legal standing to do so?

The IBA has organized the programme-monitoring procedure into several stages. First, an IBA specialist vets the proposed programme schedules and examines whether the programmes comply with the statutory requirements. In cases of doubt, the decision over the suitability of a programme for showing is referred to higher levels of control, ultimately reaching the Director General in particularly critical cases. In the *McWhirter* case,[350] decided in 1973, the Court of Appeal dealt with an injunction sought by a private individual, Mr WcWhirter, to restrain the IBA from showing a documentary on the artist Andy Warhol. Mr McWhirter had claimed that the screening would violate section 3(1)(a) of the Television Act 1964[351] because the programme was offensive to public feeling. The Court of Appeal granted an interim injunction on the grounds that (1) evidence suggested the programme to be likely to offend public feeling, and the IBA had not done its duty; (2) the Attorney General had refused to take an action ex officio; (3) there was not sufficient time for the plaintiff to bring a relator action,[352] which would have required a lengthy procedure to receive the Attorney General's necessary consent, since the programme was supposed to be shown on the same day; and (4) the members of the Authority had not viewed the programme to satisfy

---

350 Attorney-General ex rel McWhirter v. IBA, 1973 Q.B. 629.
351 Television Act 1964 (c.21). The wording of section 3(1)(a) of the Television Act 1964 is identical with the wording of section 4(1)(a) of the Broadcasting Act 1981.
352 In a relator action, the Attorney General is only the nominal plaintiff, while the relator is responsible for the actual conduct of the proceedings and for the cost of the action, which serves the assertion of a public right. It is in the discretion of the Attorney General to grant a relator action.

themselves about its suitability for showing.[353] In the final judgment, the Court once again confirmed its view that a member of the public had standing in similarly exceptional cases of last resort. At the time of the second hearing, which preceded the final judgment, the members of the IBA had made up for their delay and had personally monitored the controversial programme. They had reached the conclusion that it was suitable for showing on ITV at a late evening hour. The Court accepted this decision, arguing that »[t]he Independent Broadcasting Authority are the people who matter. They are the censors. The courts have no right whatever – and I may add no desire whatever – to interfere with their decisions so long as they reach them in accordance with law. ... my views do not matter, unless they go to show that the Independent Broadcasting Authority misdirected themselves or came to a conclusion to which they could not reasonably come.«[354]

This decision has been modified in certain respects by two later cases. In *Gouriet v. Union of Post Office Workers,*[355] the House of Lords dealt with a situation in which the Attorney General had explicitly refused to allow a relator action. The Court held that as a matter of constitutional law, no private individual had legal standing to bring an action for the purpose of enforcing a public – as contrasted with a private – right, absent any special damages suffered by him personally.[356] In dictum, the Court also rejected Lord Denning's opinion in the *McWhirter* case, stating that there was no authority for the proposition and that it was contrary to principle that a private individual could obtain an injunction if the Attorney General had not had time to consider a relator action or if he had improperly or unreasonably delayed giving leave or if he had refused to give leave in a proper case.[357]

Another case concerned itself with »Scum,« a film about life in a borstal, broadcast on Channel 4 one late night in 1983. Mrs Whitehouse, a member of the public, brought a relator action seeking judicial review of the IBA's exercise of its powers under section 4(1) of the Broadcasting Act 1981. The Divisional Court, holding that Mrs Whitehouse as a television licence holder had sufficient interest to bring the action, decided that the Director General had committed a grave error of judgment, because he had failed to refer the film to the members of the Authority to get their decision about

353 *Attorney-General ex rel McWhirter*, 1973 Q.B. at 633-36 (per Lord Denning M.R.).
354 *Id.* at 652.
355 [1977] 3 W.L.R. 300.
356 *Id.* at 313-14 (per Lord Wilberforce).
357 *Id.* at 315.

whether the controversial programme should be broadcast.[358] Also, the Court was of the opinion that the IBA itself had breached its duty to give appropriate instructions to the Director General and the staff about the circumstances in which programmes needed to be referred to the members for decision.

The Court of Appeal reversed, holding that it was up to the IBA to set up a monitoring system that it considered best adapted to meet the statutory requirements, a discretion the exercise of which the Court of Appeal refused to scrutinize as long as the Authority had not acted ultra vires or unlawfully. In contrast to the *McWhirter* case, the recent holding suggests that IBA members are under no duty to monitor personally every controversial programme.[359] These latest decisions are in line with a much older case involving a private action against a BBC programme. In 1967 a British resident of German origin sought an injunction to restrain the BBC from broadcasting further television and radio programmes allegedly containing abusive racial propaganda against Germany and Germans. The Court of Appeal held that regardless of the possible virtue of the complaint, the plaintiff had no cause of action since prosecutions due to a violation of the criminal law could only be instigated by or with the consent of the Attorney General, a consent he had refused to give in the case before the Court.[360]

On the whole, one can discern a tendency of the courts to interfere as little as possible with IBA and BBC programme-policy decisions and to restrain individual members of the public from exerting legal pressures on the broadcasting organizations' exercise of their discretionary powers. This situation would change to the disadvantage of the broadcasters if, as is presently being considered by the government, the Obscene Publications Act were extended also to apply to broadcasting. This would give individual members of the public a right of action in cases of allegedly obscene programmes, provided that the Attorney General acquiesced in the proceedings.

Before this background of the courts favouring freedom of expression on the part of the broadcasters over the right of private individuals to impose their own version of programme standards on the broadcasters, the recent developments surrounding the setting up of the Broadcasting Standards Council (BSC) can best be understood. The National Viewers' and Listeners' Association, a private organization and public pressure group chaired

358 R. v. IBA ex parte Whitehouse, The Times, Apr. 4, 1984 (Court of Appeal).
359 *See also* 6 J. MEDIA L. & PRAC. 210, 212 (1985).
360 Thorne v. BBC, [1967] 1 WLR 1104, 1109 (per Lord Denning M.R.).

by Mrs Whitehouse, had lobbied hard for higher programme control of the broadcasting organizations.[361] The 1987 Conservative Party election manifesto had also committed itself to take action on what it deemed the public concern about sex and violence on television. In early 1988, the government took decisive steps to carry through its policy by setting up what has been termed a »watchdog body.« The BSC, which is to receive statutory backing with the next broadcasting bill, will have the following functions: (1) issue a code on the portrayal of sex and violence and standards on taste and decency after consultation with the broadcasting authorities and the other bodies responsible for programme content in the broadcasting, cable and video fields; (2) monitor and report on the performance of these standards in television and radio programmes received in the United Kingdom, and in video works; (3) make findings on public complaints about matters within its frame of reference; (4) preview programmes bought by British broadcasters, particularly American films, (5) carry out research on the nature and effects on attitudes and behaviour of the portrayal of sex and violence on broadcasting and video pro- grammes; and (6) prepare an annual report.[362] One of the most powerful weapons of the new body will be its right to require broadcasters to publicise its findings on individual programmes. The BSC's first chairman, Sir William Rees-Mogg, has already made it clear that publication of the Council's criticisms at the same time and, if possible, in the same pro- gramme as the originally offensive material will be seen as essential for the effectiveness of its work.

Sir William's insistence on the previewing of imported material has met with particular opposition, the implication being that this power will be a first step towards a censoring body.[363] However, the BSC will not pre-vet programmes produced by the British broadcasters. Also, it will have no powers to prevent any programme from being shown; the BSC may only issue opinions in advance of transmissions. How the Council's programme vetting powers will be fit into the present structure of the BBC's and the IBA's corresponding powers is a question that is still unresolved. In- stitutional frictions are already built into the new system, particularly in cases in which the views of the BBC and the IBA differ from those expressed by the BSC. A marked difference of the new system clearly lies in the likelihood of an increasing politicising of programme content

---

361 *See, e.g.*, The Times, Oct. 31, 1987.
362 *See* The Times, May 17, 1988.
363 *See, e.g.*, The Times, May 13, 17, 18, 1988; Fin. Times, Oct. 1, 1987.

matters, with private individuals and organizations having a right to bring a case against broadcasters on matters of taste.

But the IBA itself has come under criticism for the extensive practice of precensorship. It has been argued that the Court's holding in the *Scum* case would justify a system under which the Authority would – except under extraordinary circumstances – only vet programmes *after* their showing on television, as long as this system would ensure a constant monitoring of programme standards and precise information on public reactions.[364] Public reprimands of programme contractors in cases of serious violations of programme standards, and ultimately the withdrawal of their television programme contract, would probably suffice in order for the Authority to execute their programme-content control functions properly. Such a system would also ensure considerably greater freedom of expression for the programme makers.

An incident that demonstrates the Authority's extensive order-making powers for remedying the showing of a programme contravening the provisions of the Broadcasting Act 1981 is the Channel 4 series »Greece.« The screening of one part of this series provoked strong public criticism that the duty of impartiality in news programmes was violated. The IBA agreed with the critics and consequently ordered Channel 4 to broadcast an apology and a balancing programme later in the year. The production company, the ITV contractor »Television South,« was ordered not to allow any repeats of this series and was prohibited from selling the programme abroad.[365]

2. *Control of Advertising*

One principle fundamental to the ITV broadcasting system is the separation between the contractors' procurement of advertisements and the IBA's ultimate control over the programme and advertising standards. This separation of functions serves the public interest by preventing advertisers from effectively influencing programme makers through the exercise of financial pressures. The public interest is further strengthened by the provision that neither the IBA nor any programme contractor may serve as an advertising

---

364 Robertson, *What Should the IBA Do?*, 6 J. MEDIA L. & PRAC. 269, 271-72 (1985).
365 7 J. MEDIA L. & PRAC. 101 (1986).

agent. Programme sponsorship is severely curtailed.[366] Spot advertisements, i.e., advertisements at the beginning or end of a programme or in natural breaks, or block advertisements may be inserted (section 8(3) and Schedule 2 of the Broadcasting Act 1981).

Schedule 2 of the Broadcasting Act 1981 imposes a number of additional requirements on television and radio advertising: The »advertisements must be clearly distinguishable as such and recognizably separate from the rest of the programme«; »successive advertisements must be recognizably separate«; they »must not be arranged or presented in such a way that any separate advertisement appears to be part of a continuous feature«; the length of the spot advertisements may »not be so great as to detract from the value of the programme as a medium of information, education and entertainment«; no advertising may be inserted »by or on behalf of anybody whose objects are wholly or mainly of a religious or political nature...« or if it »is directed towards any religious or political end or has any relation to any industrial dispute.«

In addition to these statutory requirements, which the Home Secretary may amend if he considers it necessary, the IBA has the duty to draw up a code of advertising standards. Its requirements may go beyond standards and practices prescribed by the statutory provisions (section 9(2) of the Broadcasting Act 1981). Apart from advertising standards, the IBA's Television Programme Guidelines[367] are amended from time to time to cover such matters as: offences to good taste and decency (for example, with regard to language, sex and bad taste in humour); the portrayal of violence (particularly with regard to children's programmes); the technical quality of programmes; accuracy in the presentation of programmes (particularly news programmes and programmes on medical subjects); the respect of privacy of people portrayed in programmes; decent methods of gathering information; fairness and impartiality; the presentation of politicians in programmes; the portrayal of crime and anti-social behaviour; and similar issues. It is also the responsibility of the Authority to regulate the amount of advertisements that may be carried on a channel on any particular day or

---

366 *See* Broadcasting Act 1981, sec. 8(6), *but see also* the exception clause in section 8(7) of the Act. In 1988 the IBA slightly relaxed its restrictions on sponsorship in a revised version of its guidelines on sponsorship. Under the new rules, the content of a sponsored programme may be directly related to the sponsor's commercial activities, and acknowledgments of sponsors may be carried in the middle of programmes as well as at their beginnings and ends. However, editorial control of the content and scheduling of a programme must stay exclusively with the ITV station. *See* Fin. Times, May, 25, 27, 1988. Any further liberalization of sponsorship rules would require new legislation.

367 Independent Broadcasting Authority, Television Programme Guidelines (April 1985).

during any particular programme (section 9(4),(5) of the Broadcasting Act 1981).

When ITV companies complained to the EUCM, alleging that the prohibition to accept advertisements of a political nature violated their right to freedom of expression under article 10 of the EUHR, the Commission decided that the licensing system for broadcasting envisaged by article 10(1) implied that states could also subject broadcasting to certain other legal restrictions.[368] In light of the fact that certain member states to the Convention prohibited all advertising on their broadcasting channels, the Commission held that article 10(1) of the EUHR equally justified the prohibition of certain specified categories of advertisements.

The IBA has the duty to enforce the observance of these standards either by giving general directions to a programme contractor or by interfering with the broadcast of a particular advertisement in an individual case (section 9(3) of the Broadcasting Act 1981). In practice, the Authority previews almost all of the advertising scripts before they are recorded. They number about 7,000 per year.[369]

A critical aspect of the present regulation of advertising on television is the lack of a formal complaints procedure in the interest of consumers and persons carrying on a trade or business who want to initiate proceedings against misleading advertisements. At present, it is in the discretion of the IBA to give consideration to the complaint of any such person about a television commercial. Section 43(4)(d) of the Broadcasting Act 1981 merely requires the IBA to give in its annual report a description of its arrangements with respect to advertisements and of the complaints received and its actions taken in response to them.

A different system is in effect with respect to the regulation of advertising outside the broadcast media. Here, the Advertising Standards Authority (ASA), an independent body financed by a surcharge on display advertising and organized by the advertising industry, is responsible for the drafting of the British Code of Advertising Practice specifying the rules to be followed by the advertising industry.[370] The ASA investigates outside complaints about individual advertisements and publishes its findings. If an advertiser refuses to comply with a decision of the ASA, the sanctions available against him are the withholding of advertising space or time from the advertiser, the withdrawal of the trading privileges of the advertising

---

368 Decision of July 12, 1971, (No. 4515/70), 38 COLL. DEC. 86, 88-89 (1972).
369 B. PAULU, *supra* note 165, at 70.
370 *See* P. O'HIGGINS, *supra* note 9, at 265-66.

agency and the notification of consumer-protection agencies.[371] This regulation of the complaints procedures with regard to misleading advertising outside the broadcasting area conflicts with the EC Council Directive of September 10, 1984 relating to the approximation of the laws, regulations and administrative provisions of the member states concerning misleading advertising.[372] According to the Directive, the member states shall ensure that all persons or organizations regarded under national law as having a legitimate interest in prohibiting misleading advertising have the possibility of initiating legal actions and/or have the right to bring a complaint before an administrative authority competent to decide on the complaint. Also, the member states shall confer upon the courts or administrative authorities powers enabling them to order the cession of or to prohibit the publication of such advertisements. Article 5, included in the Directive as a concession to the British regulatory system, states that the Directive does not exclude the voluntary control of misleading advertising by self-regulatory bodies in addition to a recourse to an administrative authority or court.

The ASA neither is an administrative authority nor has the power to order the cession of or to prohibit the publication of advertising. Thus, legal action on the part of the United Kingdom is required; according to article 189(3) of the EEC Treaty, a Council Directive is binding upon member states. But it is up to the member states how they want to give effect to the substantive provisions of a Directive.

In the United Kingdom, section 2(2) of the European Communities Act 1972[373] provides for the enactment of subordinate legislation to put into effect all obligations arising under the EEC Treaty that are, like a Council Directive, not directly applicable or effective. Under this section, the power to make such provisions by subordinate legislation is delegated to the Crown in Council and any Minister of the Crown or government department designated for this task by Order in Council. In order to give effect to its obligations under the Treaty, the British government is planning to implement a set of regulations under the European Communities Act giving the Director General of the Office of Fair Trading (OFT) the power to seek recourse to the High Court if he concludes that the ASA has failed to consider a complaint or has rejected a complaint

---

371 *Id.* at 267.
372 27 O.J. EUR. COMM. (No. L 250) 17 (1984) (84/450/EEC).
373 European Communities Act 1972 (c.68).

that should be reconsidered by the courts.[374] According to the draft regulations,[375] complainants must first unsuccessfully resort to the ASA before they can turn to the OFT to seek redress. At the same time article 5 of the Directive makes it possible to maintain ASA's principle functions.

The IBA had taken the position that no legislative amendment was necessary under the directive with regard to broadcast advertising.[376] To the extent that the IBA has been designed as an administrative authority controlling the ITV television system, and to the extent that it has the power to prevent the broadcasting of any misleading advertising, the IBA's position has some merit. However, the current situation is characterized by several important shortcomings: (1) since it is the IBA itself that draws up the advertising standards code, previews the overwhelming majority of advertising scripts and screens all commercials before their first showing, it sits as its own judge in cases where a person complains about a particular commercial – the complainant thus lacks legal recourse to a truly independent body; (2) the Broadcasting Act 1981 provides for no formalized complaints procedures; (3) there exists no statutory obligation on the part of the IBA to adjudicate a complaint at all. The draft regulations take care of only one of these shortcomings: paragraph 6(1) requires the IBA to consider any complaint, unless it is frivolous or vexacious. All in all, therefore, the present advertising complaints procedure in broadcasting, while it complies with the literal reading of the Council Directive, contravenes the spirit of the first cornerstone of the Community's consumer-actions policy.

The foregoing remarks have evidenced the tight and detailed control of programme and advertising standards typical of the British broadcasting system. On the other hand, the fact that the courts have shielded programme-policy issues from private actions has resulted in greater independence for the broadcasters, although the courts have indicated that the price for the relinquishment of a private right of action in this area has to be an even stronger sense of responsibility on the part of the broadcasting organizations. But the transformation of these principles into the sphere of advertising control disregards the legitimate interests of consumers for the benefit of an extremely broad discretionary power exercised by the IBA.

374 Under article 8 of the Council Directive, the changes had to be implemented into the national laws of the member states by Oct. 1, 1986. However, the United Kingdom failed to act by then. In August 1987, the Directive had still not been implemented, but the author was told by government officials that the regulations were expected to come into force by the end of September 1987.
375 The Control of Misleading Advertisements Regulations 1987 (Draft).
376 1985 IBA Annual Report, *supra* note 253, at 44.

Both the IBA and the BBC have parallel functions with respect to radio broadcasting. While in the case of the BBC the introduction of television broadcasting came about more than twenty years after the beginning of sound broadcasting, the introduction of commercial radio only followed after 17 years of commercial television had already passed. For both broadcasting authorities, however, the legal structure of radio broadcasting closely follows the pattern of television broadcasting.

D. *The Organizational Structure of Sound Broadcasting*

As with the provision of television services, the BBC provides radio broadcasts itself, while the IBA licenses radio contractors for the provision of local sound-broadcasting services.

1. *BBC Domestic Radio Services*

The BBC presently provides four national sound services (Radio 1, 2, 3, 4), four national regional services (two for Wales and one each for Scotland and Northern Ireland) and eight local services, which opt out of the regional services at certain times of the day. In addition, the BBC presently provides 30 purely local radio services in England. Although the Peacock Committee recommended the privatisation of Radios 1 and 2 and local radio in whole or in part,[377] the government's 1987 Green Paper on the choices and opportunities for radio reaffirmed the BBC's role as the provider of national and local radio services and rejected the proposals of the Committee.

The legal basis for all BBC radio services is the Corporation's Charter and the 1981 Licence and Agreement.[378] The operation of the radio stations is financed through an apportionment of the income from the television licence fees to the radio services. Any advertising on BBC radio stations is prohibited. Programme standards to be maintained in the radio services are the same as those applying to television broadcasts. The Charter also imposes an obligation upon the BBC to establish Regional Advisory Councils and Local Radio Advisory Councils in those areas where it offers regional or local radio services.[379] These councils, which have to be

---

377 1986 Peacock Report, *supra* note 216, at para. 637.
378 *See* article 3(a) of the BBC Royal Charter 1981, *supra* note 252; clause 3(c) of the BBC Licence and Agreement 1981, *supra* note 268.
379 Article 11(2) of the BBC Royal Charter 1981.

»broadly representative of the general public,« are to ensure that programmes broadcast in the respective regions or localities have full regard to the interests of the people living there. Just like the national broadcasting services, BBC local radio is committed to »help to make people better citizens.«[380] This accounts for the many educational and minority programmes offered by these services. But because BBC local radio is permanently short of funds, they also broadcast a large number of programmes from the national radio services.[381]

In 1977 the Annan Committee had expressed doubts about whether a national broadcasting organization such as the BBC were suited to offer local radio services, particularly in view of the fact that these services were financed through television licence fees collected nationwide.[382] But in the following years, the number of BBC local radio stations nonetheless rose from 20 to around 30.

2. Independent Local Radio (ILR)

The Sound Broadcasting Act 1972[383] for the first time brought commercial radio to the United Kingdom, but strictly limited it to local services, called Independent Local Radio (ILR). These private local radio stations operate under licences granted by the IBA.[384] As with television, the IBA operates the transmitters. The services are financed exclusively by advertising. Also, the stations are under the public-service obligation to inform, educate and entertain, and detailed programme obligations designed and supervised by the IBA apply. As of 1987, the IBA had granted radio licences to 50 local radio stations.[385] Most of the radio contractors have an exclusive contract for their respective localities. Despite their quasi-monopolies, a great number of them face severe difficulties in trying to raise sufficient money from the sale of advertising time on their

---

380 *See* 1977 Annan Report, *supra* note 269, at para. 8.29.
381 *Id.* at para. 8.30.
382 *Id.* at para. 8.31. In 1986 the Peacock Committee recommended the reduction of the television licence fee and the introduction of a separate licence fee to be charged for car radios but not for BBC radio services in general. 1986 Peacock Report, *supra* note 216, at paras. 632-33.
383 Sound Broadcasting Act 1972 (c.32). Its provisions were incorporated into the Broadcasting Act 1981.
384 *See* Broadcasting Act 1981, sec. 2. All details on the contractual relationship between the Independent Broadcasting Authority and a sound programmme contractor are contained in the Agreement for Appointment of Programme Contractor for Local Sound Broadcasts (Proof June 1984) (unpublished), provided to the author by Mr Kenneth Blyth, Chief Assistant to the IBA Director General.
385 A list of 48 ILR programme companies is contained in Appendix VII to the 1986 IBA Annual Report, *supra* note 304.

channels. Revenues from advertising have deteriorated due to an increasing competitive challenge from commercial breakfast television, cable television, »pirate« radio stations and a rising number of »free sheets« offering advertising space.[386] In the mid-1980s the IBA employed a number of measures aimed at relieving the ILR operators' financial burdens, such as a 10-percent cut in the level of rental payments for the use of the IBA's technical facilities in 1985, and a year later it instituted a cut of at least 26 per cent. It also changed its competition and antitrust policies to allow sound broadcasters greater freedom to diversify into other activities and even permitted mergers between neighbouring stations.[387] The IBA's main argument was that the Broadcasting Act 1981 did not prohibit such mergers and that the Authority would thus not object as long as the programme output remained local.

The ILR system as it exists now may soon come to an end altogether. The Peacock Committee, which had made a number of suggestions aimed at a reform of the present radio system, had strongly favoured the introduction of commercial national radio services at the expense of the BBC's Radios 1 and 2. But the government's 1987 Green Paper on radio rejected the privatisation of these two services. It instead proposed the introduction of three additional national commercial networks carrying music, sports, news and talkshows.

The 1987 Green Paper foreshadows some revolutionary developments in the field of terrestrial broadcasting, with important repercussions for the existing public-service concept. These implications will be the subject of the following section, which will also deal with the dramatically changing nature of the traditional broadcasting duopoly due to the IBA's and the BBC's engagement in virtually all aspects of the new media.

E. *New Programme and Value-Added Services and the Impact of the Peacock Report*

The changes in the traditional broadcasting system are taking place on all

386 *See* 1986 Peacock Report, *supra* note 216, at paras. 76, 79; 1987 Green Paper on Radio, *supra* note 221, at paras. 2.4-2.6, 2.25; 1985 IBA Annual Report, *supra* note 253, at 7. Due to the IBA's technical constraints put upon radio contractors, particularly regarding the acoustic standards to be maintained, construction costs for ILR stations are high and currently range from £ 200,000 to £ 1 million. *See* Independent Broadcasting Authority, IBA Evidence to Peacock, Airways, 8-9 (Autumn 1985).

387 1985 IBA Annual Report, *supra* note 253, at 7; 1986 IBA Annual Report, *supra* note 304, at 34-35; 1987 Green Paper on Radio, *supra* note 221, at para. 2.9.

levels, i.e., within the broadcasting organizations themselves and with regard to the activities of the ITV contractors; they also pertain to all aspects of broadcasting, i.e., they relate to the traditional programme services and also extend to the provision of data and other information services. One of the imminent and most comprehensive changes in the present broadcasting duopoly is likely soon to take place in the area of commercial radio broadcasting, where plans to introduce community radio have triggered government proposals to restructure the whole commercial radio system.

1. *Far-Reaching Implications of the Plans for a New Commercial Radio System*

The possible »fourth tier« of radio broadcasting in the United Kingdom has received wide public attention for many years. The concept of community radio is based on the idea that the present radio services, including ILR, take insufficient interest in the needs of small communities and minorities.[388] Community radio would operate with low-power transmitters for reception in small areas or communities only. It could cater to the tastes of ethical minorities and devotees of certain kinds of music and/or ensure greater personal involvement of individuals in community matters.

In the summer of 1985, the Home Secretary expressed his intention to start a two-year experiment with licences granted to some 21 community stations in different parts of the country.[389] However, these plans, which had attracted almost 280 applicants, were shelved in the following year when the Home Secretary announced that the time had not yet come to make a final judgment on the suitability of the experiments.[390] Instead, the government promised a Green Paper that would identify the pros and cons of community radio. This consultative paper, published in early 1987, not only supported the idea of community radio, but also proposed dramatic changes for the ILR system as well. It announced that new international agreements on spectrum allocation and other reallocations of spectrum users would provide many new opportunities to operate local and

388 A very critical assessment of an ILR contractor's programme policy is contained in COMEDIA PUBLISHING GROUP/LOCAL RADIO WORKSHOP, CAPITAL – LOCAL RADIO & PRIVATE PROFIT (1983).
389 1986 Peacock Report, *supra* note 216, at para. 42.
390 Fin. Times, July 1, 1986.

community stations, as well as commercial national networks. As noted above,[391] these announcements represent a milestone for freedom of communication in the United Kingdom. The diminishing spectrum scarcity for radio has also led the government to agree with the Peacock Committee about the reduced need to regulate the programme content of the private stations. The Committee had spoken out in favour of relieving the ILR stations of most of the IBA's regulatory restrictions. Under the new regime, the private radio companies were to be allowed to own and operate the transmitters in their respective franchise areas. They were to be authorized to accept any advertising on their programmes allowed in the printing press and to decide on their own over broadcasting hours, technical standards, ownership (!), sources of programme material and programme sponsorship.[392] Also, all content regulations in the form of standards – such as proper balance of subject matters, programme mix of information, education and entertainment, and the like – should be dropped, the Committee had argued. The IBA should keep only the regulatory control over frequency allocation and transmitter power and the responsibility for drafting and enforcing the general codes of conduct relating to programming and advertising.

In 1987 the government decided that a new regulatory regime should be passed by Parliament if the Conservatives won the next general elections, as they did in June of the same year. Under the new legislation, to be introduced in Parliament in the autumn of 1988, commercial radio stations, be they community or ILR stations, are likely to be no longer under the full-range programme obligations to inform, educate and entertain. On the national level, where the government envisaged the introduction of three commercial services in addition to the four national services provided by the BBC, it linked the demand for the maintenance of some kind of content control with the missing achievement of the full broadcasting market:

> While the number of frequencies suitable for national services is not so large that the concept of public service broadcasting can safely be discarded, neither is it so small that they should all be reserved for the BBC as national broadcaster. ... The key is to strike the right balance between the BBC and new competition which might operate under such a lighter system of regulation.[393]

The Green Paper advanced arguments on the basis of the same concept

---

391 *See supra* at chapter I(B)(3).
392 1986 Peacock Report, *supra* note 216, at para. 639.
393 1987 Green Paper on Radio, *supra* note 221, at paras. 4.6, 4.7.

with respect to local and community radio, where it identified many more available additional frequencies than those existing on the national level. It therefore carried the argument of a reduced need for content regulations even a step further:

> [T]here is now the prospect of enough spectrum to accommodate a large increase in the number of local radio stations, some serving small communities and others larger areas. This will over the next decade meet one of the two conditions identified by the Peacock Committee as necessary for a move away from the public service broadcasting framework. It is possible to argue that that framework is no longer needed for local radio, and that throughout the UK a pattern of local stations will come about, through the operation of normal market forces, which between them meet all reasonable audience tastes.[394]

All in all, the government did not go so far as to advocate a total abolition of content restrictions on broadcast programmes. Under the new regime the BBC, which is to maintain all its present radio services,[395] will continue to provide these services in accordance with the public-service broadcasting obligation set out in its Charter. The commercial radio stations, on the other hand – i.e., the national and the local services alike – are likely to be subject to a loosened regime of content restrictions similar to those now applying to cable programme services.[396]

The era has not yet begun in which radio broadcasters are subject to the same restrictions on their freedom of expression as journalists working for the press. But for the first time the core of the public-service broadcasting concept has been officially put into question. Liberalizing commercial radio broadcasting from the constraints of public-service content regulations represents a decisive step into the broadcasting market of the future as

---

394 *Id.* at para. 6.2.
395 However, the BBC's extended practice of simulcasting, i.e., the broadcasting of the same service on different wave lengths, is to be radically reduced in order to make more frequencies available for alternative commercial broadcasting uses. *See id.* at paras. 4.10-4.11.
396 *See* the suggestions for possible programme content obligations set out at *id.*, para. 7.7. The IBA in its response to the Green Paper pointed out that a requirement for impartiality in news programmes would not only require complex judgments not necessarily in line with the concept of a »lighter touch« but would also be difficult to maintain on a local level for small-scale neighbourhood and ethnic minorities stations. IBA, The IBA's View – The Future of U.K. Independent Radio paras. 47-49 (June 1987) (hereafter cited as IBA, Response to the Green Paper on Radio). The BBC, on the other hand, while much welcoming the Green Paper's recommendation to continue the present range of public-service broadcasting, is much concerned with its likely loss of frequencies and the end to simulcasting. *See* BBC, Choices and Opportunities: The BBC's Response to the Radio Green Paper (1987).

envisaged by the Peacock Committee. The new policy acknowledges one of the central principles formulated by the Committee, namely, that only spectrum scarcity and not a general media policy can justify special legal restrictions on the content of broadcast speech.

What is more, the new regulatory regime for community radio and ILR may even lead to the loss of the IBA's supervisory power over commercial radio broadcasting. The Green Paper presented several options without deciding the question of which institution would be the most suitable supervisory authority for a future community radio broadcasting system. Of the three possible options, namely, (1) continued regulatory competence of the IBA; (2) the setting up of a new radio authority, and (3) an extension of the Cable Authority's functions to radio, the government seems to favour the second option. The underlying rationale appears to be that allowing the IBA to supervise community radio would represent the worst possible alternative because the IBA has traditionally applied a strict regulatory regime.[397] The very spirit of the public broadcasting concept, with which the IBA justifies its existence, is widely considered as an impediment to the development of the new broadcasting era.

If the IBA were to lose its control over radio broadcasting, this decision would have a signalling effect for the future of the public broadcasting system.[398] While in the past both the IBA and the BBC have managed to extend their involvement and competence to all newly emerging media technologies, the traditional automatic extension of their functions would for the first time be stopped. The IBA's regulatory competence not only would be checked but also would effectively diminish. The government's considerations evidence the fundamental policy changes that have taken place since the days of Lord Reith.

---

397 *See* Fin. Times, Mar. 1, 1987. The IBA, on the other hand, has pointed out its long experience as a regulatory authority responsible for radio and the high costs involved in setting up and running a separate radio authority. IBA, Response to the Green Paper on Radio, *supra* note 396, at paras. 81-91.

398 On Jan. 19, 1988, the Home Secretary announced that the government had decided to establish a new Radio Authority independent of the IBA and responsible for commercial radio as a whole. The Times, Jan. 20, 1988. The plan included the licensing of several hundred community radio stations and a deregulation of ILR. At the same time, three new national commercial radio channels were to be auctioned to the highest bidder, provided that the applicant's programme plans satisfied certain minimum standards. In May 1988, however, the Home Secretary announced that these plans for commercial radio were to be shelved for some time and would not be included in the new broadcasting bill to be introduced in the autumn of 1988. As a result, the emergence of many new pirate stations is expected in Britain. *See* The Times, May 21, 1988.

2. *Developments Extending the Traditional Role of the Public Broadcasters*

The opposite tendencies, namely, the expansion of the activities and competence of the broadcasting organizations to services not directly related with the core of their tasks, is best evidenced by the developments in DBS and teletext services. When in the early 1980s the provision of a British DBS service for the first time became technically and politically feasible, the BBC strongly lobbied in support of an allocation of two of the five DBS channels to itself. It argued that because of its vast programme library it could offer attractive programme channels. Its international reputation in broadcasting would help the establishment of new services; and most importantly, such a move would ensure the BBC's continued role as the principle national instrument of broadcasting.[399] These arguments found support in the government, which decided to grant to the BBC the licence for the first two channels, for a number of years to be the only two channels allocated to any DBS operator. The project ultimately failed due to a lack of financial assistance, and in the end the BBC declined to engage in DBS at all. This meant that private companies had to be won as DBS contractors. Almost as a matter of course a DBS broadcasting system with private licensees was conceived of as a regulatory system paralleling the already existing ITV system. Consequently, the IBA's regulatory powers greatly increased when the Cable and Broadcasting Act 1984 designated it as the licensing and supervisory authority responsible for the future DBS services. In the course of the political decision-making process leading to a legal regime for DBS, the public broadcasting authorities thus played a crucial role in determining the future structure of the services.[400]

After the failure of its initial DBS plans, the BBC continued to think about venturing into satellite television. It entered into negotiations with ITV companies over a satellite television channel using a communications satellite and featuring the best of British television. This programme channel, named Superchannel, came into operation in January 1987,[401] and it is presently aimed at cable systems in 14 different countries. Under the commercial agreement with the ITV contractors, the BBC is not directly

399 Home Office, Direct Broadcasting by Satellite paras. 12.9, 12.13, 18.13 (1981) (hereafter cited as 1981 Study on DBS)
400 For more details on the history and regulation of the DBS services, see *infra* at chapter III(B)(1),(2).
401 Fin. Times, Jan. 28, 1987.

involved in the channel but contributes a great number of programmes. Any direct engagement in the channel, which carries advertisement, would probably have contravened the BBC's Charter prohibiting the provision of advertising-supported services, unless the Home Office had explicitly allowed the service. The BBC's ambitious plans to engage in satellite television did not stop there, however. Currently the Corporation is negotiating with the government over the permission to provide a world television service using a communications satellite. The channel is to be the complementary service to the BBC's foreign radio services, known as the External Services.[402] The BBC also avails itself of the programme market opportunities stemming from the widespread use of video cassette recorders (VCRs) in the United Kingdom. For some time, the thriving video cassette market has provided the Corporation with a welcomed source of additional income through the commercial distribution of video cassettes showing BBC programmes.[403] BBC video cassette sales have proved to be an exceptional commercial success.[404]

A very different sector of new services into which the broadcasting organizations have advanced by virtue of their unique position of being solely responsible for the technical provision of the broadcasting services is teletext information services. Teletext services give viewers one-way access to news and general information services via their television screens. Section 14(6) of the Broadcasting Act 1981 defines a teletext transmission as »a television transmission intended for general reception and consisting of a succession of visual displays (with or without accompanying sound) each capable of being selected and held for separate viewing or other use.« The first British teletext service, started by the BBC in 1973, is called Ceefax and is an 18-hours-a-day service of news and information with the capability to offer also subtitles for the deaf. At the end of 1986, it was estimated that three million British homes could receive the service.[405] Other information services followed. The BBC is supplying information services over the telephone, and anyone interested can call certain telephone numbers in order

402 Fin. Times, Apr. 3, 1986; Dec. 13, 1986. For more details on the External Services, see *infra* at chapter VI(B)(1). With respect to the world television service, see *infra* at chapter VI(B)(3).
403 The sales are effected by BBC Enterprises, Inc., the Corporation's commercial arm. *See* article 3(p), (u) of the BBC Royal Charter 1981. The BBC plans to sell a stake in BBC Enterprises on the stock market in order to raise its funds for programme production. Fin. Times, Oct. 22, 1987.
404 Fin. Times, Jan. 21, 1986.
405 BBC Handbook 1987, *supra* note 273, at 53. In 1982 only 300,000 receivers were in use in the United Kingdom. *See* R. MOORFOOT, TELEVISION IN THE EIGHTIES – THE TOTAL EQUATION 29 (1982).

to get live coverage of cricket scores or the latest racing information. A so-called audio-call plays pop records from each week's »Top-Twenty« record charts. These services are provided by BBC Enterprises Limited. Carfax is a BBC radio service operating on medium wave and providing drivers with traffic information through an electronic adapter connected with their car radios.[406] The BBC also announced the introduction of a new radio data service for the autumn of 1987.[407] This Radio Data System (RDS) is a digital service transmitting commands and information via the existing VHF-FM radio programme signals: RDS is automatically to tune radios to the strongest channel signals and read out the station name.

Finally, similar to the BBC, the ITV system provides a teletext service, named Oracle, with news and information and subtitles for the deaf. According to the statutory provision authorizing teletext (section 14 of the Broadcasting Act 1981), the service may contain advertisements. It is to be provided by »teletext contractors,« which may, but do not have to be, identical with the television programme contractors. In practice, Oracle Teletext Ltd., a company jointly owned by all ITV contractors except TV-am, holds the licence for the provision of teletext on ITV and Channel 4.[408] On each channel, two »spare« television lines are used to accommodate the service. The Oracle teletext provided on the ITV channel offers »newspaper«-like information, such as news contributed by ITN, and weather and sports programmes. The teletext service on Channel 4 is set up similar to a magazine carrying television programme schedules, feature sections for women, leisure, children, home finance and city information.[409] Holiday advertisements carried by Oracle have proved particularly successful. Even travel agencies regularly consult these ads to provide customers with an up-to-date service. Finally, Oracle to some degree also offers regional information services, with weather forecasts, theatre and other events, and the like. These services have been partly provided by regional ITV companies.[410]

An even more specialized service is 4-Tel. On an experimental basis several teletext pages on Channel 4 carry telesoftware relating to educational programmes. This information can be downloaded by viewers

---

406 R. MOORFOOT, *supra* note 405, at 51.
407 Fin. Times, Mar. 26, 1986. Similarly, in 1987 the IBA licensed two operators to provide stock market information on two London VHF radio bands.
408 Revenue from the sale of advertising time on the service doubled each year since its introduction in 1981. The service has by now become profitable.
409 1986 IBA Annual Report, *supra* note 304, at 33.
410 *Id.*

and used with their home computers.[411] During the 1970s, when the techniques for teletext services were first developed, both the Home Office and the Department of Industry, with its responsibility for telecommunications, allowed the broadcasting organizations and the Post Office to work closely together on these matters at their own initiative and pace.[412] The BBC and the IBA had the technical staff and equipment to develop the new services and could thus later easily claim that they should also receive the financial benefits of the services. Since the signals were conveyed via terrestrial transmitters and were received by normal television sets equipped with an adapter, the conceptualization of these information services as ancillary broadcasting services lay at hand. The BBC's succinct authorization to provide such services can be found in article 3(b) of its Royal Charter 1981. The provision empowers it, subject to the prior approval of the Home Secretary, »to provide, as public services, by means of wireless telegraphy, other services whether or not broadcasting services.«

The question whether third parties should have access to the new communications services was long not even posed. The matter-of-fact manner employed by the broadcasting organizations in taking over the information services obstructed an analysis that would have identified these services as a hybrid technology located halfway between traditional broadcasting services and individual data transmission via cable. Without that change of character provoking much public discussion, the broadcasting organizations became electronic publishers. As a consequence, the new services were automatically subjected to the regulatory schemes governing broadcasting. In particular, the services were organized as monopolies without any access rights for third parties, be they newspapers, freelance journalists or others. The content restrictions characteristic for broadcasting also applied. Section 15 of the Broadcasting Act 1981 explicitly obligates the IBA to draw up a code on standards and practices for teletext transmissions. It may be noteworthy at this point that the provision of teletext services over cable systems is not regulated under the Cable and Broadcasting Act 1984 since it is not covered by the definition of a »licensable service« as employed by the Act. The omission of these services from the definition appears to have been accidental; some people in the industry speak of an involuntary gap in the law. Be this as it may, as a result teletext

411 *Id.*
412 McDonnell, *Broadcasting Policy and the Challenge of Information Technology: The Case of British Cable Television*, in POLICY RESEARCH IN TELECOMMUNICATIONS 35, 36-37 (V. Mosco ed. 1984).

services provided over cable, like newspaper content, are only governed by the ordinary laws of the land relating to obscenity, defamation and the like.

Teletext services provide several hundred different screen pages that can be leased to different information providers. The scarcity of frequencies cannot serve as a justification for the monopolization of the services. The first sign of a recognition of such a new concept for teletext is section 47 of the Cable and Broadcasting Act 1984. It represents a striking novelty in that it authorizes the IBA to offer subscription services via teletext to paying customers. Prior to 1984, teletext had to be for general reception by the public. Now, specialized teletext services (whether encrypted or not) may be supplied to small groups of customers with particular interests. Only the provision of teletext services to closed-user groups (CUGs), i.e., groups to which only specific persons are admitted, is still prohibited. The service must be provided to anybody willing to pay the fee. Section 47 thus gives up one of the central elements defining the public broadcasting services in Britain, namely, the *general reception* by the public.

The departing from this principle prompted another important change in the traditional public broadcasting policy. In 1985 the IBA and ORACLE Teletext Ltd. considered leasing a number of the latter's screen pages to an outside company, possibly Cable and Wireless. In the end, Oracle sub-contracted two lines to Air-Call, a separate telecommunications company, which in turn subcontracts pages to other users that transmit their own, self-generated encrypted information. Parties interested in subcontracting with Air-Call include a large warehouse chain that wishes to transmit warehouse stock and staff information and similar matters to its distribution outlets and banks contemplating the communication of foreign-exchange information to their various branches. Such information may of course also be transmitted via cable networks, with the added advantage of an inter-active service. However, in cases where only one-way information channels are needed, using the teletext service is cheaper and often several times faster than information transmitted via conventional networks. Similarly, the BBC in late 1985 introduced Datacast, operating in the same way as Air-Call and aiming at large financial institutions as the primary users of the system.[413] An international news agency also plans to lease capacity to provide encrypted news services to its customers.

The services set up by both Air-Call and Datacast are, by their very nature, designed to serve CUGs, and technically this is the way they operate, with every user encrypting his signals. This not only ensures the

413 *See* BBC Handbook 1987, *supra* note 273, at 53, 69.

financial viability of the service but also serves the secrecy of the information transmitted. Legally, however, Oracle is still under an obligation to provide a decoder to anyone who is willing to pay the fees, and this poses a potential threat to the exclusivity of the information, a feature many users may be most interested in. It is therefore conceivable that the next broadcasting bill to be introduced in Parliament will again change section 47 of the Broadcasting Act 1981 to take account of the changed circumstances. For the time being, however, the Home Office takes the position that Oracle cannot supply any *confidential* services, a policy designed to get around the public-service obligation under the Broadcasting Act 1981.[414]

In the case of Datacast, it is BBC Enterprises Ltd. that provides the service. Under article 3(u) of the BBC Royal Charter 1981, the BBC may, »subject to the prior approval of Our Secretary of State ... establish companies whose objects include any of the objects of the Corporation or whose business is capable of being carried on in such a way as to facilitate or advance any of the objects of the Corporation.« The examples evidence that the latest developments have changed the nature of the teletext service to cast aside even the requirement of the availability of the services to the *public*.

What is more, the BBC has begun to venture into pure telecommunications services that have no relation whatsoever with its broadcasting functions. Since 1985 the BBC has embarked jointly with the Central Electricity Generating Board on the use of capacity on its radio transmitters in order to turn on and off the electricity supplies to domestic night storage heater circuits.[415] Similar services are typically provided over cable systems and are referred to as value-added network services (VANS). The BBC and the ITV companies have thus begun to compete not only with telecommunications service providers such as British Telecom for data-transmission ser-

---

414 Information provided to the author by Mr N.C. Sanderson, Broadcasting Department, Home Office. However, the ITV companies are pressing for a lifting of these restrictions, and the IBA appears to support their aim. Fin. Times, Aug. 13, 1987. Also, the BBC is considering launching a national paging service, a problematic venture under its present charter, because radio-paging signals are directed at single individuals. *See* Fin. Times Business Information 93/3 (1987).

415 This so-called Radio Teleswitching operates as follows: »By adding data signals to the BBC's long wave broadcasts, without affecting the audible signals, load switches and meters on electricy consumers' premises can be remotely controlled, enabling off-peak storage systems to operate without the need for electro-mechanical time-switches and flexible tariff rates to be developed. Consumers benefit from the opportunity to take advantage of favourable tariffs, while savings of up to £ 80 million a year are expected in the cost of electricity generation.« BBC, Engineering Press Release, July 23, 1987. The BBC uses Radio 4 long-wave transmitters to send the coded signals. Fin. Times, Mar. 22, 1988.

vices[416] but also with general value-added network service providers offering alarm and similar services.

By experimenting with new techniques for terrestrial transmissions, the broadcasting organizations have blurred the traditional distinction between telecommunications services and broadcasting services. This development is a special variation of the convergence of conduit and content in modern telecommunications technologies. While this expression normally describes the phenomenon whereby the entity exercising control over the conduit, i.e., a cable network, a satellite operator or a similar carrier, also exercises control over the content transmitted via the carrier system (unless the law explicitly provides otherwise), the BBC's experiments evidence a reverse development. The Corporation's primary task has been to provide the programme content, with its responsibility for the transmission facilities always having been an ancillary activity; the technical operation was justified only as a means and to the extent necessary to get the message across. Now, the interrelation between the content-related tasks and the control over the transmission system has been disconnected, and the control over the latter is also being used for the exploitation of value-added telecommunications services.

At present, the Home Office has taken no final position on the expediency of BBC telecommunications services. It supports a »gentle way forward« into these services for the broadcasting organization, arguing that the BBC's Charter is a permissive document and that clause 3(c)(iii) of the Licence covers the broadcasters' activities in this respect.[417] Problems may arise, however, from the still undefined relationship between the broadcasters (including the IBA) and the general public telecommunications service operators (PTOs) BT and Mercury. Both companies enjoy a legal duopoly on the provision of certain basic services until 1991, and the broadcasters' activities may to some extend infringe upon this duopoly. Their relationship is further complicated by the fact that BT and Mercury are under a public-service obligation with respect to the provision of telecommunications services, while the broadcasters are not. They may decide for

---

416 British Telecom operates a two-way interactive information system called »viewdata.« The service is operated under the trade name »Prestel.« The user can access centrally based computers via the telephone network, and the information retrieved is displayed on the television screen. *See* R. MOORFOOT, *supra* note 405, at 27, 29.

417 Information provided to the author by Mr N.C. Sanderson, Broadcasting Department, Home Office. The provision reads in part that the licence permits the BBC »to use the stations and apparatus aforesaid for emitting, sending, reflecting and receiving ... wireless telegraphy for purposes ancillary or related to the services aforesaid.«

themselves in which areas of the United Kingdom they want to offer any of these services,[418] a decision that entails only marginal additional costs for them because the transmitter systems already cover virtually the entire country. The provision of similar services by the PTOs generally necessitates enormous financial investments. This puts them at a serious competitive disadvantage vis-à-vis the broadcasters.

The BBC's departure from its principal programming functions is further highlighted by the Corporation's evidence to the Peacock Committee with regard to plans for »silent hours« subscription services. The new suggestions put forward by the Corporation deal with the possibilities of so-called electronic downloading of video programmes. Under one scheme the BBC would itself offer a pay-TV service as a subscription service for scrambled feature films and general entertainment using BBC transmitters in the early mornings when transmitter facilities normally lie idle.[419] The programmes would be recorded on VCRs for playback at a later hour. The provision of such a service would cast aside two principle elements of public-service broadcasting, namely, the reception of the programmes by the general public and the requirement of a balanced programme mix. The BBC argued that it could conceivably act as a common carrier by offering its transmission services to commercial distributers of video programmes, or »to transmit computer data, for example to update the price of stocking information about goods held in chains of shops.«[420] One short technical experiment of this kind has already been carried out. In July 1987, the BBC experimented in one locality with a nighttime subscription service for medical doctors. Medical organizations provided information on certain medical products. These programmes were transmitted via BBC transmitters at a nighttime hour to be stored in subscribers' video recorders for later viewing.[421] In effect, the BBC's role in this experiment was that of a

418 Information provided to the author by Mr Anthony Jennings, BBC legal adviser.
419 1986 Peacock Report, *supra* note 216, at para. 515.
420 *Id.* at paras. 117, 515.
421 Information provided to the author by Mr N.C. Sanderson, Broadcasting Department, Home Office. In October 1987, the BBC formally announced its plan to launch such a nighttime hour subscription service for medical doctors. Under the scheme hour-long specialist medical programmes would be transmitted over the BBC 2 channel after close-down to be recorded by VCRs. The programmes are to be scrambled, and a decoder would be needed for their reception. Production of the programmes will be made in conjunction with an independent television company, British Direct Television Ltd. The BBC hopes to raise £ 1 million per year with this new service. However, reports on the financing of the service were contradictory. Thus the service will possibly be financed by advertising and/or through a subscription fee payable by the medical doctors. The Home Office announced that the subscription services required new legislation. But already discussion has started to offer additional specialist subscription services for architects, lawyers, accountants and farmers. Fin. Times, Oct. 15, 16, 1987.

common carrier. If all these plans for services were executed, the BBC's traditional role as a *public-service broadcasting* organization would have come to an end, and a new regulatory concept would have to be found redefining the Corporation's obligations as a common carrier and electronic publisher and as a competitor for value-added services.

The broad variety of new activities and plans give ample evidence that the character of »the single most important cultural organization in the nation,« as the government characterized the BBC in 1978,[422] is changing rapidly. The British government has indicated that changes in the audio-visual media market particularly brought about by the arrival of cable and satellite television necessitate some fundamental changes in the regulatory regime applying to the traditional broadcasting duopoly. If these changes are enacted – the legislative measures are supposed to be presented to Parliament in the autumn of 1988 – the traditional public-service concept of broadcasting will have come to an end. However, it should be noted that the current political discussion on a new broadcasting concept focuses on media-policy issues. The public broadcasters' new activities in general telecommunications services and the impact of these services on the nature of the broadcasting organizations have thus far escaped a general public debate.

The recommendations of the Peacock Committee have spurred a lively public discussion about the future British media policy. After some initial hesitation, the government has welcomed many of the new concepts. It has given particularly serious thought to the Committee's recommendation to impose a requirement on the BBC and all ITV contractors to increase over a ten-year period to 40 per cent the proportion of programme material supplied by independent producers.[423] This new quota system would aim at stimulating the growth of the independent film production sector, a development regarded by the Committee as a crucial element for the creation of a »full broadcasting market.« The recommended new approach could also be expected to carry further the policy that already determines the programme concept of Channel 4. Its programme policy has spurred the emergence of an independent programme sector that has been called »almost certainly the liveliest in Europe,«[424] although its size is not exactly known.

---

422 1978 White Paper on Broadcasting, *supra* note 270, at para. 42.
423 1986 Peacock Report, *supra* note 216, at Recommendation 8, para. 647.
424 Fin. Times, Nov. 22, 1986. The article states that the annual turnover of this market is almost certainly much more than £ 100 million and that the new industry employs several thousand people.

The Peacock Committee's proposals found a broad political echo as a way to grant access for independent producers to the broadcasting system. However, the government criticized the 40-percent quota as being unreasonably high; the public broadcasters had complained that such a requirement would necessarily reduce their programme output and result in an indirect compulsion to shrink in size.[425] On the other hand, the government has indicated that it expects the quota system to be fully implemented within four years.[426] The government also made it known that it would favour the introduction of the quota system on the basis of voluntary agreements with the broadcasters. Failing that, it announced the likelihood of legislative measures.[427] The broadcasters, realizing that voluntary agreements would probably be more to their advantage, have presented a range of different measures, which together would ensure a contribution of 25 per cent of programmes stemming from independent producers. Their proposals include coproduction, co-financing, commissioning with costs, and pre-sale – i.e., a proportion of the costs of production in advance in return for the British broadcasting rights.[428] The ITV companies and the BBC have even partly welcomed the proposal as a way of reducing their expenditures, provided that the programmes produced by the independents could be purchased at a price considerably lower than the costs for inhouse productions.

The quota system for independent producers would effectively abolish the monopoly on the provision of programmes enjoyed for so many decades by the BBC and the ITV contractors. But the system would still be a long way from a true right of access of third parties to the broadcasting system. A quota limit of 25 per cent would from the outset severely restrict the number of potential programme suppliers. Also, the detailed content requirements characteristic for the public broadcasting system would also apply to programmes produced by independents. A liberalization of the freedom to broadcast would thus only take place to a limited extent. A greater number of people would be able to disseminate their ideas via the terrestrial broadcasting media, but the content of their speech would still be heavily regulated. Nonetheless, these latest developments reveal that even apart

---

425 The British trade unions concerned advanced particularly strong opposition against the 40-percent quota, arguing that this requirement would threaten thousands of work stations at the BBC and the ITV companies. *See* Neue Zürcher Zeitung, Sept. 18, 1986.
426 Fin. Times, Nov. 21, 1986.
427 Fin. Times, Nov. 22, 1986.
428 *Id. See also* Fin. Times, Jan. 10, 1987.

from the impact of the new media on the traditional broadcasting structure, the government's media policy is undergoing a revolutionary change. It indicates that the Peacock Committee's vision of a future »true broadcasting market« has become the guiding idea of Britain's media policy.

The sweeping changes envisaged by the Peacock Committee, though, go even further. The Committee, while supporting the idea of separate sources of financing for the BBC and the ITV systems, rejected proposals to finance the BBC partly by advertising. Yet it also advanced the informal proposal gradually to change the BBC's financing system to a voluntary subscription system once television sets are supplied with the technology to receive encrypted signals and a greater programme supply from different sources, particularly cable and DBS, is available.[429] The government gave serious consideration to these proposals. As a first step and in order to put pressure on the BBC to organize its services more in accordance with economic principles of cost efficiency, the government adopted the Committee's recommendation to index the licence fee on an annual basis to the general rate of inflation.[430]

Meanwhile, the BBC has indicated that the indexing of the licence fee would not only imply some job reductions but also be likely to result in the restructuring of certain programme divisions. As a first measure to cut future costs, the BBC reduced its cleaning and catering staff by granting the right to provide these services to outside companies. Also, the Corporation is contemplating engaging in more coproduction works under respective agreements with American, Australian and Italian broadcasting organizations, agreements that have already been in existence for a number of years. Significantly, the Corporation also announced that due to the unexpected financial constraints, it would not engage in cable and satellite broadcasting transmissions but instead concentrate on supplying programmes to these new media.[431] The indexation of the licence fee may thus have the side effect of stifling or even ending the BBC's numerous activities in areas not directly related with its broadcasting tasks. This would probably greatly satisfy the members of the Peacock Committee, who had expressed their hope that the indexation would cause the BBC »to think more carefully before embarking on peripheral activities far removed from its core obligations.«[432]

429 1986 Peacock Report, *supra* note 216, at paras. 673-81.
430 *See id.* at Recommendation 3, paras. 621-28.
431 Fin. Times, Mar. 6, 1987.
432 1986 Peacock Report, *supra* note 216, at para. 621.

As a way of assessing the benefits of BBC and possibly also ITV subscription services, the government commissioned a study from an independent consulting firm, Booz Allen and Hamilton (formerly CSP International Ltd.), asking them to determine, i.a., the technical feasibility of subscription services, to assess the benefits to be gained with respect to economic and consumer welfare and to identify the principal strategic alternatives for the introduction of such services.[433] The study identified a very strong and as yet unsatisfied demand for premium programming, i.e., particularly new, first-rate movies, among U.K. television viewers, a service for which consumers had shown a willingness to pay considerably more than they presently have to pay under the licence-fee system.[434] However, it also concluded that given the programme mix presently shown on BBC and ITV television, a pay-television system would not be viable; taking also into account that the costs of collecting the subscription fees may be nearly double those currently incurred, BBC 1 was deemed to be able to raise only half of the present running costs of the channel.[435] If only the BBC television programmes were scrambled, the channels could still not cover costs, the study concluded, and »substantial losses in consumer welfare would result as a consequence of the exclusion of non-subscribers from the benefits of BBC television viewing.«[436]

Accepting the study's findings in this respect, the Home Secretary announced that the government would not contemplate the introduction of subscription television for either the BBC or ITV for the foreseeable future.

Another proposition put forward by the study, however, may not quite so readily find acceptance with the government. Following its analysis of strong but as yet unmet consumer demand for premium programming, the consulting firm suggested that this demand be met by one of three options: (1) the BBC and the IBA could distribute pay-television services during the unused hours of their transmitters; (2) some evening and weekend transmissions of BBC 2 could be scrambled to provide extra premium films; (3) a fifth and possibly a sixth terrestrial television channel could be set up solely for the provision of such services. Option 3 may meet with the strongest opposition. Not only would such a service directly compete for BBC and ITV audiences, but it could also threaten the viability of the

---

433 Home Office, Subscription Television – A Study for the Home Office para. 1.2. (May 1987) (hereafter cited as 1987 Report on Subscription Television).
434 *Id.* at para. 4.2.
435 *Id.* at para. 11.1.
436 *Id.* at para. 11.2.

premium film channel planned as a subscription service by BSB, the contractor for the first three British DBS channels. Although no formal promises have been made by the government in this respect, BSB would be likely to argue that the duty of good faith requires the government to abstain from licensing directly competing services, at least for the initial years of operation of the channels until the DBS services have established themselves.[437]

Option 2 would undermine the fundamental programme principles now governing BBC 2. Option 1 might very well appeal to both BBC and ITV contractors, as long as they are allowed to operate the late-night or early-morning subscription services on their own account and thus accrue all the benefits. In fact, as has been mentioned, the BBC had given evidence to the Peacock Committee revealing that such plans had seriously been considered within the Corporation as a way to raise additional revenues.

In summary it may be said that the Peacock Committee's recommendation to replace the licence fee by subscription currently has no chance for implementation. The BBC's interest in providing some special subscription services in addition to its normal programming has found new political support and has raised the chances for the introduction of BBC pay-TV. It need not further be stressed that this development would lead to a further erosion of the public-service broadcasting concept.

To effect a more efficient use of resources was also the guiding light behind the Committee's recommendation to put the ITV franchise contracts to competitive tender.[438] The government has indicated that it may follow the proposal and at least partly change the present system of a levy of 45 per cent on the ITV contractors' domestic profits and a 22.5-percent levy on their export sales. One plan is to introduce a new levy system that is combined with an obligation on bidders for ITV contracts to make competitive offers of payments to the Treasury in return for the franchises.[439] The present levy system, which is additional to the corporation tax, was designed to skim off some of the contractors' monopoly profits. Both the

---

437 An explicit undertaking by the government has been given to BSB to the effect that the remaining two DBS channels were not to be assigned to any user for the first few years of BSB's operation.

438 1986 Peacock Report, *supra* note 216, at Recommendation 10, paras. 655, 656.

439 Fin. Times, Mar. 3, 1987. In order to gain time to consider seriously the proposal, the franchise period for the ITV contracts, entered into for the last time in 1981, was extended by three years and will now expire at the end of 1992. This will also allow the contractors time to assess the impact of DBS services on their own services. Broadcasting Act 1981, sec. 19 (2A), inserted by virtue of sec. 1 of the Broadcasting Act 1987 (c. 10).

Committee and the government suspected that the levy system had induced ITV contractors to inflate their costs.[440] As a result, overmanning and the high wages paid by ITV contractors put pressure on the BBC to raise its wages to the level paid by the commercial system in order to keep its talented personnel. The high production costs, it has been argued, also had negative effects on the competitiveness of ITV and BBC television programme sales in the international market. Finally, the argument was advanced that the inflated costs had resulted in very high fees for television commercials, thereby raising the costs of products for consumers.[441]

The last but equally important consideration given by the incumbent government to a restructuring of the present broadcasting system deals with the Peacock Committee's recommendation to grant Channel 4 greater independence from the IBA.[442] The Channel's financial basis, which much improved over the last few years, in the financial year to March 31, 1987 for the first time became self-supporting.[443] If Channel 4 ceased to be an IBA subsidiary, the anomaly of the IBA's dual role of being the supervisory authority as well as the owner of a channel would be removed. The decision would also set another sign that the past tendencies of the broadcasting organizations to expand their activities and competence to every new alternative form of communication are not to continue.

In the United Kingdom the great days of the broadcasting duopoly appear to be coming to an end. While the assumption that the BBC and the IBA are the cornerstones of the British broadcasting structure has thus far not been challenged, the public broadcasting organizations are being prepared for a gradual transition from a duopoly system to a »full broadcasting market« with many alternative programme sources. The changes contemplated will soon change the very face of public broadcasting in Britain. The immediate policy approach is to restrain the public broadcasting organizations from expanding their activities into new areas and gradually to expose them to more competition. At the same time, the BBC and the ITV contractors have already reacted to the challenges and have begun to compete directly

440 *See* 1986 Peacock Report, *supra* note 216, at para. 532. The ITV companies, on the other hand, contend that their high production costs are to some extent due to deliberate overmanning and greater-than-necessary studio capacity imposed upon them by the IBA in the franchising rounds in former years as a precondition to win the contracts. Information provided to the author by Ms Jane Vizard, legal adviser, ITCA, and Mr Ivor Stolliday, company secretary, ITCA.
441 *See* the government's analysis, in Fin. Times, Mar. 3, 1987.
442 1986 Peacock Report, *supra* note 216, at Recommendation 14, para. 660. *See also* Fin. Times, Jan. 12, 1987.
443 Channel Four Television Company Ltd., Report and Accounts for the Year ended 31st March 1987 10 (1987) (hereafter cited as 1987 Channel 4 Annual Report).

with private companies for the provision of satellite television services, for example. While their policy in the first half of the 1980s has been to continue to enjoy the comfortable duopoly in the area of terrestrial broadcasting, they have also from the outset of the new developments in media technology and media policy been aware of the implications and have tried hard to play a vital role in the events. It can be expected that they will continue to seek to dominate the British broadcasting system in the future. Their leading position has been challenged, but it has not yet begun to totter.

III. Video and Satellite: Old and New Concepts for New Phenomena

The new media technologies involving video and satellite have led to an explosive increase in the number of available programmes and in the variety of programme sources. These stem from satellite television channels, from cable television and also from video rentals, which enable individual citizens to put together their own home-television programme menues independent of outside organizations. The effect of this increased programme supply on the status of the public broadcasting system in the lives of the British people is considerable. Video works represent a particularly fast-growing market, which the public broadcasters themselves have begun to exploit.

A. Regulatory Framework for Video Following the Regulation of Cinema Exhibitions

By the end of 1986, just over 50 per cent of British households with a television set also possessed a video cassette recorder (VCR). Outside of Japan, the United Kingdom has the largest VCR penetration in private households. [444] The success of the video market has struck a perhaps deadly blow

---

444 *See* Fin. Times, Jan. 6, 1987. Just a little over half of all VCRs are owned by individual households, with the rest of the recorders being leased. According to a 1983 study, 1.25 million video cassettes were rented in the United Kingdom every week. *See* Kommission der Europäischen Gemeinschaften, Zwischenbericht über Realität und Tendenzen des Fernsehens in Europa: Perspektiven und Optionen, Kom. (83) 229 endg., para 95 (hereafter cited as EC Commission, 1983 Interim Report on Television).

146

to the already ailing British cinema industry. Beginning in the 1950s, television and most recently video have largely overtaken the market for cinema exhibitions in Britain. Between 1955 and 1981, cinema admissions sharply declined from 1,182 million to 84 million admissions.[445] In the same period, the number of cinemas fell from 4,483 to 877. Estimates suggest that in 1982 for the first time total revenues from video cassette rentals exceeded total revenues from cinema exhibitions.[446]

The rapidly increasing popularity of video cassettes alarmed the public and politicians alike because of the potential impact of these programmes on public morale. Unlike with respect to cinema exhibitions, government control over video works had no explicit basis in the law. Before 1984 the Director of Public Prosecutions issued a monthly list specifying those video works that the government had determined to be obscene. Some recordings on the list were successfully prosecuted under the Obscene Publications Act; in other cases, proceedings remained long pending to no avail, and in a third category of listed video works, prosecutions were never even started. Although the list was available to video retailers and trade organizations at local police stations, dealers could disregard it since it was legally non-binding and simply take the rather remote risk of being prosecuted under the Obscene Publications Act.[447] The system resulted in the distribution of many video cassettes with explicitly sexual or extremely violent contents. It was argued that this situation called for specific video regulations similar to the supervisory system governing film exhibitions in cinemas.

Cinemas need a licence for the showing of films. The licensing authorities (usually the district councils) »may grant a licence ... to such a person as they think fit to use any premises specified in the licence for the purpose of film exhibitions on such terms and conditions and subject to such restrictions as ... they may determine.«[448] Under the Cinemas Act 1985, the local authorities have broad discretion to control and regulate directly the kind of films to be shown. In practice they will hardly ever exercise this right because almost all censorship of films takes place through the British Board of Film Classification (BBFC), formerly the British Board of Film Censors. The BBFC was established as early as 1912 by the film industry as a private body with the task of convincing the licensing authorities that films with a

---

445 Monopolies and Mergers Commission, Films – A Report on the Supply of Films for Exhibition in Cinemas, Cmnd. 8858, Table 2.4 (1983) (hereafter cited as MMC, Films).
446 EC Commission, 1983 Interim Report on Television, *supra* note 444, at para. 95.
447 *Guidelines on Video Nasties*, 5 J. MEDIA L. & PRAC. 304-05 (1984).
448 Cinemas Act 1985 (c.13), secs. 1(2), 3(10).

BBFC certificate fulfilled the demands of morality and decency, making further scrutiny by public officials obsolete.[449] It thus became the first censorship body for films of its kind in the world. Nonetheless, not only have local authorities retained the last word over the showing of films, but the courts have also made it clear that the public administrations may not abrogate their right to censorship by making their own approval of a film fully dependent on a certification by the BBFC.[450] In practice, however, most local authorities have adopted the model licencing conditions for cinema licences as recommended by the Home Office. They provide, i.a., that no film shall be exhibited unless it has received the Board's certification.[451]

Film exhibitions organized wholly or mainly for children need to have the special consent of the relevant local authorities (section 2 of the Cinemas Act 1985). A number of film exhibitions are exempted from the licence requirement, like those given in private dwellings, those to which the public is not admitted or that are not promoted for private gain, or those whose sole or main purpose is to demonstrate a product, to advertise goods or to provide information or education (section 5 of the Cinemas Act 1985). Also, certain non-profit organizations need no licence publicly to show films as long as their exhibitions are not promoted for private gain.

By law, local authorities may impose any conditions and restrictions on the licensee pertaining to the kind of films to be shown, as well as those dealing with the safety precautions to be taken on the premises. This broad discretion is limited in three respects only, namely: (1) the licences need to impose special conditions for the protection of children against the viewing of films designated as works unsuitable for children,[452] (2) in granting, renewing or transferring any licence, the authorities shall, after consultation, take into consideration any observations submitted to them by the fire authority and the chief officer of police, and (3) film exhibitions have to comply with the regulations for general safety and for the health and welfare of children, which the Home Secretary may issue by statutory instruments under section 4 of the Cinemas Act 1985.

The Cinemas Act 1985 consolidated the Cinematograph Acts 1909 to 1982 and represents the primary legislation responsible for the regulation of film

---

449 *See* L. COTTERELL, *supra* note 63, at 490.
450 R. v. Greater London Council, ex parte Blackburn, [1976] 1 W.L.R. 550, 554-55 (per Lord Denning M.R.).
451 British Board of Film Classification, Annual Report and Accounts for 1985, Appendix I at i (1986) (hereafter cited as BBFC, Annual Report 1985).
452 Cinemas Act 1985, sec. 1(3)(a). The term »child« as used in the Act refers to any person under the age of 16 (section 21(1)).

exhibitions in cinemas. Like the previous enactments, it refrains from granting the BBFC any formal legal status. The BBFC examines all films to be exhibited in public cinemas in Britain. The fees charged for the submission of each film help to finance the Board. If the Board determines that a film is principally suited for public viewing, it decides on a classification to be applied to the film within one of six categories presently used, ranging from »U,« for »suitable for all,« to »Restricted 18,« meaning that films with this classification may only be shown to persons over 18 years of age in segregated premises.[453] Often the Board requires certain film scenes to be cut in order for the film to fit into a certain category.[454] The Board also censors all cinema advertisements lasting more than 30 seconds. While local authorities are free to reject the BBFC's decisions and prohibit the showing of a certified film in their boroughs, they typically have shown little interest in matters of film censorship and have usually rubber-stamped the Board's rulings.[455] On the other hand, if the Board refuses to grant a classification certificate, the film may nonetheless be submitted to the local authorities for approval. A film that has received a number of favourable local verdicts has especially good chances to be approved by the Board if resubmitted for classification. The Board gives consideration to any such positive reactions of public opinion.[456]

Because of its non-legal status, the BBFC has been particularly susceptible to government pressures, particularly during its first decades of existence.[457] As long as this private body had not earned universal recognition by local authorities and the central government, its survival greatly depended on how its practice of certification pleased the political institutions. Its standards appear for a long time to have been even stricter than the local authorities called for.[458] In the 1970s the Board became noticeably more independent from political pressures. Phelps notes that the government was now keen on not being involved in any kind of cen-

---

453 For a description of these categories, see G. ROBERTSON & A. NICOL, *supra* note 54, at 380-81; L. COTTERELL, *supra* note 63, at 491. The licensing of cinemas showing films with explicitly sexual content takes place under Part II of the Local Government (Miscellaneous Provisions) Act 1982 (c.30).

454 G. PHELPS, FILM CENSORSHIP 104-05 (1975).

455 *Id.* at 163. Phelps maintains that the relationships between the BBFC and the local authorities have always been strained. He gives examples of how the authorities, after a period of relative satisfaction with the Board's decisions, took a renewed interest in film censorship in the early 1970s. *Id.* at 161, 166-71.

456 *Id.* at 106.

457 *Id.* at 144, 158.

458 *Id.* at 109. For years, this seems to have been true particularly for the Greater London Council, which for some time even took the view that films should not be pre-censored at all. Information provided to the author by Mr Ken Penry, Deputy Director, BBFC.

sorship.[459] On the other hand, the BBFC maintains that independence from both the government and the film industry (no government grants or subsidies by the film industries are received) has been crucial to secure its unique position as uncensored censors.[460] After 75 years of operation, the Board has – if not legally, then in effect – become the authorized censor for feature films.

While the lessening political interest in the control of cinema exhibitions parallels the diminishing importance of this media as a source of public information and entertainment, the public concern over the control of video cassette content has for the same reason greatly surged in recent years. The BBFC's consolidated position in film censorship resulted in its entrustment with video censorship.

The Video Recordings Act 1984[461] established the first explicit regulatory framework for the distribution of video cassettes in the United Kingdom. Its principle function is to create an offence with regard to a person who supplies or offers to supply a video recording containing a video work in respect of which no classification certificate has been issued, unless the recording is exempted from classification (section 9(1)). The Home Secretary has the power to determine the authority responsible for the classification and has appointed the BBFC for this purpose. He also appoints to the authority the persons who have the duty to determine the suitability of video works for classification (section 4 of the Act). One President and two Vice-Presidents have been appointed under this provision. On the executive level of the BBFC, one Director, a Deputy Director and two Assistant Directors are responsible for the day-to-day work of the organization. In 1987 a total of about 20 examiners were responsible for the initial viewing and categorization of the video works. The Video Consultative Council, a Committee made up of representatives of the public, including local authorities and the video industry, has the task of providing advice.[462]

The classifying body has extremely wide powers to censor all video recordings not exempted from the scope of the Act under section 2. It is up to the BBFC to determine the criteria to be met for a classification certifi-

459 *Id.* at 158.
460 *See* BBFC, Annual Report 1985, *supra* note 451, at Appendix I, ii. The proposals advanced by the Williams Committee to end the local authorities' power to censor films and to create a statutory board for film censorship purposes was not greeted with much public support. *See* 1979 Report of the Williams Committee, *supra* note 141, at paras. 12.20, 12.29.
461 Video Recordings Act 1984 (c.39).
462 BBFC, Annual Report 1985, *supra* note 451, at 17-18.

cate.[463] The Act itself is silent on the content standards to be imposed on video works. An unclassified video work may not be supplied or kept in possession.[464] The Act contains definitions of two important terms: (1) a »video work‹ means any series of visual images (with or without sound) (a) produced electronically by the use of information contained on any disc or magnetic tape, and (b) shown as a moving picture«; and (2) a »video-recording‹ means any disc or magnetic tape containing information by the use of which the whole or a part of a video work may be produced« (section 1(2),(3)).

Certain categories of video works are exempted from classification, namely, video games and video works designed to inform, educate or instruct and works concerned with sports, religion or music, unless they depict human sexual activity or are designed to a significant extent to stimulate or encourage such activity or unless they show human genital organs or acts of gross violence towards human beings or animals. Under section 4(3) of the Act, the Home Secretary has to ensure that any person has a right to appeal any certification decision by the Authority. This appeal does not go to a court but rather to a higher internal body of the Authority, termed the Appeals Committee. It consists of persons of distinction and integrity and with independence from both the video industry and the Board.[465]

The legislative device of creating an offence that attaches to the objective criteria of certification rather than to the obscene content and the denial of any appeal of certification decisions to a court of law make the Act a swift and effective weapon against videos with offensive content. Persons charged with an offence under the Obscene Publications Act can claim the defence of artistic merit, with the hope that a liberal jury will find no

---

463 Note, *The Video Recordings Bill*, 5 J. MEDIA L. & PRAC. 74, 75 (1984); G. ROBERTSON & A. NICOL, *supra* note 54, at 383-84. However, a potential conflict exists between the powers of the BBFC and those of the Broadcasting Standards Council, created in 1988. The BSC will also draw up a code on programme content with respect to the showing of violence and sex and its authority will extend to video works.

464 Video Recordings Act 1984, secs. 9, 10. Videos that had been on the shelves before the criminal provisions of the Act came into operation on Sept. 1, 1985 were granted three years in which to seek classification by the Board, but the Board took great pains to view and classify most if not all of the »video nasties« that had been on the market within its first year of operation. Information provided to the author by Mr Ken Penry, Deputy Director, BBFC. In December 1985, the first conviction was made under section 10 of the Act, and the defendant was fined £ 400 for the possession of three unclassified video cassettes that he had kept for the purpose of supply. *See* 7 J. MEDIA L. & PRAC. 16 (1986).

465 BBFC, Annual Report 1985, *supra* note 451, at 15 and Appendix VII, containing the »Video Appeals Committee Provisions 1985.« *See also* Cameron, *Censorship and the Video Recordings Act*, 7 J. MEDIA L. & PRAC. 93, 96 (1986).

»tendency to deprave and corrupt.« The Video Recordings Act rules out such defence strategies.

The BBFC has extremely wide powers to censor the contents of video works. The only specification given in the Act with respect to the applicable standards is contained in section 4(1)(a), where the Authority is authorized to determine »whether or not video works are suitable for classification certificates…, having special regard to the likelihood of video works in respect of which such certificates have been issued being viewed in the home.« The test of »suitable for home viewing« poses the question whether films in the »18« category (i.e., certified only for persons of 18 years and over) and the »Restricted 18« (»R 18«) category (only to be viewed in specially licensed cinemas by persons of 18 years and over) could equally be released on video cassettes viewed in the home. While persons under the age of 18 can successfully be excluded from cinemas showing »18« category films, the term »home viewing« seems to imply that children have access to these films and must be taken into account as possible viewers for the purpose of a classification decision. It has been argued that a narrow interpretation of this provision could mean that certification certificates could only be granted to videos suitable for young children.[466]

This analysis reveals an intrinsic contradiction in the Act. While the Authority has to give consideration to the aspect of home viewing, the Video Recordings Act makes it clear that the Authority may issue video certificates specifying that either (1) the video work is suitable for general viewing and unrestricted supply, (2) the cassette may only be supplied to persons above a certain age and is only suited for viewing by these persons, or (3) the video work may only be supplied in a licensed sex shop.[467] This provision seems to imply that the standards to be applied to video works are expected at least roughly to compare with the BBFC's standards for cinema films. However, if the Authority were to take the »home viewing test« seriously, making category »R 18« video cassettes available for viewers in the home is problematic. For although the provision prohibiting the supply of such cassettes to persons under age is accompanied by a supporting measure, namely, the criminal sanctioning of any such video cassette

---

466 Cameron, *supra* note 465, at 93.
467 *See* Video Recordings Act 1984, sec. 7(2). The contents of the labels and markings and the position in which these labels are to be shown on video cassettes and spools are regulated by the Video Recordings (Labelling) Regulations 1985, 1985 S.I. No. 911.

supply to a minor or its supply in a place not specifically licensed,[468] the Act correctly acknowledges that films on video cassettes rented out to private homes substantially differ from films shown in cinemas: There is no public control of what is made available to children in a private home. Letting children watch restricted films at home has not been penalized under the Act.

The problems involved in this double standard for cinema and video were recognized in the parliamentary debates. The focal point of the discussion was whether it were advisable to prohibit the viewing of certain films, particularly in the »R 18« category, altogether in the home in order to protect children; the ultimately prevailing view was that parents should be expected to assume some responsibility for the benefit of the viewing opportunities of the adult population.[469]

Following this line of argument, the BBFC subsequently adopted a differentiated approach. Videos with sexually explicit scenes in the »R 18« category can be rented in licensed sex shops, and category »18« films may be supplied to adults. However, the Board repeatedly stated »that there are some scenes we would pass for the cinema which would not in our view be suitable for video.«[470] Scenes that have been cut from the cinema version of certain films in order to license them for video distribution have in particular included the showing of criminal techniques, rapes and certain horror scenes, mainly on the ground that video differs from cinema in that video sequences can be repeated endlessly out of context or analyzed in slow motion. The latter factor has caused concern to the Board, where film scenes demonstrated, for example, the making of bullets or home-made explosives, the bypassing of the ignition of a stolen car, lock-picking and similar matters. With respect to film scenes displaying sexual violence, the Board has seen the risk that such sequences might be singled out by the viewer to arouse sexual excitement with repercussions for his behaviour in real life. Finally, as regards certain horror scenes, the BBFC has »exercised a restraining influence on the explicitness of gory imagery for video because of our awareness that children and younger teenagers may be particularly

---

468 Video Recordings Act 1984, secs. 11, 12. »›Supply‹ means supply in any manner, whether or not for reward, and, therefore, includes supply by way of sale, letting on hire, exchange or loan« (sec. 1(4)).
469 *See* BBFC, Annual Report 1985, *supra* note 451, at Appendix V, xxxiii.
470 *Id.*

tempted to watch such material, if only to measure their courage and strength of stomach against the competitive claims of their peers.«[471]

Apart from the offences particularly created by the Video Recordings Act, the general criminal laws are equally applicable to the making and supply of video works.[472] With regard to the applicable copyright law, a recent Court of Appeals decision deserves attention.[473] The subject of the dispute was the promotion and sale of video recorders capable of copying prerecorded cassettes. The dispute derived its particular importance in commercial respects from the fact that in the United Kingdom the black market for video pirates is thriving.[474] The British Phonographic Industry, an organization promoting the interests of the British recording industry, maintained that the marketing and sale of such machines constituted an unlawful act for three reasons, namely: (1) the manufacturer could be said to have authorized infringements of copyright by the purchaser, (2) he breached his duty of care vis-à-vis the copyright owners, and (3) he incited purchasers to commit criminal offences contrary to section 21(3) of the Copyright Act 1956. The plaintiff manufacturer sought a declaration in court that his sales and advertising activities were lawful. The trial judge held for the defendants, arguing that the sale and advertising of recorders inviting the unauthorized copying of works protected by copyright represented a copyright infringement.

The Court of Appeal differentiated between the mere sale of the recorders and the way in which these machines were publicly promoted. It held that »mere knowledge on the part of the supplier of equipment that it would probably be used to infringe someone's copyright does not make the supply unlawful; nor does an intention to supply the market for such user.«[475] The Court expressly rejected the notion that the manufacturer owed any duty of care to the copyright owners, even if there could be no doubt that they suffered great losses as a result of the availability of these recorders on

---

471 *Id.*, and p. 9.
472 *See, e.g.*, R. v. Lloyd, R. v. Bhuee, R. v. Ali, [1985] 3 W.L.R. 30, holding that the defendants who had copied feature films onto video tapes with the help of a cinema projectionist were guilty of the criminal offence of conspiracy to contravene the provisions of the Copyright Act 1956.
473 Amstrad Consumer Electronics plc v. British Phonographic Industry Ltd., 1986 F.S.R. 159, 1985 N.L.J. 1186 (Court of Appeal).
474 To counter the black market in video cassettes and in order to promote self-regulation by the industry, the British Videogram Association, the Motion Picture Association and the Society of Distribution founded the Federation Against Copyright Theft (FACT). An organization with similar aims is the Video Copyright Protection Society, founded by the BBC, the ITV companies and representatives of the film industry. *See* R. MOORFOOT, *supra* note 405, at 115.
475 *Amstrad Consumer Electronics plc*, 1985 N.L.J. at 1186.

154

the market. With regard to the second question, whether the manufacturer's advertising campaign – which had stated, inter alia, »tape tapes at twice the normal speed,« »record from any record and make copies in half the time,« and »[y]ou could make copies of your favoured cassettes,«[476] – were unlawful, Judge Lawton took a different approach. He held that distributing advertisements and promotional literature that nearly all potential purchasers would understand to mean that the machines could be used for the copying of prerecorded cassettes could under certain circumstances constitute an incitement to commit an offence contrary to section 21(3) of the Copyright Act 1956.[477] This consideration was ultimately rejected by the House of Lords.[478]

At present, the British government is expected to impose a levy on sales of audio and video recording equipment for private use.[479] The levy on tapes would come as a reaction to the private copying of prerecorded material in breach of the Copyright Act 1956. The levy would be collected by a body independent of the government, which would then distribute the royalties to the copyright owners.[480]

The extensive use of VCRs in the United Kingdom has had a strong bearing on the role of the BBC and the IBA. VCRs allow more than just a time-shifting of the authorities' programme schedules: The thriving market for video cassettes also evidences that long before a »true broadcasting market« as envisaged by the Peacock Committee with large consumer choice among different programmes will have come into existence, the public broadcasting authorities will have lost (and are already losing) their position of a »comfortable duopoly« to a much greater extent than is reflected in the United Kingdom's penetration rate of cable television. The balanced diet of programmes designed to inform, educate and entertain is being increasingly ignored by the viewers in favour of more entertainment programmes. Video is causing the IBA and the BBC to lose their grip on what the British people ought to watch in their leisure time.

---

476 *See* 1986 GRUR/Int. 69.
477 *Amstrad Consumer Electronics plc*, 1985 N.L.J. at 1187.
478 *See* C.B.S. Songs Ltd. v. Amstrad Consumer Electronics plc, [1988] 2 W.L.R. 1191, 1208 (per Lord Templeton). This decision was made on appeal from a decision by the Court of Appeal in a separate action, C.B.S. Songs Ltd. v. Amstrad Consumer Electronics plc, [1987] 3 W.L.R. 146.
479 The Recording and Rental of Audio and Video Copyright Material. A consultative document by the Secretary for Trade and Industry, Cmnd. 9445, paras. 3.2, 10.1 (1985).
480 *Id.* at para. 7.10.

B. *Regulatory Framework for Direct Broadcasting by Satellite (DBS)*

The public broadcasting authorities and the proponents of the public broadcasting system early on recognized the threat to their public-service duopoly represented by the new media. When DBS became feasible, there was little opposition to the postulate that the BBC and the IBA should be closely involved in the provision of these services. Nonetheless, in the end this principle agreement over the basic concepts for DBS resulted in a DBS regulation that deviates considerably from the classical British model of public-service broadcasting.

1. *Historical Background*

In 1977 the World Broadcasting Satellite Administrative Radio Conference (1977 WARC-BS), an organ of the ITU, allocated to most countries in Europe, including the United Kingdom, five orbital positions and corresponding frequencies for direct-broadcasting satellites. This allocation enables each nation to provide up to five DBS television channels. The Annan Committee, which published its report on the future of British broadcasting in the same year, was not then prepared to take the prospects of DBS into consideration. With the coming to power of the Conservative government in 1979, DBS began to receive serious public attention and political significance in the United Kingdom. This was part of the new government's overall policy to spur the development of new telecommunications technologies and to secure a leading position internationally for the U.K. high-technology industry. In 1980 the government commissioned a Home Office study on the options for, and implications of, DBS.[481] The final report, published in 1981, identified five strategic options that the United Kingdom could follow with respect to DBS, ranging from a full, five-channel service beginning as early as 1987 to no DBS at all in the foreseeable future. While the study refrained from recommending any specific options, it pointed out certain advantages of a national DBS service, as well as the risks involved. In particular, it stressed the economic prospects of DBS: strong market incentives for the aerospace and electronics industries, programme makers and advertisers.[482] The study repeated the concerns advanced by British industry representatives that a late DBS start could put the British aerospace, electronics and tele-

---

481 1981 Study on DBS, *supra* note 399.
482 *Id.* at para. 1.2.

vision-rental industries at a competitive disadvantage vis-à-vis foreign competitors; the government anticipated fierce international competition in these markets.[483] The report further emphasized that while additional television services could result in adverse effects on the existing British broadcasting services, such potentially negative consequences could not entirely be avoided by a decision against the introduction of a British DBS service. Foreign DBS services, to the extent that they could be received in the United Kingdom and were attractive to British viewers, could in particular threaten the British broadcasting system and its policies.[484] Under these circumstances, the study presented the view that the provision of British DBS services could pre-empt the potential audience market in the United Kingdom, provided that Britain itself offered DBS services at the earliest time possible.[485] Otherwise, it was suggested, British viewers might invest in receiving equipment unsuited for British DBS transmissions for viewing European DBS programmes. The study identified the expected overspill into northern Europe stemming from the footprint of a British direct-broadcasting satellite as a welcomed opportunity to raise additional revenues from advertising or subscription.[486]

Turning to possible negative effects of a British DBS service on the existing broadcasting structure, the report mentioned the danger that a comprehensive competition for audiences between the established broadcasting system and new DBS services could result in an undue emphasis on programmes with mass appeal. This in turn could cause a narrowing of the total available programme range.[487] The IBA and the ITV contractors expressed concerns that a DBS service financed by advertising could substantially reduce the ITV companies' advertising revenues. Also, DBS was considered to carry the risk of siphoning programme material from the established services, thereby impoverishing them.[488] But the study also recognized that DBS could provide new opportunities for programme makers and offer new, exciting services.

The weighing of these mutually dependent risks and opportunities led the study to support cautiously an early introduction of DBS with only one or two initially operational channels, in order to allow the existing broadcasting system gradually to adjust to the changing pattern of U.K. broadcasting.

483 *Id.* at para. 18.9.
484 *Id.* at paras. 1.2, 18.24.
485 *Id.* at para. 14.15.
486 *Id.* at paras. 14.17, 14.18, 18.25.
487 *Id.* at paras. 6.37, 18.6.
488 *Id.* at para. 6.39.

In order to safeguard the public system of broadcasting, the Home Office further suggested that any new DBS service adhere to the programme standards obligatory for both the IBA and the BBC.[489] The Home Office also expressed its belief that possible exceptions to the application of equal standards could be made in the area of proper balance and wide range of programming. To the extent that a duty to adhere to these standards would inhibit the development of DBS services, the Home Office argued that a relaxation of these requirements for DBS would be conceivable. The study left open the question whether it were desirable to allow private companies to provide the new DBS services or to follow the BBC's proposal. The BBC had strongly lobbied for the apportionment of two DBS channels to itself. It had suggested that one channel could offer the »best of BBC 1 and BBC 2« and that the other channel could operate on a subscription basis.[490] Arguments in favour of granting one or two DBS services to the BBC were that the BBC should remain the principal national instrument of broadcasting and that the BBC's international reputation in broadcasting would help to establish the new services.[491] The ITV companies, on the other hand, were also regarded as being capable of making significant contributions to DBS if they were allowed to become DBS programme contractors. But the study explicitly refrained from suggesting that they have exclusive access to any new commercial DBS service.[492]

Another problem mentioned but not resolved in the report was the question whether the regulatory control over the technical and content-related operation of a DBS service were to rest in a single organization or whether the technical operation of the satellite should be in the hands of a separate entity. As a starting point of its analysis, the Home Office recalled the major features of the public broadcasting system in the United Kingdom. In its view the system was characterized by the combined responsibility for three central tasks vested in each of the two existing public broadcasting organizations, namely: (1) the provision and operation of the transmitters; (2) the appointment of the main programme makers and suppliers; and (3) the safeguarding of programme service objectives and the carrying out of programme standards.[493]

The study took the position that this combined responsibility of the public authorities relating not only to content but also to the control over the

489 *Id.* at para. 18.18.
490 *Id.* at paras. 12.13, 18.13.
491 *Id.* at para. 12.9.
492 *Id.* at para. 12.14.
493 *Id.* at para. 12.4.

technical facilities found its justification in the public-service obligation. Under this obligation the broadcasting organizations had the task to ensure not only that the public be informed, educated and entertained but also that the broadcasting services reach as much of the public as technically feasible without regard to the commercial viability of extended service areas. But because a DBS service would automatically reach into the furthest corners of the United Kingdom, the Home Office concluded that – unlike in the context of ITV – control of the satellite operation by a public authority such as the IBA would be unnecessary.[494]

The rationale of this line of argument is that private control over the conduit facilities is not objectionable per se, as long as the operation can be carried out on the basis of profit maximization and still be considered to be in the public interest; any long-term, uneconomic public-service obligation, however, can only be ensured by a public authority.

The Home Office's analysis of the differences in the technical operation of terrestrial and DBS broadcasts represented a conceptual distinction on which the Department based its support for the private control over the conduit facilities. Yet the Home Office intended to avoid a convergence of conduit and content by supporting the idea that the private satellite operator was to be an entity independent of the programme suppliers. This organizational independence would put the operator in the position of a common carrier, resulting in a number of additional organizational advantages, for example:

(a) if the satellite (or satellites) were to be used for more than one broadcasting service, each the responsibility of different authorities;

(b) if the satellite were shared with other countries which have been allocated the 31° West orbital position to provide their own DBS services;

(c) if the satellite carried other telecommunications services in addition to broadcasting services; or

(d) if it were the intention that the DBS channels themselves should also be used for the development and expansion of new types of information services, which might include information services to special classes of users, such as business or industry. Some of these services might have more of the character of commercial undertakings and possibly carry significant financial risks.[495]

The study implied that the private undertaking responsible for the tech-

494 *Id.* at para. 12.5.
495 *Id.*

nical operation would be »a major UK aerospace manufacturer« leasing the channels to the various organizations licensed to broadcast.[496]

In 1982 the British government revealed whom exactly it had in mind as the suitable DBS common carrier: with the backing of the government, British Telecom, British Aerospace[497] and GEC-Marconi had formed a consortium, named United Satellites Limited (UNISAT), with the view to designing, constructing and operating the first direct-broadcasting satellite, which was to be operational by 1986. The Home Office announced that the BBC, as the responsible programme supplier, would get the first two DBS channels on condition that it use the satellite system built by UNISAT. One channel was to offer major feature films as a subscription service; the second channel was to provide »a more general service.«[498] A number of high-quality radio channels were also planned, including the potential provision of data services.[499] The other channels would be available at a later point subject to further demand.

Thus, in the initial planning stage for a British DBS service, the proponents of the classical public broadcasting system prevailed – the system represented by the BBC as the exclusive authority with nationwide programme coverage. At the same time, the government wished to secure a dominant position for U.K. industry in the evolving, new satellite-technology market – at least in the initial stages.

The following two years were taken up by the BBC's attempt to make the financial arrangements necessary to provide the services. The government categorically refused to give any financial assistance. The BBC entered into a so-called »Heads of Agreement« with UNISAT for a system of two orbiting satellites (one as a »flying spare«) and one spare satellite on the ground. The agreements envisaged that the BBC would pay £ 12 million per channel annually for a minimum of seven years and an additional insurance fee of £ 168 million. In 1983 the Home Secretary announced that the Cable and Broadcasting Act, to be passed in 1984, would enable ITV companies and outsiders to bid for two of the three remaining unallocated DBS channels three years after the initial start of the first two BBC-supplied DBS services. These private DBS programme contractors would be placed under IBA supervision. But before this version of the Act could be passed, new developments forced the government to introduce legislative changes in the bill in an attempt to save the whole project.

496 *Id.* at para. 13.4.
497 British Aerospace is the largest U.K. manufacturer of satellite systems.
498 BBC Annual Report and Handbook 1984, Chapter on Programmes 11 (1983).
499 *Id.*

UNISAT, which had already spent some £ 50 million on the development of the satellite without a financial commitment from the BBC, announced that it would stop work unless it received financial guarantees. The BBC, unable to find institutional investors, turned to the IBA and the ITV companies and proposed to share the cost and operation of its two DBS channels. The new version of the Cable and Broadcasting Bill now contained the necessary additional legal prerequisites to allow the joint venture to go ahead. Section 42 of the Cable and Broadcasting Act 1984 contained the regulation that a Satellite Broadcasting Board, consisting of three BBC governors and three IBA members, would be responsible for the provision of the DBS services. Under a contract with the Board, a DBS contractor would provide the actual programming and make the necessary arrangements concerning the satellite transponder.[500] In addition, section 46 of the Cable and Broadcasting Act 1984 was introduced granting the IBA the power to defer the re-advertising of the ITV franchises until 1997. The idea was that a guaranteed franchise extension until that date would provide the necessary incentives to the ITV companies to embark on the risky DBS project. Serious doubts had been raised that until 1986 or 1987 too little DBS receiving equipment would be available to ensure a sufficiently sized audience and that the equipment would be too expensive to attract a fast-growing audience. The plan was that the BBC would subscribe to 50 per cent of the costs, while the ITV companies were to finance 30 per cent; for the remaining 20 per cent, five outside companies[501] agreed to provide the financing.

With the government's approval of the outside companies, the concept of strict adherence to the existing public broadcasting pattern in the DBS context had been eroded. In any event, the attempt to get the modified project off the ground ultimately failed for lack of sufficient financing.[502] The new consortium pleaded in vain with the government to allow an international tender of the satellite contract in order to reduce the estimated total costs of £ 500 million. The government also refused to extend the initial DBS franchise period from 10 to 15 years as requested by the consortium. In June 1985, the government officially announced that the

---

500 Sections 42-44 of the Cable and Broadcasting Act 1984, dealing with the provision of DBS services by the Satellite Broadcasting Board, never came into operation.

501 These companies were Thorn EMI, Granada TV Rentals, S. Pearson, The Virgin Group, and Consolidated Production. All companies prepared to join in the DBS venture, including the BBC and the ITV contractors, were referred to as the »21 Club.«

502 Two of the three members of the UNISAT consortium, namely, British Areospace and GEC-Marconi, later sued the BBC for £ 57 million to cover the costs of the initial design and manufacture of the DBS satellite undertaken by UNISAT. Fin. Times, Mar. 11, 1986.

project had failed and that the two channels originally assigned to the BBC would have to be reallocated. The ITV companies consequently did not get the benefit of extended television franchises. The Satellite Broadcasting Board, which had met a number of times, dissolved, and the IBA was instead vested with the task of inquiring about any parties interested in a British DBS service operating three of the five available channels. The franchising procedure to be followed was the one originally designed for the allocation of the three remaining DBS channels.

Following the formal advertising of the first three DBS channels at the end of 1985, a total of five different consortia applied for the franchise. In December 1986, the IBA awarded it to British Satellite Broadcasting (BSB).[503] The BSB consortium originally consisted of five British companies, namely, two ITV contractors (Anglia Television and Granada Television), Pearson, the Virgin Group and Amstrad Consumer Electronics. The latter subsequently withdrew from the consortium. According to the IBA, BSB won the franchise for two main reasons. One was the intended use of the three channels, with one channel offering premium film material on a subscription basis and the other two channels financed by advertising, offering one news and actuality channel, including the coverage of current events and sports, and one general entertainment channel. The second reason for the franchise award as advanced by the IBA was the sound financial package offered by the consortium. It was understood from the outset, however, that the initial five companies would not be able to provide all the financing but would instead find additional partners willing to invest what was indeed the bulk of the total money needed. Following the initial franchise award, BSB found seven other companies, including one non-European party, who joined the venture.[504] When these final arrangements had been made and the U.S. company Hughes Aircraft had been chosen for the provision of the satellite, the IBA and BSB signed the DBS contract in July 1987. It ensures that the original five members of the BSB consortium have voting control over the DBS contractor.

---

503 Fin. Times, Dec. 12, 1986.
504 The additional companies were the Bond Corporation Holdings (Australia), Chargeurs (EC), Reed International (U.K.), London Merchant Securities (U.K.), Next (U.K.), Innerst (Luxembourg), Trinity International Holdings (U.K.).

2. IBA Functions Relating to the Franchising Process and Programme Supervision

Under sections 37 to 41 of the Cable and Broadcasting Act 1984,[505] the IBA is charged with the provision of DBS services. Similar to the regulation under the Broadcasting Act 1981, the IBA does not itself provide these services but is responsible for the licensing of a DBS contractor and for programme supervision once the services are in operation. The franchising period for DBS television broadcasts originally was 12 years, but the government eventually extended this period to 15 years.[506] The IBA may also appoint a DBS teletext contractor.[507]

With regard to the technical operation of the satellite, the DBS programme contractor has to make the necessary arrangements and owns and operates the facilities. This sharply contrasts not only with the regulation of the ITV system but also with the 1981 Home Office study on DBS, which recommended the licensing of a separate common carrier. The potential dangers of such a unified private control over conduit and content has been somewhat mitigated by a surprisingly simple regulatory measure. The IBA, far from being devoid of any control over the technical operation of the satellite, carries the responsibility for the uplink to the British DBS satellite.[508] This ensures the IBA's ultimate control over the transmissions, a criterion identified in the Home Office's 1981 study as a major feature of the traditional public broadcasting concept. This arrangement represents a compromise between the IBA's all-encompassing control over the radio and television transmitters used for terrestrial transmission and private control over the conduit facilities. While the responsibility for the uplink places the IBA at the central coordinating point for the DBS transmissions at little expense of its own, the risks involved in the construction, launching and operation of the satellite rest solely with the private operator. If its programme transmissions did not meet the standards prescribed, the IBA could at any time and on its own account discontinue the upbeam link.

The Authority also specifies the standards of transmission and other

---

505 *Entered into force* on Apr. 1, 1986. Cable and Broadcasting Act 1984 (Commencement No. 2) Order 1986, 1986 S.I. No. 537.

506 *See* Broadcasting Act 1981, sec. 19(2)(aa), inserted by virtue of sec. 38(1)(aa) of the Cable and Broadcasting Act 1984. *See also* The Times, Feb. 17, 1987.

507 *See* Cable and Broadcasting Act 1984, sec. 37(3), and Broadcasting Act 1981, secs. 14 and 15.

508 IBA, Guidance Notes for Organizations Interested in the Provision of DBS Services, Press Release, Sept. 3, 1985 (hereafter cited as IBA, Guidance Notes on DBS).

conditions relevant to ensuring high-quality performance of the satellite transponders (section 2(1) of the Broadcasting Act 1981).[509]

DBS programme-content requirements to some degree are identical to those in force for the ITV system. In particular, nothing may be included in the programmes that offends good taste and decency or is likely to incite to crime or to lead to disorder or that is offensive to public feeling (section 4(1)(a) of the Broadcasting Act 1981). In this respect the IBA's Television Programme Guidelines are as applicable to DBS services as is its Code of Advertising Standards and Practices (sections 5, 8 and 9 of the Broadcasting Act 1981). In addition, news has to be presented with due accuracy and impartiality (section 4(1)(b) of the Broadcasting Act 1981). However, in view of the tremendous financial burdens placed upon the DBS contractor(s), Parliament granted a number of important concessions aimed at reducing some of the potential costs for DBS programme supply and designed to attract viable audiences. Section 37(2)(a),(b) of the Cable and Broadcasting Act 1984 designates that DBS programmes are exempted from the duty to maintain a proper balance and wide range of subject matters and do not need to give a sufficient amount of time to news and news features. This regulation enables the DBS contractors to focus on general entertainment programmes. Such a programme menu is believed to be best suited to induce potential viewers to invest in DBS receiving equipment and to interest them in a subscription service.

This content regulation illustrates that while the Cable and Broadcasting Act 1984 technically integrated DBS broadcasting services into the public broadcasting domain, one of the cornerstones of the concept was eroded, namely, the tripartite claim that public-service broadcasting must serve to disseminate information, education and entertainment. While the IBA now has the responsibility to guard the maintenance of high-quality programmes in both the ITV and the DBS services, its roles in the respective services are essentially different. Whereas the IBA heavily intermeddles with the programme management of the ITV contractors, its conceptual position vis-à-vis the DBS contractor(s) is a much more passive one. It is basically reduced to safeguarding that feature films, comedies and television series do not offend good taste and decency; in this it is light-years away from Lord Reith's original claim that a public broadcasting authority has the foremost task to make people better citizens.

509 With the exception of the provisions listed in section 37(2), section 37(1) of the Cable and Broadcasting Act 1984 makes all provisions of the Broadcasting Act 1981 applicable to DBS franchisee(s).

164

Furthermore, the present institutional arrangement has a built-in potential conflict of interests. To the extent that a DBS contractor finances his services by advertising, he directly competes with the ITV companies for the same sources of revenue, with the exception of purely local or regional advertisements. Under section 39(2) of the Cable and Broadcasting Act 1984, the IBA may prohibit a DBS contractor to include advertising in a subscription service. If competition for advertising income damaged the ITV companies' revenue base, this provision would allow the IBA to cut off the DBS contractors' possible mixed financing arrangements in the interest of the ITV contractors. The likelihood of this scenario depends on the wording of the DBS franchise contract and also on whether the IBA would more closely identify with the interests of its traditional television franchisees. Undoubtedly, however, section 39(2) of the Cable and Broadcasting Act 1984 was included in the Act as a safeguard for the terrestrial commercial television system in Britain. However, the IBA currently takes the position that it is up to the DBS contractor to decide whether its subscription channel should also carry advertising. It appears that at least for the moment the IBA is more concerned over the financial viability of the DBS services than with the possible effects on the ITV system. Nonetheless, the IBA also stresses that the fact that BSB's franchise application included the undertaking to provide one channel as a subscription service had been considered as a major advantage over the application of at least one other consortium, which had wanted to finance all three channels solely by advertising. The potential conflict of interests is not mitigated by the fact that the IBA strictly separates its bookkeeping with respect to the rental payments made to it by the ITV and the DBS contractors and separately manages the administrative costs for both broadcasting systems (*compare* section 40 of the Cable and Broadcasting Act 1984).

While the IBA managed to extend its control beyond the commercial broadcasting system ITV, its regulatory powers over DBS are much weaker. This is due in part to the liberalization of programme standards applying to DBS programmes. Furthermore, while the Authority holds the control over the technical facilities, its technicians are not responsible for the crucial technical operation of the satellite; this circumstance prevents the IBA from accruing all the technical know-how connected with DBS technology, and it prevents it from experimenting with the facility, a practice that could lead to a determination and pre-emption of future technical developments by the Authority.

Finally, the fact that the BBC ultimately lost its campaign for a decisive hand in DBS broadcasting services will have strong repercussions on the dominant position in broadcasting enjoyed by it for so many decades. The pluralistic broadcasting market of the future as predicted by the Peacock Committee will for a number of years be strongly influenced – if not dominated – by the DBS services, because the spread of cable television in the United Kingdom is slow and only a few private households can receive satellite programmes transmitted from communications satellites. Under these circumstances, a stake in DBS would have been crucial for the defence of the BBC's outstanding position thus far. The lost DBS battle for some time spurred the BBC's interest in the provision of programme channels transmitted via communications satellites. This is a fast-growing programme supply market, in which not only the BBC but also such other British media undertakings as the ITV companies and newspaper publishers have taken a strong interest.

C. Regulatory Framework for Programmes Transmitted Via Communications Satellites

Satellite television programmes aimed at cable networks in Europe are transmitted via communications satellites, also called low-power satellites or fixed-service satellites (FSS). The term low-power satellite is a reference to the low energy level with which the signals, picked up from an earth station, are retransmitted to the earth in a footprint usually covering several countries.[510] The low-power signals require for their reception large dish antennas generally of a diameter of three to five meters. The size and cost of these antennas explain why individual households do not normally receive these signals directly. Instead, the signals are picked up by cable network operators and then distributed via cable systems to the ultimate consumer. The British liberalization of satellite master antenna television (SMATV) in 1985 opened up a further market for satellite television programmes and particularly enabled hotels, clubs, larger apartment buildings and similar establishments to receive the channels directly.

The IBA coordinated the first pan-European satellite service experiment, Eurikon, in early 1982. The programmes were transmitted simultaneously in six languages and were received on closed-circuit television in 15 nations in Western Europe and northern Africa. A major aim of the experiment

---

510 It is understood that communications satellites with point-to-point transmission, i.e., with a narrow downlink beam aimed at the receiving dishes of one or only a few earth stations, are outside the present analysis.

166

was to carry out research on audience reaction to such an international service and to assess its main impact on existing national services.[511] Today, some seven satellite programme channels originate in the United Kingdom.[512] Operated by private companies, most of the channels are financed through advertising, while others operate as pay-TV services. They are aimed at the cable systems in Western Europe, including the United Kingdom, and reach an audience of more than 10 million homes. In addition, Satellite Television plc., the company operating the programme service Sky Channel, has even managed to reach an agreement with Hungary, which gave permission for the reception of Sky Channel in hotels in Budapest and other Hungarian cities.[513]

U.S. undertakings have heavily invested in these British satellite television companies, but British participation is also significant. Of particular interest is the financial involvement of ITV companies in these ventures. Five ITV contractors hold equity stakes in established satellite television companies.[514] The ITV contractors as a group may have felt threatened by the competition they faced from satellite television channels, particularly from those featuring general entertainment. On a long-term basis, they anticipated a shift of their audiences and advertising clients to the new programme services. Also, the companies believed it to be advantageous to get experience in the satellite television market and technologies as early as possible in order to be able to respond to any new developments from a position of strength. Their joint answer to the new challenge was the setting up of their own satellite television channel, Superchannel, which started operation at the end of January 1987. With the exception of one contractor, all ITV companies participated in the venture. They reached agreement with the BBC over programme contributions from the BBC's huge programme library with the aim of ultimately showing the »best of

---

511 Paterson, *The British Renaissance: An Assessment of Satellite Developments in the U.K.*, SATELLITE COMMUNICATIONS (Jan. 1983), reprinted in THE THIRD BIENNIAL COMMUNICATIONS LAW SYMPOSIUM. INTERNATIONAL SATELLITE TELEVISION. RESOURCE MANUAL 80, 81 (1983).

512 They are: The Arts Channel, The Children's Channel, Lifestyle, Premiere, Screen Sport, Sky Channel, and Superchannel. Cable Authority, Annual Report and Accounts 1986-87 21 (1987) (hereafter cited as 1987 Cable Authority Annual Report).

513 Fin. Times, June 6, 1986.

514 These ITV contractors are: Television South, Yorkshire TV and Granada TV with investments in the Arts Channel, Lifestyle and Music Box. *See* Neue Zürcher Zeitung, Dec. 2, 1986. However, Music Box eventually merged into Superchannel. Thames Television and Central Television have invested in The Children's Channel. 1987 Cable Authority Annual Report, *supra* note 512, at 20.

British television« on the new channel.[515] Thames Television and London Weekend Television have in addition entered into a consortium with three other large British corporations that together plan to launch two new entertainment channels, which are to carry general entertainment, films and possibly home-shopping programmes and are to be distributed via the Luxembourgian telecommunications satellite Astra.[516]

No regulatory regime applies directly to the provision of low-power satellite programmes. Neither the IBA nor the Cable Authority nor the Home Office has any power to exercise direct programme control over the channels. Since the technical operation of the services is carried out under commercial agreements between the satellite programme providers and BT, which, aside from Mercury, holds the monopoly right of access to the satellites, the satellite television companies themselves fall outside any regulatory regime both as to programme provision and technical operation.

It does not follow from the aforesaid, however, that the satellite television companies operate in a legal vacuum. The reception of their programmes by British consumers depends upon their access to the British cable systems. The licences issued to the cable operators by the Cable Authority require that programmes transmitted via cable systems comply with the standards of taste and decency set out in the Cable and Broadcasting Act 1984. In case a programme service violates the programme and advertising standards, the Cable Authority may direct the cable operator to discontinue the transmission of the service (section 15(1) of the Cable and Broadcasting Act 1984). If a satellite television channel were incompatible with the 1984 Act, the Cable Authority could be expected to prohibit all U.K.-based cable systems from further transmitting the service, thereby totally erasing the satellite channel's British audience. While these orders would be directed at the cable operators, the economic injury would effect the satellite programme provider. Together with his U.K. audience, he would lose the economic base for his business operations. If he operated on a pay-TV basis, his financial losses would be immediate and complete, unless he also distributed his programmes to cable systems in other countries. If his system were based on advertising revenues, he would lose

---

515 Fin. Times, Oct. 25, 1985. Despite an audience of 11 million homes across Europe only one year after the start of Superchannel's operations, the service faced severe losses, convincing most ITV contractors to sell their shares in the channel. The UK's Virgin Group now holds a 45-percent stake, while the remaining shares belong to three large ITV contractors, Granada, Anglia, and Yorkshire. Broadcasting, May 9, 1988, pp. 65, 66.
516 The Times, July 14, 1987; Fin. Times, Sept. 17, 1987.

advertising addressed to the British audience. He would also become less attractive to advertisers interested in a pan-European market.

The satellite television provider's access to the British cable networks thus wholly depends on the regulations governing British cable television.

IV. *The Convergence of Conduit and Content in Cable Television*

The situation in British cable television is characterized by a government policy strongly fostering private enterprise and advocating as little state involvement as possible. The cable operators' primary concern has been the provision of television programmes. This explains why numerous undertakings with backgrounds in the entertainment industry have engaged in cable television ventures. Through their involvement in cable network construction and operation, these information providers have become information distributors. At the same time, British Telecom, the privatized common carrier of the national telecommunications grid, has become engaged in cable television ventures as well; its activities have reached out from the initial purely technical network-related responsibilities to an increasing involvement in programme supply. A traditional network provider has thus undergone a transition, becoming an information provider. The dissolving functional distinctions between information providers (i.e., traditional broadcasters and the general entertainment industry) and network providers (i.e., basically the telephone systems operator(s)) is reflected in the evaporating distinction between the traditionally separated legal regimes applying to broadcasting services on the one hand and telecommunications services on the other hand. Voice and data services are generally qualified as telecommunications services, while the transmission of video services is typically referred to as broadcasting services, which until recently were solely the province of the public broadcasting authorities and were provided via terrestrial transmitters. The new cable technology allows the network provider to put his medium to alternative uses, which are subsumed under these different legal categories. On the one hand, such new technological developments as fibre-optic cables and satellites may be used for the provision of television entertainment as well as for a whole range of basic and enhanced telecommunications and information services. On the other hand, traditional voice networks are becoming increasingly digitalized, leading to the construction of integrated services digital networks (ISDNs) capable of transmitting sound as well as data and video signals. This development has been aptly termed the convergence of conduit and content.[517]

The legal regime applying to the operation of cable networks has to respond to this new factual situation dictated by the technological revolution of the past 15 years. The principle legislation applicable to cable operation in the United Kingdom is the Cable and Broadcasting Act 1984 and the Telecommunications Act 1984. They represent the first comprehensive regulatory responses to the problem of convergence, necessitating a close cooperation between the various regulatory authorities responsible for either the conduit- or the content-related rules. The novelty of the convergence phenomenon and the need first for tentative solutions in order to bring about a comprehensive regulatory scheme result in certain organizational frictions stemming from the unresolved harmonization of the interplay between the traditional and the legal concepts.

The British response to the phenomenon of convergence of conduit and content can only be understood against the background of the history of cable television in the United Kingdom. The following chapter will give the necessary historical background, to be followed by a discussion of the regulatory responses to the new technologies and an analysis of the specific conflicts and problems still unresolved.

A. *Historical Background of Cable Television*

1. *Early Developments*

The origins of television programme transmission via cable in the United Kingdom go back as far as the 1920s. Poor reception of radio broadcasts in many parts of the country and high costs of radio receivers encouraged private entrepreneurs to distribute radio programmes over wires attached to simple loudspeakers in private homes. These subscription services enjoyed increasing popularity, because they could not only relay the BBC programmes but also foreign radio services, such as Radio Luxembourg and

---

517 *See, e.g.,* Schnurr, *Conduit-Content Convergence: Its Causes and Effects*, 53 TELE-COMMUNICATION JOURNAL 537 (1986).

Radio Normandy.[518] Before 1936 even services with only one-channel capacity were allowed to relay foreign programmes as long as their services contained at least some element of BBC programmes.[519] Between 1929 and 1935, the number of subscribers rose from about 8,500 to well over 233,000, while the number of relay companies grew more than tenfold from 34 to 343.[520] As has already been described in the context of the principles determining freedom to broadcast in the United Kingdom,[521] these relay services faced strong opposition by the BBC. The corporation feared for its broadcast monopoly if relay companies were allowed to transmit their own programmes via cable. The BBC was also concerned that its programme policy would be undermined by the common practice of relay systems operators replacing parts of BBC programmes with foreign material while retaining other parts.[522] The introduction of »must-carry rules« for BBC (and later IBA) programmes and the prohibition of services originated by the relay operators decided the conflict for several decades in favour of the public broadcasting system.

The lost battle of relay operators in the 1930s led to a stagnation of growth in this industry until World War II, when defence-related government measures resulted in a deteriorating quality of private signal reception. This created a renewed demand for signal enhancement over wire.

When television was later introduced in the United Kingdom, the relay operators soon realized that it was commercially viable and necessary to offer this new service over wire as well. But again they were prohibited from offering programme services themselves. In the 1950s and 1960s, the relay of television services (soon including ITV programmes) had a stimulating effect on the relay industry.[523] Relay systems existed mainly in urban areas, where subscriber density made the capital-intensive business viable. However, improvements in the number of transmitters and changes in transmission standards diminished the necessity of wired signal enhancement in many parts of the country. Some systems became obsolete due to the new technologies, and in the 1970s many relay operators lost a large number of subscribers. The new financial pressures on relay operators led to increasing tendencies of concentration in the relay industry. The relay of television programmes had already necessitated

---

518 *See* B. PAULU, *supra* note 165, at 20.
519 T. HOLLINS, *supra* note 169, at 40.
520 R. COASE, *supra* note 173, at. 84.
521 *See supra* at chapter I(B)(3).
522 BBC Yearbook 1933, *cited in* B. PAULU, *supra* note 165, at 20-21 and n. 56.
523 Between 1966 and 1972, the number of people receiving their television signals by cable rose from about 1 million to some 2.3 million. *See* T. HOLLINS, *supra* note 169, at 42.

enhanced capital investments in wire technology, and larger companies began to dominate the business. Many of these companies had strong commercial interests in the radio and television rental business, because relay services and television rentals were mutually stimulating businesses. These early developments account for one of the present characteristics of the cable television market in the United Kingdom: Companies with this kind of business background, like Rediffusion, Visionhire, Telefusion or Radio Rentals, have gained significant stakes in the newly evolving cable industry.[524]

In summarizing the first fifty years of cable transmission in Britain, one can discern several characteristics: (1) an early stifling of alternative programme supplies via cable reinforced the public-service monopoly and restricted relay services to the role of mere signal enhancement; (2) relay services became increasingly superfluous with enhanced terrestrial transmitter service coverage; (3) increasingly expensive wire technology and diminished profits from relay services supported market concentration, with a small number of firms engaged in the television rental, electronics, computing and broadcasting businesses dominating the market and having at their disposal important cable technology know-how gained over several decades; (4) the Post Office, despite its monopoly in telecommunications services, had only insignificantly become engaged in cable relay services, preparing the way for an independent development of the market for cable television services. In 1973 about 2.3 million households (13 per cent of the population) were connected to cable. There existed some 9,000 cable systems, most of them small master antenna services (MATV). The company Rediffusion accounted for 50 per cent of the market, while the second-largest operator controlled 16 per cent of the market. Most of the small systems were run by the Post Office, city councils, residents' associations, dealers, and the like.[525]

2. *Experiments with Community Television*

In the early 1970s, the idea of cable services in Britain was revitalized by a debate on the merits of community television. At the heart of the issue was the call for public access to the cable media. Local cable relay systems should be used, it was widely argued, to enable citizens to communicate with each other. This was to be achieved through locally originated programmes. The idea was

524 *See*, *e.g.*, *id.* at 48 (Table II); Adam Smith Institute, Omega Report – Communications Policy 25 (1984), *citing* The Economist, Mar. 27, 1982.
525 P. LEWIS, COMMUNITY TELEVISION AND CABLE IN BRITAIN 12 (1978).

that such programmes could be made either by television professionals or by the locals themselves on any matters of local concern. Politically, the movement received support from two different sides: There were those who had in mind article 19 of the Universal Declaration on Human Rights guaranteeing freedom of expression and the right »to receive and impart information and ideas through any media.«[526] They argued that greater freedom of choice for viewers, closer personal involvement in the production of programmes, and increased access to the means of communication were of vital importance to any free, informed and democratic society.[527] On the other hand, the cable relay industry also supported the movement. For many years they had lobbied in vain for the introduction of pay television.[528] In supporting the idea of community television they were hoping not only to attract more subscribers but also to set a precedent for the introduction of alternative programmes on cable systems, with the long-term aim of supplying a whole range of pay-TV programme services. The concerted efforts of these two conceptionally diverse camps were aptly referred to as the »alliance of the mercenaries and the missionaries.«[529]

In 1972 the Minister of Post and Telecommunications announced that he would license five experiments with community television on existing cable systems under sections 89 and 90 of the Post Office Act 1969.[530] These licences were subsequently granted to a variety of companies, such as Rediffusion, British Relay, Wellingborough Traders TV Relay,[531] and a subsidiary of a Canadian cable company, Albion Cablevision, for cable relay systems in Bristol, Sheffield and Wellingborough. The fifth experiment in Swindon received particular public attention because of its

---

526 Council of Europe, Swindon Viewpoint – A Community Television Service, CCC/DC (76)98 8 (1977).

527 *Id*. at 8-9.

528 There had only been one two-year experiment with pay-TV in two suburbs of London and in Sheffield between 1966 and 1968, with subscribers using slot meters to pay for individual – mostly feature film – programmes. Despite the commercial success of the experiment, its licence was not extended by the government. *See* T. HOLLINS, *supra* note 169, at 44-45.

529 P. LEWIS, *supra* note 525, at 16.

530 Five community sound-only experiments were also authorized. *See* 1978 White Paper on Broadcasting, *supra* note 270, at para. 176. Two examples of the licences for a local relay service and a local programme service, both issued in 1973, are reprinted in J. HEYN, *supra* note 214, at 428-38.

531 The ownership structure of the Wellingborough cable system differed from the other successful cable licence applicants in that the system had been set up and operated since 1958-59 by local businessmen. In order to finance their community television service, they sold 50 per cent of the shares of the licensed company to a Canadian enterprise, Selkirk Communications, with experience in cable television. This was the second Canadian company to get involved in the British community television experiments. *See* P. LEWIS, *supra* note 525, at 55.

unique features. Thorn EMI Ltd., a company with diversified business interests in communications but without its own cable system, set up a separate company, Swindon Viewpoint, and received a licence for the use of one channel of the Swindon cable network, owned by Radio Rentals. Swindon Viewpoint's staff was completely free from any editorial interference by Thorn EMI, and local citizens were greatly encouraged to initiate and produce their own, mostly uncensored, programmes. For this purpose, seven video cameras and ancillary equipment were available free of charge to any community member wishing to produce a programme item.[532]

On the average, the various community programme experiments produced 14 hours of programming per week. However, the experiments were severely restricted by their licence conditions: No public money was provided, all programmes had to be locally originated, no advertising or sponsorship was allowed, programmes had to »maintain a high general standard of quality,« and »due impartiality« was to be observed on »matters of political or industrial controversy or relating to current public policy, provided that [...] a series of programmes may be considered as a whole.«[533] Also, the Minister of Posts and Telecommunications (after 1974, the Home Secretary) retained ultimate control over the programmes and could at any time prohibit the showing of any particular programme item. While the local programmes were generally well received by the viewers and proved particularly successful in significantly raising the information level of the local population on local political issues,[534] the experiments were doomed to failure after a few years, if only for lack of financial support. The expectation of the cable operators that their investment would pay off in the long run once the government also licensed pay-TV channels was disappointed when a Labour government came to power in 1974. It looked much less favourably upon the cable companies' ambitions. Although the new government finally gave permission in 1975 to include advertising in the local programmes, some licensees took the position that this was »too little and too late.«[535] By 1976, when the sixth and last community television experiment was licensed in Milton Keynes,[536] only one of the original five pro-

532 Council of Europe, *supra* note 526, at 10-12.
533 *Id.* at 9-10.
534 *Id.* at 23.
535 *Id.* at 16.
536 Milton Keynes was a new town built on the basis of a development project. The cable system was owned and operated by the Post Office, which also provided a grant for the purchase of the initial studio equipment. Operating expenses were provided by the development corporation, while the board of the separate community cable company consisted of nine local residents. *See* P. LEWIS, *supra* note 525, at 64-65.

jects was still in full operation, while three had already closed down completely for lack of money.[537]

The situation of cable services in the 1970s was thus characterized by strong political currents emphasizing the potential of cable technology for freedom of information on the local level and by a cable industry willing to put considerable money into corresponding experiments in order to get their feet into the door of pay TV. The debate over new forms of communication by cable was limited to the formulation of a new broadcasting policy, while interest in other kinds of cable services, such as data transmission or voice services, played no role in the discussions. At the same time, community television was designed in such a way as to avoid any potential conflict with the established broadcasting system: The obligation to provide only locally originated programmes and the prohibition on showing feature films or carrying any advertising ensured that the new programme services were a mere supplement to, and not competitive with, BBC or ITV programmes. At the same time, a stringent government policy on broadcasting spanning a considerable number of years was missing, not in the least due to the change of governments from Conservative to Labour.

The Labour government took the position that it was best to postpone any decision on broadcasting issues until the Annan Committee on the Future of Broadcasting, set up by the Home Secretary in 1974, had issued its report. This report was finally published in 1977. It recommended the maintenance of the established broadcasting system and rejected proposals to authorize pay television on cable systems. The Committee's central argument against pay TV stemmed from its perception of the U.S. and Canadian cable television markets: »[W]e were not persuaded that Pay TV of itself generated new programme material. What it did was to distribute material from broadcasting organizations, feature films and some live sport. It was therefore a ravenous parasite. It lived off those who produced television and films.«[538] According to the almost hostile position of the Annan Committee, any additional programme supply on private cable networks tended to threaten the overall programme standards of BBC and ITV programmes, forcing the broadcasters to compete for audiences.[539] Although the subsequent 1978 Government White Paper took a more favourable though very cautious stance on pay TV,[540] the cable operators

---

537 The experiments are described in detail in J. HEYN, *supra* note 214, at 161-257.
538 1977 Annan Report, *supra* note 269, at para. 14.50.
539 *Id.* at para. 14.52.
540 *See* 1978 White Paper on Broadcasting, *supra* note 270, at paras. 177-79.

had to wait until 1979 for a major revision of broadcasting policies when a Conservative government once again came to power.

3. *Telecommunications Policy in the First Half of the 1980s*

In 1980 the Home Office licensed 13 pilot pay-TV systems on existing cable networks.[541] The licences were originally issued for a two-year term only, in order to gain time for the investigation of public demand for pay TV and the repercussions on the existing broadcasting structure and cinemas. The services offered an extra film channel in return for the payment of an additional subscription fee, ranging from £ 6.50 to £ 12. However, the trials experienced great difficulties in various respects. Programme material proved very difficult to achieve at reasonable prices, and repeats were thus frequent. For most systems, subscription rate for pay-TV services was considerably lower than expected. By 1984 only 17.7 per cent of the subscribers had taken the additional services,[542] and channel operators faced heavy financial losses.

As part of the major review of the country's telecommunications policy, the government set up a permanent Information Technology Advisory Panel (ITAP), consisting of members of the information-technology industry. Its task was to advise the government on all aspects of information technology, in particular, on market needs and opportunities.[543] The ITAP's first longer study, submitted in 1982, dealt with the potential role of cable systems in the United Kingdom.[544] It focussed attention on the economic aspects of cable television. Emphasizing the economic stimulus that heavy investment in cable technology could give to a wide range of industry sectors, the ITAP implored the government to take speedy action to encourage the rapid growth of this industry. The government responded swiftly by setting up a committee with the responsibility of reporting on the broadcasting aspects of cable technology. This committee was chaired by Lord Hunt of Tanworth and completed its report six months later in September 1982.[545] The Hunt Committee took a very favourable stance on the introduction of new television channels on existing and newly built

---

541 A compilation of these systems, including data about the ownership structure and the number of subscribers, is contained in T. HOLLINS, *supra* note 169, at 48 (Table II).
542 *Id.* at 49.
543 *Id.* at 52.
544 Cabinet Office, Information Technology Advisory Panel, Report on Cable Systems (February 1982) (hereafter cited as 1982 ITAP Report).
545 Home Office, Report of the Inquiry into Cable Expansion and Broadcasting Policy (October 1982) (hereafter referred to as 1982 Hunt Report).

176

cable systems. It concluded that under certain arrangements »cable television and public service broadcasting can co-exist without unnecessary inhibitions on the development of the former and without damage to the essentials of the latter.«[546] As a last step before passing new legislation on the basis of these findings, the Home Office and the DTI prepared a White Paper describing the government policy on cable television and the broadcasting media in general and outlining the envisaged new legislation.[547] This preparatory work culminated in the passage of the Cable and Broadcasting Act 1984 and certain parts of the Telecommunications Act 1984.

The fundamental policies underlying the 1984 enactments were industrial, economic and labour-market concerns. In contrast to the ideas that had led to the community television experiments in the 1970s, considerations of media policy were no longer the driving force behind the new developments in cable television. Symptomatically, neither the Hunt Report and the 1983 White Paper nor the Cable and Broadcasting Act gives any prominence to concerns for public access to cable channels or community programming. The key element of the official policy has instead been aptly described as the »technology opportunity syndrome.«[548] It was hoped that the encouragement of the cable industry would generate a great range of economic activities, such as new developments in optical-fibre technology, consumer electronics, office technology systems, and the like. In addition to stimulating the home market, the government wanted to seize an opportunity to encourage the export of information technology. In this area, it saw great commercial potentials as a result of an increasing world demand for high technology in telecommunications.

The government's cable-systems policy has to be seen in the immediate context of its general telecommunications policy since the early 1980s. Since its coming to power, the Conservative government has made the fostering and reorganization of telecommunications services one of its primary policy goals. As a first step, it liberalized the markets for terminal equipment and value-added network services. It also provided for the organizational separation of the Post Office from the newly created company BT, which became the provider of the national telecommunications network. As a further step, it also licensed Mercury, a private company, to

546 *Id.* at para. 102.
547 1983 White Paper on Cable Systems, *supra* note 208.
548 Gibbons, Hartley, Evans, Metcalfe & Simnett, *Technology and Policy in Cable TV Development in the UK*, 8 TELECOMMUNICATIONS POLICY 223 (1984) (hereafter, Gibbons, et al.).

provide additional basic telecommunications services on a competitive basis with BT, thus establishing a legal duopoly in basic network services. As a final move, British Telecom was privatized through a public offering of shares on the stock market. This privatization process in turn was in line with the privatization of other public enterprises, such as Cable and Wireless, Britoil, British Aerospace, British Steel, British Gas and British Airlines. The underlying political concept that led to these measures was the belief that economic recovery required the reform of nationalized industries.[549]

The promotion of consumer choice across a broad range of industry sectors became the primary goal. Industrial and commercial decisions were to be determined by the market rather than through state intervention. In line with this market-economy approach, the development of local cable systems was to take place on the basis of consumer demand, leaving it up to private enterprises to seek out franchised areas and to finance the cable systems without public subsidies. The system of local franchises was designed to encourage the coexistence of a great number of independent franchisees. According to this policy, development of cable services was to be consumer-led, that is, the market was to determine what price consumers were willing to pay for certain services. This in turn, it was believed, would determine the level of technical sophistication of the cable systems as well as the kind of services to be offered. This policy has been termed the »demand pull« approach, in contrast to the »technology push« strategy.[550] The latter policy is characterized by the government laying the cables without concrete knowledge of consumer demand in the hope that the technical availability of certain services will create a demand for them. West Germany and France are examples of this kind of policy approach.

As has rightfully been pointed out,[551] in the United Kingdom the introduction of network competition through the licensing of private cable systems was not founded on a predetermined concept of what an optimal telecommunications network structure should look like. A policy based on network structure might, on the one hand, have favoured two or more independent communications networks, with network operators competing with each other on the whole available range of services; on the other

---

549 *See* Jonscher, *Telecommunications Liberalization in the United Kingdom*, in TELECOMMUNICATIONS REGULATION AND DEREGULATION IN INDUSTRIALIZED DEMOCRACIES 153, 156 (M. Snow ed. 1986), *citing* THE CONSERVATIVE MANIFESTO 1983.
550 Gibbons, et al., *supra* note 548, at 226.
551 Jonscher, *supra* note 549, at 156.

hand, one common carrier might have provided basic functions with an obligation to make the network available to anybody wishing to offer enhanced or information services. Instead, the underlying considerations for the British policy were broad market-economy concerns, with an emphasis on consumer demand and consumer choice. Thus, the government wanted to encourage private companies to build and operate local cable systems separate from and additional to the existing and potential telecommunications networks operated by BT and Mercury. In view of the fact that a private – though limited – market in cable television relay systems already existed in the United Kingdom, the new policy in some respects amounted to an extrapolation of historical developments. On the other hand, two new dimensions were added to the cable operators' legal status. On the programme side, their authorization to supply privately originated programmes in addition to the public broadcasting channels put them in competition with the public broadcasting authorities. On the telecommunications side, the additional telecommunications services (i.e., basic, enhanced and interactive services), which can be offered particularly by wideband cable systems, made it necessary to redefine the relationship between the general network operators BT and Mercury and these private cable operators.

With respect to the cable technology to be used for the local networks, several options had to be considered, ranging from the traditional tree-and-branch system (TAB) to the most advanced switched-star system, as well as a number of hybrid technologies in between. While the TAB system represents a mature technology capable of transmitting 25 to 30 video channels to a subscriber plus any kind of interactive services with the exception of a universal telephone service, the switched-star system offers greater up-stream capacity as well as the potential of a full video-phone service.[552] At the time the government had to make the decision on the most desirable cable technology, the switched-star system was expected to be first technically feasible on a large scale in two or three years. In light of the rapid developments in cable technology and the delays in the setting up of new cable systems expected from a general requirement of switched-star technology, the government decided to allow cable operators a choice of cable technology and cable material (i.e., fibre-optic or coaxial cables). The technical sophistication of these systems was to be

---

552 1983 White Paper on Cable Systems, *supra* note 208, at para. 20. *See also* the diagrams showing the construction of the various system technologies; *id.* at pp. 19-21.

determined by the market forces.[553] The government imposed only the requirement that all newly constructed underground ducts should have a star configuration in order to facilitate any possible future upgrading of the systems.

In view of these overriding technological and economic concerns, the attention paid to the relationship between cable television operators and the traditional broadcasting system appears to have been of only secondary importance. The 1983 White Paper acknowledged that the introduction of cable television channels additional to the BBC and ITV public-service channels »challenges the assumptions on which broadcasting policy has hitherto been founded.«[554] The broadcasters and their political supporters in particular had argued that alternative television channels would lead to a fragmentation of audiences and to financial pressures on the BBC as well as on the ITV companies.[555] They had protested that ITV contractors would need to compete for advertising revenues with the cable operators, while decreasing audiences would call into question the BBC licence-fee system. This in turn would result in the need to reduce the production of high-cost quality programmes and increasingly to compete for maximum audiences with mass-appeal programmes to the detriment of minority and current-affairs programmes. The bottom line of the criticism was that broadcasting policy had been subordinated to industrial objectives.[556]

Against this background, the 1983 White Paper avoided a systematic examination of the future relationship between the old and the new television media. It postponed any definition of the new relationship and gave no clear statement on the changing concept of public-service broadcasting in light of competition. Instead, it quoted the succinct assertion of the Hunt Committee that public-service broadcasting and cable could coexist if certain safeguards were taken.[557]

Government and industry assigned a particularly important role to additional entertainment programmes. In their view, the development of British cable systems not only would be »consumer-led« but also »entertainment-led,«[558] in the sense that consumer demand – at least initially – would call for additional entertainment programmes rather than enhanced telecommunications services. Underlying the government's

---

553 *Id.* at paras. 24, 27.
554 *Id.* at para. 85.
555 Severe criticism came, for example, from the Greater London Council. *See* Greater London Council, Cabling in London, Report by the Economic Policy Group (December 1982).
556 McDonnell, *supra* note 412, at 42.
557 1983 White Paper on Cable Systems, *supra* note 208, at para. 83.
558 Gibbons, et al., *supra* note 548, at 226.

policy was the conviction that private companies needed the profit-making incentives of pay TV in order to take the risk and be able to finance technologically advanced cable systems that could later also be used for a wide variety of advanced telecommunications services.

Still, the future of cable television in the United Kingdom has been looking rather gloomy for several years. Since the granting of the first interim franchises in 1983, the development of cable has been very slow. At the end of 1986, only seven of the original eleven franchises were operating, and of the additional eleven granted by the Cable Authority since 1984, only one appeared prepared to start operation within the next twelve months, and indeed did so in April 1987. For some time, the number of homes linked to cable had even been declining, mainly due to the closing down of old relay systems; in early 1987, only a total of about 193,000 homes subscribed to cable in all of Britain.[559] Between January 1986 and April 1987, the number of homes connected to cable systems increased by 52 per cent.[560] Still, even the Cable Authority itself acknowledged that the slowness of cables development had been »frustrating.«[561] It identified the lack of confidence of the business community in the future returns of cable television and the subsequent difficulties in raising the necessary financing for new systems as the primary problems in promoting cable. While investment in cable construction (not taking into account programming and similar matters) from 1985 to 1987 had been on the order of £ 60 million, the Authority made it clear that total investment should have been five times as high to meet the government's original expectations at the time of the passage of the Cable and Broadcasting Act 1984.[562]

Considering the small number of households subscribing to cable, cable television in Britain cannot be expected to represent a serious challenge to the traditional broadcasting system in the near future. The 1983 White Paper's strategy was to appease the proponents of public-service broadcasting, inter alia, by stressing this very fact. Having emphasized the government's commitment to the high programme standards of the public broadcasting system, the White Paper pointed out the government's »duty to

559 1987 Cable Authority Annual Report, *supra* note 512, at 11. The total number of homes passed was 1,190,000. *Id.* By early 1988 a little over 250,000 homes subscribed to cable television. However, only 40,000 subscribers were connected to the new broadband cable systems, while the rest subscribed to the old relay systems that were carrying new cable services. 16 franchises granted since 1983 had taken up services. Fin. Times, Feb. 20, 1988.
560 1987 Cable Authority Annual Report, *supra* note 512, at 12.
561 *Id.* at 2.
562 *Id.*

enable new technology to flourish and fulfil its potential unfettered by unnecessary restrictions.«[563] The arguments put forward by the government in the White Paper can be summarized briefly as follows: (1) cable systems need a significant time to develop before they can represent a true alternative to present television services in large parts of the country, thus leaving the broadcasting organizations with sufficient time to adjust to the new situation; (2) the public-service broadcasters start from a position of strength and thus have a competitive advantage over cable television; (3) the public broadcasters may participate in the exploitation of the new media, including cable and DBS, and can thus appropriate some of the advantages of these systems to themselves; and (4) the BBC will continue to be financed through the licence fee, while competition between cable and the ITV companies for advertising revenues will be mitigated by the requirement that cable may only carry as much advertising per hour on the channels as is allowed to the ITV and ILR companies.[564] The underlying conviction of the government was that while cable was still an infant industry, it represented no practical threat to the present broadcasting system. As long as no practical necessity existed, there was no need to redefine the basic concepts constitutive for the traditional British broadcasting system.[565] The rules applying to the traditional public broadcasting system thus more or less remained unchanged with the passage of the two fundamentally new pieces of legislation, the Cable and Broadcasting Act 1984 and the Telecommunications Act 1984.

B. Two Regulatory Schemes Applying to Cable Television

1. The Cable Authority and the Cable and Broadcasting Act 1984

The Cable and Broadcasting Act 1984 established the Cable Authority as a body corporate (section 1 and Schedule I) independent of the government and with the duty to discharge the functions listed in the Act, in particular, the issuance of licences. The Act mostly deals with the content-related aspects of cable network operation. The technical operation of the

563 1983 White Paper on Cable Systems, *supra* note 208, at para. 87.
564 *Id.* at paras. 89-90, 97.
565 This approach is well reflected in the following statement: »Whatever changes may be warranted in the longer term the Government believes that the introduction of cable in no way justifies any amendment at this stage of the duties and obligations of the public service broadcasting organizations.« *Id.* at para. 89.

systems is regulated in a telecommunications licence issued by the DTI and the Office of Telecommunications (OFTEL).

The creation of an independent body to supervise the development and execution of cable television in the United Kingdom was regarded by the government as necessary to ensure that the granting of licences to and the control of cable operators would be competent, efficient and objective. In light of the prognosis that due to the financial investments involved most cable systems would be factual (though not legal) monopolies, it was felt that special consideration should be given to these aspects of the licensing procedure, a function that up to that point had not been assigned to any governmental unit involved in cable franchising.[566] Also, certain aspects of the U.S. and Canadian experiences with cable television, which the Hunt Report had denounced, convinced the government that responsibility for cable franchising in the hands of local authorities was undesirable; the British government took it as a warning that the United States had experienced long delays in many franchising processes, unreasonable demands on the part of local authorities, and unfulfillable promises made by the franchise applicants.[567] Finally, since the interests of ITV broadcasters and cable operators could potentially conflict and programme standards differed, the IBA was deemed inadequate as the supervisory authority for both media systems, and a specialized authority for cable television – the Cable Authority – was favoured.[568]

The Cable Authority's structure is largely modelled on that of the IBA. It consists of a chairman, a deputy chairman and three to ten other members, all appointed by the Home Secretary for five-year terms.[569] The members are prohibited from simultaneously holding office as BBC Governors or as members of the IBA or the Welsh Authority. They are also precluded from being members of the House of Commons or the Northern Ireland Assembly. Any member of the Cable Authority who has a direct or indirect interest in any cable franchise to be granted has immediately to disclose this fact to the Authority and is thereafter disqualified from taking part in the franchising decision.[570] The members of the Authority appoint its officers and employees. Under the lead of a Director General, who is responsible for the running of the Authority, a Director of Services with

566 *Id.* at para. 40.
567 *Id.*
568 *Id.* at para. 41.
569 Cable and Broadcasting Act 1984, sec. 1(2),(3) and Schedule I. Presently, the Cable Authority has seven members altogether.
570 *Id.* at Schedule I.

experience in broadcasting takes care of programme control; there exists a Controller of Advertising, a Director of Finance and Operations, a Controller of Programmes and a Secretary to the Authority.[571]

When the Cable Authority was first set up in December 1984, it gave priority to the granting of franchises under the new 1984 legislation and advertised the first five areas for cable franchises in February 1985. In accordance with the market-led environment envisaged by the legislators, the Cable Authority usually leaves the identification of franchise areas to the market and then decides on the priorities to be set in the application processes. While the government had put a ceiling of 100,000 homes on the size of the franchise areas for the pilot projects,[572] the Cable Authority has set no maximum limit to the size of franchise areas but requires that each area be large enough to support some sort of local service, such as teletext or – preferably – video programmes. The largest area yet franchised is Edinburgh, whose grid can access 180,000 homes. Generally, franchise areas encompass between 70,000 and 130,000 homes.[573]

Licences from the Cable Authority are required for any »licensable« service, as defined by section 2(2) and (3) of the Cable and Broadcasting Act 1984. Any person running a licensable service without the necessary licence commits a criminal offence under section 3 of the Act. A licensable service means »a cable programme service which consists wholly or mainly in the sending by any person, by means of a telecommunication system (whether run by him or by any other person), of sounds or visual images or both.« Thus, the Cable Authority carries no statutory responsibility for the licensing of voice or data transmission services, which fall outside the definition. Such services need a licence under section 7 of the Telecommunications Act 1984. As has been pointed out earlier, falling outside the definition of a licensable service are teletext transmissions; this creates a regulatory gap between the control of teletext services provided by the broadcasters and those provided by cable operators, who are only subject to the general laws of the land.

The Cable and Broadcasting Act 1984 distinguishes between three basic kinds of licensable services, namely, »diffusion services,« »prescribed diffusion services« and »restricted services.« The latter refers to cable programme services »for reception, by whatever means, at a place in the

---

571 1987 Cable Authority Annual Report, *supra* note 512, at 6.
572 *See* 1983 White Paper on Cable Systems, *supra* note 208, at para. 246.
573 1987 Cable Authority Annual Report, *supra* note 512, at 16-19. In February 1988, the Cable Authority advertised the as-yet largest cable franchise: The cable contractor for Birmingham is to connect 400,000 homes. Fin. Times, Feb. 20, 1988.

United Kingdom for the purpose of their being presented there either to members of the public or to a group of persons some or all of whom do not have a business interest in hearing or seeing them« (section 2(2)(b)). Services falling under this narrow definition will represent only a small part of all licences granted by the Authority; educational organizations and similar institutions using cable programmes for instructions are expected to be typical applicants for such licences.

Most practical importance attaches to those systems defined as diffusion or prescribed diffusion services. A diffusion service is a cable programme service »for simultaneous reception, otherwise than by wireless telegraphy, in two or more dwelling houses in the United Kingdom.« A »prescribed diffusion service« is a diffusion service in which sound and television programmes are relayed directly to 10,000 or more homes (*compare* section 2(3)). Licence applications for these large-scale cable systems take preference over any licence applications for small-scale diffusion services. The legislative aim is to promote advanced cable technology capable of offering a great variety of services. In order to safeguard the development of large-scale wideband systems, the Act provides that the maximum licence period for any diffusion service is 8 years, as opposed to 15 years for prescribed diffusion services (*compare* section 4(4) of the Cable and Broadcasting Act 1984). This provision also serves to ensure that the licensing of smaller cable systems does not prejudice the promotion of more sophisticated systems.[574] In line with these policies, the Home Office, in granting licences for the 11 pilot projects in 1983, had also given priority to applications offering systems with advanced technology and a comprehensive range of programme services plus the capability for interactive services.[575] The 1983 Home Office Guidance Note had allowed for licence terms of 12 years. The telecommunications licence could be extended to 20 years if switches were installed. The licences for the pilot projects had provided that contract provisions would be modified and amended once the new legislation had been passed. This gave the Cable Authority and OFTEL a hold on these franchisees and enabled them to adjust the old licences to the terms imposed on wideband diffusion services licensed after the passage of the 1984 Acts. Also, the Cable Authority and OFTEL received jurisdiction over previously licensed cable systems generally.

---

574 *See* Cable Authority, Licensing of Cable Diffusion Services – Notes for the Guidance of Prospective Licensees 1 (May 1985) (hereafter cited as Cable Authority, 1985 Notes for Prospective Licensees).
575 *See* Home Office, Cable: Interim Licensing of Pilot Projects: Guidance Note 1 (July 15, 1983).

As has been mentioned in the context of freedom to broadcast, the Cable Authority has made it known that it does not envisage the granting of licences for prescribed diffusion services to any additional operators in an already cabled franchise area for the foreseeable future. Such systems will therefore at least enjoy a factual monopoly position.[576]

Special provisions apply to the licensing of prescribed diffusion services, such as the Authority's responsibility to call for competitive applications for such franchises, to publish information about the applicants, to ascertain and to take into account the opinions of the public in the respective licence areas and to encourage suggestions by members of the public in the franchise areas about the services that should be offered (section 5 of the Cable and Broadcasting Act 1984). However, public reaction to the first five franchised areas advertised by the Cable Authority was minimal, and the Authority received only a »handful« of letters from members of the public.[577]

With regard to those diffusion services not qualifying for the definition of large-scale wideband systems, a legal distinction is drawn between (a) systems, old or new, that only relay BBC and ITV broadcasting services, (b) Satellite Master Antenna Television (SMATV) systems distributed to between two and 10,000 premises, and (c) systems for domestic households (TVROs). Systems qualifying under (a), i.e., »classical« relay systems, are exempted from the licence requirements under both the Cable and Broadcasting Act 1984 and the Wireless Telegraphy Act 1949[578] and only need a licence under section 7 of the Telecommunications Act 1984 for signal transmission. The DTI has announced its intention to issue a class licence for all these systems, which would make individual authorization unnecessary.[579]

In May 1985, the government also eased the way for SMATV, small satellite reception systems aimed at transmitting television programmes from low-power satellites. Systems serving no more than one dwelling house or single set of premises (TVROs) were completely exempted from the licence requirements under the Telecommunications Act 1984 and the Cable and

---

576 Cable Authority, Guidance to Franchise Applicants para. 16 (March 1985).
577 Cable Authority, Annual Report and Accounts 6 (1986) (hereafter cited as 1986 Cable Authority Annual Report).
578 A licence under the Wireless Telegraphy Act 1949 is issued by the DTI. It is needed for apparatus receiving satellite transmissions. *See* Wireless Telegraphy Act 1949, sec. 1.
579 *See* Cable Authority, 1985 Notes for Prospective Licensees, *supra* note 574, at 2.

Broadcasting Act 1984 and are only licensed under the Wireless Telegraphy Act 1949 for the reception of low-power satellite transmissions.[580] About 2,500 TVRO licences had been granted by the DTI by mid-1987.[581] In addition, because of the size of the receiving dishes for TVROs, planning permission from local authorities may be required. If a system is designed for more than a single set of premises, however, it needs a licence under both 1984 Acts. The same is true for any upgraded relay systems. About 70 licences for SMATV and upgraded systems had been issued by the Cable Authority by mid-1987.[582]

The liberalization of SMATV particularly benefits hotels, pubs, clubs, hospitals and similar establishments, many of which may find the investment in the expensive satellite receiving dishes a viable service for customers.

Many of the initial licences seem to have been awarded to former Master Antenna Television (MATV) systems, which connect several television sets to one master antenna for the reception of terrestrial broadcasts. These systems have often been upgraded to become compatible with SMATV technology. Such conversions were expected to make up a large part of the initial SMATV market.[583] By November 1985, the Cable Authority had granted the first four licences to operators of larger SMATV systems, the largest licence serving an area of 10,000 homes in a town in Cheshire. Under the latter licence, cable programme channels were offered on an existing narrowband relay system.[584] In some of these cases, operators were allowed to discontinue the retransmission of the BBC and ITV programmes and to use the four- or six-channel capacity for the transmission of satellite television programmes, while subscribers were supplied with aerials for the reception of the terrestrial broadcasting channels.[585] All of these SMATV licences carry with them several restrictions designed to bring them in line with the overall cable television policies. The Cable Authority will only grant a SMATV licence in an area in which no licence for a prescribed diffusion service has already been granted or is being consid-

---

580 Department of Trade and Industry, Press Notice (May 23, 1985) (hereafter cited as DTI, Press Notice). *See also* Telecommunications Act 1984, sec. 6(2)(b), exempting the running without authorization by a person of a telecommunications system on a single set of premises from the statutory offence under sec. 5(1). *See also supra* at chapter I(C)(2).
581 Information provided to the author by Mr Jon Davey, Director General, Cable Authority.
582 *Id.*
583 Cable & Satellite Europe (June 1985).
584 Broadcast 13 (November 15, 1985).
585 1986 Cable Authority Annual Report, *supra* note 577, at 8.

ered.[586] This policy ensures that the wideband cable operator will face no competition from other systems operators and will be able to attract a maximum number of subscribers in the franchise area. However, TVROs do not fall under this restriction and may thus operate in the franchise area of a wideband cable system.[587] In order not to prejudice the franchising of any wideband cable system in any part of the country, SMATV licences are granted on rolling terms and are subject to termination with three years' notice.[588] Also, all SMATV operators have to observe the »must-carry« rule. It requires them to include for reception in the relevant licence area all BBC and ITV programmes broadcast plus the British DBS services, as soon as these become operational. While SMATV licensees are required not to cause any harmful interference to other users of the radio spectrum, they themselves receive no protection for their systems from radio interference from other sources,[589] a rule that underlines once again the conceptually preliminary nature of SMATV systems.

The rationale behind the liberalization of SMATV and TVROs primarily lies in its stimulating effect for the manufacturing industry producing satellite dishes and ancillary equipment. In fact, private satellite programme providers and equipment manufacturers were the most insistent lobbyists in support of the deregulation of SMATV.[590] Most of the satellite equipment manufacturers that had spoken out in favour of the measure were small, high-technology companies, whose innovative entrepreneurship the government meant to support. Since the attractiveness of cable services moreover depends greatly on the quality of the programmes shown, and quality programmes are expensive, the development of the cable television market is a direct function of the number of subscribers to such programmes. Deregulation of SMATV thus

---

586 Cable Authority, 1985 Notes for Prospective Licensees, *supra* note 574, at paras. 6 and 9. The Cable Authority's decision to ask the government to permit the broadcasting of cable television programmes by local multi-microwave distribution systems (MMDS) in cable franchise areas does not contradict its policy to reduce potential competition for broadband cable systems. On the contrary, since MMDS is capable of broadcasting between 10 and 12 television channels over a radius of several miles, it would enable new cable franchisees to distribute their programme services throughout their franchise areas before the laying of all cables would have been completed. With this capability, the Cable Authority expects to ease the ailing finanical difficulties of most cable operators and to reduce their high capital requirements. However, the Authority plans to ensure the imposition of time limits for the operation of MMDS in order not to discourage the speedy completion of the cable systems. *See* Fin. Times, Oct. 5, 1987.
587 *See* DTI, Press Notice, *supra* note 580.
588 1987 Cable Authority Annual Report, *supra* note 512, at 3-4.
589 Cable Authority, 1985 Notes for Prospective Licensees, *supra* note 574, at para. 4.
590 *See, e.g.*, Cable & Satellite Europe (June 1985).

represented a measure to encourage faster-growing audience sizes, particularly in the interim period until a considerable number of wideband cable systems have come into full operation.

Both the cable systems and the DBS lobbies were opposed to the liberalization of SMATV. The former feared competition with their systems, particularly if hotels and similar establishments could install their own systems in cable television franchise areas. The latter was concerned about the attractiveness of their future DBS services, if their potential viewers were given the right and the equipment to receive low-power satellite programmes. But general industrial-policy concerns aimed at stimulating the high-tech manufacturing industry outweighed the objections of the cable and DBS industries.

In evaluating the merits of a licence application, the Cable Authority is under a statutory obligation to take certain matters into account. Section 7 of the Cable and Broadcasting Act 1984 lists the relevant criteria as to programme matters in the following order: (1) range and diversity of programmes; (2) programmes originating within the EC and performed by EC nationals; (3) an increasing proportion of such programmes; (4) educational programmes, programmes with particular appeal to persons living in the franchise area, and programmes giving such persons an opportunity to participate therein; (5) programmes produced by persons other than the franchise holder or his associates; (6) programmes prepared by local voluntary associations with the licensee's assistance; (7) special programmes for the deaf; (8) the provision of related services. None of these aspects, including the proportion of non-EC programme material and local access programmes, represents any absolute requirement. They are only guidelines for the Cable Authority, with particular relevance in the decision-making process following the competitive bidding for a franchise area.

The natural-monopoly situation existing for cable television systems in the United Kingdom poses the question to what extent third parties have access to cable channels in order to provide programming. A cable operator holding a licence under the Cable and Broadcasting Act has the exclusive right to provide television services – subject, of course, to the must-carry rule, which ensures the access of the BBC, the relevant regional ITV operator and Channel 4 to the system. In its 1983 White Paper, the government explicitly rejected any proposal to reserve certain channels for community access, for example.[591] Instead, it decided that

---

591 1983 White Paper on Cable Systems, *supra* note 208, at para. 131.

the Cable Authority's obligation under section 7 of the Cable and Broadcasting Act 1984 to take account of the range and diversity of the envisaged services and of the plans for community programmes and local access set out in the franchise applications would suffice to ensure programme packages »in the best interests of the whole community.«[592]

But section 7 is a very weak instrument to enforce access by third parties to the programme channels. The provision merely represents a list of considerations relevant for judging the merits of a particular franchise application. It is not a compulsory catalogue of undertakings to be entered into by the applicant. It also gives no right to an individual to demand from the cable operator access to the system. It is up to the Cable Authority to ensure compliance with the legislative provision. But there is no guarantee that in cases of competitive bidding a candidate who intends to grant local access to cable programme channels will always be favoured over an applicant with no such intentions. If the Cable Authority grants a licence to a franchisee who undertakes to grant community or other general access to his channels, the Cable Authority can direct the cable operator to fulfill his promises.[593] Nevertheless, the cable operator is under no legal obligation to enter into such contractual obligations with the Cable Authority.

The Authority, acknowledging its statutory obligation to take into account any proposals for local programmes in a franchise application, has shown full understanding for the financial difficulties for operators to provide such services, particularly in the early stages of their operations:

> [T]here is a common view, which is shared by the Authority, that it is unrealistic to expect substantial amounts of money to be devoted to these services until the basis of a successful business has been established. The Authority hopes to see local services developing steadily, but this must be undertaken in a properly cautious way consistent with the need not to jeopardize the main business on which they will inevitably depend.[594]

The passage cited clearly reflects a view on the chances and capabilities of cable systems that is much more cautious and pessimistic than the view the government had expressed a few years earlier. It echoes the general disappointment over the willingness of the financial community to invest in cable television.

Under the existing financial constraints, local news programmes in the form

---

592 *Id.*; *see also* Cable and Broadcasting Act 1984, sec. 7(2).
593 *See* Cable and Broadcasting Act 1984, sec. 4(5),(6).
594 1986 Cable Authority Annual Report, *supra* note 577, at 19.

of text services are likely to find a viable market more easily than locally produced video (news) programmes. Of the eight, new broadband cable systems franchised since 1983 and in operation in 1987, five systems offer their own local television channel, with three of them producing the local programmes mostly themselves and the two others showing programmes under arrangements for community access. A sixth operator offers a locally produced Hindi cable radio channel, while most of the others offer local text services either exclusively or in connection with the local television services.[595] In one case, the text service was provided by a newspaper subsidiary.[596]

The right of cable operators to provide monopoly television services evidences that the government focussed on the stimulation of a wide range of programme services, but neglected considerations of freedom of communication – not only the right to receive, but also the right to impart, information.

Aside from the licensing of cable systems, the Cable Authority has to ensure that cable operators comply with the statutory requirements of the Cable and Broadcasting Act 1984 and the codes of conduct issued thereunder by the Authority (sections 10-14 of the Cable and Broadcasting Act 1984). These statutory and regulatory requirements relate to programme content, advertising, sponsorship, the protection of public-service broadcasting, and similar issues. Unlike the Broadcasting Act 1981, the Cable and Broadcasting Act 1984 establishes only a few positive requirements as to programme content and advertising. It sets certain minimum standards, which have only rudimentary resemblance with the detailed public-service obligations imposed on ITV contractors.

Section 10(1)(a) of the Cable and Broadcasting Act 1984 requires »that nothing [be] included in the programmes which offends against good taste or decency or is likely to encourage or incite to crime or to lead to disorder or to be offensive to public feeling.« While this provision copies the corresponding obligation imposed on ITV programme contractors by section 4(1)(a) of the Broadcasting Act 1981, most of the Act's other detailed programme-content provisions for public-service broadcasting are missing, namely, requirements for »proper proportions« of news programmes and minority programmes. Only with regard to »all news given (in whatever form) in programmes which originate in the United Kingdom«

595 1987 Cable Authority Annual Report, *supra* note 512, at 16-18, 21.
596 Information provided to the author by Mr Jon Davey, Director General, Cable Authority.

do the cable operators have to observe »due accuracy and impartiality« (section 10(1)(c)).

Instead of the public-service broadcasting obligation to observe »due impartiality« in all political matters, cable operators are only required not to give »undue prominence« in their programmes »to the views and opinions of particular persons or bodies on religious matters or matters of political or industrial controversy or relating to current public policy« and to exclude »all expressions of the views and opinions of the persons providing the service on religious matters or on matters (other than the provision of diffusion services) which are of political or industrial controversy or relate to current public policy« (section 11(3)). Undue prominence of political views is judged on the basis not of individual programmes but of the cable programme mix as a whole. Finally, the Cable Authority has drawn up a code relating to the showing of violence, particularly with respect to films likely to be watched by large numbers of children and to films appealing for donations (section 11(1)(a),(b)).[597] The code to be issued by the Cable Authority may also deal with »such other matters concerning standards and practice for programmes as the Authority may consider suitable for inclusion in the code« (section 11(1)(c)). The regulation evidences that with regard to cable and satellite television, the extent of government control of, and the programme vetting by, the regulatory institutions is diminishing. The diversity of potential programme sources places a factual limit on the extent of possible regulatory control. In particular, the Cable Authority has no monitoring procedures; its supervisory powers are reactive rather than preventive. Thus, the Authority is prepared, for example, to screen a controversial programme if it receives complaints by members of the public. But in the first two years covered by the Authority's annual reports, no public complaints had been received by the Authority.

In marked contrast to the ITV system, programme sponsorship on cable television is allowed, subject to the rules issued by the Authority in a code of conduct.[598] This code allows the underwriting of programmes, i.e., the

---

597 *See, e.g.*, Cable Authority, Cable Programme Services: Inclusion of Feature Films (November 1985) warning operators that »care and sensitivity is needed in deciding the time at which a film may be included in a cable programme service, bearing in mind that the BBFC's categories were accorded in the context of the control of the age of admission to cinemas and cannot be linked so effectively to the time at which children and young persons are likely to be watching television in the home.« These guidelines were of a preliminary nature. The final Code on Violence in Cable Programmes, which reflects the above-cited reasoning, is reprinted in 1986 Cable Authority Annual Report, *supra* note 577, at 33-34.

598 The Code of Practice on Programme Sponsorship is reprinted in 1987 Cable Authority Annual Report, *supra* note 512, at 4-5.

sponsoring, without editorial control, and commissioning of a programme, a method permitting the sponsor to exercise an influence over programme content and selection. Political organizations are totally prohibited from any kind of programme sponsorship, however. News and current-affairs programmes are, moreover, not able to be sponsored, unless the Authority gives special approval. In addition, cable operators may of course also carry general advertising on their channels, subject to specific content standards that for the most part are the same as those relating to advertising on ITV. One fundamental difference in the rules applying to ITV and to cable operators has to do with the Cable Authority's liberal view regarding the amount of advertising and the nature of advertising breaks permissible on cable programmes. This approach is well reflected in the following statement made by the Authority:

> The Authority came to the view that since cable was not designed as a public service, but was intended to found itself on a much more direct relationship between the service provider and the consumer, such matters as the scheduling of advertisements could be left to market forces to determine. The programme provider and cable operator were in the business of providing a service which consumers would be willing to buy, and in the circumstances it is inappropriate for the Authority to intervene to say whether frequent advertising breaks, or longer breaks less frequently, interfere with the quality of the service being provided.[599]

One restriction regarding the amount of advertising on cable channels is contained in section 12(3) of the Cable and Broadcasting Act 1984. It provides that a channel calculated to appeal to tastes and interests that are generally catered to by ITV may not carry more advertising than ITV is allowed to carry. Presently, the Cable Authority, after having consulted with the IBA, has made the determination that Sky Channel and Superchannel should fall under this restriction.[600] All other channels, including foreign and locally originated ones, may carry as much advertising as they please.

Under section 15 of the Cable and Broadcasting Act 1984, the Authority has the right to give directions to the cable operators ordering them to exclude any programme or advertisement from a licensed service. For the purpose of exercising its statutory functions, the Authority has the right to demand any relevant information from the cable operator (section 16). In

599 1986 Cable Authority Annual Report, *supra* note 577, at 17.
600 1987 Cable Authority Annual Report, *supra* note 512, at 6.

case of a violation of a licence obligation, the Authority is entitled to revoke the licence after having granted a reasonable opportunity to the cable operator to defend his case and after having consulted with the DTI and OFTEL on aspects concering the telecommunications licence (section 17). The power to revoke a licence extends to cases in which the cable operator fails to provide the services outlined in his franchise application.[601]

In addition to a licence under the Cable and Broadcasting Act 1984, a cable operator needs another licence for the technical operation of the cable system under the Telecommunications Act 1984.

2. *The Office of Telecommunications (OFTEL) and the Telecommunications Act 1984 in the Context of Cable Television*

The Telecommunications Act 1984 created OFTEL, a non-ministerial government department. This independent regulatory body is headed by a Director General of Telecommunications appointed by the Secretary of State of Trade and Industry for a five-year term (section 1 of the Telecommunications Act 1984). OFTEL's functions are set out in Parts I to III of the Telecommunications Act 1984. These sections regulate the provision of telecommunications services.[602]

Anybody running a telecommunications system needs a licence under section 7 of the Telecommunications Act 1984; without such licence, his activities constitute a criminal offence under section 5 of the Act. Since satellites operate from outside national territories and since other telecommunications systems may be located outside the United Kingdom, the definition of what constitutes a »telecommunication system« under the Act is designed to address possible jurisdictional difficulties.[603] Section 4(2) of the Act subjects to the Act all telecommunications apparatus situated in the United Kingdom that »(a) is connected to but not comprised in a telecommunication system; or (b) is connected to and comprised in a telecommunication system which extends beyond the United Kingdom.«

Section 7(1) provides that a licence may be granted by the Secretary of State of Trade and Industry after consultation with the Director General of OFTEL, by the Director General himself with the consent of the Secretary

---

601 *See* Cable Authority, 1985 Notes for Prospective Licensees, *supra* note 574, at para. 31.
602 According to sec. 4(1) of the Telecommunications Act 1984, a telecommunications service includes the conveyance, through the agency of electric, magnetic, electro-magnetic, electro-chemical or electro-mechanical energy, of speech, music and other sounds, and of visual images.
603 *See* Mostehar, *Satellite Communications*, 1986 LONGMAN INTELLIGENCE REPORTS 26.

194

of State, or under a general authorization from the DTI. So far, the DTI has retained the power to license telecommunications systems. This is probably due to the political implications involved in these decisions. But OFTEL expects to become responsible in due course for the granting of telecommunications licences, with the exception of those licences designating the network operator as a public telecommunications operator (PTO).

It is OFTEL's primary task to ensure that holders of telecommunications licences comply with their licence conditions. As a result of the abolition of BT's monopoly and the licensing of Mercury, OFTEL has from its start been particularly busy with the supervision of the proper transition of the old telecommunications structures into the new regulatory environment.[604] OFTEL holds a key position in the definition and arrangement of the relationship between cable operators and the basic network operators BT and Mercury. It is also responsible for licence amendments. This is done either by agreement with the licence holder (section 12 of the Act) or, failing that, by reference to the Monopolies and Mergers Commission (MMC) under section 13. The MMC has to decide whether the matters referred to it relating to the running of a telecommunications system or the supply of telecommunications apparatus operate, or may be expected to operate, against the public interest and if so whether these negative effects could be remedied by a modification of the licence conditions. The public-interest concept as used in this context has to be interpreted in light of the catalogue of the general duties of the Secretary of State and the Director of OFTEL as specified in section 3 of the Act.[605]

Section 3 represents the general framework of British telecommunications policy. It requires the DTI and OFTEL to ensure: (1) the satisfaction by telecommunications service providers of all reasonable demand, including emergency services, public call-box services, directory information services, maritime services and services in rural areas; (2) efficient financial resources on the part of the service providers; (3) the promotion of the interests of consumers and purchasers in the United Kingdom with respect to the prices charged and the quality and variety of services and apparatus provided; (4) the maintenance and promotion of effective competition between persons engaged in commercial activities connected with telecommunications in the United Kingdom; (5) the encouragement of

604 Information provided to the author by Mr Warlow, OFTEL.
605 See Telecommunications Act 1984, sec. 13(8).

efficiency and economy on the part of such persons; (6) the promotion of research into, and the development and use of, new techniques by such persons; (7) the international competitiveness of U.K. producers of telecommunications equipment.

The first two criteria are to take preference over all other considerations.[606] In particular, the protection of consumers plays a crucial role in OFTEL's functions. This is emphasized by its task to investigate complaints by users of telecommunications systems and apparatus (section 49). OFTEL is obligated to take appropriate action in relevant cases in the interest of the complainants. The complaints procedure is an informal one. Consumers may directly address themselves to OFTEL, but they are advised first to contact the provider of the service and, as a next step, to seek help from the local Posts and Telecommunications Advisory Committees (PATACs).[607] About 170 of these voluntary bodies exist throughout the United Kingdom, representing the interests of consumers of telecommunications services in their respective areas. Consumers may also turn to the courts to remedy any personal negative effects suffered from a violation of obligations by the systems operator. Regional advisory bodies additionally represent the interests of consumers vis-à-vis OFTEL (section 54(1),(2)). Also, the Director General has set up a special advisory committee representing the interests of small businesses as users and purchasers of telecommunications apparatus and as suppliers of services and equipment to the telecommunications industry.[608] Another advisory committee deals with matters affecting disabled and elderly people.[609] Representation of the public is thus institutionalized by means of formal committees with advisory functions. As has been demonstrated earlier, this is a favourite British solution to the problem of how to check the exercise of power by public institutions in the communications sector. At the same time it is an efficient way to channel any potential public criticism into institutional paths.

For the purpose of specifying licence terms or of enforcing the observance of licence conditions, the Director General has extensive order-making powers under the Act (section 7(6)). Enforcement of an order necessitates his taking civil action in the courts.

Apparently, the prevailing view in both government and Parliament was

---

606 Cable Authority, 1985 Notes for Prospective Licensees, *supra* note 574, at Part 3, para. 8.
607 OFTEL, A Guide to the Office of Telecommunications (1985).
608 *See* Telecommunications Act 1984, sec. 54(4)(a); OFTEL, BACT – The Advisory Committee on Telecommunications for Small Businesses (December 1986).
609 *See* Telecommunications Act 1984, sec. 54(4)(b); OFTEL, DIEL – The Advisory Committee on Telecommunications for Disabled and Elderly People (October 1985).

that the liberalization of the telecommunications sector demanded the establishment of a new and specialized regulatory agency. This institution was to be vested with special regulatory powers and was to have particularly close ties to the telecommunications industry as well as to consumers. The setting apart of the new regulatory authority from the remaining government bureaucracy emphasized the government's determination to encourage the development of the telecommunications industry based on market stimulation rather than on centralized planning. Still, the Department of Trade and Industry retained supervisory powers. This evidences the cautious character of the new policies and the residual hesitance to cast off completely long-established organizational structures.

A licence to run a telecommunications system specifies a number of matters, such as: the conditions regulating the means of running the system; the connections of the system to other specified telecommunications systems or apparatus; the telecommunications services to be provided by the network operator; and any other conditions that appear to the DTI or OFTEL to be requisite or expedient in light of their duties under section 3 of the Act (section 7(4),(5)).

Special obligations arise in connection with the designation of a cable system as a public telecommunications system and the operator as a PTO (section 9). All new wideband cable systems are expected to receive this designation. A cable operator that is also a designated PTO closely resembles the major telecommunications network providers BT and Mercury, and his licence is modelled on the terms of the latter licences.[610] The Telecommunications Code under Schedule 2 of the Telecommunications Act 1984 applies to all PTOs (section 10), including cable operators. The Code confers special powers upon a PTO, for example, the power to acquire land compulsorily, to do necessary streetwork, and similar matters. In return for the conveyance of these powers, the PTO undertakes special obligations relating to both consumers and potential competitors for the provision of services (*see* section 8). For example, cable system operators with a PTO designation have to publish codes of practice for consumers, informing them of charges and terms and conditions for the reception of telecommunications services. In case the PTO additionally provides voice telephony services, it is also required to establish free directory inquiry services for the blind and other disabled persons (section 8(2),(3)).

---

610 *See* OFTEL, PTO Contract Terms and Conditions – A Consultative Document 1 (1987).

The DTI intends to include in all licences for cable operators with a PTO designation »conditions which will provide for interconnection of major systems so as to ensure that British Telecom subscribers can send messages to Mercury customers and so on.«[611] Apart from the duty to connect certain other telecommunications systems to its own system, a PTO may be required to carry on its system services provided by others or by a cable operator with whom it cooperates. In these cases, a PTO may not show undue preference for or undue discrimination against the outside service providers and against consumers wishing to receive the services. This issue concerns the right of access of third parties for the provision of tele-communications services other than cable programme services.

Section 8(1)(b),(c) of the Act deals with certain special conditions to be in-cluded in a cable network operator's licence. The provision requires it to (1) connect to its network any other telecommunications system and apparatus specified in its licence and (2) permit any telecommunications system operator connected to the cable system to provide via the cable system those services to consumers permitted in its licence. Alternative (1) may, for example, apply to private branch systems in office blocks. If an operator of such a system re-quests the cable operator to connect his system, the latter is under an obliga-tion to reach an agreement over the connection of the two systems. Failing that, the Director General of OFTEL will define the terms and conditions for the interconnection.[612] In addition, a relevant licence provision directs the ca-ble network operator to allow any operator of a telecommunications system connected with a cable system to offer services not falling within the section 4(3) definition of telecommunications. This condition serves to ensure that third parties have the possibility to provide value-added data services (VADS), like banking or information services, over the cable system.[613] How-ever, telecommunications licences also contain an escape clause in favour of the cable network operator, whose own business interests may be damaged by the competitive VADS: »[T]he obligation does not arise where he [i.e., the ca-ble operator] thinks that allowing someone else to provide services in this way would so interfere with his own plans as to impede the sound commercial de-velopment of the cable system.«[614]

The original policy of providing a right of access for VADS as a general

---

611 Cable Authority, 1985 Notes for Prospective Licensees, *supra* note 574, at Part 3, para. 14.
612 *See id.* at Annex A (Structure of the Draft Telecommunications Licence for Cable Systems), Condition 8.
613 *Id.* at Condition 10.
614 *Id.*

rule and employing the escape clause as an exception has meanwhile been reversed. Existing cable franchisees insisted to the government that the viability of their operations depended on their right to enter into exclusive arrangements with banks, mail-order companies and the like. The government, faced with the greatly disappointing development of cable systems, accepted this view.[615] As a result, cable operators now may claim a monopoly for the provision not only of entertainment services but also of VADS. The policy change may be explained by the government's expectation that the exclusivity rights conferred upon cable operators would entice more potential investors to apply for cable franchises. In July 1987, after 17 months during which no franchise area had been advertised at all, the Cable Authority advertised the first two new franchises. At this point, the Director General of the Cable Authority expressed his belief that in the near future a considerable rise in the number of franchise applications could be expected because the interest of investors had shifted to some degree from providing entertainment programmes to providing VADS.

At this stage of the development of British cable systems, it appears that the political and economic concession the government has been willing to make to spread cable in Great Britain was the waiver of its original demand that cable systems foster a lively competition for VADS. Considering that the promotion of competition for the provision of value-added services had once been at the heart of the government's telecommunications policy, this waiver represents an admission of the failure of the original policy approach. Curtailing competition in cable networks is the price the government pays for its determination not to spend any public money on cable projects. This is complemented by the Cable Authority's declared policy to refrain as a matter of practice from granting additional cable franchises in already cabled areas and thus to guarantee factual monopolies.

The only exception to the policy of no governmental aid for cable systems has been a parliamentary grant of £ 5 million over five years to encourage the introduction of novel forms of interactive services on broadband cable systems, like common alarm systems. Depending on the degree of novelty involved, cable operators can receive funding for up to 50 per cent of the costs for introducing such a service.[616] But aside from this one-time grant, costly cable technology has to be privately financed. Since financing arrangements with European banks and other European investors have

---

615 Information provided to the author by Mr Jon Davey, Director General, Cable Authority.
616 Information provided to the author by Mr Warlow, OFTEL.

proven to be extremely difficult to achieve, it comes as no surprise that the Cable Authority has strongly spoken out in favour of abolishing the nationality requirement of section 8(1)(a),(b) of the Cable and Broadcasting Act 1984, which prohibits the granting of a franchise to any non-EC applicant. The Authority would welcome the interest that particularly North American investors have shown in the British cable market.[617]

The subscription fees charged to consumers presently are left to the discretion of the cable operator and are to be regulated by market forces.[618] In the long run, however, price regulation by the market will only work if systems operators are required to grant access to their systems to all kinds of service providers (including cable programme suppliers), who may then compete with each other on the systems.

While the Cable Authority will grant licences under the Cable and Broadcasting Act 1984 for a period of 15 years from the start of the services on the system (with 8-year renewal periods following a readvertising of the franchise), the DTI licences will be 15 years for non-PTO licences and 23 years for the most sophisticated systems.

3. *Convergence Leading to Institutional Frictions*

The dual character of cable systems, in which elements of conduit and content converge, necessitates the close coordination of the policies and individual actions of the various regulatory authorities responsible for the systems. The 1984 enactments make explicit provision for a number of such joint procedures. But as has rightfully been pointed out, the existence of a multitude of institutions involved in the franchising and supervision of cable television in the United Kingdom is likely to lead to institutional frictions capable of frustrating the liberalization of the telecommunications market.[619]

In addition to the newly created regulatory bodies OFTEL and the Cable Authority, the DTI and the Home Office have retained controlling powers. While the two ministerial departments may want to put into effect their own departmental policies through the Cable Authority and OFTEL respectively, the different regulatory regimes under which both supervisory

---

617 Information provided to the author by Mr Jon Davey, Director General, Cable Authority.
618 *Id.*
619 *See, e.g.*, Bruce, Cunard & Director, *Country Report: United Kingdom*, in II REPORT OF THE STUDY OF TELECOMMUNICATIONS STRUCTURES. FROM TELECOMMUNICATIONS TO ELECTRONIC SERVICES. A GLOBAL SPECTRUM OF DEFINITIONS, BOUNDARY LINES AND STRUCTURES 90-91 (International Institute of Communications 1985) (hereafter, Bruce, et al.).

bodies are set up bear inherent policy conflicts. By law, the Cable Authority and OFTEL are required to coordinate their licensing procedures. The applicant for a cable television franchise submits his application for both licences to the Cable Authority, which then has to consult with the DTI, as the department responsible for the granting of the tele-communications licence, and OFTEL with regard to the merits of the applicant (*see* section 6(2)(a) of the Cable and Broadcasting Act 1984 and section 7(10A) of the Telecommunications Act 1984). While each regulatory body has to examine the application on the basis of its respective enabling Act, the Cable Authority's responsibility is fully aimed at the promotion of cable television, while OFTEL's responsibilities also include the furtherance of common carriers, such as BT and Mercury.

To the extent that cable applicants may want to offer interactive and value-added services, they will directly compete with BT and Mercury. The potential conflicts of interest between the general network providers and cable operators will have to be decided by the DTI and OFTEL as the responsible licensing authorities. There has already been some speculation whether OFTEL, on occasion, might not side with the general PTOs against the cable industry. If cable television operators needed the pro-vision of additional VADS in order to guarantee the financial viability of their services as a whole, the Cable Authority would certainly strongly favour such plans; however, if this were likely to result in a serious loss of customers to BT and Mercury, OFTEL might refuse the licences need-ed.[620]

OFTEL's broad range of activities also requires it to set priorities as to what issues will receive most careful scrutiny.[621] Depending on OFTEL's involvement with BT and Mercury, cable operators' concerns might not always appear to OFTEL to be of primary importance.

OFTEL, with its far-reaching responsibilities for the protection of consumer interests, has been given certain related responsibilities regulated under the Fair Trading Act 1973[622] and the Competition Act 1980.[623] According to section 50(1) of the Telecommunications Act 1984, the Director General of Fair Trading may request the Director General of OFTEL to exercise the functions of the former under Part III of the Fair Trading Act 1973 »so far as relating to courses of conduct which are or may be

---

620 *See, e.g.*, A. HEUERMANN & H. NEUMANN, DIE LIBERALISIERUNG DES BRITISCHEN TELEKOMMUNIKATIONSMARKTES 284 (1985).
621 Bruce, et al., *supra* note 619, at 98.
622 Fair Trading Act 1973 (c.41).
623 Competition Act 1980 (c.21).

detrimental to the interests of consumers of telecommunication services or telecommunication apparatus, whether those interests are economic or interests in respect of health, safety or other matters.« Part III of the Fair Trading Act 1973 authorizes the Director of Fair Trading to take certain actions against any person carrying on a business who has embarked on a course of conduct detrimental to the interests of consumers. In such cases, the Director has to use his best endeavours to get a written assurance from the person to the effect that the conduct complained of will cease (section 34(1) Fair Trading Act 1973). If the requested assurance is neither given nor, if given, observed, then the Director may bring proceedings against that person before the Restrictive Practices Court (section 35 of the Act). The Court in turn can order the person to cease with the objectionable behaviour. These functions of negotiating with a service provider over an assurance, and, failing that, of initiating the procedures before the Court may be, but do not have to be, delegated by the Office of Fair Trading (OFT) to OFTEL, either generally or in particular cases. In other cases, OFTEL assists and advises OFT on certain matters. For example, when BT wanted to buy a 51-percent stake in the Canadian telecommunications manufacturer Mitel, it needed to negotiate with OFT over the precise terms of the conditions for the takeover. In setting the legal requirements to be met by BT, OFT worked closely with OFTEL.[624]

The question may be posed as to which authority would be responsible to consider the practices of a cable operator unfairly treating consumers with regard to the provision of television programmes. Such behaviour could, for example, relate to discriminatory pricing, linked sales of programmes and decoders, and similar matters. The broad term »telecommunication service« as used in section 7 of the Telecommunications Act 1984 encompasses in addition to general network services and VADS the provision of radio and television programmes (section 4(3),(1)(a),(b) of the Telecommunications Act 1984). In principle, the DTI, OFTEL and OFT thus enjoy jurisdiction over these services. Yet the Cable Authority, too, is committed to the protection of consumer interests. While the Cable and Broadcasting Act 1984 does not speak of »consumer interests,« section 7(2)(d) of the Act, detailing the matters to be taken into account by the Cable Authority in the franchising process, requires the Authority to give due regard to the inclusion of »programmes calculated to appeal specially to the taste and outlook of persons living in the area and programmes in which such persons are given an opportunity to participate.«

624 *See* Fin. Times, Jan. 28, 1986; Jan. 30, 1986.

Section 7(2) of the Cable and Broadcasting Act 1984 implies that the Cable Authority bears the sole responsibility for programme content. If a cable programme licence condition required a cable operator to provide certain programmes in the interest of particular consumer groups, only the Cable Authority could enforce compliance with the condition. On the other hand, if the provision of such services violated the interest of consumers in economic, safety or health aspects, OFT or OFTEL would be competent to take appropriate action.

But the Cable Authority is not only the »moral watchdog« over programme services; it is also closely involved in the business operation of a cable operator. Under section 8 of the Cable and Broadcasting Act 1984, the Authority is responsible for the enforcement of ownership restrictions imposed by the Act. This responsibility potentially conflicts with section 50(2) of the Telecommunications Act 1984, which requires the Director General of OFTEL to exercise certain other functions under the Fair Trading Act 1973 concurrently with the Director General of OFT. According to the relevant provisions, OFTEL may require any person supplying telecommunications services to furnish to the Director any business information necessary, if the Director has grounds for believing that a monopoly situation exists or may exist in relation to commercial activities connected with telecommunications. If it then appears to the Director that a monopoly situation exists or may exist in the supply of goods or services of any description, he may make a monopoly reference to the Monopolies and Mergers Commission (section 50(1) of the Fair Trading Act 1973). The MMC will then issue a report determining whether a monopoly situation exists and, if so, whether it operates, or may be expected to operate, against the public interest (section 54 of the Fair Trading Act 1973). The report may recommend actions to be taken in order to remedy the situation, in which case the Secretary of State may ask the Director to request an undertaking from the enterprise concerned (section 88(1) of the Fair Trading Act 1979). The Secretary of State may also make an order prohibiting the objectionable practice or remedying its adverse effects (*see* sections 88(3), 56, 73 of the Fair Trading Act 1973). The Cable Authority's powers over a cable contractor's ownership structure thus overlap with OFTEL's and OFT's powers relating to the operator's commercial activities; the implications of these regulatory peculiarities cannot as yet be assessed.

Finally, section 50(3) of the Telecommunications Act 1984 gives the Director General of OFTEL the responsibility of investigating anti-competitive practices under sections 2 to 10 and 16 of the Competition Act 1980 »so far as relating to courses of conduct which have or are intended to have or are likely to have the effect of restricting, distorting or preventing competition in connection with the production, supply or acquisition of telecommunication apparatus or the supply or securing of telecommunication services.« This investigative procedure closely follows the mechanisms described above in the context of the Fair Trading Act 1973 and includes a reference to the MMC in relevant cases. The Director of OFTEL carries out the functions under the Competition Act 1980 in concurrence with the Director of OFT. Each Director is obligated to exercise his authority under section 50(2) and (3) of the Telecommunications Act 1984 only after having consulted with the other Director. All in all, there exist at least five institutions concerned with consumer protection and enforcement of competition laws: the Cable Authority, OFTEL, OFT, the Restrictive Practices Court, the MMC, and to some extent the Home Office and the DTI.

These examples evidence the intricate intertwining of responsibilities of the Cable Authority, OFTEL and OFT. The latter two, on the one hand, and OFTEL and the Cable Authority, on the other hand, will have to develop particularly close working relationships. A regulatory environment charging a multitude of institutions with the responsibilities for various facets of consumer protection and competition risks serious institutional frictions detrimental to the legislative aim of liberalizing both the broadcasting and the telecommunications markets. The future will show whether these concerns are well-founded.

C. *Transition from Network Providers to Information Providers and Vice Versa*

1. *New Roles for British Telecom and Mercury Communications*

Following the development of digital techniques and microchips and as a consequence of the rapidly growing demand for data storage and access to information stored in remote computer systems, the »plain old telephone« network of the Post Office was gradually restructured to provide voice as well as data services and technically can now even carry television programmes.[625] Similarly, the wideband cable system operators with a PTO designation responsible for the programme supply as well as for the provision of VADS and even voice telephony services thus are the most prominent examples of the progressing extent of convergence of conduit and content in cable television technology.

In the old days, the Post Office served solely as a common carrier for television programmes relayed for the benefit of the BBC and the IBA. Unlike today's wideband cable systems, this service necessitated special cables unrelated to the general telephone network, because the early telephone networks were technically unsuited for signal transmissions of a different kind.[626] The old technologies also allowed programme links via microwave transmissions. The IBA and the BBC have made extensive use of BT's services in this respect. BT has leased the links to the broadcasting organizations both for the dissemination of programmes from the studios to the broadcasting transmitters and for the connection of remote studios and outside broadcast sites to the central control rooms.[627] Until 1981, when BT assumed its duties, the Post Office had been engaged in the setting up of programme links from the beginnings of sound and television broadcasting. A 1974 Post Office study stated that the Post Office network of permanent programme circuit links included 15,000 cct/km of vision links and 59,200 cct/km of long-distance sound programme links, this representing the overwhelming majority of all vision and sound programme circuits then existing in the United Kingdom.[628]

Until 1984, when BT lost its exclusive privilege to provide telecommunications services, the Broadcasting Act 1981 had explicitly authorized the IBA to take care of the distribution of programmes from broadcast relay stations in ac-

625 *See* Schnurr, *supra* note 517, at 538-39. The Post Office and its successor BT seized the business opportunities connected with data processing and storage. The interactive information service Prestel, offered by BT, is only one example of the network provider's extended activities. These activities also encompass letter-processing facilities for customers, management and calculation of business accounts and payrolls, and the like. *Id.* at 541.

626 *Id.* at 538.

627 A complete list of all vision- and sound-link facilities existing in the United Kingdom in 1982 is contained in Schedule IV of the Television Contract, *supra* note 349.

628 Post Office Telecommunications, Evidence to the Government Inquiry into the Future of Broadcasting para. 1.3 (1974). In exceptional cases where a television broadcasting transmitter is remote from the Post Office microwave network and cannot directly receive the programmes from a main transmitter, the IBA and the BBC were allowed to provide their own microwave links between the relay broadcasting transmitter and the point where the main broadcast transmitting station could be received. *Id.* In April 1988, the BBC threatened to set up a BBC-run telecommunications system unless BT agreed to lower substantially its charges for the use of its cable and microwave links by the BBC. The Times, Apr. 2, 1988.

cordance with arrangements made for this purpose with BT.[629] Under the initially reformed legal regime, however, the Authority had the power to make such arrangements with »operators of telecommunications code systems,« which thus acknowledged the introduction of competition in this industry sector.[630]

As regards cable television, the Post Office seized the opportunity to extend its operation into the new medium starting with the first experimental cable television licences granted in the 1970s. It became the licensed operator for the community television service in Milton Keynes; a separate company acted as the programme supplier.[631] The Post Office's and, later, BT's exclusive involvement in the cable system was for a number of years characterized by their purely *technical* operation. BT acquired interests in a number of the large cable franchises granted in the early 1980s and has an interest in four of the eleven new multichannel cable networks, including a majority stake in Coventry Cable and 100-percent ownership of Swindon Cable.[632] Mercury, BT's only licensed competitor for general network services, proceeded in a similar way but on a much smaller scale. It is a founding shareholder of East London Telecommunications (ELT), the cable company holding the franchise for parts of the City of London. It also has a stake in Cable Camden, the franchisee for Camden in London.[633]

BT's involvement in the local cable franchises to some degree runs counter to the government's policy of promoting competition in telecommunications wherever possible. But under the assumption that competition in cable network services on the local level might never become viable, Mr Bryan Carsberg, the first Director General of OFTEL, made it known as early as 1985 that BT's participation in cable television ventures might have to be encouraged despite the negative effects on competition.[634] Presently, the government's policy is that BT's en-

---

629 Broadcasting Act 1981, sec. 3(1)(c). *See also* British Telecommunications Act 1981 (c.38): Under section 15 of this Act, the Secretary of State had the power to grant telecommunications licences to other persons without infringing upon BT's exclusive privilege. In such cases, he had to consult with BT prior to the granting of a licence. He could also order or authorize BT to grant licences to specific persons.

630 Broadcasting Act 1981, sec. 3(1)(c), *as amended by* Telecommunciations Act 1984, Schedule IV, para. 81(a). The amendment was superceded, however, by the Cable and Broadcasting Act 1984, sec. 57(1), Schedule V, para. 40(1).

631 T. HOLLINS, *supra* note 168, at 48 (Table II); J. HEYN, *supra* note 214, at 224-27.

632 Fin. Times, Apr. 29, 1986. *See also* 1987 Cable Authority Annual Report, *supra* note 512, at 16-18.

633 Fin. Times, Feb. 6, 1986; Sept. 18, 1986.

634 *See* Williamson, *Cable and DBS Industries in a State of Disarray*, Telephony, May 27, 1985, at 16.

gagement in cable should be limited to one-third of the total market share.[635] In view of BT's already existing engagement in wideband cable franchises, the Cable Authority thus does not expect to grant any new franchises to BT in the near future.

As a measure to safeguard competition, BT has been required to operate its cable franchises through a separate subsidiary operating at arms length.[636] For the same reason, both BT and Mercury are prohibited from using their basic telecommunications systems for the transmission of entertainment programmes to private homes.[637]

As stated earlier, BT had originally resigned itself to the role of a mere network provider and had left the programming supply to others. An example for such an arrangement is Westminster Cable, the company holding the cable franchise for the City of Westminster. BT and Westminster Cable jointly hold the telecommunications licence. Under a commercial agreement with Westminster Cable, BT plans, constructs and maintains the cable system.[638]

But before long, BT began to engage in the programme supply market as well. BT justified its new programme supply ventures with the argument that the great financial difficulties encountered by most cable systems operators forced it to look for additional revenue sources.[639] Schnurr,[640] for instance, has suggested that information market value is proportional to the bandwidth required to contain that information. On this basis, he advanced the proposition that the provision of video information by the network provider could generate revenue on an impressive scale. Thus, BT became a substantial shareholder in Home Video Channel (HVC), a company delivering video cassettes to cable operators. In August 1986, BT also launched a similarly operating, but alternative, premium film channel, Star Channel, for cable television systems, reaching agreement with the U.S. film studios MGM/UA, Paramount and Universal over the supply of films for

---

635 Information provided to the author by Mr Jon Davey, Director General, Cable Authority, and Mr Warlow, OFTEL.

636 *See* Department of Trade and Industry, The Development of U.K. Communications Systems. Discussion Document 3 (Apr. 9, 1987) (hereafter cited as DTI, 1987 Discussion Document). The subsidiary mainly engaged in the cable ventures is Broadband Ventures Ltd.

637 *Id.* at 4.

638 Westminster Cable Television, unpublished company profile, dated Mar. 11, 1985.

639 *See, e.g.*, Cable & Satellite News, Apr. 19, 1985. In 1986 a sharp rise in the penetration rate, i.e., the percentage of homes passed by cable that actually subscribed to its services, from 14.5 per cent to 16 per cent gave new hopes to the ailing industry that British cable television might offer certain investment prospects despite initial setbacks. Fin. Times, Sept. 11, 1986.

640 Schnurr, *supra* note 517, at 542.

the channel.[641] Shortly after Star Channel had begun operations, it merged with the movie channel Premiere, with the Mirror Group Newspapers as majority partners, and Home Video Channel as part of a restructuring of the satellite television supply industry.[642] In March 1986, BT also acquired a one-third stake in Children's Channel, a low-power satellite television channel aimed at cable systems.[643] In mid-1987, BT entered into a joint venture with Robert Maxwell's Mirror Group Newspapers and an American company, Viacom International, for the provision of a new music channel, »MTV,« to be distributed via the INTELSAT V satellite to cable systems in Europe. BT holds a 25-percent stake in the channel.[644]

BT's engagement in the satellite television business is particularly problematic, because the corporation – together with Mercury – continues to hold the monopoly for the provision of the uplink facilities to the satellites. With respect to the satellite television channels operating from the United Kingdom, BT thus serves as the common carrier for signal transmission. For this purpose, BT has entered into commercial agreements with the satellite television companies, and it leases frequencies on INTELSAT and EUTELSAT satellites to the programme providers; BT in turn leases these frequencies from the international satellite organizations.[645] BT is the United Kingdom signatory to both the International Telecommunications Satellite Organisation (INTELSAT)[646] and the European Telecommunications Satellite Organisation (EUTELSAT).[647] BT, with a 10.7-percent stake, is the second largest shareholder in INTELSAT.[648] BT has made use of INTELSAT's offer to lease television capacity to its members on a long-term, full-time basis. During the past few years, possibilities to lease such channels subject to flexible conditions have even in-

641 Fin. Times, Apr. 29, 1986.
642 1987 Cable Authority Annual Report, *supra* note 512, at 20.
643 1986 Cable Authority Annual Report, *supra* note 577, at 14.
644 1987(8) MEDIEN BULLETIN 37.
645 Ford, *Bringing the World to Your Door: The Role of British Telecom*, 4 INTERMEDIA No. 2 40, 42 (1986).
646 Founded in 1964, INTELSAT is an international consortium with 110 member states. These countries have to be also members of the ITU. With 16 satellites presently in operation, INTELSAT runs the world's most extensive global satellite network and transmits telephone calls as well as data services and television programmes to all parts of the world. *See* Pelton, *INTELSAT: Global Telecommunications for the 21st. Century*, 4 INTERMEDIA No. 4/5 52 (1986).
647 EUTELSAT is an organization founded in 1977 by 20 European PTOs for the purpose of achieving greater independence from the INTELSAT system for EC member states. The European Space Agency (ESA), to which the United Kingdom is also a party, surveys the operation of EUTELSAT's satellites. *See* Hardman, *Into the Future with EUTELSAT*, 4 INTERMEDIA No. 4/5 59 (1986).
648 Ford, *supra* note 645, at 40.

creased due to considerable spare capacity on the INTELSAT system.[649] Similarly, BT has leased spare capacities on ECS satellites set up by EUTELSAT. In 1983, for example, Sky Channel negotiated a three-year agreement with BT over the lease of one channel on the ECS 1 satellite. Under the contract, Sky Channel paid an uplink and a downlink fee to BT, which in turn passed the downlink fee on to EUTELSAT.[650]

In March 1987, BT entered into a joint-venture agreement with the private company Société Européen des Satellites (SES) for the lease of the 16 satellite channels available on the Luxembourgian medium-power satellite Astra, which was launched successfully at the end of 1987. Under the terms of the contract, to market eleven of Astra's sixteen channels BT will lease the necessary transponders and then enter into leases with satellite television companies located in the United Kingdom.[651] The satellite's footprint covers central Europe, from Madrid in the West to Berlin in the East, and from Great Britain (without Scotland) in the North to central Italy in the South. In contrast to signals transmitted from low-power satellites, Astra's signals can be received by relatively small dish antennae of sizes between 85 and 96 centimeters in diameter. With slightly larger dishes, the signals can even be received in all of Western Europe and parts of Eastern Europe. Despite its signal strength, the satellite has been registered with the ITU as a communications satellite.

The Astra agreement secures BT's dominant position as a common carrier for satellite services. This position could be challenged by privately operated satellite transponder service providers, such as SES, a company licensed by Luxembourg. But the era of private competition to the INTELSAT and EUTELSAT systems is only gradually coming into existence, and Astra presently represents the most important private project in this respect. With the joint-venture agreement, BT has probably cemented its common-carrier monopoly for the near future.[652]

---

649 *See* Wall Street Journal, Sept. 16, 1985.
650 Information provided to the author by Mr Heath, Sky Channel Network Marketing Manager.
651 Neue Zürcher Zeitung, Mar. 19, 1987; The Times, Dec. 2, 1987.
652 In early 1988, BT's and Mercury's duopoly position on satellite uplinks was indeed challenged by the U.S. company Pan American Satellite of Connecticut (PanAmSat), a private company planning to launch the first intercontinental telecommunications satellite independent of the IN-TELSAT and EUTELSAT systems. PanAmSat, having failed to reach an agreement with either BT or Mercury to link it with British customers, engaged the support of the U.S. government in an attempt to put pressure on the British government to liberalize the legal regime governing satellite communications in the United Kingdom. OFTEL eventually ruled that BT could not boycott PanAmSat's operations. Fin. Times, Mar. 23, 1988. OFTEL's decision may have been

BT's engagement in the programme supply side evidences that the convergence of conduit and content has spread from the cable television medium to satellite services. Current U.K. legislation puts no ceiling on BT's permissible investment in satellite programme providers. Before 1984, the Home Office could have made use of section 6(6)(b) of the British Telecommunications Act 1981[653] if it had felt that BT's engagement in the programme supply side was contrary to the public interest. The provision vaguely stated that the Home Secretary had the power to direct BT to dispose of any of its assets in another company. Absent any such veto by the government, BT's various activities in satellite services create the danger of severe market distortions.

In addition to its monopoly on the uplink facilities, which it shares only with Mercury, BT is also planning to enter into the market for the reception of satellite television programmes, i.e., the SMATV market. Thorn EMI, the largest U.K. entertainment and electronics enterprise, until 1986 had stakes in various satellite television programmes, such as Premiere and Musicbox. Before it pulled out of most of these enterprises, it had announced plans to set up a national network of franchisees with the right to distribute these entertainment channels – but no other directly competing channels – using SMATV reception equipment leased from Thorn EMI.[654] Following this announcement, BT made it known that it was also looking for opportunities to offer a similarly comprehensive package, including programme provision, encryption, billing, the sale of TVRO earth stations, and the wiring of all kinds of SMATV systems.[655]

The legal system has thus far failed to respond to these activities, which are threatening to engulf all aspects of communication in Great Britain. BT's use of the opportunities offered by the new technologies and the ineptness of legislators to respond swiftly to the inherent threats to a pluralistic information society may soon result in the emergence of a company having more power and influence in communications than ever before. The

influenced by PanAmSat's request to the U.S. government to block the expansion of the British company Cable and Wireless in the United States in retaliation for BT's refusal. Only one month earlier, the Department of Trade and Industry had let it be known that it would licence up to six additional operators offering specialized satellite services to specific user groups. However, unlike the services that BT and Mercury may offer under their respective licences, the new licences will be restricted to one-way transmissions. Also, the British government emphasized that BT's and Mercury's duopoly on the provision of basic network services would remain unchanged. Fin. Times, Feb. 17, 18, 1988.
653 British Telecommunications Act 1981 (c.38).
654 New Media Markets, Mar. 19, 1985, 4, 6.
655 New Media Markets, May 29, 1985, 1, 8.

convergence of conduit and content in cable and satellite services has allowed BT to penetrate into areas far beyond its traditional scope of competence. This finding also holds true for other undertakings that have ventured into the new media. However, in the case of BT the problem of convergence is particularly fatal because of both its traditional monopoly rights, parts of which have survived the liberalization process, and its financial strength and factual control of large parts of the existing markets.

BT's privileged position in cable services has also been maintained with respect to general telecommunications services. This in turn means that the convergence of programme providers into general telecommunications service providers has not succeeded and progressed to the same degree as BT's transition from a network provider to an information provider. BT and Mercury have retained the exclusive right to provide basic telecommunications services on wideband cable systems capable of offering telephone services.

Present cable network licences for sophisticated networks issued under the Telecommunications Act 1984 require that voice telephone services by means of cable systems may only be provided in conjunction with either British Telecom or Mercury.[656] In September 1986, Mercury announced that for the first time it had reached agreement with a cable television operator, East London Telecommunications (ELT), the cable company holding the cable franchise for parts of the City of London and the London Docklands, for the use of ELT's cable television network. Mercury is to offer local telephone and data services to business and domestic customers in competition with BT.[657]

The government justified BT's and Mercury's right to engage in cable systems with the argument that it wished to utilize the expertise and know-how in cable technology accumulated in BT and Mercury as well as the financial resources of these two companies for the speedy development of local cable systems.[658] But it also defended the general PTOs' privileged position with respect to basic network services by way of BT's duty to provide such general services to all parts of the United Kingdom, including non-profitable rural areas. In order to offset these and other loss-making activities and to prevent »cream skimming,« the government felt it

---

656 1983 White Paper on Cable Systems, *supra* note 208, at para. 185; *see, e.g.*, condition 15 of the licences granted to Croydon Cable Television Ltd., Windsor Television Ltd., and Swindon Cable Ltd. The licences granted under the Telecommunications Act 1984 may be inspected at OFTEL's headquarters in London.
657 Fin. Times, Sept. 18, 1986.
658 1983 White Paper on Cable Systems, *supra* note 208, paras. 183-84.

necessary to go even further: Cable operators planning to provide data services in the particularly profitable business centres – the City of London, the Boroughs of Westminster, Camden (central London), Manchester and Birmingham – need to cooperate with BT or Mercury for an initial period of twelve years.[659]

Finally, BT and Mercury enjoy the exclusive privilege to interconnect different cable systems and to transmit cable programmes to local franchise areas using microwave links. The latter privilege was challenged by a cable operator in London. The company had applied to the DTI for the allocation of unused video microwave frequencies in the 14-gigahertz band for the exchange of local programmes between different cable systems in London. The company had argued that BT's charges for the microwave links were too high for the cable operators.[660] But the DTI rejected the complaint and upheld the duopoly of the general PTOs.[661]

2. *New Horizons for the Information Suppliers*

There is also ample proof for the reverse trend of a transition from general entertainment providers, including broadcasters, to network providers. In 1985, the British newspaper magnate Robert Maxwell, for example, bought British Cable Services (BCS) from Rediffusion. BCS was one of the old television and radio relay systems operators. Under the new cable television policy of the 1980s, many of these relay systems had been upgraded to provide also privately originated entertainment channels. Maxwell announced that he would further restructure the existing cable networks and develop new cable franchises. In addition to his stake in the old BCS networks in 40 towns, he became engaged in a number of newly awarded cable television franchises, making him the single most important investor in cable television in the United Kingdom.[662]

Furthermore, Grampian Television, one of the ITV contractors, is a shareholder in Cablevision (Scotland), the company holding the cable franchise for Edinburgh.[663] Thames Television and two other ITV companies have acquired stakes in SES, the technical operating company leasing or selling transponders on the medium-power satellite Astra.[664] Even BBC

659 *See id.* at para. 186.
660 Fin. Times, Mar. 14, 1987.
661 Information provided to the author by Mr A.C. Warlow, OFTEL.
662 Fin. Times, May 27, 1986.
663 Fin. Times, Feb. 6, 1986.
664 Fin. Times, Jan. 10, 1987; Neue Zürcher Zeitung, Jan. 29, 1987; 1988(3) MEDIEN BULLETIN 32.

212

Enterprises Inc., the BBC's commercial arm, at one point in the early 1980s had engaged in cable television as a programme supplier, under the name »Showcable,« for Visionhire Cable, the licensed systems operator in various locations of London.[665] However, in this case the BBC had resigned itself to the role of programme provider and had left the network operation to others. The experiment with Showcable was discontinued when its unprofitability became clear.[666]

The interlocking activities of the PTOs, on the one hand, and those of the traditional programme providers, on the other hand, are a consequence of the new media technologies. Whoever controls the conduit medium controls its content. Due to the legal regulation of British cable television, the reverse is also true – whoever wants to control the content is best served if he carries responsibility for the conduit.

In summarizing, the convergence of conduit and content in the context of the new media may be characterized by the following main elements: (1) BT (formerly the Post Office) gradually changed from a pure network provider to an information distributor in order ultimately to become an information provider; (2) BT also changed from a common carrier of satellite services to a satellite programme supplier; (3) its provision of information services gradually extended from mere data services to broadcasting programmes; (4) the new roles of BT and Mercury have put them in direct competition with other cable systems operators, both as to data as well as to video services, while they have retained some privileges vis-à-vis the latter; (5) information providers have increasingly become network operators.

Thus far the legal system has ignored both the dangerous implications for freedom of information and the constraints on a competitive information supply market stemming from the rapidly proliferating convergence of conduit and content. In particular, BT's growing vertical integration as network and information provider poses a threat to a free information market. This situation is only partly mitigated by the fact that the corporation enjoys no monopoly in cable television services; its market strength and technical know-how guarantee its dominance in telecommunications services, which threatens also to engulf the general information market. BT's privileges, namely, those relating to satellite transponder access and voice-telephone services, which have been carried over from the era when it was the single public telecommunications network provider, further strengthen its position. The government, bowing to what it called the practical

665 T. HOLLINS, *supra* note 169, at 48 (Table II).
666 Information provided to the author by Mr Anthony Jennings, BBC Legal Adviser.

necessities of sufficient private financing for cable systems, strongly favours BT's involvement in cable television ventures. While the government feels that the stimulation of growth of cable penetration due to BT's engagement outweighs the negative effects on competition in telecommunications services, it overlooks the ensuing dangers for freedom of information. This situation is aggravated by the fact that no third-party access rights exist for the provision of radio and television programmes on cable systems and that, even with respect to VADS, cable operators have been able to convince the government of the need to enter into exclusive contracts. The future relationship between the traditional broadcasters and the satellite and television programme providers is as unresolved as is the relationship between the cable systems operators and the national PTOs, BT and Mercury.

D. *Towards a New Separation of Conduit and Content?*

The aforementioned crucial shortcomings were identified by the Peacock Committee, which offered a long-term solution to these problems. Vital to the understanding of the Peacock Committee's recommendations is its perception of the impact of the new telecommunications technologies on the future pattern of U.K. television. Pointing to the growing importance of cable and satellite television, the Committee recognized that the continued viability of the »comfortable duopoly« would necessarily be called into question due to the increasing competition for audiences stemming from these new media. The Committee stated that »[c]onvergence is occurring across a range of electronic based [sic] technologies including broadcasting,«[667] and concluded that for the period of the later 1980s to mid-1990s

> [a] key strategic development in this period is the introduction of optic fibre cables in parts of the telecommunications network but this is unlikely to have any direct impact on the end user of broadcasting services in this period. The other significant development is the transition from a world of information conveyed in analogue form to one in which information is conveyed in digital form ... these trends [are graphically reproduced] from the mid 1990s well into the next century where the digital form of information has pervaded most of the networks and fibre optic cables have become the bearer of a wide range of telecommunication and broadcasting services into many businesses and homes. The impact of fibre optic cable is

---

667 1986 Peacock Report, *supra* note 216, at para. 425.

likely to be tempered by the progressively more difficult economics with reducing geographical population density. This underlines the complementary nature of cable networks and direct broadcasting by satellite. [668]

The Report gives ample evidence that the Committee was well aware of the threat to the freedom of communication represented by the convergence of conduit and content. The Committee defines two basic legal pillars on which to build a »free to all« telecommunications system: (1) separation of conduit and content coupled with an anti-discrimination provision; and (2) control of concentration of ownership.

With these recommendations, the Committee questioned the basic principles underlying the cable television policy of the incumbent government. The proposals represent a fundamental retreat from the concept of competition by a multitude of private cable network operators with monopolistic local franchise areas and from the present right of cable operators exclusively to provide any kind of entertainment programmes and VADS to pay for the investment in the cable networks. Under the envisaged legal regime, the supplier of the cable grid would have the status of a common carrier responsible for every aspect of the system's technical operation but without the right to determine the content of any programme or the kind of service transmitted. Also, the common carrier would be under an obligation not to discriminate against any potential users of the available channels. In addition, the Committee advanced the idea that prices for network access could be subject to some kind of government supervision. [669] Regulated access prices could ensure easier access to the grid for small individual programme producers. Under the present system, anybody has the legal right to apply for a cable licence, but the initial capital investment necessary for the cable technology allows only a few financially potent undertakings to make use of their right to communicate over cable. The present broadcasting situation is characterized not only by natural limitations in terrestrial transmission due to spectrum scarcity but also by economic impediments in cable television. In contrast, the legal framework as envisaged by the Committee would subject the cable grids to a set of rules similar to those applying to the present basic telephone network systems.

The Committee also attached an important role to the competition laws.

668 *Id.*
669 *Id.* at paras. 506-07, 666.

First of all, it advocated a dominant-firm provision prohibiting one undertaking from controlling more than a given number or a given proportion of channels.[670]

The Committee's vision of a national grid preferably consisting fully of fibre-optic cable does not necessarily presuppose a single common carrier. Such a network could also be operated by a variety of common carriers, as long as these cable systems were compatible with each other and the operators would be obligated to interconnect their systems. In light of the financial difficulties faced by the existing cable franchisees, however, the Committee expressed doubt whether a national fibre-optic cable grid could be put in place purely on the basis of a network of interconnected, independent local cable operators.[671] Because of the enormous investments that such a national cable network would require, the Committee discussed the use of public funds to finance the national grid.[672] But this idea was not cast into a formal recommendation. Instead, the Committee recommended that national telecommunications systems operators, like BT, Mercury and other subsequent market entrants, should have the right to act as common carriers[673] but would have to divest themselves of their present cable franchises, which include the right to provide programme services and VADS.[674] In 1985, BT operated some 42,500 miles of optical-fibre networks in the United Kingdom, and plans existed to make its national network fully digital by 1988.[675] It would therefore be in a good position to act as the national common carrier. According to the Committee's recommendations, the provision of a variety of services, possibly including the actual assignment of channels to independent publishers, would be the responsibility of local or regional cable franchisees operating under a licence from the Cable Authority.[676] But these franchises would be devoid of any control over the cable network itself.

Despite its preference for one national grid, the Committee expressly refrained from suggesting the withdrawal of present local cable franchises. Taken to their logical conclusions, however, the Committee's suggestions

---

670 *Id.* at para. 508.

671 *See id.* at paras. 494, 666.

672 *Id.* at para. 506.

673 *Id.* at para. 665, Recommendation 15.

674 *Id.* at para. 666. In case of a victory in the 1987 national elections, the Labour Party had announced plans to renationalize BT. Had they won, the idea of the establishment of one national wideband cable grid might, from the Peacock Committee's point of view, have found rather unexpected support from this side of the political spectrum.

675 Fin. Times, Dec. 12, 1985.

676 1986 Peacock Report, *supra* note 216, at para. 666.

would indeed necessitate a legal separation of the licence holders for the cable grid and the licence holders under the Cable and Broadcasting Act. In the coming years such a proposition seems politically unfeasible. The present regulatory system for cable television is closely tailored to the needs of private initiative and private financing of cable systems. Even a cautious and purely theoretical public debate about the pros and cons of this particular Committee recommendation might have the effect of scaring away other private investors contemplating a cable franchise. Nonetheless, the DTI has commissioned a study on the development of Britain's communications network over the next two decades. The study, supervised by a government Steering Group, is expected to recommend methods of dealing with problems stemming from the increasing convergence between the traditional telecommunications networks and the new communications media, including satellite communications, fibre-optic cables, mobile-radio services and microwave transmissions. The study, expected to be published in early 1988, is to comment on whether a unified broadband delivery system, as recommended by the Peacock Committee, would be more desirable than reliance on several competing types of services.[677]

In a 1987 discussion document inviting interested parties to provide comments on the subject of the study, the DTI outlined its own position on the issue, arguing that »it is not clear that the actual recommendation made by the Peacock Committee is the most practicable way to achieve these objectives [i.e., economies of scale for information service providers and manufacturers of hardware stemming from a very limited number of network suppliers], nor that it would do so without unacceptable damage to other objectives.«[678] The key objections of the government to the recommendation may be summarized as follows: (1) The Peacock vision of a national fibre-optic grid may be an attractive concept, yet the most efficient way presently to fulfill an as yet indeterminable market demand for a range of potential services cannot be assessed; British cable policy therefore needs to maintain a flexibility of response. (2) A major review of the government's telecommunications policy is due no earlier than 1990; any previous major policy changes would be destabilizing, destroying confidence of present cable system suppliers and possibly upsetting the cabling process in Great Britain altogether. (3) There exists no willing candidate for the role of common carrier, and the government could not

---

677 Fin. Times, Apr. 11, 1987.
678 DTI, 1987 Discussion Document, *supra* note 636, at 5 (explanation in brackets added).

compel private sector companies like BT or Mercury to act in such capacities.[679]

The separation of conduit and content as recommended by the Committee would constitute an important milestone in the creation of a free information market. Whether this step will ever be taken in the United Kingdom appears doubtful. The more the present cabling policy progresses the less likely a policy reversal appears to be practical. Under these circumstances, the existing regulatory framework of the competition and antitrust laws as they apply to the media as a whole and to the new media in particular can provide a crucial insight into the present state of the competitiveness of the British media market and the existing potentials for its future development.

V. *The Impact of Competition and Antitrust Laws on the British Media*

English competition law as it applies to the media has taken special safeguards for the protection of the free expression of opinion. This approach acknowledges that media conglomerates can not only cause market restraints but also lead to a monopolization of public opinion. Numerous ownership restrictions applying to newspapers as well as to commercial broadcasters and cable operators reflect a policy to prevent a monopolization of public opinion by private entities. While the general competition and antitrust laws can provide an important contribution to those media sectors where a true market of ideas exists, these laws are for the most part inoperational in those areas where, like in terrestrial broadcasting, there exist legal monopolies. In order to safeguard some degree of plurality of opinion with respect to the public broadcasting system, special rules apply that regulate programme content and ensure the representation of the public in advisory councils internal to the structure of the broadcasting organizations. Nonetheless, the general competition laws to a certain degree complement the special regulatory regime applying to broadcasting as regards the relationship between the public broadcasters and third parties or the relationship between the various private ITV companies. Moreover, the principles guiding the operation of long-established media markets, like the newspaper market, may serve

679 *Id.* at 9-12.

218

as a basis for the structuring of an integrated media market, which would include broadcasting, that has been brought within reach with the era of the new media.

A. The Special Concepts Regulating Competition Between the Two Public Broadcasting Systems and Their Relation to Third Parties

1. The Concept of »Competition in Excellence« Between the BBC and the IBA

The relationship between the BBC and the IBA and ITV companies is based on principles of competition, principles that are unique in a number of ways. The end of the BBC's monopoly and the creation of a broadcasting duopoly in the United Kingdom in 1955 brought a competitive thrust to the U.K. television system. Initially, the BBC and its supporters were strongly opposed to the idea of a second broadcasting authority, arguing that commercially supported television would be fully dependent on the need to please audiences by focussing on popular favourites and light entertainment. The BBC had traditionally defined its role as an institution »satisfying the requirements of an educated democracy in the making.«[680] There was fear that competition would lower programme standards, eliminate educational, cultural and minority programmes and waste resources. That is why in the first stages of the duopoly a number of BBC officials maintained that because of different objectives of the IBA and the BBC both broadcasting organizations were not really in a state of competition.[681]

This attitude disappeared when the BBC faced heavy audience losses shortly after the ITV system had begun operations, with 70 per cent of viewers watching ITV. Such a development threatened the BBC's claim as the only true national broadcasting authority. It also endangered its ability to attract the best talent and made it difficult politically to justify to British viewers the payment of a licence fee for BBC services in the face of free ITV programmes. The BBC therefore decided »to fight back« and gradually won back its audience.

---

680 B. PAULU, *supra* note 165, at 42.
681 *Id. See also* A. BRIGGS, *supra* note 285, at 104-05. For a discussion of the transition from the monopoly to the duopoly system in broadcasting, see also P. BLACK, THE MIRROR IN THE CORNER – PEOPLE'S TELEVISION (1972).

In 1980 it received about 50 per cent of all viewing time.[682] Although some argued that general programme standards had suffered and few debated that ITV had brought an end to the BBC's initial paternalistic broadcasting concept, the majority view in Britain even among BBC staff today appears to be that the competitive challenge brought about by ITV released many talented forces within the BBC, encouraged greater creativity and generally stimulated innovative impulses.[683] As a result, many believe that the variety and quality of British television on the whole greatly improved. Significantly, the Annan Committee described the relationship between the two authorities as »[c]ompetition in excellence.«[684]

Two key factors are generally attributed to this positive effect of competition on programme standards: (1) while the two broadcasting organizations are competing for audiences, they depend on two completely separate sources of income; and (2) the BBC Charter and the Broadcasting Act 1981 both commit the broadcasting authorities to the public-service concept of broadcasting, imposing a number of severe constraints on the amount and nature of their competition. The ultimate findings of the Peacock Committee – set up by the government in 1985 to report on the pros and cons of alternative methods of financing the BBC and on replacing the licence fee system with advertising, sponsorship or subscription – confirmed this traditional concept of the relationship between the two public broadcasting systems.

The setting up of the Committee had spurred a heated public debate[685] in which BBC, IBA and ITV companies found themselves on the same side. The BBC emphasized that competition between separate broadcasting organizations with different and relatively secure means of funding would encourage differences in programmes, while competition between identically structured broadcasting systems for mass audiences and an elastic revenue source would foster monotony and thus deprive British

682 B. PAULU, *supra* note 165, at 42-43. Studies for the year between July 1984 and June 1985 show a BBC average audience share of viewing of 45.7 per cent. Independent Television Companies Association, Financing Broadcasting 13 (1985). With regard to the arts programmes and series, the BBC and ITV/Channel 4 traditionally have avoided competing for the same audience at the same time, programme controllers of both television systems regularly conferring to avoid clashes. The Times, Sept. 2, 1987.

683 B. PAULU, *supra* note 165, at 43-44.

684 1977 Annan Report, *supra* note 269, at para. 7.5.

685 An interesting impression of the arguments advanced in defence of the BBC and the traditional notion of public-service broadcasting as well as those arguments attacking the traditional role of the BBC can be obtained from Smith, *Licences and Liberty: Public Service Broadcasting in Britain,* in THE BBC AND PUBLIC SERVICE BROADCASTING 1, 4-21 (C. MacCabe and O. Stewart eds. 1986).

broadcasting of its programme variety and high standards. IBA and ITV companies were particularly concerned about possible heavy revenue losses if both broadcasting systems had to share in a relatively fixed total advertising budget. The advertisers themselves were split in their opinions as to whether advertising on BBC would further their interests. Repeated public opinion polls, however, showed that about two-thirds of British viewers preferred advertising on the BBC to increased licence fees, so long as it was properly regulated.[686]

When the Peacock Committee publicised its report in July 1986, there was an immediate sense of relief on the part of the proponents of the present licence system that the Committee had unequivocally spoken out against the introduction of advertising on BBC television and radio. To begin with, the Committee agreed with the evidence submitted by the BBC, ITV companies and others that even if the BBC financed only part of its services by means of selling advertising time, an undesirable narrowing of the now existing programme range and a deterioration of programme quality on all channels would be likely. In the words of the Commission, »[t]he main defect of a system based on advertising finance is that channel owners do not sell programmes to audiences, but audiences to advertisers.«[687] The Committee expressed its conviction that competition for advertising revenues would force the broadcasters to compete for high audience ratings, thereby neglecting minority and experimental programmes with small audiences. At the same time, particularly the smaller ITV companies would need to fight for their survival despite the likely modest growth of total television advertising expenditure.[688] Likewise, the introduction of advertising on some or all BBC radio services would, in the Commission's opinion, seriously damage the already financially weakened ILR stations and lead to an undesirable wave of mergers and an eventual decrease in the amount of local news and information services.[689] The Commission mentioned the same reservation with regard to sponsorship of BBC programmes. Not only would revenues from sponsored programmes by their very nature represent but a fraction of all income needed for BBC services; as is shown by the U.S. experience with sponsorship, sponsors would be much more likely than general advertisers to assert an undesirable editorial interest in the programmes.[690]

---

686 *See* Sunday Times, Oct. 20, 1985.
687 1986 Peacock Report, *supra* note 216, at para. 617.
688 *Id.* at paras. 322, 327, 329, 330, 416-20. The Commission evaluated the possible negative effects of BBC advertising on the press and on cable and satellite television operators as modest. *Id.* at paras. 341-44.
689 *Id.* at paras. 386-89.
690 *Id.* at paras. 405, 408.

Just as it had clearly rejected the introduction of advertising on BBC television and radio, the Peacock Committee expressed the view that the present British broadcasting system was far from ideal and should in the long run be replaced by a consumer-oriented system. Criticizing the present broadcasting structure for what it termed the »comfortable duopoly,«[691] the Committee pointed to the negative side effects of a situation in which the duopolists' revenues did not directly depend on consumer choice: A lack of incentives to be cost conscious and cost efficient and an overriding aspiration to win the praise of fellow professionals in the form of film and similar awards rather than the approval of the ultimate consumer of these productions characterize the inherent shortcomings of the present system.[692]

The ensuing recommendations of the Peacock Committee, particularly with regard to an indexation of the licence fee and later on a transition to subscription services, have been discussed at an earlier stage in some detail.[693] In the present context the existing rules and regulations organizing the »competition in excellence« between the public broadcasting organizations will be analysed in detail.

The Home Secretary can make regulations prohibiting exclusive arrangements by either broadcasting authority for the coverage of sporting or other events of national interest (section 30 of the Broadcasting Act 1981). Also, the BBC and the IBA voluntarily cooperate to a certain degree in matters such as audience research, school programmes, trade union problems, and the like.[694] The Secretary of State may order the BBC and the IBA to share in the use of their respective technical facilities, such as transmitters or other installations (section 31 of the Broadcasting Act 1981). Traditionally, due to the common public-service obligation, this technical cooperation has been very extensive, with both the BBC and the IBA being responsible for about half of all existing transmitter facilities respectively. In these cases the relationship between the BBC and the IBA vis-à-vis a transmitter site is that of landlord and tenant. However, with the diminishing distinction between the provision of the traditional broadcasting services and the new telecommunications services, an area into which both broadcasting organizations increasingly advance while

---

691 *Id.* at paras. 183-201, 645.
692 *Id.* at paras. 197-98.
693 *See supra* at chapter II(E)(2).
694 For more details, see B. PAULU, *supra* note 165, at 44-45.

leaving behind the concept of a service to the general public, they might soon find themselves in antagonistic positions.[695]

The most extensive cooperation between the two public broadcasting systems, however, is their joint engagement in the satellite television channel Superchannel. Under their television franchises, the ITV contractors needed IBA approval for their financial engagements in the satellite television channel.[696] The IBA approved the venture despite the possible negative effects on competition between, on the one hand, the ITV contractors themselves and, on the other, the ITV system as a whole and the BBC.[697] Similarly, under the BBC Licence and Agreement, the Home Office raised no objections to the cooperation agreement. Apparently, the threat to the ITV system's revenue base from cable and satellite was deemed to outweigh any possible adverse consequences for the »competition in excellence,« which has always been said to define the relationship of the broadcasters in the traditional duopoly.

The IBA, however, advances a different view on the reasons that lead to cooperation on the channel. It contends that Superchannel is primarily a »service to foreign countries.«[698] In other words, its primary goal is the exploitation of foreign markets. Due to the very limited spread of cable systems in the United Kingdom, Superchannel is presently not considered as having a significant impact on the competitive situation of the two public broadcasting systems in the United Kingdom. However, if Superchannel could be received by a considerable number of people in the domestic market, the IBA might take a different stance on the expediencies of the current cooperation arrangements.[699]

Sky Channel, Superchannel's direct rival for audiences, however, raised a complaint to the EC Commission in June 1986. The company argued that the refusal of the BBC and the ITV companies to supply Sky Channel with programme material and their joint operation of Superchannel constituted

---

695 Opinion provided to the author by Mr Chris Daubney, Head of Engineering Secretariat, IBA.
696 See Broadcasting Act 1981, sec. 20(5), and Television Contract, supra note 349, at clause 1(4)(g).
697 The potential problems for the competitive relationship between BBC and ITV companies are well illustrated by the remark made by Mr David Plowright, Chairman of the ITCA. He talked of the need to »attend to the minimum requirements of vanity« between the traditional rivals. One of the controversial issues was, e.g., how to accommodate the conflicting aims of the BBC and the ITCA to show their respective news programmes on the new channel. Fin. Times, Oct. 25, 1985.
698 Information provided to the author by Mr Kenneth Blyth, Chief Assistant to the IBA Director General.
699 Id.

an abuse of their dominant trading position contrary to the EEC Treaty.[700]

To the extent that their cooperation and coordination affects third parties and may qualify as an uncompetitive practice, both broadcasting organizations are subject to general competition laws. An illustrative example is the »Dallas affair,« where the OFT at one stage considered the possibility of an official inquiry into the BBC and the ITV companies' programme purchasing policies.[701] The OFT acquired interest in the matter, when, in late 1985, an American programme distributer complained to OFT that the British broadcasters had tried to keep prices for American programmes low by coordinating their bidding. Pursuant to sections 1 and 6 of the Restrictive Trade Practices Act 1976,[702] all agreements restricting trade in goods need to be registered with the OFT. It is then up to the Restrictive Practices Court to determine their validity on the ground of whether they operate in the public interest (section 1(3) of the Restrictive Trade Practices Act 1976).[703]

Thames Television, one of the private television programme companies contracting with the IBA, had outbid the BBC for a number of episodes of the television series »Dallas.« The BBC, which had broadcast all previous episodes of Dallas shown in the United Kingdom, bitterly complained to the IBA and to Thames Television, arguing that Thames had broken a »gentleman's agreement« that the BBC and the ITV companies not outbid each other. The BBC's public pressure on Thames Television was successful: Thames finally transferred all rights for the broadcast of the contested television episodes to the BBC, and the ITV company's responsible managing director resigned.[704]

In the end, the OFT did not pursue the matter any further. This may have been partly due to difficulties in proving the existence of the informal understanding. More likely, however, the OFT was advised by the government not to cause any detriment to the public broadcasters' film purchasing

---

700 *See* 7 J. MEDIA L. & PRAC. 99 (1986).
701 Fin. Times, Nov. 7, 1985.
702 Restrictive Trade Practices Act 1976 (c.34). The Act is the governing statute for horizontal agreements. *See also* Restrictive Trade Practices Act 1977 (c.19) and Restrictive Practices Court Act 1976 (c.33).
703 The government is presently evaluating plans to change the Restrictive Trade Practices Act. According to a 1988 government Green Paper, the Act is too formalistic. The review proposes changing the law to make it more consistent with EC competition law. According to the proposals, the new legislation, to be introduced in 1989-90, would prohibit agreements with anti-competitive effects and purposes, and the registration system would be abolished. Department of Trade and Industry, Green Paper, Cmnd. 331 (1988).
704 Fin. Times, Nov. 11, 1985.

portfolio, at least not in a case in which solely a non-EC distributor was affected.

Confronted with increased competition from other national and international television service suppliers, both BBC and ITV companies have increasingly felt it desirable to expand their cooperation beyond the traditional scope. For example, the two broadcasting organizations negotiated jointly on the fees for the dissemination of their programmes over Belgian cable systems and are also currently taking a joint position in the respective negotiations with Irish cable systems operators.[705]

The conduct of the broadcasting organizations documented by the »Dallas affair« could possibly constitute an abuse of a dominant position under article 86 of the EEC Treaty, if EC nationals were affected. In a case before the European Court of Justice, the plaintiffs, representatives of the film industry, had accused the three national French broadcasting organizations of having forced producers of cinematograph films to accept unreasonably low fees for the broadcast copyrights of their films.[706] The EC Commission had previously held that as a matter of principle a conduct of the kind complained of could violate article 86 of the EEC Treaty. The Court of Justice, without explicitly analysing the question, appears also to have assumed the applicability of article 86 to broadcasting organizations. However, its final decision upheld the Commission's conclusion that the evidence in this particular case did not support a finding that the French broadcasters had forced unreasonably low prices on the film makers.

The case touched upon the difficult problem of the general applicability of the EC antitrust and competition laws to national broadcasting organizations. This question has provoked conflicting statements from the EC Commission and the Court of Justice. The crucial provision in this context is article 90 of the EEC Treaty. Under article 90(1), member states may grant special or exclusive rights to certain undertakings. While the creation of such a monopoly in itself is not incompatible with article 86,[707] the business conduct of these privileged undertakings has to comply with the EC competition laws.[708] Undertakings entrusted with the operation of services

---

705 Information provided to the author by Mr David Williams, Assistant to the BBC Legal Adviser.
706 Comité des Industries Cinématographiques des Communautés Européennes v. EC Commission (case 298/83), 1986 GRUR/Int. 49.
707 Preliminary ruling in Sacchi (case 155/73), 1974 E.C.R. 409, 430; S.A. Centre Belge d'Etudes de Marché-Telemarketing v. S.A. Compagnie Luxembourgeoise de Télédiffusion (»RTL«) (case 311/84), 1985 E.C.R. 3261, 3275.
708 E.-J. MESTMÄCKER, EUROPÄISCHES WETTBEWERBSRECHT 647 (1974).

of general economic interest may be exempted from the competition laws, if the fulfillment of their special obligations would otherwise become impossible (article 90(2)). It falls within the exclusive competence of the Commission to decide whether the exception clause of subsection 2 is applicable to a particular undertaking in an individual case.[709]

In its Green Paper on Television Without Frontiers,[710] the EC Commission took the view that the exception clause of article 90(2) is totally inapplicable to broadcasting organizations, because the media laws in the various member states regulate broadcasting as a service of general cultural and social but not of general economic interest.[711] This analysis led the Commission to conclude that all broadcasting organizations, whether set up by Royal Charter, legislative act or otherwise, are subject to the Community competition laws without qualification.

In the *Sacchi* case, the Court of Justice indeed made a presumption in favour of the applicability of the competition laws to the Italian broadcasting organization RAI.[712] In this case, the Court took the position that »if certain Member States treat undertakings entrusted with the operation of television, even as regards their commercial activities, in particular advertising, as undertakings entrusted with the operation of services of general economic interest, the same prohibitions apply, as regards their behaviour within the market, by reason of Article 90(2), so long as it is not shown that the said prohibitions are incompatible with the performance of their tasks.«[713] The Court's wording »even as regards their commercial activities« implies that, in contrast to the Commission's opinion, article 90(2) is all the more applicable to the activities of broadcasting organizations carried out in the general cultural interest.[714] As Mestmäcker has pointed out, the distinction between a general economic interest and a general cultural and social interest overlooks that the rationale for the assignment of special tasks to public undertakings as described in article

---

709 *See* the comments on the European Court of Justice's decision in »Telemarketing« (case 311/84) of Oct. 3, 1985 by Mestmäcker, *Anmerkung*, in II RECHTSPRECHUNG ZUM URHEBERRECHT, ENTSCHEIDUNGSSAMMLUNG EuGH 12, 37, at p. 39 (E. Schulze ed. January 1987).
710 Television Without Frontiers, The Establishment of the Common Market for Broadcasting, Especially by Satellite and Cable, EC Green Paper, Com. (84)300 final/2 (hereafter cited 1984 EC Green Paper).
711 *Id.* at Part 5 E I 3.
712 1974 E.C.R. at 430.
713 *Id.*
714 Mestmäcker, *supra* note 709, at 41.

90(2) can typically be found in the need to ensure the execution of a whole variety of economic as well as social and cultural policy goals.[715]

Both the BBC and the IBA are thus subject to national as well as to the EC competition laws, a circumstance easing the way to the »full broadcasting market« as envisaged by the Peacock Committee.

An example of the application of the Competition Act 1980 to the public broadcasters is a 1985 report of the MMC on BBC and ITV copyright practices with respect to programme schedules. These schedules are entitled to copyright protection as literary works under section 2 of the Copyright Act 1956.[716] Under so-called copyright notices, both the BBC and Independent Television Publications Ltd., a company set up by the ITV programme contractors with the consent of the IBA, have severely restricted the right of any newspaper or magazine to publish BBC or ITV programme schedules in advance. British television viewers or radio listeners wanting to get information on programmes more than one day ahead of time have to buy *Radio Times*, the BBC publication on BBC television and radio programmes, and/or *TV-Times* and *Look-In*, the corresponding publications sold by Independent Television Publications Ltd. The sale of these programme magazines represents a valuable source of revenue for the BBC and the ITV contractors. Because of these strong commercial interests, they have in the past vigorously enforced their copyrights in court in cases of any infringements of the copyright notices by newspapers and magazines.[717] In January 1985, the Director General of Fair Trading made a reference to the Monopolies and Mergers Commission under section 5 of the Competition Act 1980, following his report under section 3 of the Act. This report stated that BBC and ITV copyright practices constituted an anti-competitive practice.[718] After an initial tie vote, the Commission, via the deciding vote of its Chairman, reached the conclusion that the practice did not operate and was not expected to

---

715 *Id.* This view is also supported by the EUCJ's decision in *Telemarketing*, 1985 E.C.R. at 3275.

716 Section 48(1) of the Copyright Act 1956 defines a »literary work« as including »any written table or compilation.«

717 *See, e.g.*, Independent Television Publications Ltd. v. Time Out Ltd. and Elliott; BBC v. Time Out Ltd. and Elliott, 1984 F.S.R. 64; *see also* Sunday Times, Nov. 3, 1985.

718 Monopolies and Mergers Commission, The British Broadcasting Corporation and Independent Television Publications Ltd. A report on the policies and practices of the British Broadcasting Corporation and Independent Television Publications Limited of limiting the publication by others of advance programme information and of not granting licences which would allow others to publish such information beyond certain specified periods, Cmnd. 9614, para. 1.1. (1985), (hereafter cited as MMC, BBC and ITV Copyright Practices).

operate against the public interest.[719] Such a negative conclusion precludes the Commission by law from making any formal recommendations to the Secretary of State advising him on the possible exercises of his order-making powers under section 10 of the Competition Act. Section 10 enables the Secretary of State to prohibit a person from engaging in any specified anti-competitive practice where the MMC has reported that there was an anti-competitive practice that operated or might be expected to operate against the public interest.

In this particular case, however, the Commission did feel the need to deal with the question of what advice it would have given had it reached an adverse finding. It stated that it would have felt unable to recommend that action be taken by the government against the BBC and the ITV companies. Pointing to the Secretary of State's limited powers under the Competition Act, the Commission noted »the difficulty of adapting them to a case in which the anti-competitive practice consists of the refusal of the owner of a copyright to grant licences.«[720] Even if, the Commission continued, a way to remedy the situation could be conceived of, the introduction of a compulsory licensing system was undesirable.[721] The Commission expressed its worries in this context that a compulsory licensing system might conflict with the United Kingdom's obligations under the Berne Copyright Convention, because it rules out the imposition of compulsory copyright licences by means of the competition laws.

The case evidences the potentially conflicting aims of the copyright laws and the competition laws: while the former grant to the copyright owner the right to restrict the supply of the copyright works, this very restriction may constitute an abuse of a dominant position under the competition laws. In the present case, the conflict could only have been resolved by new legislation providing for some kind of compulsory licensing system in the case of programme schedules. It has been argued that with growing competition from the private (cable) television market, such statutory reform is becoming more likely, since restrictions on competition in programme information could be regarded as a reflection of the public broadcasting duopoly; if competition were introduced in the primary mar-

---

719 *Id.* at para. 6.41. The public-interest concept applied by the Commission in this case has been strongly criticised. *See* Johnson, *Competition, Copyright and the Public Interest*, 1986 BUS. L. REV. 6-7. The author implies that the Commission would have decided differently had it not dealt with the practice of a public corporation like the BBC but with that of a private company.

720 MMC, BBC and ITV Copyright Practices, *supra* note 718, at para. 6.42.

721 *Id.* at para. 6.43.

ket, competition on the secondary market of programme information would necessarily follow.[722]

The examples given above document the extent and the limits of general competition laws for the regulation of the relationship between the two public broadcasting systems and between them and third parties. Competition in programme supply is moreover artificially restricted by a number of specific provisions devised to serve the public-service concept of broadcasting.

2. *Rules Restricting Programme Competition and Competition for Advertisements*

Until the introduction of cable television, ITV companies had faced no competition for advertising revenues from other audio-visual enterprises. This had been one of the cornerstones of the British public-service concept of broadcasting. The situation changed considerably with the spread of cable television franchises in the United Kingdom. Although in contrast to ITV franchises cable services operate only locally, increasing revenue losses for ITV stations were predicted as a consequence of a progressing territorial spread of cable franchise areas in different localities. In addition to that coming from the cable television operators, which could be expected to include advertisements in their channels, competition for advertising revenues was also expected from the mounting number of satellite television companies, which found more and more audiences as a result of the mounting number of cable systems.

In order to mitigate the negative effect of such competition for the ITV franchise holders, the Cable and Broadcasting Act 1984 struck a compromise. Cable television channels with a nature and character resembling ITV channels are restricted in the total amount of advertising time per day and hour to the amount of time allowed for ITV stations. They are the programme channels most likely to compete directly with the ITV stations for audiences. Cable channels »calculated to appeal to tastes and interests which are generally catered for by local sound broadcasting services« are bound to respective rules governing the ILR system (section 12(3)(b) of the Cable and Broadcasting Act 1984). Since this regulation contains restrictions only for channels directly competing with ITV or ILR, cable operators are free to set up specialist cable channels or advertising

---

722 Frazer, *Unchanging Times: The Monopolies and Mergers Commission Report on the BBC and ITP*, 7 ECLR 96, 108 (1986). For a discussion of the conflict of EC copyright and competition laws, see *supra* at chapter I(C)(1).

programmes (as contrasted with spot advertising) that could be built around commercial messages.[723] In its 1983 White Paper, the government specifically acknowledged that because the cable medium could offer a variety of advertising services not covered by the public broadcasting system, such as classified advertising, flexible rules relating to the amount and content of advertisements on cable channels should apply. Under the 1984 Act, the Cable Authority has the responsibility to draw up and enforce a code of advertising standards for cable television. In order to account for the different natures of possible advertisements on cable, the Authority is obligated to get the advice of the IBA as to advertising standards on channels similar to ITV and ILR services and the advice of the ASA to the extent that classified advertising or similar commercials resemble the kind of print advertising carried by newspapers.[724]

While these rules protect the ITV companies' revenue base, other legal provisions are designed to secure the reception of the public broadcasting channels by all customers of cable television services. The »must-carry« rule of section 13 of the Cable and Broadcasting Act 1984 restricts the cable operator's freedom to transmit programme channels on his cable system entirely at his will. Section 13 requires the cable operator to relay simultaneously and completely all BBC and ITV radio and television services provided for his franchise area. From this requirement, the Home Office has allowed some exceptions: Diffusion services need not include any BBC or ILR radio broadcasts at all, unless they include (at a time when they also transmit television services) any other radio service, in which case they also have to transmit at least one BBC or ILR service.[725] Section 13 ensures the supply of public broadcasting services to all cable television consumers and enables local planning authorities to prohibit roof antennae in cabled areas.

The provision also clearly favours the interests of the domestic public broadcasting system over the interests of other domestic – and particularly foreign – television programme suppliers. The EC Commission has indicated that in its view articles 59 and 62 of the EEC Treaty prohibit national rules that grant domestic channels better slots on cable systems than foreign services.[726] The Commission argued that instead of rules explicitly favouring national over foreign broadcasts, such neutral criteria

---

723 *See* 1983 White Paper on Cable Systems, *supra* note 208, at para. 100.
724 *See* Cable and Broadcasting Act 1984, sec. 12, and 1983 White Paper on Cable Systems, *supra* note 208, at paras. 91-103.
725 *See* the Cable (Excepted Programmes) Order 1984, 1984 S.I. No. 1993.
726 1984 EC Green Paper, *supra* note 710, at Part V B I.

as signal strength should apply if a cable system could not accommodate all available programmes and a choice would have to be made among them. However, in the United Kingdom a rule relying on signal strength would again lead to a preferential treatment of BBC and IBA programmes. Their terrestrial broadcasting monopolies ensure for the time being that the strength of their signal transmissions surpasses that of other domestic and foreign programme competitors. As a consequence, the inclusion of BBC and ITV programmes on all cable systems would again be guaranteed.

British cable operators also face certain restrictions with regard to those programmes that they would like to offer on a pay-per-view instead of a pay-per-channel basis. The Hunt Committee identified the potential danger that popular events might be bought up for subscription television with the effect of syphoning such programmes away from the programme range available to the public broadcasting system. Since large numbers of the public could for the foreseeable future be expected to depend solely on public broadcasting television, the Committee recommended a total ban on all pay-per-view services.[727] The 1983 White Paper, in contrast, spotted a worthwhile market for pay-per-view programmes that would not threaten programmes typically available on the public-service broadcasting channels, namely: events specially staged for cable; theatre and opera events never shown on public-service channels; sporting and other events of purely local interest; very recent feature films not made available to the broadcasters by distributors under current arrangements; and certain specialist programmes.[728]

On this basis, the Cable and Broadcasting Act 1984 strikes a compromise between the broadcasters' interest in showing events of national interest and the cable operators' interest in the acquisition of exclusive rights to certain events for the realization of premium profits with the pay-per-view method. Section 14 prohibits the inclusion in a diffusion service of »listed« or »protected« events on pay-per-view terms. Listed events are sporting or other events of national interest defined as such by the Home Secretary; a protected event is a sporting or other event so designated by the Cable Authority. The designation is to ensure that the broadcasting authorities will not be deprived of the right to broadcast any programmes that they typically broadcast before the arrival of cable television. Twenty-four hours after an original recording has been made, cable operators are free to

---

727 1982 Hunt Report, *supra* note 545, at paras. 50-51, 68-70.
728 1983 White Paper on Cable Systems, *supra* note 208, at para. 113.

include all such programmes in their services on a pay-per-view basis (section 14(5) of the Cable and Broadcasting Act 1984).

The aforementioned restrictions document that the British broadcasting market in terms of programme supply is still heavily regulated. The rationale for these restrictions can be traced back to a single concern that always dominated British media policy: Because of their impact on »the life of the nation,« the broadcast media in principle should not be left to the control of market forces but needs close supervision and guidance by the legislature. Moreover, with respect to the control of the private ITV and ILR companies, the IBA enjoys broad discretionary power to regulate the conduct and business affairs of the franchisees.

3. The IBA's Control over the Business Affairs of the Contractors

In principle, the private television and radio programme contractors are subject to the general competition laws. However, their relationship to each other and to third parties is to a large extent defined by the Broadcasting Act 1981 and the television contracts thereunder. The 1981 Act assigns to the IBA a number of supervisory and regulatory functions deeply intruding into the business activities of the contractors and overlapping with some of the powers of the OFT, the MMC and the Secretary of State of Trade and Industry under the general competition laws. The limits of the various functions assigned to these different bodies are not always clearly defined, a situation typical of the complex and frequently illogical system of U.K. competition law policy.[729]

A case in point is a 1984 report by the Director General of OFT on certain business practices employed by Thames Television vis-à-vis advertisers and advertising agents.[730] The OFT had initiated the investigation following a complaint by an advertising agency against the television contractor alleging anti-competitive practices in connection with the conditions imposed on advertisers for the purpose of receiving favourable terms on advertising time and expenditure. At the end of a long and detailed report, the Director General reached the conclusion that none of the contractor's policies regarding the granting of advertising time and space amounted to an anti-competitive practice within the meaning of section 3 of the

---

729 *See* the critical assessment of British competition law policy by R. MERKIN & K. WILLIAMS, COMPETITION LAW: ANTITRUST POLICY IN THE U.K. AND THE EEC 17 (1984).

730 Office of Fair Trading, A Report by the Director General of Fair Trading on an Investigation Under Section 3 of the Competition Act 1980. Thames Television Ltd. (Feb. 3, 1984).

Competition Act 1980.[731] The Director General then noted that »[a] practice which is not anti-competitive in terms of the Competition Act may nevertheless be discriminatory.«[732] He concluded that the practices investigated by the OFT discriminated between advertisers and advertising agencies and went on to state:

> [The] report draws attention (...) to the duty of the Independent Broadcasting Authority to secure compliance with certain statutory rules as to advertisements, including a rule against »unreasonable discrimination either against or in favour of any particular advertiser« and a rule about the publication by contractors of their charges. The Authority has hitherto refrained from pronouncing on the principle of share-deal schemes (...). I propose to bring this report to the attention of the Authority, so that it may consider whether further action is necessary in context of its general duty under section 8 of the Broadcasting Act 1981.[733]

The paragraph evidences that the Director General of OFT had reached the limits of his power under the Competition Act. All that was left to him was recourse to a non-binding recommendation to the IBA. If the IBA refused to take action, not even the Home Secretary could order the IBA to issue guidelines on share-deal schemes, because the government's order-making powers in relation to the IBA are limited to a number of well-defined subjects (*compare* sections 28-31 of the Broadcasting Act 1981).

The IBA imposes on the contractors many detailed contractual obligations and requirements concerning the nature and characteristics of their businesses. Thus, before entering into a contract, the franchisee has to make a written declaration »as to certain matters concerning its affairs.« This document is formerly incorporated into the franchise contract.[734] This non-public document apparently describes the business of the contractor in some detail, because the television contract itself provides that if the representations made in the document later prove to be false or inaccurate in any material aspect, the Authority has the right to terminate the contract. The IBA generally reserves the right to terminate the contract by notice in writing if »any change affecting the nature or characteristics of the body corporate or any change in the person having control over or interests in the body corporate« take place »after the conclusion of the contract, which, if it had occurred before the conclusion of the contract, would

---

731 *Id.* at para. 10.1.
732 *Id.* at para. 10.2.
733 *Id.*
734 Television Contract, *supra* note 349, at clause 1 and Preamble.

have induced the Authority to refrain from entering into the contract.«[735] This means that all business decisions and decisions of the controlling owners of the television contractor affecting in any way its nature or characteristics need the prior written consent of the Authority unless the company wants to risk the loss of the franchise.[736]

Without prejudice to the generality of this principle reservation, the contracts with the television programme contractors contain specifications as to the activities that automatically need the prior approval of the Authority. Among these activities are: the issuance and transfer of any voting share in the contractor's capital or the change of its beneficial ownership; the acquisition of any share or loan capital of another television programme contractor by the contractor or any of its directors; the contractor's financial or other engagement in cable, satellite or subscription television or in the video cassette or video disc business; the engagement in these latter activities by any holding company of the contractor or any person or company having a material interest in the company, or by a director of the contractor or a director of the holding company; and the contractor's engagement in any other business or activity not directly incidental to its functions and obligations as a television programme contractor.[737] The contractor's engagement in cable or subscription television or in the video cassette business needs no approval by the Authority if these activities are carried on wholly outside the United Kingdom, the Channel Islands and the Isle of Man and do not relate to programmes or transmissions receivable in the United Kingdom.[738]

Since neither the Broadcasting Act 1981 nor the television contracts contain any definition as to the expected or preferred characteristics that a television programme contractor should meet, the Authority has almost unrestricted discretion with regard to the criteria to be applied in the approval process. The Authority's decisions have thus sometimes come unexpectedly and have even startled independent observers, as the row over the proposed takeover of Thames Television by a manufacturer of television and video equipment in late 1985 exemplifies. In this case, Thames Television had received a very lucrative offer for 94 per cent of its voting shares. The hold-

---

735 Broadcasting Act 1981, sec. 20(5). Under the Act, the IBA may only terminate an agreement if the contractor has broken the contract on at least three occasions and the Authority has conveyed particulars in respect of each of those breaches to the contractor within one month from the time the Authority received notice of the breach. *Id.* at sec. 21(2)(b).
736 Television Contract, *supra* note 349, at clause 1(2).
737 *Id.* at clause 1(4).
738 *Id.* at clause 1(5).

ers of these shares, two large diversified companies, had been most willing to sell. Initial talks with the IBA apparently gave the impression that it would consent to the transfer.[739] After the contract between the proposed buyer and the two majority shareholders was concluded, the IBA's Director General suddenly announced that the bid was unacceptable on the ground that it would lead to »a major change in the nature and characteristics« of a viable ITV company.[740] No further public explanations were given. Thames Television could have challenged the IBA's decision under the judicial-review procedure only on the ground that the Authority had acted in an arbitrary or capricious way, objections extremely difficult to substantiate before a court of law.

In certain cases, the courts may even decline to grant such a limited judicial review of an IBA decision. When the Rank Organisation attempted a takeover of Granada Television in early 1986, the IBA again refused to consent to the purchase, arguing summarily that this major change in control of a viable programme contractor would be unacceptable. The IBA's decision prevented the Rank Organization from voting more than 5 per cent of its shares in Granada, because Granada's articles of association specified that no shareholder was to vote more than a 5-percent holding unless it was a person approved by the IBA. When the Rank Organisation challenged the IBA's decision in the High Court, Judge Mann dismissed the complaint. He argued that he could only review Authority decisions that were based on a statutory power conferred upon the IBA. The present decision, the Court reasoned, had not been authorised by section 20(5) of the Broadcasting Act 1981; instead, the Authority had exercised an adjudicatory power conferred upon it by Granada's articles of association. The Court then argued that the fact that the IBA had a statutory power to act in such an adjudicatory capacity did not make the decision a matter of public law or open it to judicial review.[741]

In the case of the failed takeover of Thames Television, the press consequently published various opinions about the possible motives that had led the IBA to oppose the deal. According to some speculations, the IBA had deferred to pressures put upon it by the incumbent management and the employees of the television contractor, who were believed to have

---

739 *See*, *e.g.*, The Scotsman, Oct. 8, 1985; Fin. Weekly, Oct. 11, 1985; The Times, Oct. 12, 1985.

740 *See*, *e.g.*, Fin. Times, Oct. 11, 1985.

741 R. v. Independent Broadcasting Authority ex parte Rank Organisation PLC (Q.B., Mar. 13,1986), Fin. Times, Mar. 14, 1986. The Rank Organisation appealed the decision, but the Court of Appeal upheld the previous decision. Leave to appeal to the House of Lords was refused. Judgment of Mar. 26, 1986 (per May, L.J.).

objected to the takeover.[742] In the Rank takeover bid, the management had been opposed to the transfer, and the IBA had evaluated this as a material factor for its decision, because of the Authority's concern that »the morale of key staff was seriously affected by the prospects of the bid succeeding, and that, if it did succeed, many of the senior management of Granada Group would leave the company and several of the key programme staff would leave Granada T.V.'s service.«[743] Others pointed out that the IBA, during the last franchising round in 1980, had made it clear to the two majority shareholders that Thames should broaden its share-base and in particular give the public a chance to invest directly; the proposed takeover would have had the opposite effect of reducing the number of owners by one, although the proposed buyer had announced its intention eventually to offer shares in its own company to Thames employees and other members of the public.[744] A third explanation offered was that the IBA had wanted to set a precedent and had intended to ensure that a viable television contractor in franchise mid-term would as a matter of principle not be for sale, with the IBA's emphasis being on the fact that a *viable* contractor was not to change hands.[745] In its Annual Report of 1986, the Authority for the first time became more explicit about the underlying reasons for its policy: »The IBA's position is that its responsibilities under the 1981 Act are incompatible with programme contracts being available to the highest bidder, whether at the time of contract award or subsequently.«[746] This statement was probably meant as an answer to the Peacock Committee's proposition to put ITV contracts out to competitive tender.

The initial criticism of the IBA's policy approach was that it would unduly restrict the transferability of a profitable ITV company and would inhibit the flow of capital into the industry.[747] However, these pessimistic predictions did not materialize in the following months. The IBA approved a comprehensive plan to broaden Thames Television's share ownership. Under the plan, around 40 per cent of these shares were offered in a public flotation, reducing the combined stakes of the two majority shareholders to

742 The Times, Oct. 11, 1985; The Scotsman, Oct. 11, 1985.
743 Affirmation of Lord Thomson of Monifieth, IBA Chairman, in the High Court of Justice, Queen's Bench Division, in the matter of R. v. Independent Broadcasting Authority ex parte Rank Organisation PLC, Crown Office Reference No. 350/86 (Mar. 10, 1986) (unpublished).
744 Daily Telegraph, Oct. 11, 1985; The Guardian, Oct. 11, 1985.
745 Fin. Times, Oct. 11, 1985, Daily Mail, Oct. 11, 1985.
746 1986 IBA Annual Report, *supra* note 304, at 8.
747 Fin. Times, Oct. 11, 1985; Yorkshire Post, Oct. 12, 1985; Sunday Times, Oct. 13, 1985.

around 58 per cent. In return, both companies gave undertakings to the IBA not to reduce further their share bases until the expiration of the current franchise in 1991. Thames' employees received preferential rights for over 10 per cent of the shares, and the IBA imposed the condition that no new single shareholder was to acquire more than a 10-percent stake. The offer for sale, made in mid-1986, was oversubscribed twenty-six times and resulted in the allocation of shares to almost 48,000 investors.[748] The great success of Thames' public flotation induced several other ITV contractors, namely, TV-am, Yorkshire TV and Border TV, to follow suit. In all cases, the share offers were heavily oversubscribed and substantially broadened the companies' shareholder bases.[749]

The public flotations have opened a way for the ITV contractors to raise substantial capital in franchise mid-term despite the severe restrictions on ownership transfer imposed upon them by the IBA. The examples also evidence the IBA's main policy objectives. While the Authority refuses to release the major shareholders from their responsibilities in mid-franchise, it welcomes the sale of minority stakes to the general public and to a contractor's employees. This approach may be seen in line with the government's wider policy of introducing »popular capitalism.«

Whereas the ITV broadcasting market is thus subject to a number of severe regulatory restraints unheard of in other market sectors, other legislative provisions are specially designed to safeguard a certain degree of intramedia as well as intermedia competition. These rules have traditionally applied to the newspaper market; some of the principles developed in this context also extend into other competitive media markets.

B. Safeguards for Intra- and Intermedia Competition

1. The Public-Interest Test Applied to Newspaper Mergers

The classical liberalized media market in the United Kingdom is the newspaper market, including the market for books and magazines and similar publications. Here, the MMC has played an important role under the Fair Trading Act 1973 in formulating the objectives to be served by the competition and antitrust rules for the preservation of a pluralistic and competitive information market.

---

748 *See, e.g.*, Fin. Times, Dec. 19, 1985; June 18, 1986; June 19, 1986, p. 26; June 27, 1986; July 3, 1986.
749 *See, e.g.*, Fin. Times, July 16, 1986; Sept. 1, 1986; Oct. 24, 1986.

Special legislation applies to the mergers of press undertakings. These legislative enactments, first introduced by the Monopolies and Mergers Act 1965, were the response to a noticeable trend in the concentration of press ownership in the United Kingdom. While the circulation figures for individual newspapers in Britain are among the highest in the world,[750] the total number of newspapers has markedly declined since the end of World War II. At the same time, there have been fewer independent newspaper proprietors and an increasing number of newspapers in the hands of large national groups.[751] The number of local weekly and biweekly newspapers fell between 1965 and 1979 by about 10.5 per cent,[752] while at the same time concentration of ownership of provincial morning and evening newspapers took place on a moderate scale only.[753] Parallel to this development, the number of titles of weekly newspapers owned by major national groups controlling 18 or more weeklies rose between 1965 and 1978 from 172 to 249.[754] Another 1981 statistic shows that eleven undertakings controlled over a third of the local weeklies, representing well over a third of the total circulation.[755] The concentration of ownership is most significant with regard to the national daily and Sunday newspapers. Four conglomerates publish 70 per cent of the national daily newspapers and 80 per cent of the national Sunday newspapers.[756]

Newspaper mergers are now controlled by sections 58 to 62 of the Fair Trading Act 1973. According to section 58(1) of the Act, the transfer of any newspaper or newspaper assets to a newspaper proprietor[757] is valid

---

750 1985 THE EUROPE YEAR BOOK: A WORLD SURVEY (Vol. I) 997. For an overview of the national and provincial daily and weekly newspapers published in the United Kingdom in 1984, see *id*. at 997-99; *see also* STAMM, PRESSE- UND MEDIENHANDBUCH 5/42 (37th ed. 1984).

751 *See* Monopolies and Mergers Commission, West Somerset Free Press *and* Bristol United Press Ltd., H.C. No. 546 3-4 (1980). *See also* the account given by J. TUNSTALL, *supra* note 315, at 69-88.

752 The Monopolies and Mergers Commission, St. Regis International Ltd. *and* Reed International plc, H.C. No. 402 5 (1982).

753 The Monopolies and Mergers Commission, The Observer *and* George Outram & Company Ltd., H.C. No. 378 4 (1981).

754 The Monopolies and Mergers Commission, The Berrow's Organization Ltd. *and* Reed International Ltd., Cmnd. 8337 3 (1981) (*quoting* the annual reports of the Press Council).

755 Monopolies and Mergers Commission, South Wales Argus (Holdings) Ltd. *and* Express Newspapers Ltd., Cmnd. 8385 4 (1981) (*quoting* the annual reports of the Press Council).

756 G. ROBERTSON & A. NICOL, *supra* note 54, at 321.

757 A »newspaper proprietor« is the actual owner of a newspaper, a person with a controlling interest (i.e., with the control of at least 25 per cent of the voting rights), or any company in which the newspaper proprietor has a controlling interest (Fair Trading Act 1973, sec. 57(1)(b),(4)).

238

only with the written consent of the Secretary of State for Trade and Industry, if the average daily circulation of the combined newspapers amounts to 500,000 or more copies. This provision contrasts sharply with the general regulation of mergers under the Fair Trading Act, because such mergers are principally valid until and unless the Secretary of State has prohibited the transfer. In contrast, in the case of newspaper mergers, the Secretary's consent is constitutive for the legal validity of the transaction.

An unauthorized transfer constitutes a criminal offence under section 62. Newspapers covered by the provision are those circulating wholly or mainly in the United Kingdom or in a part of the country (section 57(1)(a)). The circulation figures are calculated on the basis of actual sales in the United Kingdom (section 57(3)).

The Secretary of State's refusal to grant his consent to a newspaper merger presupposes that he has first referred the matter to the MMC and has received its report[758] due three months from the date of the reference (section 60(1)). But the Secretary of State is not bound by the findings of the Commission. Also, under certain conditions specified in section 58(3) and (4) of the Act, he may permit a merger without a previous reference to the Commission. This is the case when the Secretary »is satisfied that the newspaper concerned in the transfer is not economic as a going concern and as a separate newspaper,« and (1) when the newspaper is to continue as a separate newspaper and the case is one of urgency; or (2) when the newspaper concerned has an average daily circulation of 25,000 copies or less (section 58(4)). If he is satisfied that the newspaper is *not* intended to continue as a separate newspaper and the newspaper is uneconomic as a

---

758 Fair Trading Act 1973, sec. 58(2). The Monopolies and Mergers Commission has published the following reports on newspaper mergers: Thompson Newspapers Ltd. *and* Crushar & Son Ltd., H.C. No. 273 (1968); George Outram Company Ltd. *and* Hamilton Advertiser Ltd. and Baird and Hamilton Ltd., H.C. No. 76 (1970); The Berrow's Organization Ltd. *and* The County Express Group, H.C. No. 224 (1972); Westminster Press Ltd. *and* Kentish Times Ltd. et al., H.C. No. 460 (1973); Courier Printing and Publishing Co. Ltd. *and* Associated Newspapers Group Ltd., H.C. No. 108 (1974); Scott Ltd. *and* Guardian & Manchester Evening News H.C. No. 249 (1975); Surrey Advertiser *and* Guardian & Manchester Evening News, H.C. No. 100 (1979); J. Andrew and Co. Ltd. *and* United Newspapers Ltd., H.C. No. 724 (1980); West Somerset Free Press *and* Bristol United Press Ltd., H.C. No. 546 (1980); The Observer *and* George Outram & Company Ltd., H.C. No. 378 (1981); The Berrow's Organization Ltd. *and* Reed International Ltd., Cmnd. 8337 (1981); South Wales Argus (Holdings) Ltd. *and* Express Newspapers Ltd., Cmnd. 8385 (1981); Benham Newspapers Ltd., St. Regis International Ltd. *and* Reed International plc, H.C. No. 402 (1982); Birmingham Post and Mail Holdings plc *and* Yattendon Investment Trust Ltd., Cmnd. 9516 (1985); United Newspapers plc *and* Fleet Holdings plc, Cmnd. 9610 (1985); Courier Press (Holdings) Ltd. *and* EMAP plc., Cmnd. 120 (1987).

going concern, he must give his consent unconditionally (section 58(3)(b)).[759]

In preparing a report, the MMC decides whether the intended transfer may be expected to operate against the public interest. For the purpose of this determination, the Commission takes into account »all matters which appear in the circumstances to be relevant and, in particular, the need for accurate presentation of news and free expression of opinion« (section 59(3)). The Commission has formulated several criteria to be considered in the public-interest test, namely:

(1) The economic prospects of the merged newspaper if the transfer would not take place. In cases where the present proprietor had announced his intention to sell the newspaper under all circumstances, the Commission has only made an evaluation of the suitability of the purchaser in terms of how he compared with other conceivable purchasers.[760]

(2) Efficiency gain. The Commission has always examined the respective efficiencies of the buyer and the purchased newspaper(s), noticing favourably any envisaged improvement in production methods and the like without giving decisive weight to the prospects of efficiency gains.

(3) Effects on employees. In this context the Commission has attached great importance on assurances given by the purchaser that no redundancies would take place.

(4) Accurate presentation of news and free expression of opinion. In this context the Commission has usually been satisfied if the purchaser had a history of non-interference with the editorial freedom of his other newspapers. The declared intention of the purchaser to continue the emphasis on local news was another factor relevant for the Commission on this point.

(5) Aspects of inter- and intramedia competion. Most of the Commission's reports have dealt with takeovers of local newspapers by large national groups and the possible threat to small newspaper proprietors in the locality due to the economic power of the purchaser. With one exception[761] the Commission, while recognizing the additional risk for the local proprietors when faced with a strong competitor, has rejected the likelihood of predatory pricing methods. In one of its most recent reports,

---

759 It has rightfully been pointed out that these provisions constitute an important loophole reflected in the following statistic: Between 1965 and 1987, 91 cases were referred to the Secretary of State, who referred only 18 to the MMC while granting his unconditional consent in 73 cases. Only one application was eventually refused. *See* 8 J. MEDIA L. & PRAC. 117 (1987).

760 *See Scott Ltd.*, H.C. No. 249 (1975); *Surrey Advertiser*, H.C. No. 100 (1979).

761 *The Berrow's Organization Ltd*, Cmnd. 8337 (1981).

the Commission introduced a new dimension into its examination of possible impacts on the competitive situation of the newspapers. It took aspects of intermedia competition into consideration. Noting that »[t]he growth of local media, the beginnings of cable television, and the expansion of orthodox television transmission through breakfast television and ITV 2, are widening the scope of sources of information and advertising media in ways which weaken the importance of newsprint generally, and paid-for newspapers in particular,«[762] the Commission showed understanding for the newspapers' need for financial gains through economies of scale and efficiency improvements.[763]

(6) Concentration of press ownership. In its early reports the Commission had expressed concern over concentration of press ownership on the local level but had refrained from basing any recommendation against a proposed newspaper merger solely on this ground. In *West Somerset Free Press and Bristol United Press,*[764] the Commission adopted a new approach. Making the concerns over press concentration previously expressed by the Royal Commission on the Press[765] its own, the MMC stated that »there are *prima facie* reasons on public interest grounds against any individual acquisition of a local newspaper which would carry the process of concentration further.«[766] It continued that »the reduction in the number of companies owning papers in the provinces that is to be deplored applies in principle to acquisitions by regional newspaper groups as well as to those by national groups.«[767] The Commission expressly refrained from criticising the behaviour of the newspaper companies involved in the proposed merger but nonetheless plainly concluded that the transfer was contrary to the public interest. This result rested on the concept that concentration of ownership was *per se* objectionable.[768] The holding reversed the burden of proof to the disadvantage of the purchaser. While under the Commission's previous approach additional negative factors were necessary to render a merger contrary to the public interest, the parties involved in the merger now had affirmatively to establish favourable circumstances outweighing the negative impact on press concentration and thus balancing the public-interest test in their favour. However, since this report, the Commission has failed to adhere to its own test. In the proposed takeover

762 *Benham Newspapers Ltd.*, H.C. No. 402 at paras. 8.8, 9.6.
763 *Id.*
764 H.C. No. 546 (1980).
765 *See* Final Report, Cmnd. 6810, para. 14.11 (1977).
766 *West Somerset Free Press*, H.C. No. 546 at para. 7.18.
767 *Id.* at para. 7.19.
768 *Id.* at paras. 7.20, 7.25.

of *St. Regis International* by *Reed International*, the majority of the Commission approved of the merger despite the resulting concentration of ownership and despite the absence of public benefits.[769] Two Commission members dissented, stating that the takeover should only go ahead if exceptional circumstances and obvious public-interest benefits justified further concentration of ownership.[770]

The MMC's public-interest test criteria reflect the Commission's limited jurisdiction. It is only called upon to decide in cases where two newspapers with a certain size of circulation merge. Mergers involving intermedia concentration between newspapers and undertakings operating in other media markets fall outside its jurisdiction. Interestingly, when the Commission did consider aspects of intermedia competition in the *Benham Newspapers* case,[771] it used the emergence of alternative information markets as a justification for further press concentration. There exist no examples evidencing that the MMC would have included in its public-interest test an evaluation of the purchaser under aspects of his market power through ownership in other media undertakings, such as the film, video, cinema, commercial television or satellite television industries, although such an integration of enterprises has a long-standing history in Britain. A 1970 study evidenced concentrations of ownership extending beyond the print media into commercial video and television as well as into the film industry.[772] These phenomena have persisted to the present. For example, the American press magnate Rupert Murdoch not only owns seven British newspapers, the most important being *The Sun, The Sunday Times* and *The Times,* but also the British satellite television company operating Sky Channel.[773] Robert Maxwell, the British publisher of the Mirror Group Newspapers, holds the majority stake in Premiere and half of the shares in MTV, two other satellite film channels. He is also the most important single investor in cable television. No special antitrust laws apply to the acquisition of satellite television channels by newspapers or any other undertakings.

One of the five members of the consortium that won the three-channel

---

769 H.C. No. 402 at paras. 8.9-8.12.
770 *Id.*, Note of Dissent, para. 9 (by Mr D. Churchill and Mr B.C. Owens). For an analysis of the various public-interest tests applied by the Commission, see also E.-J. MESTMÄCKER, MEDIENKONZENTRATION UND MEINUNGSVIELFALT 71-74 (1978); R. MERKIN & K. WILLIAMS, *supra* note 729, at 275-80.
771 *Benham Newspapers Ltd.,* H.C. No. 402 (1982).
772 A. SILBERMANN & E. ZAHN, DIE KONZENTRATION DER MASSENMEDIEN UND IHRE WIRKUNGEN 220-25 (1970).
773 *See* 1984(1) NEUE MEDIEN 140-42; 1985(3) NEUE MEDIEN 124-33.

DBS franchise in 1986 is the Pearson Group, publishers of the *Financial Times*. Newspaper share ownership in ITV and ILR contractors has also been frequent. In cases of newspaper shareholdings in DBS, ITV or ILR contractors, however, the IBA and the Home Secretary have statutory powers to limit the ownership base and to prevent an undesirable degree of intermedia concentration.

2. *Ownership Restrictions Applying to Newspaper Shareholdings in DBS, ITV, ILR and Cable Contractors*

The Pilkington Committee, set up by the government in 1960 to consider the future of the broadcasting services in the United Kingdom, seriously warned of the *»threat* to democracy« if two of the media of mass communication, namely, the press and commercial television, were owned in some measure by the same people.[774] The Committee pointed to the danger of an excessive concentration of power to influence public opinion and a one-sided presentation of affairs of public concern. In 1960 many newspapers had invested in ITV stations.[775] The Pilkington Committee expressly noted that these investments by the press had been made solely for commercial reasons and that no bias in the ITV programmes had resulted from these shareholdings. Yet the threat to democracy was seen as a potential risk that necessitated the setting of some limits to press participation. Some had argued that the press should not be treated differently than the cinema and the theatre industries, since both were media of mass communication. But the Committee rejected this view by pointing out that while there was no difference in principle between these various media, there was an »immense difference of degree.«[776] While the Committee had felt it unnecessary to recommend a total ban on press ownership in television contractors, it demanded that in no company »should the press interest be dominant‹: »By ›dominant‹, we do not mean ›holding more than half the voting shares‹; we mean rather that it should not be the largest single interest.«[777]

The Television Act 1964[778] incorporated this recommendation two years after the Pilkington Committee had published its report (*see* section 12 of the Television Act 1964). Today, the corresponding provision is contained in section 23 of the Broadcasting Act 1981. It authorizes the IBA

774 1960 Pilkington Report, *supra* note 172, at paras. 627-632.
775 *See* the statistics at *id.*, para. 623.
776 *Id.* at para. 632.
777 *Id.*
778 Television Act 1964 (c.21).

to suspend or terminate a television licence if it appears to the Authority that newspaper shareholdings in a contractor have led or are leading to results that are contrary to the public interest. According to the IBA's present policy, public-interest concerns will generally exist if shareholdings by the press exceed 25 per cent, although in 1976, for example, one single press holding in Southern Television amounted to 37.6 per cent, while a second press shareholding in the same company was 24.8 per cent, making the combined press ownership 62.4 per cent.[779] Since the IBA, unlike the MMC, publishes no formal findings elaborating the public-interest test as contained in section 23 of the Broadcasting Act 1981, the 25-percent figure is a rule of thumb unsubstantiated by any case law. It may perhaps be assumed that the IBA has silently adopted the considerations put forward by the Pilkington Committee. However, in 1987 no single press shareholding in any ITV contractor amounted to more than 21 per cent,[780] making this kind of intermedia concentration »no longer an issue.«[781]

When independent local radio was first introduced in 1972, the newspaper lobby had been very concerned about possible losses in advertising revenues particularly for local newspapers as a result of the new competition from ILR stations.[782] Although the government refused to guarantee majority stakes by local newspapers in the ILR stations operating in their respective distribution areas, the Independent Broadcasting Authority Act 1973[783] contained a preferential right in favour of local newspapers to purchase shareholdings (section 18 of the Act). The provision applied to newspapers with a circulation representing a substantial proportion of the population in the locality of the ILR station, unless the IBA were satisfied that the local radio service was »unlikely to have a materially adverse effect on the financial position of the newspaper.« Free-sheets and newspapers published less frequently than once a week were excluded from the right of pre-emption. According to section 18(5) of the Independent Broadcasting Authority Act 1973, the IBA had to offer any relevant newspaper proprietor an opportunity to acquire shares in the ILR contractor, subject, however, to terms approved by the Authority.

---

779 Royal Commission on the Press, Final Report, Appendices, Cmnd. 6810-1, Appendix B at Table 1 (1977).
780 Independent Broadcasting Authority, ITV Companies – Schedule of Principal Corporate Shareholdings (June 1987) (unpublished).
781 Statement of Mr Kenneth Blyth, Chief Assistant to the IBA Director General.
782 *See* B. NOWOTTNY, RUNDFUNK BüRGERNAH – REGIONALISIERUNG, LOKALE SENDER UND PRIVATFUNK IN GROßBRITANNIEN 188 (1982), *citing* comments by the Newspaper Society for the Home Office Working Party on Local Radio 1 (1979).
783 Independent Broadcasting Authority Act 1973 (c.19).

Local newspapers in a monopoly or dominant position in the particular locality were prohibited from obtaining control over the sound programme contractor.

Local newspapers made use of their pre-emptive right: They acquired interests in 18 out of the 19 original ILR contractors.[784] When evidence suggested that newspaper circulation had remained unchanged in areas in which ILR stations had taken up services and that newspapers' advertising revenues had principally not been affected,[785] the Annan Committee in 1977 recommended the abolition of any right of pre-emption for local newspapers.[786] In addition, the Committee favoured a prohibition on a more than 10-percent interest in an ILR station by any one newspaper; total press shareholdings were to be limited to about 25 per cent.[787] While the Broadcasting Act 1980 refrained from introducing any precise limits to newspaper shareholdings, it abolished the pre-emptive right for local newspapers. Section 23 of the Broadcasting Act 1981, which gives the IBA the authority to prohibit certain shareholdings by newspaper proprietors in television contractors if they are deemed to be contrary to the public interest, now extends to shareholdings in sound programme contractors.

Yet newspaper proprietors continue to invest in ILR. Radio Tay, for example, which had been franchised for the first time in the early 1980s, had a press interest of 42.4 per cent, with the largest single newspaper shareholding being 20 per cent.[788] On the average, newspapers in 1980 held a 21-percent interest in ILR stations, with single shareholdings averaging 13 per cent.[789]

The British concern over the integration of media enterprises involving newspapers is also reflected in section 8(2)(c) of the Cable and Broadcasting Act 1984. The provision requires the Cable Authority to secure that a person who is, or is an associate of, the proprietor of a local newspaper circulating wholly or mainly in the area covered by the cable programme licence does not become or remain the cable licence holder. This constitutes a prohibition of a total identity between the cable operator and

---

784 B. NOWOTTNY, *supra* note 782, at 189.

785 *See id.* at 191. The author suggests that advertisers probably spent additional sums on local radio advertising instead of withdrawing parts of their funds previously allocated to newspaper advertising.

786 1977 Annan Report, *supra* note 269, at para. 14.18.

787 *Id.*

788 B. NOWOTTNY, *supra* note 782, at 194, *citing* IBA, Nov. 26, 1981.

789 *Id.* at 189, *citing* IBA, Press Holdings in Existing ILR Stations, Feb. 29, 1980. However, radio and television contractors are, anomalously, not precluded from owning and publishing newspapers in their areas of operation.

the newspaper owner. If a newspaper proprietor is a principal participant in a cable contractor, i.e., if he holds not less than one-twentieth of the shares, the Cable Authority is obliged to examine whether the share ownership may be adverse to the public interest, in which case it has to terminate the licence unless the cable franchisee's ownership structure is changed (*see* section 8(3)(b),(5)(b),(7) of the Cable and Broadcasting Act 1984). These provisions have not prevented the British newspaper magnet Robert Maxwell, through his Pergamon Press Group, from becoming a major participant in British cable television by acquiring the company Rediffusion, now British Cable Services (BCS).

Finally, with respect to a DBS contractor, the public-interest concerns of section 23 of the Broadcasting Act 1981 equally apply (*see* section 37 of the Cable and Broadcasting Act 1984). The extension of section 23 to DBS services is surprising in light of the fact that no ownership restrictions regarding the participation of ITV companies in DBS contractors apply, although the ITV companies compete even more directly than newspaper proprietors on the same market with DBS contractors. Yet, no public-interest test can be used to prevent an integration of the ITV and DBS television markets. On the contrary, from the beginning ITV participation in a DBS venture was officially encouraged. The guiding rationale for the limitation of newspaper shareholdings in ITV and ILR contractors with the same service area has been a strong concern about a monopolization of opinions, particularly in local and regional markets. However, the present regulation enables ITV contractors to reinforce their regional broadcasting monopolies and to extend their dominant position to the national television market. The ITV companies' position is further strengthened by the fact that they have been allowed to provide programme services for cable systems via communication satellites, a possibility they have already seized by means of the satellite programme Superchannel.[790]

While concerns over the monopolization of opinions determined the regulation of the local media markets, the different regulatory approach in the DBS context may have its roots in concerns about the possible adverse effects of competition between ITV and DBS contractors for the same advertising clients. However, this line of argument is difficult to justify: newspapers, local radio stations, cable contractors and regional television contractors also compete at least partly for the same advertising revenues.

---

790 Yorkshire Television and Granada Television also held a 20-percent stake each in Music Box, another cable television channel that was distributed over the communication satellite ECS-I. Fin. Times, Apr. 19, 1986. Due to severe financial losses, Music Box eventually merged with Superchannel.

Furthermore, while the applicability of the public-interest reservation of section 23 of the Broadcasting Act 1981 to DBS may become particularly relevant with respect to newspapers with a national distribution area, the one-sided privileging of ITV contractors overlooks that (1) through a participation in DBS, the ITV contractors can reinforce their regional monopolies; and (2) the ITV network operators whose programmes are regularly disseminated nationwide are already present in the national television market and are able to strengthen further their position.

When the IBA, after failure of the UNISAT project, advertised three of the five DBS channels at the end of 1985, five different consortia applied for the DBS franchise. Two of the five members of BSB, the company which won the franchise,[791] are ITV contractors, namely, Anglia Television and Granada Television. The latter company is also involved in other media markets, such as television rentals. Only one other DBS applicant, DBS UK, a consortium with seven equity participants, had among its members an ITV contractor, namely, London Weekend Television (LWT).[792]

The problem of intermedia concentration between ITV and DBS contractors and satellite television companies raises the question how the law generally treats cross-ownership between broadcasters and cable operators on the one hand and other media undertakings on the other hand and whether it takes safeguards against horizontal conglomerates involving various broadcasters or different cable contractors.

3. *Other Ownership Restrictions Applying to Media Undertakings*

Rules protecting intermedia competition beyond the integration of newspapers and television contractors are contained in section 20 of the Broadcasting Act 1981. Certain persons are totally disqualified from holding licences for the provision of commercial television or local sound broadcasts. With regard to ITV contractors, these persons are individuals or bodies corporate carrying on business as advertising agents or having control over advertising agents or persons acting as directors or officers of such enterprises (subsections 2(a), 6(c)). The prohibition gives expression to the legislative aim to prevent advertisers from exercising influence over the ITV contractors' programme policy. With respect to ILR contractors,

---

791 *See supra* at chapter III(B)(1).
792 *See* Fin. Times, Aug. 30, 1986. Next to Pearson, the Virgin Group holds a stake in the venture, while Amstrad Consumer Electronics, which originally was part of the consortium, ultimately withdrew. All are U.K. companies. They have a controlling stake in the venture, while a number of other companies that joined the consortium after the franchise had been awarded play a subordinate role, although they provided most of the financing. For more details, see *supra* at chapter III(B)(1).

subsection 8 disqualifies as licence holders (1) manufacturers of records or publishers of musical works; (2) persons promoting the broadcasting of sound recordings or the performance of musical works; or (3) persons obtaining employment for theatrical performers or for persons taking part in television or sound broadcasting programmes. Again, the guiding rationale for the restrictions is the securing of an independent programme policy guided by journalistic rather than purely commercial concerns.

While legal identity between an ITV and an ILR contractor operating in the same or partly the same service area is prohibited (section 20(1) of the Broadcasting Act 1981), the IBA also has to secure that no ITV contractor acquires control of such an ILR contractor and vice versa (section 20(3)). Finally, cross-ownership between various ITV or ILR contractors also runs counter to the legislative aim to securing »adequate competition to supply programmes between a number of programme contractors independent of each other both as to finance and as to control« (section 20(2)(b)). Section 26 of the Act contains a further safeguard against ILR conglomerates. Under this provision, the IBA may refuse to grant an ILR licence to an applicant if the franchise would give an aggregate interest to the benefit of two or more sound programme contractors.

In the early 1980s, the share base of ILR contractors in accordance with the legislative aim was indeed widely spread, and local participation was significant.[793] Some larger companies, like advertising agencies and ITV contractors, had also invested in various ILR franchisees, but their combined average interest amounted to only 19 per cent.[794] Mounting financial difficulties by ILR contractors and a struggle for plain survival by some of them convinced the IBA in the mid-1980s that mergers between certain smaller ILR stations were necessary to safeguard their existence.[795] Also, cooperation between a number of ILR stations, for example on programme exchange, increased with the approval of the IBA.[796]

Section 8 of the Cable and Broadcasting Act 1984 contains certain other ownership restrictions aimed at preserving intermedia competition as well

793 G. NOWOTTNY, *supra* note 782, at. 195-96.
794 *Id.* at 197.
795 *See* Fin. Times, Oct. 22, 1986. This trend continues into the late 1980s. In March 1988, e.g., the IBA gave permission to the London-based ILR contractor Capital Radio to buy minority stakes in 13(!) other ILR stations. *See* Fin. Times, Mar. 25, 1988. According to the article, Capital Radio held more than 20 per cent in two of the ILR stations, while most of the other stakes remained under 10 per cent. At about the same time, the two biggest ILR stations in the West Midlands announced merger plans in order to offer a larger audience to potential advertisers. *See* Fin. Times, Feb. 6, 1988.
796 *See* 1985 IBA Annual Report, *supra* note 253, at 35; 1986 IBA Annual Report, *supra* note 304, at 34-35.

as the independence of cable television from local authorities and religious bodies.[797] The provision distinguishes between the complete identity of the licence holder and any of these public institutions or competitors, and their equity participation in a cable franchisee. With respect to the former alternative, section 8(1) and (2) excludes the following persons from holding a cable franchise: (1) local authorities and bodies »whose objects are wholly or mainly of a religious or political nature«; (2) persons or associates of persons who are (a) ITV programme contractors; or (b) local radio contractors; if the ITV and radio licences refer to the same or any part of the area covered by the cable franchise. This absolute prohibition, so far as it applies to intermedia competitors, is restricted to the group of people or enterprises directly competing with a cable franchisee on the same local market. Furthermore, bodies corporate in which local authorities, religious or political institutions or the BBC or IBA hold shares are equally precluded from holding cable franchises (*see* section 8(3)).

Equity participation in a cable franchisee by any of these persons is generally possible, subject, however, to a public-interest test to be applied by the Cable Authority (section 8(3)(a),(4)). It is questionable what amount and kind of participation by these bodies might be regarded as contrary to the public interest. In principle, any fraction of share ownership by the said institutions may call into question the entitlement of a cable franchise applicant or cable franchisee to hold a cable licence. The Act distinguishes between a participant and a principal participant, the former being a person entitled to less than one-fifth of the voting power.

With respect to the second group of (legal) persons, the public-interest test applies if they are principal participants in a cable operator. The section is applicable to persons who are (1) principal participants in other operators of a diffusion service; (2) programme contractors, or advertising agents; (3) the producers, distributors or exhibitors of cinematograph films; (4) manufacturers of records or the publishers of musical works; or (5) the promoters of the broadcasting of sound recordings or of other musical works (section 8(5)).

The Act lacks a definition of the term »public interest,« and the Cable Authority has so far refrained from specifying it. Clearly, it is the influence on programme policy and public opinion that follows from share

---

797 These restrictions do not apply to SMATV operators that only require a licence under the Wireless Telegraphy Act 1949 or to cable systems solely relaying the broadcasts of one of the broadcasting authorities (*see* Cable and Broadcasting Act 1984, sec. 8(6)).

ownership, and not the influence on purely economic matters, that is of greatest relevance for the public-interest test. Judging from the fact that in the case of partial share ownership by local authorities or the broadcasting authorities a percentage of less than 20 per cent may be problematic, a minor legal and factual possibility to exercise an influence on company policies (and particularly a blocking minority) could possibly run counter to the public interest as envisaged by the Act. Presently the Cable Authority holds the informal position that the merely theoretical possibility of exercising control over a cable operator would not suffice to trigger the public-interest test; instead, some particular anti-competitive measures stemming from the ownership participation should be likely.[798] Generally, the public interest has to be determined in light of the circumstances existing at the time the decision is made and on the basis of the facts of each individual case, independent of whether the legislature may have envisaged a certain situation at the time of the passage of the Act.[799]

Section 8(5)(a) is to prevent a concentration of ownership of cable systems throughout the United Kingdom in the hands of a few enterprises. Also, the potentially strong overlap of interests between producers, distributors, exhibitors and publishers of musical works on the one hand and cable programme providers on the other hand has been identified as a factor possibly furthering the restraint of intermedia competition through increasing proportions of vertical integrations of industries. It should be noted that in the context of participation of share ownership, the restrictions may apply regardless of whether the relevant shareholder directly competes with the cable programme operator in the same locality or whether he is active in a different market territorially. But the criteria of different local markets may become relevant for the determination of the impairment of the public interest. The MMC's observations made in the context of concentration of press ownership may shed some light on possible approaches. Also, the experiences by the IBA in its role as the guardian of competition between ITV programme contractors could help the Cable Authority to define the public-interest concept in particular cases. Yet it appears from the above-mentioned informal position taken by the Cable Authority that it is presently prepared to take a more relaxed view on ownership restrictions than has traditionally been taken by the IBA. This would correspond with the »lighter regulatory touch« applied to cable television generally. The guiding provision for the IBA, i.e., section

798 Information provided to the author by Mr Jon Davey, Director General, Cable Authority.
799 *See* Cartwright v. Post Office, [1968] 2 All E.R. 646, 651; *aff'd.* [1969] 1 All E.R. 421.

20 of the Broadcasting Act 1981, however, has already served as a model for the drafting of the corresponding provision on ownership restrictions in the Cable and Broadcasting Act 1984.

Similar to the ITV franchises, ownership restrictions applying to cable operators are enforced in mid-franchise by means of a licence condition requiring the cable operators to notify the Cable Authority of any significant changes in shareholdings.[800] If the cable franchisee ignores the Cable Authority's views on any change of ownership, the Authority may ultimately revoke the licence in accordance with section 17(1)(b) of the Cable and Broadcasting Act 1984. Furthermore, a general clause in sub-section (c) of section 17(1) enables the Authority to revoke a licence if »any change affecting the nature or characteristics of the body corporate, or any change in the persons having control over or interests in the body corporate, takes place ... which, if it had occured before the granting of the licence, would have induced the Authority to refrain from granting the licence.«

The Cable Authority presently supports a liberal policy with respect to changes of ownership in mid-term of the franchises. In light of the enormous difficulties faced by the cable industry, any other position would be likely to lead to a total stifling of the cabling process. In several in-stances the Authority has already permitted such ownership changes, in-cluding Thorn EMI's sale of the total Swindon franchise and a large stake in the Coventry cable system to BT. As long as the new ownership struc-ture does not represent an outright violation of cogent provisions of the Cable and Broadcasting Act 1984, the Cable Authority will not prohibit the transfer.[801]

Equally, competition-law policy concerns have not always taken preference over other considerations. When the dramatic decline in the number of cinemas led to a strong concentration of ownership in cinemas, no official measure was taken to counteract this development, because the cinema industry was still ailing. In 1983 the MMC, following a reference by the Director General of Fair Trading, held that a complex monopoly situation under section 6(1)(c) of the Fair Trading Act 1973 existed in favour of cer-tain film distributors in Great Britain.[802] The Commission found that two companies together with their distributors had effective control of about 60 per cent of the film exhibition market and of even more than two-thirds of

---

800 Cable Authority, 1985 Notes for Prospective Licensees, *supra* note 574, at Part I, para. 24.
801 Information provided to the author by Mr Jon Davey, Director General, Cable Authority.
802 MMC, Films, *supra* note 445, at paras. 8.4., 8.5.

the film distribution market.[803] Holding that both monopolies operated against the public interest, the Commission recommended a number of changes in the way new films were to be distributed to the cinemas. Considering, however, the »decline in cinema audiences, the continuing need to close cinemas, and the fact that some surviving cinemas are making losses,« the Commission expressly refrained from also advising in favour of the divestment of the two dominant companies.[804]

While the ownership restrictions described above evidence a detailed system of competition and antitrust laws designed to safeguard intermedia competition, there exist a number of other ownership restrictions spread throughout various legislative enactments with a very different aim. The ownership restrictions in question limit foreign participation in British media ventures. Instead of furthering competition, these rules attempt to shield British companies from foreign competition and to keep the broadcast media under British control. Section 20(6) of the Broadcasting Act 1981 disqualifies any person as an ITV contractor who is neither »(i) a national of a member State who is ordinarily resident within the European Economic Community, nor (ii) ordinarily resident in the United Kingdom, the Isle of Man or the Channel Islands.«[805] The same provision defines a disqualified body corporate as a corporation that is neither »(i) a body formed under the law of a member State which has its registered or head office or principal place of business within the European Economic Community, nor (ii) a body incorporated under the law of the Isle of Man or the Channel Islands«. The same provision applies with respect to ILR contractors (*see* section 20(8) of the Broadcasting Act 1981).

Still, the provisions do allow some minority form of foreign equity participation in ITV or ILR contractors. When the majority of ILR stations went through great financial difficulties in the mid-1980s, the IBA even welcomed the purchase by two Australian broadcasting organizations with vast experience in radio broadcasting of stakes in 14 ILR stations. The expectation was that the know-how of the Australian companies stemming from the highly competitive Australian radio market would help to improve the

---

803 *Id.* at para. 8.17.
804 *Id.* at para. 8.22.
805 Section 20(7) of the Broadcasting Act 1981 further specifies a »national« in relation to the United Kingdom as a person »(a) who is a citizen of the United Kingdom and Colonies or a British subject not possessing that citizenship or the citizenship of any other Commonwealth country or territory, who, in either case, has the right of abode in the United Kingdom; or (b) who is a citizen of the United Kingdom and Colonies by birth or by registration or naturalisation in Gibraltar, or whose father was so born, registered or naturalised.«

marketing management of the ILR stations.[806] Australian companies have also invested in ITV.[807]

Similarly, under section 20(2)(a),(6) of the Broadcasting Act 1981, which is applicable to DBS contractors, these contractors have to be either nationals of an EC member state or bodies corporate formed under the laws of a member state. When the Australian media magnet Holmes à Court and his Bell Group showed an interest in the British DBS franchise and acquired a 45-percent stake in one of the DBS applicants, the IBA made it known that it had no objection to the Bell Group holding a minority stake in a DBS applicant.[808] Another non-EC company, the Bond Corporation of Australia, owned shares in a third DBS applicant, and an American company, News International, held a financial stake in yet another DBS applicant. Since the government had also dropped its requirement that a British-built satellite be used, a number of foreign companies involved in satellite construction had also approached the IBA and potential DBS applicants to explore their market chances.[809] In its Guidance Notes for applicants, the IBA became explicit about its attitude towards foreign involvement in British DBS:

> With regard to the source of satellite provision, it is assumed that there would be freedom to consider proposals from suppliers either in this country or overseas. But it is also to be assumed that the Government would be opposed to any proposal in which an overseas supplier was quoting prices which were less than cost in order to gain access to the British DBS market, and *that the nature and prospective size of the net industrial benefit to the U.K. of proposals will be a consideration to be taken into account by Government in deciding whether to proceed.*[810]

806 Fin. Times, Oct. 22, 1986.
807 However, when a newspaper report in early 1988 revealed that members of the Saudi royal family held an indirect share in TV-am, the breakfast television station, this created a great public irritation and prompted the IBA to take counter-measures. Since the summer of 1987, Beaverbrook Investmensts, a 14.9-percent shareholder of TV-am, has been controlled by Saudi interests. Apparently, the fact that Beaverbrook was controlled by non-EC shareholders had been disclosed to the IBA, but the identity of the ownership had not been revealed, a circumstance that appears to have caused particular anger within the IBA. This in turn suggests that the Authority carefully distinguishes between favourable and unfavourable non-EC investments. The IBA ultimately ordered Beaverbrook to reduce its investment in TV-am to less than 10 per cent, making it clear that TV-am's licence could otherwise be in jeopardy. See Fin. Times, Feb. 22, 26, 1988; Apr. 6, 1988.
808 Fin. Times, Apr. 14, 1986.
809 COMSAT, the U.S. satellite organization; EUROSATELLITE, the Franco-German-led satellite manufacturing group constructing the French and German DBS satellites TV-Sat-1 and TDS-1; and Britsat, a British company offering American satellites, had shown interest in becoming the system supplier. See Fin. Times, Feb. 4, 1986; Feb. 21, 1986; June 18, 1986. Ultimately, BSB signed a contract for the provision of the satellite with the U.S. company Hughes Aircrafts.
810 IBA, Guidance Notes for Organizations Interested in the Provision of DBS Services, Press Release, Sept. 3, 1985 (emphasis added).

Clearly, industrial-policy considerations weighed at least as heavily in the decision-making process as did programme-policy concerns. The final franchise award for the BSB consortium may thus have been closely linked to the fact that all its controlling members are British companies, although it was agreed after the awarding of the franchise but before the actual signing of the contract that a number of other, partly non-European companies could join in the venture to provide the bulk of the financing, with the control over BSB remaining with the British partners, however.

Similar to the ownership restrictions of the Broadcasting Act 1981, the Cable and Broadcasting Act 1984 contains restrictions aimed at fending off foreign, particularly American, competitors. Section 8(1) of the Cable and Broadcasting Act 1984 prohibits the granting of a licence for the provision of a diffusion service to an individual who is neither a national of an EC member state ordinarily resident within the EC, nor an individual ordinarily resident in the United Kingdom, the Isle of Man or the Channel Islands. Equally, bodies corporate have to be incorporated under the law of a member state and need to have their registered or head offices or principal places of business within the EC. The Cable Authority's Guidance Notes for franchise applicants contain the following pertinent passage:

> Companies with overseas shareholders are not precluded from applying for telecommunications licences and overseas companies are not barred from the ownership of cable systems. However, in no case will a telecommunications licence be issued to a company in which the ownership of more than 50% of the voting shares lies outside the European community and, where ownership is fragmented, the Government would normally expect non-European community participation to be no more than 30%. In cases where the shareholdings in a cable company are particularly fragmented, a still lower holding might be required if, in the Government's opinion, a shareholding of less than 30% could, nevertheless, bestow a dominant influence over the policy of the proposed licence holder.[811]

The Peacock Committee took the view that the present restrictions prohibiting the grant of local cable franchises to non-EC companies had unnecessarily inhibited the growth and spread of cable television in the United Kingdom and should therefore be abolished.[812] In particular, the Committee took favourable note of the interests American investors with large expertise in the U.S. cable television market had shown in British

---

811 Cable Authority, 1985 Notes for Prospective Licensees, *supra* note 574, at Part I, para. 25.
812 1986 Peacock Report, *supra* note 216, at para. 667.

cable television. The Cable Authority shares this view and would like the foreign ownership restrictions to be removed.[813] This is not surprising in light of the very slow and disappointing development of British cable television systems and the enormous difficulties potential cable operators are still facing in trying in find British investors.

But as pointed out earlier, the Peacock Committee's main concern with respect to cable television was its ultimate goal to promote the establishment of an integrated national common-carrier cable grid instead of a network of local cable franchises in the hands of a variety of different owners. In the final stage of a »full broadcasting market« with general access rights to the national grid as suggested by the Committee, the special relationship between the BBC and the ITV system would be abolished. They would be in the position of »normal« electronic publishers along with other programme providers, and unified competition laws could apply in order to prevent market distortions through uncompetitive practices or concentration of ownership. Until the realization of this final goal – which appears unlikely in view of the position presently taken by the government – British competition and antitrust law as it applies to the media will to some extent be characterized by a variety of differing and partly conflicting rules. A totally consistent system of the principles governing competition does not go with a heavily regulated media market in which the public broadcasting organizations enjoy privileged positions. Still, in the 1980s the British media market has on the whole become more competitive. The original plan to allocate two of the five DBS channels exclusively to the BBC failed for financial reasons, as did the following project to divide responsibilities equally between the BBC and the ITV companies. The final competitive tender of the DBS franchise led to the participation of diversified companies in the venture, although two ITV contractors also participate. Increasingly, non-EC companies have invested in ILR and ITV, and the cable and low- and medium-power satellite television markets dramatically increased the number

---

813 Information provided to the author by Mr Jon Davey, Director General, Cable Authority. Thus, the Authority did not object to the £ 57 million investment by the U.S. company Prudential Bache in the cable franchise operator City Centre Cable that holds the franchise for the Royal Borough of Kensington and Chelsea in London. However, despite the fact that the investment gave Prudential Bache about a two-thirds stake of the equity in City Centre Cable, voting control remained with a U.K. company. Fin. Times, Feb. 11, 1988. A Canadian cable television operator has also demonstrated a vivid interest in Robert Maxwell's British Cable Services and is negotiating for a 49-percent stake in that company. *Id.*

and variety of participants in the broadcast media. Finally, the creation of Channel 4 and the latest government initiative to enforce on the public broadcasting channels some minimum quotas for programmes made by independent programme producers has further spurred the emergence of a lively new television programme production market. It is to be hoped that, before too long, the competition law will provide rules defining the relationship between these new market entrants and the established media undertakings.

VI. *The International Dimension of British Broadcasting*

The relevance of international law for the structure and functioning of the British media system has been demonstrated in many contexts throughout this treatise. In particular, the importance of the European Convention on Human Rights for the regulation of freedom of expression in the United Kingdom and the impact of the competition and antitrust laws of the EEC Treaty on the British media market have been discussed. The following chapter will focus on the effect of the law of international treaties and customary international law, which is solely addressed to sovereign states and obligates them to conduct their broadcasting activities in a certain way. The analysis will tackle the problem of how the United Kingdom gives effect to its international obligations and what position it takes in the context of the legality of transborder broadcast transmissions. Two elements of the international legal regime deserve separate treatment: (1) the technical operation of U.K. broadcasting, extending from frequency assignment to the enforcement of technical standards; and (2) the content-related side of broadcasting dealing with the sending of programmes across national frontiers. Finally, the chapter will also deal with the way the British broadcasting system, including cable, is legally able to open up to the international broadcasting markets by including foreign programmes in its services and the extent to which it itself contributes to the internationalization of broadcasting markets through cooperation with foreign broadcasters and through programme export.

A. The Relevance of the International Legal Regime for the Technical Operation of the Broadcasting Media

1. Frequency Assignment

The emission of electromagnetic waves across national frontiers is a legally relevant event under international law because of the principle of territorial integrity. As a ground rule, the deliberate transmission of electromagnetic waves onto the territory of a foreign state without that country's prior consent violates its territorial integrity, unless the transborder transmission is the result of an inevitable overspill due to the uncontrollability of signal spreading.[814] The United Kingdom is bound by article 35 of the ITU Convention 1982,[815] obligating it to prevent harmful interferences with the radio services of other member states or recognized operating agencies. With respect to the relationship between the United Kingdom and other ITU member states this treaty obligation takes preference over the above-stated rule of customary international law requiring prior consent.

The international allocation of frequencies to member states by ITU Administrative Conferences serves the harmonization of the international use of the frequency spectrum according to the spirit of article 35 of the ITU Convention. The ITU Radio Regulations, issued by the Administrative Conferences, specify the frequency allocations in detail. Under article 35(2) of the ITU Convention 1982, member states further bear the responsibility that private operating agencies authorized under national law observe the international obligations.

U.K. government control over the civil use of the frequency spectrum is ensured by the Wireless Telegraphy Acts 1949 and 1967. According to section 1 of the Wireless Telegraphy Act 1949, the use of any station for wireless telegraphy or the installation or use of any apparatus for wireless telegraphy is subject to a licence requirement. A violation of the requirement constitutes a criminal offence under sections 1(1), 14 of the Wireless Telegraphy Act 1949. In these cases the government may also issue forfeiture orders in respect of equipment used in connection with the radio station, including the forfeiture of loudspeakers, but not of records

---

814 *See* Engel, *Das Völkerrecht des Telekommunikationsvorgangs*, 49 RABELSZ 90, 99 (1985).
815 ITU member states that have not signed the 1982 Convention are bound by the corresponding provision of the ITU Convention of 1973.

and cassettes.[816] Also, the obligation to »observe the provisions of the International Telecommunication Convention and of any International Convention or international agreement relating to broadcasting to which Her Majesty or the Secretary of State may be or become a party« is expressly included, e.g., in clause 8 of the BBC Licence and Agreement 1981. Similarly, the requirement imposed by article 39(1) of the Radio Regulations 1979 on broadcasting stations not to employ power exceeding that necessary to maintain an economically effective national service of good quality is reflected in clause 9 of the BBC Licence and Agreement 1981.

While many government departments, such as the Ministry of Defence and the Home Office, participate in U.K. radio regulation, it is the Radiocommunications Division (RD) (formerly the Radio Regulatory Division) of the Department of Trade and Industry that carries the main responsibility. It enforces the Wireless Telegraphy Acts 1949 and 1967 on behalf of the Secretary of State and controls any interference. This department also specifies the basic technical standards to avoid radio interference. The interdepartmental work is coordinated by the Cabinet Office. While the Home Office carries the responsibility for assigning the broadcasting frequencies to the IBA and the BBC, the RD licences other non-Crown users on behalf of the Secretary of State for Trade and Industry. For a long time the RD was part of the Home Office, but following a recommendation of the 1983 Government Report of the Radio Spectrum, the powers under both Wireless Telegraphy Acts were transferred from the Home Secretary to the Secretary of State of Trade and Industry.[817] The change was effected because the government felt that greater coordination between the DTI's various divisions – which are responsible for telecommunications policy and also for sponsoring the interests of the electronic manufacturing industries – and the RD was desirable.[818]

RD officers participate on behalf of the United Kingdom in all international negotiations on the use and allocation of radio frequencies and on the technical and operating standards for radio communication services.[819] The RD then formulates equipment performance specifications

---

816 *See* Secretary of State v. Rudd, 1987 W.L.R. 786.
817 *See* 1983 Report of the Radio Spectrum, *supra* note 306, at para. 13.31.
818 *Id.* at para. 13.23.
819 1986 Annual Report of the Radio Regulatory Division, *supra* note 263, at 10-12.

and other technical criteria and licences all non-Crown users of radio. They also formulate the frequency planning policy.

The actual assignment of frequencies to individual users under the Wireless Telegraphy Acts 1949 and 1967 takes place on the basis of the U.K. National Frequency Allocation Table drawn up as a result of interdepartmental coordination. The table used to be a classified document until 1985, when it was published for the first time following the recommendation of the Merriman Committee[820] for greater openness of the system of spectrum allocation.[821] It identifies the international allotment[822] and compares it with the assignment of frequencies in the United Kingdom.[823] The 1983 Government Report of the Radio Spectrum alleged that »[i]n most cases this follows the international allocations but differs in some cases to meet the UK's special requirements, provided that there is no infringement of the international radio regulations.«[824] This approach complies with the corresponding wording in article 6(4) of the Radio Regulations 1979. In some cases, however, governments may exercise some discretion, for example, if a spectrum band is used for several services internationally – provided that the national variations are made known in footnotes to the International Table of Frequency Allocations. In other cases the country may reserve some discretion through statements made in the Final Acts of Administrative Conferences. The United Kingdom has on various occasions made use of these possibilities and has departed from the international allocations.[825]

In 1985 the Department of Trade and Industry launched a study to determine a new method for assigning frequencies. The study was conducted by a communication consulting firm, which was reviewing plans that suggested that private companies should be allowed to administer at least parts of the radio spectrum.[826] Supporters of this system believed that commercial pricing would result in a more speedy development and allocation of spectrum frequencies for new users, such as cellular radio

820 1983 Report of the Radio Spectrum, *supra* note 306, at para. 9.10.
821 Department of Trade and Industry, Table of Radio Frequency Allocations (1985).
822 *See* article 6(2) of the Radio Regulations 1979, obligating member states to effect all frequency assignments to stations capable of causing harmful interference to the services of the station operated in another member state in accordance with the Table of Frequency Allocations.
823 1983 Report of the Radio Spectrum, *supra* note 306, at para. 6.7.
824 *Id. See also* E.G. WEDELL, *supra* note 266, at 65-68.
825 Department of Trade and Industry, Deregulation of the Radio Spectrum in the UK para. 2.3 (study produced by CSP International) (1987) (hereafter cited as DTI, Deregulation of the Radio Spectrum).
826 *Id.*

operators.[827] The results of the study, published in 1987, were favourably received by the DTI; the day-to-day administration of gradually increasing parts of the frequency spectrum would be transferred from the DTI to new private-sector frequency planning organizations (FPOs) under 20-year franchises. Competing FPOs would then be allowed to sell their frequencies on the open market to the highest bidder. Existing heavy users of the frequency spectrum, like the BBC, the IBA, BT or Mercury, would keep most but not all of their frequencies and could administer them themselves. Suggestions that the frequencies be auctioned to the potential FPOs were rejected by the study, which instead recommended that the initial allocation of frequencies to FPOs should take place on the ground of merit rather than on the basis of the highest price paid.[828]

The study put forward the hypothesis that spectrum scarcity is the result of the present method of allocation and that the frequency spectrum is not a scarce resource that only the government could be expected to administer in the public interest. The study alleged that under the present system, frequencies have been allocated in an arbitrary manner on the ground of the government's perception of need rather than on the ground of genuine market demand, a system that, according to the study, has also encouraged wasteful hoarding of under-utilized capacity. The government has let it be known that it intends to introduce legislation along the lines of the main recommendations of the study.[829] If the changes come about, the United Kingdom will be the first country in the world to privatise its radio spectrum.

2. *Transformation of International Technical Standards*

Of great importance in the context of telecommunications systems is the setting of technical standards regulating the equipment used to run the systems and the apparatus attached to it. Much of this standard setting is done by international bodies. Their work is aimed at a harmonization of national standards in order to facilitate the international trade in telecommunications goods and services. These activities are partly based on international treaties and partly result from the voluntary cooperation of

827 *See* Adam Smith Institute, *supra* note 524, at 6-9.
828 *See id.* at para. 9.1, pp. 131-33.
829 The Times, Apr. 3, 1987; Fin. Times, Apr. 3, 1987. It also appears likely that the government will proceed more carefully than proposed in the study. It is being considered to privatise the radio-licensing department of the DTI as a first step to introducing an element of market forces into the frequency assignment in the U.K. *See* Fin. Times Business Information, Telecom Markets 100/8 (1988).

private and governmental organizations. For example, the International Consultative Committee on Telegraph and Telephone (CCITT) and the International Organization for Standardization (ISO) are important international bodies responsible for the drafting and adoption of international technical standards. Also, the General Agreement on Tariffs and Trade (GATT) has negotiated a Standards Code dealing with a wide range of standards-related issues and aimed at preventing governments from using standardization procedures for the creation of excessive restrictions to trade.[830] Another example is article 5 of the Radio Regulations 1979: all transmitting, receiving and similar equipment used in connection with stations should, as far as practicable, be based on the most recent technical advances, as indicated, inter alia, in the Radio Recommendations issued by the International Radio Consultative Committee (CCIR) (see articles 5(4)(c) and 11(1) ITU Convention 1982). Under section 12(A) of the Wireless Telegraphy Act 1949,[831] the Secretary of State of Trade and Industry may issue regulations specifying the technical requirements to be complied with in the case of apparatus used in connection with wireless telegraphy. Subsection 4 of this provision requires the Secretary of State not to prescribe any technical requirements unless he is satisfied that they are compatible with the international obligations of the United Kingdom.

The necessary flexibility to ensure the use of the latest technical achievements by the broadcasting authorities is provided, for example, by clause 5(2) of the BBC Licence and Agreement 1981, allowing the Secretary of State to give orders at any time with regard to the technical measures and processes to be used.

Of further importance in this context is the standard setting effected by the Conference of European Posts and Telecommunications Administrations (CEPT), operating at intergovernmental levels and issuing non-binding recommendations. The United Kingdom participates and takes note of this standard setting.[832]

Standard setting binding upon member states may also take place at the level of the EC Council. According to article 100 of the EEC Treaty, the Council, acting on the recommendation of the Commission, may issue directives for the harmonization of legal or administrative regulations of the member states directly affecting the establishment or the functioning of the Common Market. If the Commission concludes that existing

---

830 *See* Mostehar, *supra* note 603, at 52-53.
831 This section was included by virtue of section 78 of the Telecommunications Act 1984.
832 1983 Report of the Radio Spectrum, *supra* note 306, at para. 6.6.

differences in these regulations lead to a distortion of competition between member states, it may enter into consultations with the member states (article 101). In case these consultations fail to result in the removal of the distorting effects, the Council may then issue the necessary directives. In certain instances, technical standards may form such barriers to trade in goods between member states. But in many member states, including the United Kingdom, technical standards are mostly issued by independent bodies with no sovereign powers of their own. Their recommendations therefore do not have the status of legal or administrative regulations, the existence of which is a prerequisite for the jurisdiction of the Council under article 100 of the EEC Treaty. However, the Council's jurisdiction is generally accepted in cases in which at least one member state regulates the technical standards for the matters considered by the Council by way of legal or administrative regulations.[833] On this basis, the EC has, for example, issued a directive on radio interference caused by electrical household appliances, portable tools and similar equipment.[834] The 1978 regulation on household appliances, portable tools, and the like,[835] issued under section 10(1) of the Wireless Telegraphy Act 1949, is an example of how an EC directive on technical standards relating to spectrum management was formally incorporated into U.K. law.[836]

Another way of giving effect to obligatory international standards is contained in section 22(6) of the Telecommunications Act 1984. According to this provision, the Secretary of State of Trade and Industry or, under his general authorization, the Director of OFTEL may designate standards to which apparatus must conform if they are to be approved for connection to a telecommunications system.[837] This section has particular relevance

---

833 *See* Langeheine, in E. GRABITZ, KOMMENTAR ZUM EWG-VERTRAG article 100, para. 19 (May 1986).

834 Council Directive of Nov. 4, 1976, 19 O.J. EUR. COMM. (No. L 336) 1-21 (1976) (76/889/EEC); *see also* Council Directive of Aug. 18, 1983, 26 O.J. EUR. COMM. (No. L 247) 10 (1983) (83/447/EEC). The EC Commission has also issued Proposals for Council Directives on standardization in the field of information technology and telecommunications and on the mutual recognition of type approval for telecommunications terminal equipment ((COM) (85) 230 final). If adopted, they would provide the basis for promoting common technical standards among member states that would be compatible with other international standards.

835 1978 S.I. No. 1267, *as amended by* 1985 S.I. No. 808.

836 Regulations with respect to the resistance of interference are now regulated by section 12 A of the Wireless Telegraphy Act 1949, included by virtue of section 78 of the Telecommunications Act 1984. This provision explicitly requires the Secretary of State to ensure the compatibility of the technical regulations with the international obligations of the United Kingdom.

837 These powers were delegated to OFTEL by the DTI on Dec. 1, 1986. *See* OFTEL News, No. 5, p. 8 (1986).

with regard to telecommunications systems and apparatus that have already been approved. It enables the DTI or OFTEL to change the standards for already licensed equipment, provided that they have given prior notice to the systems operator enabling him to make representations or raise objections (section 22(8)Telecommunications Act 1984). An interesting example of how use is made of the authorization in section 22(6) is condition 37(1) of the licence granted by the Secretary of State of Trade and Industry to Racal-Vodafone Ltd., a cellular radio operator, under section 7 of the Telecommunications Act 1984. The condition provides that the DTI may require the systems operator to incorporate into or remove from his system any apparatus designated by the DTI (or to ensure that his system conforms or is to conform to any standard designated in a DTI directive), »provided always that the power of direction here under shall be exercised only for the purpose of securing compliance with any requirement of European Community law.« This provision implies that the DTI has no authority to enforce Racal-Vodafone's compliance with (later) ITU recommendations, for example. Licence conditions similar to the kind described above are normally used to ensure the transformation of international standards into already existing licences.[838] However, no such conditions are contained in licences granted to cable systems operators.[839]

As a matter of last resort, section 94(1) of the Telecommunications Act 1984 further authorizes the Secretary of State of Trade and Industry, after consultation with the person concerned, to »give to that person such directions of a general character as appear to the Secretary of State to be requisite or expedient in the interests of national security or relations with the government of a country or territory outside the United Kingdom.« The scope of the provision encompasses any kind of directions the Secretary of State may think necessary. It is not limited to the formulation of technical standards. The section rather represents a means of enforcing certain conditions vis-à-vis a licensee as a way for the government to respond to new developments unforeseen at the time of the drafting of a licence.

Conversely, international standards may be used by systems operators to protect their systems against third parties. For example, British Telecom's licence, granted by the DTI, provides that BT may refuse to enter into an agreement with anybody wanting to make use of BT's system, if it cannot

---

838 Information provided to the author by Stephen R. Temple, Assistant Secretary, Telecommunications Division of the Department of Trade and Industry.
839 *Id.*

be secured that the signal quality of the messages complies with »any obligations and recommendations of the International Telecommunication Union,«
provided that these standards have been accepted by the U.K. government
(condition 13(4)(g)).[840] This is also an example of a formal acknowledgement
of non-binding ITU recommendations by a U.K. governmental department.

In 1983 the EC Council took another initiative aimed at establishing a procedure for the exchange of information in the field of technical standards and
regulations.[841] Under the directive, the Commission and certain specified
national and EC standards institutions have to be informed each year of
the standards programmes drawn up by the national standards institutions.
The two European standards institutions mentioned are the European
Committee for Standardization (CEN) and the European Committee for
Electrotechnical Standardization (CENELEC), both located in Brussels.
These institutions promote the cooperation of the European
standardization institutions. The British institutions addressed in the
directive are the British Standards Institution (BSI) and the British
Electrotechnical Committee (BEC).[842] Both institutions take an active
part in CEN and CENELEC.[843] The aim of the Council directive is first to
make the necessary information available to the Commission and the relevant institutions before appropriate technical provisions can be adopted by
the Council.

Administrative regulations setting technical standards of the kind of those
dealing with household appliances and portable tools or in the form of
formal directives under section 22 of the Telecommunications Act 1984 are
the exception in the United Kingdom. In most cases, standard setting in
the area of telecommunications is done by the BSI.[844] The BSI standards
are implemented by the British Approvals Board for Telecommunications
(BABT), which is a wholly owned subsidiary of the British Electrotechnical
Approvals Board, a non-profit company limited by guarantee. BABT is
responsible for the testing and assessment of telecommunications

---

840 With respect to BT's general telephone network, it will be the International Consultative
   Committee for Telegraphs and Telephones (CCITT) rather than the International
   Consultative Committee for Radio (CCIR) that will issue the recommendations relating to
   the relevant standards; with respect to cable television systems, the recommendations may be
   supplied by both bodies. *See* G. CODDING, JR. & A. RUTKOWSKI, THE INTERNATIONAL
   TELECOMMUNICATION UNION IN A CHANGING WORLD 235 (1982).
841 Council Directive of Mar. 28, 1983, O.J. EUR. COMM. (No. L 209) 8-12 (1983) (83/189/EEC).
842 *Id.* at Annex.
843 British Standards Institution, Annual Report 1983-84 5 (1984).
844 With regard to equipment approval, BT has so far enjoyed a monopoly on the approval of
   telecommunications equipment to be linked to its network by private contractors. OFTEL is
   planning to abolish this monopoly right. *See* Fin. Times, Apr. 2, 1988.

264

subscriber apparatus for connection to telecommunications systems run by the PTOs. If the Board is satisfied that the apparatus submitted for approval meets all necessary requirements, the DTI issues a »Certificate of Approval.« BABT then grants a licence on payment of a fee and makes an entry in its list of approved apparatus (*see* sections 22, 23 and 84 of the Telecommunications Act 1984). The BSI, on the other hand, takes care of the setting of standards against which all types of telecommunications equipment are tested.

Under section 8 of the Trade Description Act 1968,[845] the Board of Trade may by order require that certain goods be marked with recognized trade descriptions, such as a BABT certificate of approval. The supply of these goods without the necessary description or the application of false trade descriptions constitutes a criminal offence (sections 1, 8(2)). Section 10(1)(b) of the Act requires the Board of Trade to ensure that its orders are compatible with the United Kingdom's international obligations. These provisions ensure the legal backing of the work of the standardization bodies.

The adoption in the United Kingdom of non-binding recommendations – be they made by CCIR, CEPT, CEN or any other international body involved in standardization – thus is basically done by way of an informal adoption procedure employed by the BSI in cases that it sees fit. As a next step, BABT uses the BSI's standards to test all telecommunications equipment submitted to it. In some cases, usually in safety-related matters, the Secretary of State for Trade and Industry formally approves the apparatus under the relevant provision of the Telecommunications Act 1984, thereby giving legal effect to the international recommendations. Other BSI standards are not legally binding and only have the quality of recommendations.

The telecommunications licences issued to cable operators require that BABT approval is only needed for attachments with an interactive capability that facilitate access to any public switched network.[846] No such obligations apply where attachments relate to services restricted to subscribers to the cable system. This method grants network constructors more leeway on the types of equipment they want to use; however, in view of potential expansions of local interactive services to the national level,

---

845 Trade Description Act 1968 (c.29).
846 Cable Authority, 1985 Notes for Prospective Licensees, *supra* note 574, at Annex A, Structure of the Draft Telecommunications Licence for Cable Systems, Condition 16.

the government strongly recommends prior BABT approval of such attachments.[847]

In general, the setting of national standards may ensure a competitive advantage of national manufacturers over foreign suppliers. The United Kingdom appears to be well aware of this effect. In line with its policy to boost the British telecommunications industry, the DTI set up a Technical Working Group on Standards for Wideband Cable Systems in 1982.[848] It is the task of the Working Group to examine all British standards applying to telecommunications services (with the exception of conventional voice telephony) and to draft new standards where necessary. The setting up of the Working Group was the result of a recommendation made by the Technology Advisory Panel in 1982. This body had been explicit about a major rationale of the Working Group: »The recommended design standards should offer maximum potential to United Kingdom manufacturers and operators and should anticipate, and be compatible with, developments in communications technology. ... The Department of Industry should create an effective forum in which all those interested in cable systems can come together to unify their efforts to the benefit of the United Kingdom.«[849] The standards drafted by the Working Group go through the regular BSI procedures and thereby receive the normal quality of »British Standards.«[850] The telecommunications licences granted to cable operators explicitly require that the systems conform to the standards drawn up by the Working Group.[851]

In assessing the merits of the cable franchise applicant, the Cable Authority, the DTI and OFTEL appear to place great weight on the British origin of the technology intended to be used by the franchisee for the cable network. An indication of the importance attached to British equipment origin may be seen in the Westminster Cable Company's company profile.[852] On its 2-1/2 typewritten pages, the company four times emphasizes that the system is based on British technology manufactured by British industry.

The policy to favour British industry appears to be nowhere explicitly stated in any official document. On the other hand, where British standards would impede the industry's international competitiveness,

---

847 *Id.*
848 *See* 1983 White Paper on Cable Systems, *supra* note 208, at para. 31.
849 1982 ITAP Report, *supra* note 544, at para. 8.11(v), (vi).
850 1983 White Paper on Cable Systems, *supra* note 208, at para. 31.
851 Cable Authority, 1985 Notes for Prospective Licensees, *supra* note 574, at Annex A, Structure of the Draft Telecommunications Licence for Cable Systems, Condition 16.
852 Unpublished document provided to the author by the company.

compliance with them does not appear to be indispensable. The Cable Authority's Guidance Notes to cable franchise applicants in this context read: »The Government's general policy on standards is that use should be made of suitable British Standards where these reflect international market requirements.«[853]

B. Principles Applying to Incoming Foreign and Outgoing British (Broadcast) Programmes

In contrast to the principle of territorial integrity applying to the technical use of the electromagnetic radio spectrum, international law has traditionally recognized that the transmission of radio broadcast programmes across borders enjoys a legal privilege.[854] While certain programme contents, such as the propagation of genocide, may violate international law, the international community has for the most part tolerated even the deliberate transmission of radio programmes onto the territory of foreign states. The right of the originating state to broadcast across frontiers has been deemed to be counterbalanced by the right of the receiving state to jam the transmissions.[855] This state practice with respect to radio programmes has found its most prominent expression in the permanent international broadcasting services set up in some 80 countries. The United Kingdom provides such an international service, called the External Services, for listeners in all parts of the world.

1. BBC External Services

The aim of the External Services is to bring the British view of national and international events to a worldwide audience. The BBC has been assigned with the task of providing these services under close government supervision. Originally, the establishment of the service was the idea of Lord Reith, the BBC's first Director General. When the »Empire Service« first came into operation in 1932, its English-language programmes were directed at Asia and Australia with the view to preserving and enhancing the political, cultural and economic ties with the Empire.[856] But the government soon realized the wider political potentials for British prestige

853 Cable Authority, 1985 Notes for Prospective Licensees, *supra* note 574, at Annex A, Structure of the Draft Telecommunications Licence for Cable Systems, Condition 16.
854 Engel, *supra* note 814, at 100.
855 *Id.* at 102.
856 B. PAULU, *supra* note 165, at 374.

and influence in world affairs that the new service could bring about and supported the introduction of broadcasts in foreign languages to an even wider range of countries. With the beginning of World War II, the service for the first time took on an explicitly political character, which it has retained ever since.[857] While the BBC Home Services are subject to all the rules of editorial independence described above, a very different set of rules relating to programme content and financing applies to the External Services.[858] The services are financed by a grant-in-aid, paid by the Foreign and Commonwealth Office, of £ 116.5 million for the year 1987-1988.[859]

Various government departments cooperate in the designation of the countries in which the External Services are to be received. These departments are responsible for the approval of the installation and equipment of all stations for wireless telegraphy necessary within the United Kingdom and abroad and grant the requisite licences and concessions to the BBC. They also determine the languages in which and the times at which the broadcasts take place.[860]

Although the BBC itself claims that the External Services are editorially independent,[861] and the government has repeatedly publicly acknowledged the BBC External Services' editorial independence,[862] this assertion is not supported by its Licence and Agreement. The pertinent licence provision reads in part: »The Corporation shall consult and collaborate with the Departments so specified and shall obtain and accept from them such information regarding conditions in, and the policies of Her Majesty's Government aforesaid towards, the countries so prescribed and other countries

857 *Id.* at 377 and n. 15, *citing* C.CURRAN, BROADCASTING FROM WEST OF SUEZ 4 (1968).

858 Territorially, the Home Services are restricted to the United Kingdom of Great Britain and Northern Ireland, the Channel Islands, the Isle of Man and the territorial waters thereof, and to ships and aircraft registered in the United Kingdom; services within the Commonwealth and other countries are defined as External Services. BBC Royal Charter 1981, article 3(a).

859 Foreign Affairs Committee, Fourth Report 1986-1987, Cultural Diplomacy, H.C. No. 24 (600 i and ii (1985-86)) para. 17 (May 1987) (hereafter cited as 1987 Report on Cultural Diplomacy). The Committee, pointing to the importance of cultural diplomacy for the representation of British cultural values overseas, strongly recommended that the government should spend more money on cultural diplomacy »in line with the importance which it deserves as a central element of Britain's diplomatic effort.« *Id.* at para. 26.

860 BBC Royal Charter 1981, article 3(h); BBC Licence and Ageement 1981, clause 13(5).

861 *See* Mytton, *Audience Research for International Broadcasting*, 14 INTERMEDIA 35 (March 1986).

862 *See* 1987 Report on Cultural Diplomacy, *supra* note 859, at Memorandum by BBC External Services 76, 77.

as will enable the Corporation to plan and prepare its programmes in the External Services in the national interest.«[863]

The revelation by *The Observer* in 1985 about the daily briefings of BBC journalists in the Foreign Office did therefore not come as a great surprise. The Ministry admitted that according to a »normal« and long-standing practice, those journalists responsible for the news programmes in the External Services were informed daily about secret state matters in order to allow them the preparation and presentation of the radio news programmes »in the national interest,« as the Foreign Office phrased it.[864] These secret briefings parallel the »lobby system« used by the government for its daily briefings of certain carefully selected British newspaper reporters.[865]

The apparent contradiction and tension between the legally existing government supervisory powers and the BBC's claim to editorial independence in its External Services, which – as has been described earlier – is typical of the relationship between the broadcasting media and the government in the United Kingdom, are dealt with in a typically British way probably unsuited for most other countries. The key word in this context is a »gentleman's agreement.« Its central elements have been described as the BBC's commitment to pay »due regard« but not exclusive attention to the mainstream of the government's foreign policy; in turn, the government refrains from issuing formal orders and settles any disputes over programme content in a friendly manner.[866]

This arrangement appears to work well. Worldwide the External Services enjoy a high reputation for their accuracy. The BBC staff takes great pains to ensure that their news and current-affairs programmes, the English version of which are broadcast once every full hour, 24 hours a day,[867] bring only confirmed stories.[868]

An important factor for the gathering, assessing and compiling of news is the BBC's extensive practice of monitoring a great number of foreign broadcasts in many different languages. This task has been formally in-

---

863 Licence and Agreement 1981, clause 13(5). *See also* clause 13(3) and (4), permitting the government to request the BBC to broadcast certain ministerial announcements or to refrain from broadcasting certain matters.

864 Frankfurter Allgemeine Zeitung, Sept. 5, 1985.

865 *See supra* at chapter I(B)(2).

866 B. PAULU, *supra* note 165, at 385.

867 *See BBC World Service – London Calling.* This is the title of the monthly BBC External Services Programme Magazine for the English-language programmes.

868 *See* the comment made by Mr Terry Heron, Editor of the BBC External Services in London, in *The Sunday Times*, Nov. 3, 1985, arguing that the BBC's reputation in its External Services depends on »getting it right.«

corporated into the BBC's Licence and Agreement 1981[869] and is further specified in detailed government orders. The BBC's heavily staffed Monitoring Service cooperates with the Deutsche Welle and the Foreign Broadcasting Information Service of the United States' Central Intelligence Agency (CIA).[870] The BBC and these two other organizations focus their monitoring activities on different parts of the world and exchange the information gathered.

From 1955 to 1987, the total number of weekly broadcasting hours in the External Services rose from 558 to 734.[871] Nonetheless, while in the 1960s the United Kingdom ranked first among nations with respect to the total number of broadcasting hours in its international services, it has since fallen to rank five,[872] the United States, the Soviet Union, China and the Federal Republic of Germany preceeding in this order of sequence. But only the United States, West Germany and the United Kingdom achieve substantial audiences on a worldwide basis.[873] An estimated 120 million people regularly listen to the BBC's External Services: 25 million make use of the English-language service, while about 100 million tune in to one of the BBC's services broadcast in 36 other languages.[874]

The practice of international programme exchange and technical co-operation goes back to World War II. During that period, particularly American broadcast services retransmitted the BBC's World Services to their American audiences, and the BBC made transmitters available for American transmissions to mainland Europe.[875] These historically close ties between the BBC External Services and American radio broadcasters extend well into the present. In 1986 the BBC reached an agreement with the U.S. Public Broadcasting System (PBS), the non-commercial American radio broadcasting system. According to the arrangements, PBS will take over up to 40 news and current-affairs programmes from the BBC's daily English World Service. The programmes will be made available free of charge and will be transmitted to the United States via satellite. The PBS stations may then choose for themselves those programmes best suited for

---

869 Licence and Agreement 1981, clause 13(5).
870 B. PAULU, *supra* note 165, at 390. *See also* BBC External Services Publicity Unit, Voice of the World. The Work of the BBC External Services 26-27 (1982).
871 Mytton, *supra* note 861, at 36; 1987 Report on Cultural Diplomacy, *supra* note 859, at Memorandum by BBC External Services 76, 102.
872 Neue Zürcher Zeitung, Sept. 25, 1986; BBC Handbook 1987, *supra* note 273, at Appendix II.
873 Mytton, *supra* note 861, at 37.
874 *Id.* at 38; BBC Handbook 1987, *supra* note 273, at 111.
875 B. PAULU, *supra* note 165, at 379-80.

270

their purposes.[876] Since the autumn of 1986, programmes from the External Services have also been transmitted via Danish cable systems to listeners in Denmark.[877] A major step to enlarge the audience of the BBC World Service has been taken through the agreement with BT in August 1987 to use the EUTELSAT satellite for the transmission of two 24-hour radio programmes.[878] The two channels, one in English and one offering programmes in studio quality in about 20 different languages, aim at cable systems in Europe but are sometimes even received by individuals in Eastern European countries, such as Poland, where privately owned satellite receiving equipment is not illegal.[879]

The BBC's plans also to start a television version of the World Service have so far failed, not least due to the government's refusal to grant extra funds to the External Services for this purpose.[880] While Eastern European countries could not be expected to relay the service to their citizens, the BBC anticipates that the United States, Canada, New Zealand, Australia, Singapore, Hong Kong and some Caribbean islands would be interested in receiving such a service.[881]

The BBC's transmission standards in the External Services are relatively modest. In contrast to the well-financed U.S. service Voice of America, they usually allow only for a few hours of broadcasts a day in any of the non-English services. While the Home Services are financed by the licence fee system, the External Services receive annual grants from the Foreign and Commonwealth Offices.[882] For example, 6-1/4 hours of broadcasts per day are in the Russian language and are aimed at the Soviet Union. These transmissions have until recently been heavily jammed by the Soviets.[883] The British government regularly protested to the Soviet Union against this practice on the ground that the jamming »contravenes the spirit and letter of the Helsinki Final Act as well as article 35 of the Convention of the International Telecommunication Union of

---

876 Neue Zürcher Zeitung, Nov. 6, 1986.
877 Information provided to the author by Mr David Williams, Assistant to the BBC Legal Adviser. Belgium, Dutch and Norwegian cable systems followed. Fin. Times, Jan. 12, 1988.
878 Neue Zürcher Zeitung, Aug. 20, 1987.
879 Fin. Times, Jan. 12, 1988.
880 Fin. Times, Mar. 3, 1988. The BBC is now seeking private-sector financing to contribute to the envisaged service.
881 Fin. Times, Oct. 7, 1987.
882 *See* Licence and Agreement 1981, clause 17(1); *see also* Sunday Times, Nov. 3, 1985.
883 The BBC's Russian service has been jammed for 24 years in its 40-year history. The Polish-language service has equally been jammed. 1987 Report on Cultural Diplomacy, *supra* note 859, at Memorandum by BBC External Services 76, 86, 102. On occasion, the Soviet Union stopped the jamming as a sign of goodwill but later resumed the practice. *See* G. MANSELL, LET TRUTH BE TOLD – 50 YEARS OF BBC EXTERNAL BROADCASTING 262-63 (1982).

which the Soviet Union is a signatory.«[884] As a demonstration of renewed goodwill, the Soviet Union unexpectedly discontinued the jamming of the Russian-language programmes of the BBC's External Services in mid-January 1987, while it continued to jam other international radio service programmes, like the Voice of America and Radio Free Europe, for example.[885]

The United Kingdom itself has a long-standing history of non-interference with foreign radio broadcasts. In the 1930s and 1940s, the British government strongly disfavoured all foreign commercial radio broadcasts, like Radio Luxembourg and Radio Normandy, because they competed with the BBC radio programmes, but no formal measures were taken to prevent these services from being received in the United Kingdom via aerials.[886] On the other hand, when Radio Luxembourg, which produced its English-language programme in London for later transmission from its Luxembourg-based station, requested to lease a network line from the British Post Office in order to facilitate the sending of its recordings from London to the station, a lease was refused by the British government. This policy was only changed in the early 1980s, when BT was set up as a company separate from the Post Office.[887] As has already been mentioned in the context of freedom to receive broadcasts,[888] the British government refrained from jamming any of the German political-propaganda programmes aimed at British listeners during World War II. There seems to have been only one instance when Britain departed from its policy of non-interference, when it jammed radio broadcasts from Greece and Egypt to Cyprus in 1956 on the ground that they incited violence on the island.[889]

The above-described practice of tolerating foreign broadcast programmes presupposes that the foreign broadcast station is a station duly licensed under the domestic law of the country of origin. Broadcast transmissions from unlicensed »pirate« stations are subject to a totally different legal regime.

---

884 BRITISH YEARBOOK OF INTERNATIONAL LAW 1984 566 (1985).
885 Neue Zürcher Zeitung, Feb. 5, 1987. The effect of the new Soviet policy, attributed to Mikhail Gorbachev's course of *Glasnost*, was that the BBC's weekly audience in the Soviet Union increased from an estimated 14 million to an estimated 16 million. Fin. Times, Apr. 25, 1988.
886 B. PAULU *supra* note 165, at 21 and n. 62. *But compare supra* at chapter IV(A)(1) about the legal difficulties in relaying such programmes via cable relay services.
887 *See infra* at section B(3).
888 *See supra* at chapter I(C)(2).
889 B. PAULU, *supra* note 165, at 389-90.

2. *Regulation of »Pirate« Stations*

Persons operating unauthorized stations and transmitting from the territory of the United Kingdom may be prosecuted under the Wireless Telegraphy Act 1949. In the mid-1980s, the British government began to take increasing action against numerous »back-room« pirate stations operating in various communities throughout the country,[890] because they were making more and more use of frequencies solely designated for emergency-service purposes. While this crackdown on the pirates affected particularly left-wing and minority groups, the Conservatives' programme to go ahead with community radio at the same time gave recognition to the need for such services, even though the party's main objective may have been to introduce competition on all broadcasting levels.

An entirely different matter is the regulation of pirate stations operating outside the territory of the United Kingdom but transmitting programmes for reception by the British public. In 1967 the United Kingdom ratified the European Agreement for the Prevention of Broadcasts Transmitted from Stations Outside National Territory, signed in Strasbourg on January 22, 1965.[891] This treaty deals with broadcasting stations installed on board ships or aircraft outside national territories and transmitting broadcasts intended for reception or capable of being received within the territory of a contracting state (article 1). The Agreement, drafted under the auspices of the Council of Europe, was designed to achieve greater legal unity within the member states and to support the prohibition against the establishment and use of broadcasting stations on board ships and airplanes outside national territories.[892] It was primarily a response to the fact that such broadcasts took place at all and caused harmful interference with lawful users of the radio spectrum; opposition to actual content of these broadcasts was of minor importance in the political deliberations.

The Marine, & c., Broadcasting (Offences) Act 1967[893] transformed the United Kingdom's international obligations into domestic law. The British legislation closely follows the pattern of the European Agreement. Until

---

890 In the financial year 1985 to 1986, the Radio Investigation Service (RIS) of the DTI, the part of the RD responsible for enforcing the provisions of the Wireless Telegraphy Act, carried out 217 actions on 69 land-based unlicensed broadcasters; the year also saw 124 criminal convictions. 1986 Annual Report of the Radio Regulatory Division, *supra* note 263, at 26-27.

891 *Ratified by* the United Kingdom on Nov. 2, 1967; *entered into force* Dec. 3, 1967; Cmnd. 3497, T.S. No. 1 (1968).

892 *See id.* at Preamble.

893 Marine, & c., Broadcasting (Offences) Act 1967 (c .41).

the passage of the 1967 Act, the Post Office had only been able to prosecute people who had operated an unauthorized station for wireless telegraphy on the territory of the United Kingdom or within its territorial waters (*see* section 1(1) Wireless Telegraphy Act 1949).[894]

The Marine, & c., Broadcasting (Offences) Act 1967 prohibits any broadcast from a ship or aircraft or from certain marine structures. The term »broadcast« as used in the Act includes radio as well as television transmissions intended for general reception, not including signals sent in connection with navigation or for safety purposes (section 9(1)). Offences are punishable by an unlimited fine or two years in prison or both. With one exception the Act strictly applies the territoriality and the nationality principle of international law: The scope of the Act includes broadcasts made from a ship or aircraft while it is in or over the United Kingdom or within its external waters,[895] and broadcasts transmitted from a ship or aircraft registered in the United Kingdom, the Isle of Man or the Channel Islands (section 1(1)). With respect to broadcasts made from outside the territorial waters and from foreign ships and aircraft, British subjects operating or participating in the operation of the station or who procure such a broadcast are also subject to British jurisdiction under the Act (section 3). Respective provisions apply to persons broadcasting from a marine structure affixed to the seabed and located in the external waters or in the tidal waters of the United Kingdom, or to British subjects participating in the broadcast from such structures located in international waters. The Act also attempts to undermine the maintenance of any off-shore pirate stations by making it an offence to supply any goods or material to the station from British territory (section 4). Furthermore, it is an offence to supply from the United Kingdom any cinematograph films or records with the intent that they be broadcast in contravention of the Act, or to make a literary, musical or dramatic work available for this purpose (section 5(1),(3)(a),(b)). The latter provision is mainly directed against British advertising agencies producing advertising spots to be in-

---

894 *See* Post Office v. Estuary Radio, Ltd., [1967] 3 All E.R. 663, where the central legal issue had been whether the unauthorized radio station, which had operated from a tower located in the Thames estuary, could be deemed to have transmitted from a place within the British territorial waters. The answer to this question depended on the calculation of the correct base line from which the three-mile zone of territorial waters was to be measured. *See also* Territorial Waters Order in Council 1964, *made on* Sept. 25, 1964, *entered into force* Sept. 30, 1964, *amended by* the Territorial Waters (Amendment) Order 1979, *made on* May 23, 1979.

895 The external waters end at the seaward limits of the territorial waters. *See* Marine, & c., Broadcasting (Offences) Act 1967, sec. 9(1).

cluded in the unauthorized broadcast programmes. A person who advertises is also punishable under the Act (section 5(3)(e)). In this context, the effects doctrine of international law helps to provide the necessary jurisdiction over persons responsible for advertising programmes broadcast from the high seas: »For the purpose of this section advertising by means of a broadcast shall be deemed to take place as well wherever the broadcast is received as where it is made« (section 5(5)). This provision would seem to extend jurisdiction to any non-British citizen broadcasting advertisements for reception in the United Kingdom from outside British territory. Also, anybody within the territory of the United Kingdom who procures another person to advertise or to make an advertising spot outside the United Kingdom for the purpose of contravening the Act is guilty of an offence (section 5(2)). Finally, a British citizen who participates in a broadcast from the high seas as an announcer or a performer and who is actually present on the ship or structure during the broadcast is equally punishable under section 5(3)(d) of the Act. As has rightfully been pointed out, however, this provision, by demanding physical presence, contains a loophole for British programme announcers who prerecord their announcements on cartridge tapes,[896] a practice already widely used by radio stations in the United States. This method enables the organizers to manage the broadcasts by remote control, so that no programme maker actually needs to be present at the broadcast site.

When a British citizen, who had been convicted under section 5(3)(f) of the Act for promoting the interests of a pirate station by displaying a sticker on his car window, appealed to the EUCM, the Commission rejected the complaint. It held that since article 10(1) of the EUHR specifically made provision for a licensing system of broadcasting, it was legitimate for a state to pass laws regarding persons avoiding or promoting the avoidance of the licensing requirements.[897]

With respect to unwelcomed broadcasts from pirate stations outside British jurisdiction, the British government has additionally embarked on a number of practical measures to prevent effectively such broadcasts. It

---

896 D. SMITH, INTERNATIONAL TELECOMMUNICATION CONTROL 89 (1969).
897 Decision of Dec. 4, 1978 (No. 8266/78), 16 DR 190, 192. The stickers had been displayed by a disc jockey helping to operate a mobile disco. The prosecution argued that the aim of the disco was to plug the pirate station Radio Caroline. *See* News of the World, Dec. 11, 1977. The Radiocommunications Division of the DTI is taking the position that »if evidence is found in the future of a similar commercial promotion of an illegal broadcasting station, then the Crown Prosecution Service would consider taking similar action.« Letter to the author by Mr K.R. Tomlin, Radiocommunications Division of the DTI, dated Sept. 9, 1987.

refrained from jamming the broadcasts, which it could have easily done by placing a British ship in front of the pirate for this purpose. Although harmful interference and the irrational use of radio frequencies are prohibited under the ITU Convention, these principles do not seem also to prohibit the jamming of broadcasts of pirate stations on the high seas.[898] Still, jamming the pirates would have been difficult to justify, because it would most likely have resulted in no less interference to other radio stations than the government had claimed was caused by the unauthorized transmissions. Apparently, there has only been one case: in April 1970, the British government jammed the transmissions of an unauthorized floating station.[899]

In 1985 the DTI in at least one case considered using diplomatic pressure to put the main pirate radio stations, »Laser 558« and »Radio Caroline,« out of business. These stations operated from ships under Panamanian flags. A plan was seriously contemplated, according to which the Foreign Office was to request the Panama Shipping Bureau to withdraw the registration of the ships.[900] At about the same time, however, another practical strategy proved sufficiently effective to get rid of the pirates. For a few months the DTI lay siege to the two ships by stationing a surveillance vessel nearby and photographing all visiting vessels, monitoring the transmissions and gathering material for possible prosecutions. The living conditions on board the ships soon became unbearable, because the presence of the government vessels had deterred suppliers of food, water and fuel. Soon, advertising revenues had almost completely subsided, and several disc jockeys had left the ships. When one of the vessels had sent out a distress call during a storm, the surveillance ship towed »Lazer 558,« which was owned by a New York company, into Harwich harbour in order to enable British officials to interview the crew and investigate possible offences under the Marine, & c., Broadcasting (Offences) Act 1967.[901]

In summary it may be said that the 1967 Act penalized most of the activities carried on from British territory or by British citizens on the high seas in support of unauthorized broadcast stations. Foreign ships with a foreign crew that stay outside British territorial waters and are supplied from overseas sources do not normally contravene British law.

---

898 *See* Hondius, *International Control of Broadcasting Programs in Western Europe*, in E. MCWHINNEY (ed.), THE INTERNATIONAL LAW OF COMMUNICATIONS 69, 77 (1971).
899 *Id.* at 75.
900 The Guardian, Oct. 28, 1985.
901 *See* Daily Telegraph, Nov. 7, 1985; 1986 Annual Report of the Radio Regulatory Division, *supra* note 263, at 26-27.

3. *Transborder Transmissions of Audiovisual Broadcast Programmes*

While the transmission of radio programmes directed at audiences in foreign countries has enjoyed a privileged position under the principle of territorial sovereignty in international law, the extension of this privilege to television is heavily contested.[902] During the era when audiovisual broadcasting aimed at the general public was technically feasible only via terrestrial transmissions, the problem of the applicable principle never became pressing; terrestrial transmitters have only a very limited range, such that they cannot be used to set up an international television service matching to any extent the coverage of external radio services. Only in the furthest Western corners of the United Kingdom, for example, can British citizens receive a foreign television service, namely, the Irish television programmes. This situation dramatically changed with the advent of DBS technology, making it theoretically possible to transmit directly receivable television programmes to a worldwide audience with only three DBS satellites based in geostationary orbit. Because of the intense impression of television pictures on the minds of viewers and because of almost insurmountable economic and practical difficulties to jam such transmissions, many countries, in particular the Socialist states, have argued that DBS transmissions differ in substance from sound broadcasts. They therefore support the prior-consent principle of international law as the guiding principle governing DBS broadcasts, as opposed to the principle of freedom of information supported by most Western countries. The prior-consent principle requires that any country subjected to television transmissions by another country must formally agree in advance to such activities.

The 1977 ITU World Administrative Radio Conference on direct broadcasting by satellite (1977 WARC-BS) represented a limited but practical solution to the conflict in the spirit of the prior-consent principle, because it allocated to all European states, including the Soviet Union and the Asian countries, generally five DBS channels each on non-interfering varying orbital positions. It also established the requirement that the footprints of these DBS satellite services – apart from inevitable overspill due to technical difficulties – would only cover the national territories. This international agreement, while only referring to the technical aspect of DBS, effectively prohibited countries from providing DBS services aimed at in-

---

902 *See, e.g.*, Engel, *supra* note 814; Frank, *Völkerrechtliche Probleme des Satellitenrundfunks*, in HANS-BREDOW-INSTITUT, INTERNATIONALES HANDBUCH FüR RUNDFUNK UND FERNSEHEN 1986/87 G 40-G 46 (1986); White, Jr. & Lauria, *International Space Law and Direct Broadcast Satellites*, 3 SPACE COMMUNICATION AND BROADCASTING 321, 330-35 (1985).

ternational audiences. This may explain why in 1979 the United Kingdom, in a working paper submitted to the Legal Subcommittee of the UN Committee on the Peaceful Uses of Outer Space (COPUOS), took the position that in light of the 1977 WARC-BS no further regulation was necessary on the issue of prior consent. The study implied that the consent principle had effectively become part of international law.[903] Still, due to considerable potential overspill on U.K. territory, particularly from French and Irish DBS satellites,[904] and constantly improving receiving equipment capable of picking up DBS signals outside the actual footprint, concerns continued to be raised in the United Kingdom over the possible establishment of a European commercial »DBS super station« directed at a European audience and threatening to undermine the British public-service broadcasting system and syphon off British advertising revenues.[905] On the other hand, the possible financial advantages of advertising revenues stemming from the overspill of a potential British DBS service into Europe were warmly welcomed by the British DBS lobby and the government.[906]

Because of the fact that the United Kingdom decided to adopt the D-Mac standard for high-definition television, while Germany and France opted for the D2-Mac standard as their transmission standard, receiving continental European DBS signals in Britain and vice versa regrettably will meet with considerable technical difficulties – even if the problem that all DBS satellites will transmit from different orbital positions could be overcome. This deplorable situation of non-compatible HDTV standards is even aggravated by the fact that the ITU member states at the 1986 meeting of the CCIR plenary conference could not agree on the proposed Japanese HDTV production standard as a world standard. This agreement failed foremost because of European, including British, objections. Their main concern was that the Japanese HDTV standard could be more easily and efficiently converted to the present Japanese and American television standards, as it operated on a 1,125 lines and 30 pictures/second basis, their present standard being 560 lines and 30 pictures. However, 75 per cent of the world, including the European countries, operate their television systems on a 625 lines and 25 pictures/second basis. With the Japanese

---

903 Dalfen, *Principles Governing Direct Satellite Broadcasting*, in I MANUAL ON SPACE LAW 283, 293 (N. Jasentuliyana & R. Lee eds. 1979). Many countries contested this legal opinion. *Id.*
904 *See* the instructive diagram of Western Europe DBS footprints shown in the 1981 Home Office Study on Direct Broadcasting by Satellite, *supra* note 399, at Figure 2, p. 11.
905 *Id.* at paras. 14.3., 14.15.
906 *Id.* at paras. 14.16.-14.18.

HDTV production standard as the universal standard, all studio equipment would have had to be changed, the Europeans had argued, and for each programme so produced, a complicated and expensive operation of »down-converting« the signal for transmission would have been needed. This would have resulted in considerable loss of picture quality for television systems operating on the 625 lines and 25 pictures basis, the argument was. However, counter arguments were also made. They pointed out that if the Europeans could come up with their own production standard (a great effort that Eureka has already embarked upon – so far with little success), new production studio facilities and the down-converting of signals for transmission would also be necessary.[907] In addition, over time the technical methods of down-converting would greatly improve both as to quality and price, while the possibility of worldwide, cinema-quality television reception on home screens as large as three to five meters in diameter would be safeguarded. Opponents to the Japanese standards countered this argument by saying that it could not be expected that home television screens of more than one meter in diameter would ever become commercially viable, so that the very sophisticated but expensive Japanese system was not needed and the evolutionary system supported by the Europeans, which would provide excellent-quality HDTV pictures on television screens not wider than one meter, would suffice to satisfy future demand.[908]

The presentation of the pros and cons of the HDTV standard battle would be incomplete without a mention of the economic interests involved. The Japanese had since the early 1970s experimented with HDTV and had invested large sums of money. Understandably, they wanted to see the financial return for these investments and thus maintained that they would not agree to any other standard as a world standard. The Europeans, on the other hand, did not like the idea of having to pay for the Japanese patents. They preferred to exploit Eureka's patents instead. No matter what line of argument one might be inclined to follow, the fact remains that at the 1986 CCIR conference a great opportunity to advance the interests of a world television market was lost.

907 In fact, to some extent down-converting already takes place today because the European broadcasters produce their programmes at a better, cinema quality than can be transmitted with the present transmission standard.
908 The arguments for and against the Japanese HDTV production standard were kindly explained to the author by Mr Chris Daubney, Head of Engineering Secretariat, IBA.

Still, the development in satellite technology that has taken place since the 1977 WARC-BS conference, in particular, the emergence of medium-power satellites, and much-improved receiving equipment have made the emergence of European commercial »super stations« again a realistic possibility. The Luxembourg-based Astra satellite project is the most prominent example. It has been registered as a communications satellite with the ITU and thus falls outside the international regime governing DBS. In particular, like many low-power satellites, its footprint will cover most of Western Europe.[909] The British government itself, in conjunction with the BBC, plans to take advantage of the improved technical possibilities and opportunities of the satellite technology. The BBC decided in 1986 to transmit its BBC 1 television service via satellite to European cable networks. It also began the satellite transmission of two radio programmes in its External Services.[910] The service began operation in June 1987: It is distributed via the INTELSAT V satellite and is offered to cable television networks and national broadcasters all over Western Europe.[911] Programmes are available eight hours a day. The internationalization of audiences is further supported by the spread of cable television in the United Kingdom and the liberalization of SMATV, which has greatly increased the British audience for foreign satellite television transmissions from communications satellites.

Before the background of the still-unresolved question of which principle

---

909 However, it appears likely that the programmes to be transmitted via the Astra satellite will not all share the same transmission standard and will thus not all be receivable across Europe. Some channels seem determined to use the British D-Mac standard as their transmission standard. While television decoders capable of receiving D-Mac signals will also be able to receive D2-Mac, viewers in mainland Europe would be excluded from those programmes aimed at the British market. Fin. Times, Feb. 23, 1988.

910 The legal authorization for the provision of satellite television broadcasts as part of the External Services has also already been incorporated in article 3(a),(h) of the BBC Royal Charter 1981. However, ITN, the ITV news service, also announced that it is interested in providing such a service and asked the government to put any such contract out to tender. Fin. Times, Dec. 13, 1986.

911 Fin. Times, June 9, 11, 1987. A good example of the increased concern foreign governments may feel about the reception of foreign broadcast signals due to the better reception quality resulting from the new technologies is an incident reported in the *Neue Zürcher Zeitung* in January 1988. The BBC had arranged for the transmission of its External Services radio programmes, distributed via satellite, into local cable systems in Finland. Within a short period of time, the Finnish listening audience of the service had increased threefold. The BBC strategy prompted a visit by Finnish government officials in London expressing their concern over the British activities on Finnish territory. *See* Neue Zürcher Zeitung, Jan. 28, 1988. On the other hand, Great Britain will also be increasingly the target of foreign broadcasts. For example, a broadcasting venture based in Ireland between an Irish broadcasting organization and Radio Luxembourg is planning to launch a commercial radio channel aimed especially at the U.K. audience. Fin. Times, Nov. 25, 1987.

of international law should govern the content-related aspect of satellite television transmissions, the United Kingdom's approach is differentiated. Regarding the overspill of European DBS services into Britain, the U.K. government has early on favoured negotiations and international agreements on the admissible programme content of such services.[912]

The 1984 Recommendation of the Committee of Ministers of the Council of Europe on Satellite Use[913] also found British support. The Recommendation sets out certain basic principles on satellite use, in particular, programme standards. A second recommendation by the Council of Europe deals with standards of television advertising.[914] Both recommendations apply to television broadcasts via both DBS and communications satellites.

In its Green Paper on Television Without Frontiers, the EC Commission took the view that rules subjecting broadcasts from other member states to domestic content regulations constituted a de facto discrimination of foreign broadcast programmes contrary to article 56(1) of the EEC Treaty.[915] The Commission further argued that the monitoring of such foreign broadcasts by a member state could not be justified by article 56(1), which could have permitted the application of special regulations to foreigners on grounds of public order; the expansion of the total programme supply in a member state due to additionally available foreign broadcast programmes represented no threat to the member state's public order, even if it regarded broadcasting as a public-service function.

The EC Commission's position on the scope of the anti-discrimination provisions of articles 59 ff. in the context of broadcasting has not been shared by the Court of Justice. Despite the fact that a requirement imposed on broadcasters with an international service area to comply with the national laws of all receiving states may seriously impede the provision of

912 1981 Home Office Study on Direct Broadcasting by Satellite, *supra* note 399, at para. 14.23. The United Kingdom did not become a signatory to the 1974 Convention Relating to the Distribution of Programme-Carrying Signals Transmitted by Satellite, *reprinted in* II MANUAL ON SPACE LAW 87 (N. Jasentuliyana & R. Lee eds. 1979). In any case, this Convention does not lay down any programme standards but is mainly concerned with the protection of copyright holders against unauthorized distribution of programme carrying signals transmitted by satellite.

913 Recommendation No. R (84) 22, adopted by the Committee of Ministers on Dec. 7, 1984, at the 378th meeting of the Ministers' Deputies.

914 Recommendation No. 12 (84) 3, adopted by the Committee of Ministers on Feb. 23, 1984, at the 367th meeting of the Ministers' Deputies. On July 15, 1983, the General Assembly of the European Broadcasting Union (EBU) also unanimously adopted a »Declaration of Principles Regarding Commercial TV Advertising Broadcast by DBS.«

915 1984 EC Green Paper, *supra* note 710, at Part 5 B III 1 d. *See also* Schwartz, *Broadcasting Without Frontiers in the European Community*, 6 J. MEDIA L. & PRAC. 26 (1985).

such services across frontiers, the Court has interpreted article 59 in a restrictive way:

> In view of the particular nature of certain services such as the broadcasting and transmission of television signals, specific requirements imposed upon providers of services which are founded upon the application of rules regulating certain types of activity and which are justified by the general interest and apply to all persons and undertakings established within the territory of the said Member State cannot be said to be incompatible with the Treaty to the extent to which a provider of services established in another Member State is not subject to similar regulations there.[916]

The holding indicates that the EEC Treaty allows member states to subject foreign broadcasts to the same content regulations as domestic programmes.

The Commission had also taken the position that because the European Convention on Human Rights was ratified by all EC member states, it formed part of the legal regime governing the Community as such.[917] This view had been supported by the Court of Justice's holding in the *Rutili* case.[918] Here, the Court had interpreted the public-order reservations contained in various provisions of the EEC Treaty in light of the EUHR. While the Court in its latest judgment on the interplay between the EUHR, and in particular article 10, and Community law confirmed the principle that it had the duty »to ensure observance of fundamental rights in the field of Community law,« it rejected the Commission's far-reaching conclusions.[919] The Court added that it was impermissible for the Court to decide upon the compatibility of the EUHR with a member state's national legislation with respect to a subject matter, such as media law, if its regulations lay within the purview of the national legislature.[920] This holding has far-reaching implications for the effectiveness of the principles of the European Convention on Human Rights in the context of the interpretation of Community law. With respect to procedural law, the Court clarified that it refused to accept a concurring jurisdiction over EUHR issues in conjunction with the EUCM and the EUCT.[921] The hold-

---

916 Procureur du Roi v. Debauve (case 52/79), 1980 E.C.R. 833, 856, [1981] 2 C.M.L.R. 362.
917 1984 EC Green Paper, *supra* note 710, at Part 5 B III 1b.
918 Rutili v. Ministre de l'Intérieur (case 36/75), 1975 E.C.R. 1219, [1976] 1 C.M.L.R. 140.
919 Cinéthèque S.A. v. Féderation Nationale des Cinémas Français (cases 60 and 61/84), [1986] 1 C.M.L.R. 365, 386.
920 *Id.*
921 *See* the comments on the European Court of Justice's decision of July 11, 1985 (cases 60-61/84) by Mestmäcker, *supra* note 709, at EuGH 11, 43, at p. 47.

ing leaves open whether the Court would exercise the same self-restraint if it were concerned with an area of the law in which member states are under an obligation to implement compulsory Community law into national law and may not exercise any discretion.[922] In any event the Court's holding in the *Cinétèque* case weakened the Commission's attempt undertaken in its Green Paper partly to justify a common regime of media law within the Community by reference to article 10 of the EUHR. This policy initiative had found strong support with the European Parliament.[923] A Draft Directive prepared by the EC Commission and repeating inter alia the principle that a common market for broadcasting prohibited the imposition of domestic content regulations on broadcasts from other member states had taken up the arguments of the Green Paper.[924]

The Draft Directive faced strong opposition by the U.K. government and other EC member states, including France, Denmark, West Germany and the Netherlands. The U.K. government's main objection was directed against the Commission's proposal to introduce a quota restriction on national broadcasters, requiring them to include a minimum of 60 per cent of EC-originated material in their programmes at the end of a three-year period and to commission a minimum of 10 per cent of all programmes from independent producers.[925] The quota restrictions were seen to threaten particularly the commercial success of the British DBS project. The DBS service, it was argued, would need to offer a film channel that would include non-EC, particularly American, programmes in order to cover costs. Another reason why the U.K. government in conjunction with the BBC and the IBA opposed the Draft Directive was that they rejected any attempt by the EC aimed at a harmonization of broadcasting standards that would touch upon issues of regional and national identity.[926]

Therefore, when the twelve media and broadcasting ministers of the

---

922 *Id.*

923 European Parliament, Resolution on a framework for a European media policy based on the Commission's Green Paper on the establishment of the common market for broadcasting, especially by satellite and cable of Oct. 10, 1985, 28 O.J. EUR. COMM. (No. C 288) 113 (1985); *see also* European Parliament, Resolution on the economic aspects of the common market for broadcasting in the European Community of Oct. 10, 1985, 28 O.J. EUR. COMM. (No. C 288) 119 (1985).

924 EC Commission, Proposal for a Council Directive on the coordination of certain provisions laid down by law, regulation or administrative action in Member States concerning the pursuit of broadcasting activities of Apr. 30, 1986, 29 O.J. EUR. COMM. (No. C 179) 4 (1986).

925 Fin. Times, Nov. 14, 1986; Dec. 10, 1986; Neue Zürcher Zeitung, Feb. 15/16, 1987. *See also* House of Lords European Communities Committee 4th Report, 1987: European Broadcasting H.L. 67, condemning the EC proposal as unrealistic.

926 Fin. Times, Nov. 14, 1986.

member states of the Council of Europe met in December 1986, it was not surprising that the United Kingdom played a leading role at the conference in supporting the view that the Council of Europe was a body more appropriate than the EC for the provision of an international framework for the future of European broadcasting. The conference consequently agreed on drafting an international agreement binding upon the member states of the Council and regulating, in particular, issues of programme and advertising standards, sponsorship and copyright.[927] This resolution has greatly weakened the EC Commission's initiative and has made a common market in broadcasting as designed by the Commission a matter of the distant future.

The Council of Europe recommendations on general programme and advertising standards mentioned above established the principle that the legality under international law of transborder broadcasts should depend on the broadcasters' compliance with the law of the originating state. In case of advertisements, this general principle was qualified by the codicil that »depending on the proportion of the audience which is in another country, [the advertiser] should take due account of the law of that country.« The recommendations set out that the countries whose competent authorities make a satellite channel available to a programme company should satisfy themselves that the programme makers respect the principles on programme and advertising standards. As has been noted above, no content-related legal regime applies to programmes broadcast by communications satellites in Britain. Content control of these programmes under the Cable and Broadcasting Act 1984 only comes in at the moment the programmes are retransmitted via British cable systems. It is theoretically possible that a satellite television service originating in the United Kingdom would not be distributed anywhere in Britain and would reach an audience only in mainland Europe, for example.

If the rule that compliance with the law of the country of origin as well as the responsibility of that country for compliance with certain programme standards became a recognized principle of international law defining the prerequisites to the validity of the principle of free flow of information across national borders, the United Kingdom would be under an obligation to amend its laws correspondingly. This principle appears to have good chances to become the rule of law at least between the member states of the Council of Europe in the treaty on satellite use now being drafted. The member states of the Council of Europe share a common heritage of ideals

---

927 *See* Neue Zürcher Zeitung, Dec. 18, 1986.

and principles. As between these countries, the principle of responsibility of the country of origin for the satellite television companies' compliance with the domestic law could replace the prior-consent principle.

The United Kingdom has given some, although not totally consistent, indications that it could consent to such a rule of international law. With regard to outgoing satellite programme transmissions originating in the United Kingdom, the government, recognizing the legal possibility of such stations to evade compliance with British programme standards, stated its policy in the following way:

> All satellite transmissions will invariably produce some overspill into Europe, and our neighbours are, understandably, interested in the implications for their own broadcasting and cable policies. One approach would be to leave each country to determine its own rules on the reception and distribution of these services. Given, however, that all satellite transmissions from this country require frequencies which only the Government can make available, the principle of good neighbourliness together with the concerns which have already been expressed within the Council of Europe point to the need for some additional safeguards; ... The Government is willing therefore to use its own powers over the use of the frequency spectrum to ensure that no television service or part of a service shall be transmitted by satellite if the Cable Authority certifies that it would be unsuitable for distribution by a cable operator in this country. ... the government would wish to be able to seek the advice of the Cable Authority on the compliance of the service with the usual cable channel rules before agreeing to license the use of the necessary frequencies.[928]

As has already been pointed out in the context of freedom of expression, this informal certification practice violates article 10(2) of the EUHR, because all restrictions on freeedom of expression need to be »prescribed by law.«[929]

It is noteworthy, however, that in face of a still-undecided controversy surrounding the validity of the prior-consent principle and the principle of freedom of information in the context of satellite television transmissions, the U.K. government takes recourse to the principle of good neighbourliness in international relations to argue the case for some kind of satellite programme-content control by its own authorities.

In the absence of a binding European treaty on satellite broadcast content,

---

928 1983 White Paper on Cable Systems, *supra* note 208, at para. 162.
929 *See supra* at chapter I(B)(3).

European countries also occasionally require reciprocity as a precondition for the permission of domestic cable systems to retransmit any foreign satellite programmes. When in 1983 the British company Satellite Television asked the Swiss government for permission to transmit Sky Channel over Swiss cable networks, the Swiss wanted to know whether as a matter of reciprocity a Swiss programme transmitted via satellite would be accepted for distribution by U.K. cable systems as well. In a letter to the satellite company stating its position in light of the Swiss government's request, the British Home Office declared that foreign television services would be accepted as long as they complied *in most respects* with the cable operators' licences. The letter continues:

> [B]ut since the normal assumption will be that such services will be subject to control in the country of origin, and in the interests of the free flow of information, not all the requirements of the licence concerning U.K. programmes will be insisted upon. For example, the news service from other countries will be acceptable notwithstanding that it may not treat news with accuracy and impartiality by United Kingdom standards.[930]

The official position expressed in the Home Office letter to the company represented a softening of the government's attitude towards foreign satellite programmes, a position it had still favoured only eight months earlier. In its 1983 White Paper on Cable Systems, which prepared the ground for the Cable and Broadcasting Bill, the government had taken the position that

> [t]he Cable Authority will ... need to maintain an interest in the programme content of channels distributed to cable systems by satellite. In the last resort it will have the power to rule against the relaying over cable of material contrary to the normal guidelines. In the case of any programmes distributed by foreign telecommunications satellites the Authority will apply the same rules as if the services originated within this country; the case for some flexibility is less than in the case of non-British DBS services primarily aimed at the audience of the country concerned.[931]

The Cable and Broadcasting Act 1984 incorporated the view expressed in the Home Office letter. Its section 10(1)(c) contains the principle that all news programmes »which originate in the United Kingdom« are presented with due accuracy and impartiality. The provision formally recognizes that in the interest of free flow of information, standards for foreign pro-

---

930 Letter of the Home Office dated Jan. 3, 1984 to Mr Patrick Cox, Managing Director of Satellite Television plc. The letter was provided to the author by the company.
931 1983 White Paper on Cable Systems, *supra* note 208, at para 162.

grammes need not necessarily comply with the full range of the internal laws. It is important to note, however, that the provision on news programmes is the only legislative recognition of this principle in the United Kingdom. With respect to the (in practical terms) very important area of advertising, for example, the 1984 Act does not differentiate between the standards to be observed by advertisements originating in the United Kingdom and those originating elsewhere.

In the context of advertising, the Swiss government in considering Satellite Television's request had taken a position similar to the one pronounced by the Council of Europe. Having received the company's assurance that the Sky Channel programme complied with the broadcasting regulations in the United Kingdom,[932] the Swiss government insisted that the company should observe the main advertising provisions applying to Swiss channels.[933] These provisions – contrary to British law – prohibited any interruption of individual programmes with advertising and also interdicted commercials for tobacco, alcohol and medicines. Sky Channel, on the other hand, retained the right to include advertising spots at each programme junction throughout the entire evening programme with no exceptions on Sundays and bank holidays, a right that was in line with the IBA's code on advertising practices but that contradicted the stricter Swiss law.

In its White Paper on cable systems, the government proposed requiring the Cable Authority to draw up content-related rules specifically addressing non-British channels.[934] The underlying concern was that foreign, particularly American, satellite channels or channels showing for the most part American programmes would be a serious competitive threat to the (more expensive) channels showing European programming. This competition, it was feared, could lead to an alienation and erosion of the British broadcasting structure.[935] The government felt generally less concern over European programme channels:

> In the case of the proportion of British/European Community programme material the Cable Authority will usually be able to take a relaxed view: most non-British services receivable in this country are likely to come from one of our fellow Community members and even where a channel contained a higher than normal proportion of non-Community material the Cable Authority ought not readily to consider

---

932 In 1983 Sky Channel voluntarily complied with the IBA's code of advertising practices.

933 Telex of Nov. 9, 1983 from the Swiss General Directorate of PTT, Radio Regulatory Division, to Satellite Television plc. The telex was provided to the author by the company.

934 1983 White Paper on Cable Systems, *supra* note 208, at para. 154.

935 *See also* 1981 Home Office Report on Direct Broadcasting by Satellite, *supra* note 399, at para. 14.22, expressing the fear that an »uncontrolled commercial exploitation of overspill [of DBS services] would threaten European pluralism and cultural values.«

restricting its relay. Nevertheless, if the situation were to arise in which a non-British station intended to broadcast a high proportion of programme material from outside the Community with the intention of circumventing the general rules for cable channels it would be right for the Cable Authority to have some power to intervene.[936]

The Cable and Broadcasting Act 1984 vested this right to intervene with the retransmission of foreign programmes in the government. Section 49(2) of the Act reserves the right to interdict the retransmission of foreign programmes made for reception in the United Kingdom »[i]f it appears to the Secretary of State, after consultation with both broadcasting authorities, that it is requisite or expedient to do so in the interests of public service broadcasting in the United Kingdom.« Subsection 3 states that the retransmission of programmes may be prohibited if they (a) include the whole or any part of protected events; or (b) are of a nature that would disqualify them as television or sound broadcasting services provided by the IBA. The thrust of this provision is twofold. Under the first scenario, the foreign programme contains a sporting or other event of national interest for which the BBC or the IBA have traditionally held the broadcasting rights. The legislative intention is to prevent a foreign broadcaster from aquiring the exclusive broadcasting rights for this event. Under the second scenario, a foreign programme service might enjoy such great popularity as to threaten a viable national audience for the British public broadcasting system; if such a channel had to comply with all regulations applying to ITV contractors, the channel's profile would probably be brought into line with the typical programme menues of the public broadcasters far enough as to give the BBC and the ITV companies a better standing in the competition for audiences.

Section 49(2) of the Cable and Broadcasting Act 1984 could be referred to as the »lex Radio Luxembourg,« because it represents the reaction to the government's concern over the popularity of the radio channel among British listeners. For a long time, the English-language programmes were produced in London, recorded on tape and subsequently flown to Luxembourg to be transmitted from there to the United Kingdom. When the company had asked to lease a permanent line from London to Luxembourg in order to be able to transmit its London programmes to the radio station in a quicker and less expensive manner, the lease was refused

---

936 1983 White Paper on Cable Systems, *supra* note 208, at para. 154.

due to the government's position that it could not to be expected to help in the transmission of the unwanted foreign programmes.[937] When BT was set up as an independent commercial undertaking separate from the Post Office, refusing to allow Radio Luxembourg to lease a line might have constituted an anti-competitive practice. The lease was therefore eventually granted, but the government ensured that it could still step in if it felt it necessary to do so. The provision can be applied both to radio and to any form of television transmission. So far, however, no use has been made of the provision.

Since particularly programme-content rules imposed on ITV contractors are stricter than those applying generally to cable contractors under the Cable and Broadcasting Act 1984, the government could theoretically ban a foreign programme even if it complied with all provisions regulating the programme content of domestic cable channels. Section 49(2) allows the United Kingdom to subject foreign channels to more stringent conditions than domestic (satellite) programmes. This regulation would thus seem to violate the anti-discrimination provisions of the EEC Treaty.[938] Moreover, section 49 of the Cable and Broadcasting Act 1984 appears to be superfluous in light of the fact that the Cable Authority can prohibit cable operators to relay programmes showing listed or protected events (section 14 of the Act). Also, the Authority, acting on its power to impose quota restrictions on cable programme channels, can ban foreign satellite television channels showing high proportions of or exclusively non-British programme material. The last-mentioned authorization has to do with the British quota system applying to foreign films, a regulatory measure with a long-standing history in Britain.

C. *International Programme Exchange*

1. *The Quota System for Foreign Programme Material*

For several decades cinemas were subjected to a quota system on foreign films. Section 1 of the Films Act 1960[939] required cinemas to show a certain percentage of British films. In 1983 this quota system was sus-

---

937 Information provided to the author by Mr N.C. Sanderson, Broadcasting Department, Home Office.
938 *See also* Schwartz, *supra* note 915, at 37.
939 Films Act 1960 (8 & 9 Eliz. II, c.57).

pended;[940] it was finally abolished by the Films Act 1985. The 1985 Act also brought to an end the need for the maker or distributor of a film to register the film as a British or foreign film with the Board of Trade. By the 1980s cinema attendance had deteriorated to such an extent that cinema exhibitions now played only a negligible role in the whole media market. At first the public broadcasters, followed by video and cable television, had increasingly determined the viewing habits of the British public. Under these circumstances, the quota system threatened the continued economic viability of the already ailing cinema industry more than it could have effectively protected the British film industry. This led to the abolition of the quota system. Also in line with the general market-economy approach of the Conservative government, the Films Act 1985 terminated the so-called Eady Levy, which had been imposed on cinemas to subsidize British film producers. This measure handed the film industry over to the market forces.[941]

The British television film industry, however, continues to enjoy the shelter of legislative protection. The presentation of programmes of foreign origin on British television is strictly confined to a quota system. Since the very beginnings of commercial broadcasting in the 1950s, the IBA was under a statutory duty to ensure »that proper proportions of the recorded and other matter included in the programmes are of British origin and of British performance« (section 4(1)(c) of the Broadcasting Act 1981). The reasons for the quotas on foreign programme material have been twofold: (1) maximum employment opportunities in the British programme-making industry; and (2) a proper reflection of British culture and interests on the screen. There exist no legislative specifications on »proper proportions« of British material, and the term has been left to the IBA's interpretation and judgment. Under the current regulation not more than an average of 14 per cent of overseas programmes may be included on ITV area services, TV-am or Channel 4 over a six-month period.[942] The 14-percent margin is only a basic figure; certain non-British material is exempt from the quota system and is not subject to any quantitative restrictions. Quota-exempt material can be roughly divided into two categories: material exempt because of its country of origin, and material exempt because of its par-

---

940 Films Act 1980 (c.41), sec. 7, provided the basis for this suspension.
941 *See* M. DICKINSON & S. STREET, CINEMA AND STATE – THE FILM INDUSTRY AND THE BRITISH GOVERNMENT 1927-1984 225, 248 (1985).
942 IBA, Notes for Reference – British and Overseas Acquired Material on Independent Television (dated Aug. 7, 1985). These reference notes, though not published, are made available to any interested parties.

ticular value to British viewers. With respect to the former category, the IBA in 1978 excluded all EC material from the quota system in order to comply with the provisions on freedom of goods and services under the EEC Treaty. At the same time, the Authority partly withdrew the preferential treatment it had previously accorded to Commonwealth material. Since 1983 Commonwealth material has again become exempt, however, at least for up to 1.5 per cent of total transmission hours. This relaxation of the quota system followed demands by Commonwealth governments for some kind of reciprocity. These countries had argued that they deserved favourable treatment from the United Kingdom because they themselves showed large quantities of British programme material on their television channels.[943]

The second category of quota-exempt material basically comprises all informational, news, sports and educational programmes and any other material of outstanding quality with a particular cultural or educational value. It is up to the IBA to decide whether the content and volume of a programme intended for showing on ITV justifies its exemption from the quota system under these standards. In all cases of doubt, the material has to be cleared with the IBA in advance of scheduling. In addition, the IBA maintains a constant monitoring system with respect to programme transmissions. The trade unions of the British broadcasting industry themselves also check the amount of imported material on ITV schedules and regularly meet with the IBA to advance any complaints.

The quota system for foreign programmes has had the effect that British television presents a greater percentage of home-made material than television stations in most other countries, with the exception of the United States and the Soviet Union. This observation remains valid if one also takes the BBC programme schedule into consideration. The BBC has voluntarily committed itself to quota restrictions similar to those applicable to the ITV system. This commitment was reaffirmed in a resolution passed by the Board of Governors in 1981. By way of reference the commitment became part of the BBC's list of programme obligations set out in its Licence and Agreement 1981.[944] In the year 1985, quota material on ITV amounted to 13 per cent of all transmissions, while quota-exempt material

943 *See* The Guardian, May 27, 1985.
944 *See* BBC Licence and Agreement 1981, Preamble and Annex.

made up 11.5 per cent on Channel 4 and 6.25 per cent for the rest of ITV.[945] Despite the abolition of all restrictions on EC material, programmes with EC origin play only a subordinate role on British television screens. They comprise not more than 1 per cent of total transmissions.[946]

As a direct extension of the concepts underlying the quota system of the public broadcasting organizations, section 10(1)(d) of the Cable and Broadcasting Act 1984 requires the Cable Authority to do all that it can to secure »that there are included in the programmes proper proportions of recorded and other matter which originates within the European Economic Community and is performed by nationals of member States.« Despite this authorization, the Cable Authority has thus far refrained from establishing quota restrictions on foreign material. Instead, even British-originated satellite television channels like Sky Channel include great proportions of American programme material in their services. The main reason for the failure effectively to establish a quota system may be found in the great difficulties encountered by programme suppliers in acquiring enough reasonably priced programme material in order to put together full programme channels. The American film studios and their distribution subsidiaries still provide the best market for programme material in terms of both volume and price. If the Cable Authority were to establish rigid foreign quotas at the present stage, the still feeble British cable industry would possibly experience even more severe financial difficulties than it faces at present. Of the British satellite television companies, probably only Superchannel, which is fed from the vast British-made programme libraries of the BBC and the ITV companies, could survive on the British cable television market. At the present stage, therefore, legal specifications aiming particularly at a limitation of American television programmes remain little more than wishful thinking.

Not least due to the immense quantity of British programme output produced by the public broadcasting system, export of BBC and ITV

---

945 1985 IBA Annual Report, *supra* note 263, at 33. Under the impression of massive political pressure to reduce the amount of violent and sexually explicit programmes on television, both the BBC and the IBA announced measures to limit the showing of foreign, in particular American, programme material deemed to be especially offensive. The IBA, e.g., urged ITV companies to reduce the amount of imported material during peak viewing time from 5-1/2 hours to four hours a week. The Times, Sept. 30, 1987.

946 Out of the 6.25-percent quota-exempt material shown on ITV, another 1.5 per cent consisted of extra Commonwealth material, and the rest stemmed from all other countries in the world combined. The Guardian, May 27, 1985.

material plays an important role in financing these television services. Because of the strength of the trade unions in the British television industry and the severely limited amount of relatively cheap foreign material that can be bought to fill the programme schedules, total production costs for television in Britain are high and rising at a considerable rate.[947] The sale of British-made programmes to foreign broadcasters represents an efficient way to reclaim parts of these production costs. The following section is therefore dedicated to the regulation of British participation in international programme exchange and BBC and ITV television programme export.

2. *Programme Export and International Cooperation*

The United Kingdom is the second largest exporter of television films in the world, surpassed only by the United States. To put matters into perspective, it should be added, however, that the United States exports programmes at a value 15 times as high as that of the United Kingdom.[948] With the ratification in 1961 of the 1958 European Agreement concerning Programme Exchanges by means of Television Films,[949] the United Kingdom removed obstacles to the assignment of broadcast rights in television films between its own and foreign broadcasting organizations that had existed due to the different legal natures national copyright laws assign to television films. The Agreement states that any broadcasting organization under the jurisdiction of a party to the Agreement has the right to authorize in the other member countries the exploitation for television of television films of which it is the maker (article 1).

Authorization for the BBC's programme export derives from its Royal Charter. The BBC effects its export of television programmes through its commercial arm, BBC Enterprises, Inc., and exports to countries as politically diverse as the United States and the People's Republic of China.[950] Also, the BBC sells its BBC 1 programmes to cable systems in different European countries as a direct-relay service. The cable networks

947 For example, in 1984 ITV production costs rose by about 10 per cent. The Guardian, May 13, 1985.
948 An OECD statistic in 1986 showed U.K. television exports worth $22 million, while the U.S. exports were valued at $450 million. OECD Observer, No. 141 23 (July 1986).
949 *Signed by* the United Kingdom on July 13, 1960, *entered into force* July 1, 1961, T.S. No. 88/1961, Cmnd. 1509.
950 In 1986, e.g., BBC Enterprises, Inc. signed an agreement with China Central Television (CCTV) to show a variety of BBC television programmes on Chinese television. Fin. Times, Aug. 13, 1986.

receive the programming for simultaneous transmission and pay a fee for the broadcasting rights calculated on the basis of the number of homes subscribing to the service.[951]

The ITV companies as well sell their programmes to foreign broadcasting organizations. They can do this without the prior consent of the IBA if the programmes have been previously shown on ITV or Channel 4 or have at least been offered to both systems for broadcasting.[952] Implied in this last alternative is the condition that the programmes offered for broadcasting comply with the content provisions of the Broadcasting Act 1981. If a programme is deemed to be unbalanced, for example, the IBA feels authorized to prohibit the export of a programme item despite its having been offered for broadcasting on the ITV system by the ITV contractor responsible for its production.[953] This system ensures that ITV contractors primarily produce programmes for the British market; programme export may only come as a by-product of these activities. This regulation still allows the contractor to produce programmes in cooperation with foreign investors, like American video companies,[954] as long as the programmes are first shown on ITV before they are supplied to the foreign market. No IBA approval is needed, however, if the contractors' activities are carried out wholly outside the United Kingdom and do not relate to programmes or transmissions receivable in the United Kingdom. If a contractor were to acquire a foreign television company, however, this decision would need IBA approval. The IBA presently takes the position that it would generally not interfere with such activities of the ITV contractors.[955] The activities of the ITV foreign subsidiaries would not be controlled by the Authority as long as their transmissions were not aimed at the British market.

ITN, the company owned jointly by the ITV companies and providing the news service, has entered into a contract with Japanese broadcasters, according to which part of its news programmes are shown on Japanese television. Also, World Television News (formally United Press International Television News) is jointly operated by ITN, the U.S. television channel ABC, and the Australian Channel 9. The service grants ITN quick access to news programmes produced by the other two corporations, and it sells huge

---

951 Information provided to the author by Mr David Williams, Assistant to the BBC Legal Adviser.
952 Television Contract, *supra* note 349, at clause 1(4)(g) and (5)(f)(vi).
953 *See* 7 J. MEDIA L. & PRAC. 101 (1986).
954 Such an arrangement was entered into by Yorkshire Television. *See* Fin. Times, Apr. 18, 1986.
955 Information provided to the author by Mr Kenneth Blyth, Chief Assistant to the IBA Director General.

parts of its programmes to television stations in all parts of the world.

ITV contractors have shown a growing interest in extending their activities to foreign countries. Granada Television, for example, holds a stake in Canal Plus, the French subscription television channel. Anglia Television joined a consortium with the plan to apply for one of the franchises for the proposed new channel of commercial television in Israel.[956] The increasingly international outlook particularly of the more affluent among the ITV contractors is further evidenced by their provision of the satellite television service Superchannel aimed at cable systems in Europe and the investment by some of them in the Luxembourg-based satellite company planning to launch the 16-channel, medium-power television satellite Astra.[957] So far, Thames shareholdings are in SES, the company responsible for the technical operation of the satellite. However, Thames has joined a consortium with another ITV contractor, London Weekend Television (LWT), and with Carlton Communications, Sacchi & Sacchi and Dixons for the provision of two programme channels to be transmitted via Astra. Since Astra's programmes would also be directed at the British market, Thames and LWT need IBA permission for the venture. However, this permission is not all too likely to be forthcoming. The IBA has let it be known that its permission to run Superchannel did not set a precedent for its willingness also to permit other competing satellite channels operated by ITV companies.[958] The IBA is concerned over the possible adverse effects of any new, particularly medium-power, satellite television channels that could be expected to compete directly with the infant industry of U.K. DBS services. The ITV companies, on the other hand, take the position that they should not be at a disadvantage with other satellite television providers in the United Kingdom.[959] They are hoping for support from the government and its policy to promote competition in broadcasting.

Channel 4, on the other hand, has chosen a different way to extend its operations beyond the British market. In 1985 it joined five other European broadcasting organizations in setting up the European

---

956 Fin. Times, Oct. 31, 1986. Capital Radio, the London-based ILR contractor, bought a 60-percent stake in Riviera Radio, a station based in Monte Carlo with a largely English-speaking audience. Fin. Times, Mar. 25, 1988.

957 In the beginning, only Thames Television held a 5-percent stake in Astra. At a later stage, Thames increased its sharebase to 10 per cent, and two other ITV contractors, Television South West Holdings and Ulster Television, acquired two per cent each in the venture. 1988(3) MEDIEN BULLETIN 32.

958 Information provided to the author by Mr Kenneth Blyth, Chief Assistant to the IBA Director General.

959 Information provided to the author by Ms Jane Vizard, Legal Adviser, ITCA, and Mr Ivor Stolliday, Company Secretary, ITCA.

Co-Production Association. The Association will coproduce programmes with a strongly European content. Programmes will be aimed at the European and world markets at a fraction of the cost, it is hoped, which each television organization would have to incur individually.[960]

Cooperation in the form of programme exchange between the BBC and the IBA on the one hand and other European broadcasting organizations on the other hand has a long-standing history. In 1950 the BBC together with French broadcasters organized the first broadcasts across the Channel from Calais to the United Kingdom. This was followed by the foundation of the Anglo-French Television Liaison Committee, which became responsible for the bilateral programme exchange between France and Britain. In the same year, the BBC joined the Union International de Radiodiffusion (UIR), which was later renamed the European Broadcasting Union (EBU). Membership of the EBU is confined to broadcasting organizations from ITU member countries.[961] The EBU is a private organization. It has its headquarters in Geneva and is governed by Swiss law. Today, apart from the separate membership of the BBC, the IBA and ITCA hold joint membership in this organization. The EBU's objects are to support the interests of its members, assist the development of broadcasting in all its forms, foster the exchange of information between members, assist members in any negotiations, and finally, and perhaps most importantly, promote the television and radio programme exchange by all possible means.[962] This programme exchange is most significant in the area of news, sports and special events. Under the patronage of the EBU, Eurovision, a system of international daily programme exchange, has been set up and operated since 1954. In 1979, 30 television services in 23 European and northern African countries were connected to this system via cable.[963] The BBC and ITV both participate regularly and extensively in Eurovision. In 1983 the BBC contributed 60 programmes amounting to 184 hours of transmissions and in turn received 179 programmes with a total duration of about 386 hours; the ITV system contributed 10 programmes lasting about 16 hours and received 110 programmes with 212 hours of duration.[964] While the EBU promotes programme exchange, it places no requirements on programme content. It has never been in the position to formulate binding international

---

960 Fin. Times, Apr. 18, 1986.
961 Statutes of the European Broadcasting Union 1982, article 3.
962 Id. at article 2.
963 HANS-BREDOW-INSTITUT, *supra* note 902, at G 21. Eurovision is also connected with Intervision, the Eastern European version of Eurovision, and – via INTELSAT satellites – with numerous non-European television services. *Id.*
964 *Id.*, *citing* EBU Review No. 3 (May 1984).

programme standards. Instead, it is up to its member organizations to decide which programmes they want to supply and to receive from the Eurovision system. Sceptical about the financial viability of Europa-TV – a satellite television channel started on the initiative of the EBU in February 1985 and providing European information and entertainment programmes for European cable systems – the BBC did not join the Italian, Irish, Portugese, Dutch and German national broadcasting organizations in setting up and operating the channel. Presently, however, the BBC is taking a greater interest in the discussions for an EBU-sponsored satellite sports channel that would commercially exploit the EBU-held broadcasting rights for major sporting events.[965]

As long as the quota restrictions on foreign cinema films applied, foreign film makers could achieve an exemption from the quota system if they made the films in accordance with the provisions of one of the various bilateral coproduction agreements that the United Kingdom had entered into over the years. These bilateral treaties reflect the spirit of the 1954 European Cultural Convention,[966] to which the United Kingdom is a party. It invites the contracting states to facilitate the movement and exchange of persons and objects of cultural value among them (article 4). The so-called Films Co-production Agreements specify that any film that has been approved as a coproduction film by the relevant authorities in the contracting states shall enjoy all the benefits accorded to national films under their respective national laws.[967] By Order in Council, these bilateral treaties were transformed into British law.[968] These agreements specify the conditions that the British and the foreign film makers who jointly produce a film have to meet in order to qualify. Specifications relate to the national origin of the

---

965 Information provided to the author by Mr Anthony Jennings, BBC Legal Adviser. Under the present proposals, a number of EBU member organisations would enter into a 50-50 joint venture with Rupert Murdoch's Sky Channel to provide the new sports channel »Eurosport« in direct competition with »Screen Sport.« Fin. Times, Dec. 1, 1987.

966 *Signed* Dec. 19, 1954, *entered into force* in the United Kingdom on May 5, 1955, T.S. 49/1955, Cmnd. 9545.

967 *See, e.g.*, Films Co-production Agreement Between the Government of the United Kingdom and the Government of the Kingdom of Norway, *signed* Dec. 8, 1982, T.S. 46/183, Cmnd. 9007; Films Co-production Agreement Between the Government of the United Kingdom and the Government of Canada, *signed* Sept. 12, 1975, T.S. 8/1976, Cmnd. 6380; Films Co-production Agreement Between the Government of the United Kingdom and the Government of the Federal Republic of Germany, *signed* Jan. 20, 1975, T.S. 103/175, Cmnd. 6155. Other bilateral coproduction agreements were made with Italy and France in 1967 and 1965, respectively.

968 *See, e.g.*, Films Co-production Agreement (Norway), Order 1983/610; Films Co-production Agreement (Canada), Order 1975/1838; Films Co-production Agreement (Federal Republic of Germany), Order 1975/623.

individuals taking part in the film, the origins of the film script and the music, the location of the shooting of the film, the production costs and the percentage of neutral participation in these costs, etc. With the abolition of the quota system, these agreements have not become moot. Coproduction films may be eligible for governmental grants. Also, while films of EC origin are treated as British films from the outset, films made under coproduction agreements with non-EC member states may become eligible for preferential tax treatment under the Finance Act 1982.[969]

At times, bilateral cultural cooperation agreements between the United Kingdom and other countries promote the interests of their mutual film industries by stating that the contracting parties shall facilitate the entry and exhibition in their respective territories of documentary, artistic and educational films originating from each country[970] or stating that better knowledge of the other's culture shall be encouraged through exhibitions, theatrical productions, musical recitals and cinema festivals.[971]

On the whole, these treaties represent only piecemeal progress on the establishment of an international market for audiovisual media. Yet the new media, particularly satellite television, put the international community increasingly on the spot to formulate a viable international legal regime accommodating both the interests of the sovereign countries as well as the needs and interests of private information providers and the public. With respect to the free flow of satellite television transmissions, the British view still leans towards the prior-consent principle and the requirement that foreign channels comply with the domestic law in the receiving country. However, if the European countries could agree on binding rules relating to programme and advertising standards, exclusive broadcasting rights and the like, the United Kingdom might be ready to dispense with its reservations against foreign satellite transmissions, at least in relation to programmes originating in member states of the Council of Europe. In the interest of an uninhibited access of the contemplated BBC international television service to cable networks around the world, the U.K. government might even find it desirable to take a more liberal general attitude towards the free flow of satellite television transmissions.

---

969 *See* Films Act 1985, Schedule I, para. 4(5), and Finance Act 1982 (c.39), sec. 72. *See also* Films (Certification) Regulation 1985, 1985 S.I. No. 994.

970 *See, e.g.*, Basic Convention for Cultural Co-operation between the Government of the United Kingdom and the Government of the Republic of Venezuela, *signed* Dec. 16, 1983, T.S. 51/1984, Cmnd. 9271.

971 *See, e.g.*, Cultural Convention between the Government of the United Kingdom and the Government of Costa Rica, *signed* Dec. 7, 1978, T.S. 64/1984, Cmnd. 9334. These treaties do not normally grant national treatment to the other parties' cultural products.

However, this interest would conflict with the British desire to protect and preserve the public broadcasting structure and specific British cultural values.

The Peacock Committe had felt less anxious about the potential loss of the British national character, which many fear could result from the introduction of a truly liberalized international media market. The Committee instead designed a three-stage plan to open the British media market fully to the realm of freedom of information and free entrepreneurship.

VII. *Outlook*

According to the recommendations of the Peacock Committee, radio broadcasting could become the forerunner of a »full broadcasting market.« The plans for the new legal regime applying to broadcasting and now strongly favoured by the government evidence the erosion of the public broadcasting concept and the cautious discharge of the dogma that governed the British broadcasting media for many decades.

Stage 1 of this gradual transition of the present media system as envisaged by the Peacock Committee would last until about the early 1990s and would end with the fading out of all special provisions relating to broadcasters and regulating obscenity,. defamation, blasphemy, and the like. These rules would be replaced by the normal laws of the land.[972] According to the Committee's time schedule, the responsibility as »publishers« in the legal sense would simultaneously be transferred from the IBA to the ITV companies and to ITN. This would then directly result in a reduction of IBA pre-vetting of programmes.[973] In Stage 2, to begin in the 1990s, the Committee advised the replacement of the BBC licence fee with subscription.[974] In this phase the BBC would be primarily financed through subscription, while the ITV companies would predominantly rely on advertising revenues. However, all broadcasting organizations would be free partly to turn to other sources of income as well. The concept of sub-

---

972 1986 Peacock Report, *supra* note 216, at para. 669. For a critical review of the recommendations by the Peacock Committee, see Barendt, *Freedom of Speech and Broadcasting*, 8 J. MEDIA L. & PRAC. 91-97 (1987).
973 1986 Peacock Report, *supra* note 216, at para. 670.
974 *Id.* at para. 673.

scription services is a crucial element of the Committee's recommendations. It is supposed to enable consumers to make individual channel and/or programme choices, thereby expressing their viewing preferences.

If these changes came about, Stage 2 would already begin at a point in time earlier than that recommended by the Committee. In Stage 2 as proposed by the Committee, the new public-service concept of broadcasting in the form of direct public sponsorship of certain experimental and minority programmes would also come into being. As soon as a sufficient diversity of independent programme suppliers would be achieved, all content restrictions on broadcasting services would be dropped.[975] Finally, in Stage 3, beginning with the 21st century, technological, legal and economic developments would be such as to allow a »full broadcasting market.«[976]

In light of the total change of the present broadcasting structure supported by the Committee and the powerful social and political role played nowadays by the two broadcasting authorities, it is no wonder that the Peacock Report initially met with strong political opposition even among Conservative politicians. After the first public outcry had abated, however, some senior government officials began to consider in more detail the possible consequences of the technological scenario and the important political and social implications of the analysis. An interdepartmental committee with members from the Home Office, the DTI and the Treasury was set up to conduct a broad review of the future of U.K. broadcasting before the background of the Peacock Report.[977]

The extent to which the Peacock Report will make an imprint on the British broadcasting structure in the near future is difficult to foresee. Political opposition is quite strong. This may explain why the government announced that it would refrain from carrying through any of the Committee's short-term proposals before the general elections in the summer of 1987. Had the Labour Party come to power, the traditional concept of public-service broadcasting and strong misgivings about any attempt to introduce a truly consumer-oriented broadcasting system could have been very likely to prevail for a number of years. But even then, the growing internationalization of media markets would have forced the United Kingdom to clarify its positions.

---

975 *Id.* at paras. 691, 693.
976 *See id.* at paras. 701-06.
977 *See* Fin. Times, Aug. 5, 1986. The Prime Minister personally chaired the committee. Fin. Times, Sept. 11, 1986.

Since the Conservative government won the elections, many of the Peacock Committee's recommendations are likely to be put into practice. Yet the political fate of a number of recommendations is still uncertain. Nonetheless, the Report's immediate significance and most important contribution lies in the fact that it provides an enlightened insight in the legal and social implications accompanying the present telecommunications revolution. The Committee can be credited for having looked beyond the everyday problems and political quarrels over the financing of the existing broadcasting system and for having directed wide public attention to the fundamental changes that the new media have brought about and will even more so invariably bring about in the not-too-distant future. The public outcry and in part misunderstanding over the recommendations that prevailed immediately after their publication only evidenced a lack of public awareness concerning the significance of the new broadcasting technologies.

The new 1984 legislative enactments primarily took care of the most pressing problems of the day. They lack a comprehensive integration of the different media and a coherent concept and definition of their harmonious coexistence and mutually stimulating interaction. The 1984 Acts are concerned with the problem of encouraging the development of an (until then) almost nonexistent and ailing cable television industry and of laying the legal groundwork for the introduction of DBS technology. While the Cable and Broadcasting Act 1984 contains guidelines favouring interactive cable technology with a view to promoting the fullest possible range of services for consumers, the Act neither sets up an absolute preference for this technology nor tackles the problem of how increased competition by an increasing number of cable and satellite programme providers will effect the two broadcasting authorities and the present public broadcasting system as a whole.

A dynamic development of alternative means of television programme supplies has already begun. With competition from other programme sources, the role of the present broadcasting organizations must necessarily diminish. The Peacock Report has given evidence of the need to set the proper course of these developments in telecommunications well ahead of time.

Another important merit of the Report is its focus on the implications for freedom of information stemming from the new technologies. In the early 1980s, the debate over the promotion of cable and satellite services was dominated by concerns over industrial and labour-market policies: high-technology industries in Britain were to be boosted, technological know-how suitable for export was to be developed, and new work stations were to be created. In contrast, the Peacock Committee puts the emphasis on the significance of the new technologies for the right to freedom of expression. It does not argue outright that British law necessarily requires an immediate liberalization of the rules governing the communication of ideas by electromagnetic means. Instead, the Committee recalls the beginnings of the era of the print media, where censorship in Britain appeared to be a matter of course. Later, when the new technology had matured, the view was gradually accepted that a free and democratic society presupposed freedom of the press. From the analogy to the print media, the Committee deduces the validity of the principle of freedom of communication in the area of broadcasting. The analogy to the printing press is all the more justified the more alike the actual characteristics of the print and broadcast media become. In the final stage of a national optic-fibre cable grid, any difference in the nature of the two media would have disappeared: an infinite number of channels would make possible the public expression of opinions by an infinite number of publishers and at reasonable costs. Paper publishing and electronic publishing would only differ in the technology used to transfer the message from the publisher to the consumer.

The right to freedom of information encompasses the right to receive the information from any available source, including foreign sources. An overriding public interest to (pre-)censor electromagnetic information flows may be present whenever unavoidable natural and/or economic conditions are such as to prevent a pluralistic market of opinions. This is the situation still partly characterizing the present broadcasting market: spectrum scarcity is one obstacle to a multitude of broadcasting channels. The often prohibitively high investment costs to set up new cable networks are the other impediment. They automatically exclude the majority of would-be publishers from this market, at least as long as the cable operators enjoy factual local monopolies on programme distribution. Both these reasons have in the past contributed to the justification of the public-service broadcasting concept with its requirements of programme diversity, balancing of opinions and the like. The concept was the best conceivable way to strike a balance between the public's right to diverse information and the division of the few available spectrum bands and the cable operators' interest in recovering their high investment costs by en-joying monopoly positions.

The Peacock Committee boldly argues that the present public-service concept is only a second-best solution. Paramount is the right to freedom of communication, which must prevail as soon as and whenever the actual situation allows for a true consumer market of ideas, i.e., whenever a new era of communication technologies has »matured.« Under this approach, public-service broadcasting needs a justification; a »full broadcasting market« does not. Implied though not directly expressed in the Committee's understanding of freedom of communication is the conviction that the government is under an obligation actively to further the establishment and development of a full broadcasting market: the Report repeatedly requests the government to take all necessary steps today to pave the way for a quick and comprehensive development of cable technology for the future.

Another facet of the Committee's concern for freedom of communication is its astute analysis of the dangers of what may be phrased the convergence of conduit and content characteristic of the new telecommunications technologies. While up until now national law has placed the control of the limited resource of the radio spectrum and the right to frequency assignment with the government, the builder and operator of a cable network has control over the use and thus the content of channels available in the grid, unless the lawmakers actively step in and provide otherwise. Much has been argued about the question whether a cable network is a natural monopoly.[978] Even if this were true and the high capital costs of such systems would generally make them viable only if just one cable existed in a given area, this cirumstance is not necessarily a barrier to a full broadcasting market. The latter depends on the kind of technology provided in the cable, i.e., the number of available channels, and the regulation of access rights to these channels. It is the combination of these two elements that decides whether the monopoly control over the conduit is paralleled in the control over the content. The Peacock Committee has identified these two elements as the focal points for the development of a full broadcasting market. Fibre-optic cable creates an almost unlimited resource of channels for a large variety of usages and thus represents the optimal answer to the problem of spectrum scarcity. Of even greater importance are the legal rules preventing the abuse of the control over the channels. Breaking away from the present policy of placing control over conduit and content in the hands of a single operator, the Committee supports a system in which control over the two elements would be totally separated. The undertaking

---

978 *See, e.g.*, C. VELJANOVSKI & W.D. BISHOP, CHOICE BY CABLE – THE ECONOMICS OF A NEW ERA IN TELEVISION 71-76 (1983).

supplying a cable would be fully excluded from its use and would solely act as a common carrier. At present, only the BBC, the ITV companies and Channel 4 are protected against the cable operators' monopoly power under the must-carry rule. Freedom of communication, however, necessitates the protection of any would-be publisher against the exclusionary powers of cable monopolies.

Once the legal separation of conduit and content were achieved, the merger and competition laws would have to step in to ensure that no unwelcomed concentration of ownership or anti-competitive practices would take place among content suppliers. The Committee has identified well the important functions of the competition and antitrust laws in this context. Furthermore, it suggests a number of accompanying measures, such as channel limitation for single users and financial support for experimental and other programmes with little mass appeal, in order to counteract tendencies of market concentration.

Unsurprisingly, protest against the Committee's proposal of a rule requiring a separation of control over conduit and content was raised soon after the publication of the report. BT publicly stated that the viability of a national cable grid as envisaged by the Committee and operated by BT would also necessitate BT's control over the services offered on the system.[979] In line with BT's position, all other natural cable monopolists can be expected also to defend vigorously the status quo and the benefits accruing from it in the months and years to come.

The problems and dangers of the present new broadcast era have been duly identified. It is now up to the political institutions to face the challenges and to shape the broadcasting market of the future.

979 Fin. Times, Sept. 13, 1986.

NATIONAL REPORT QUESTIONNAIRE*

Part 1: Telephone services

A. Regulation of transborder telephone services

    I.   Basic regulations of domestic telecommunications law for transborder telephone services[1]
        1. Transformation of international regulations into domestic law and practice
            a) Survey of the relevant international law
                aa) Multilateral agreements
                bb) Bilateral agreements
            b) Scope of questions of transborder telephone services reserved for national regulation
            c) Domestic regulatory power to transform international regulations into domestic law and practice
                aa) Power to issue regulations affecting the domestic sphere[2]
                    aaa) Legislature
                    bbb) Public administration (administrative agencies)
                    ccc) Operating companies (providing telephone services)
                bb) Power to issue regulations affecting foreign states[2]
                    aaa) Legislature
                    bbb) Administrative agencies
                    ccc) Operating companies
            d) Contents of the international regulations as transformed into domestic law (including their application and construction)
        2. Domestic law unaffected by international law
            a) Regulatory power[2]
                aa) Legislature
                bb) Administrative agencies

* The Questionnaire was prepared by a Work Group at the Max Planck Institute in Hamburg. Under the direction of Prof. E.-J. Mestmäcker, the Group consisted of Thomas Born, Reinhard Ellger, Beate-Katrin Graben and Detlev Witt.

cc) Operating companies
b) Survey of the contents of the domestic law
(including application and construction)

II. Legal relations between domestic carriers (networks) providing transborder telephone services and domestic users of those services

1. Use of telephone services
a) Public networks (common carriers)[3]
aa) Who operates public networks?
bb) Legal requirements for establishment and operation of
public networks
aaa) Contents of the requirements
bbb) Power to regulate the requirements, to license
operating companies, etc.
ccc) Judicial review or other legal recourse against regulatory decisions
cc) What services may be offered? What services are actually
available?
dd) Requirements for access to and conditions for use of
public networks[4,5]
aaa) Who has access to the networks?[6]
(1) Ultimate consumers
(2) »Resellers« of transmission services (lessees of
network capacity)
(3) Power to regulate access to networks
bbb) Setting of tariffs
(1) Tariff principles
(2) Power to regulate tariffs (or market pricing?)
ccc) Liability (of operating company for malfunction,
etc.)
ddd) Technical standards (especially standards for terminal equipment and its usage)
(1) Power to regulate standards (source of regulation: international/national, governmental/pri-
vate?)
(2) Contents of technical standards
eee) Judicial review or other legal recourse against regulatory decisions

b) Private networks
    aa) Who operates private networks?
    bb) Legal requirements for establishment and operation of private networks[6]
        aaa) Contents of the requirements[7]
        bbb) Regulatory power[7]
        ccc) Judicial review or other legal recourse[7]
    cc) What services may be offered? What services are actually available?
    dd) Are private network operators allowed to sublease networks? If so, under which conditions?

c) Networks operated by closed user groups
    aa) Who operates closed-user-group networks? (e.g., SITA, SWIFT)
    bb) Legal requirements for establishment and operation of closed-user-group networks[6]
        aaa) Contents of requirements[7]
        bbb) Regulatory power[7]
        ccc) Judicial review or other legal recourse[7]
    cc) What services may be offered? What services are actually available?
    dd) Requirements for access to and terms of usage of closed-user-group networks[6,7]
        aaa) Who can become a member of the »user group« and thereby gain access to the network?
        bbb) Setting of tariffs
            (1)   Tariff principles
            (2)   Who sets the tariffs?
        ccc) Liability (for errors, malfunction, etc.)
        ddd) Technical standards
        eee) Judicial review or other legal recourse; government supervision

2. Admission of terminal equipment to the network[8,9]
    a) What terminal equipment is part of the network – according to domestic telecommunications law – and therefore subject to the regulatory powers governing the telephone services?
    b) Who regulates the admission of terminal equipment to the network?
        aa) Administrative agencies

bb) Network operators

c) Criteria for admission (e.g., technical compatability)[5]

d) Judicial review or other legal recourse

III. Legal relations between domestic and international or foreign network operators

    1. Access of domestic networks to and terms of usage of foreign networks

        a) Requirements of domestic telecommunications law[6] for access to the international network[10,11]

            aa) Contents of the requirements

                aaa) International law (multilateral/bilateral agreements) and domestic implementation thereof

                bbb) Domestic law unaffected by international law

            bb) Regulatory power

                aaa) International organizations

                bbb) Bilateral coordination

                ccc) Domestic legislature

                ddd) Domestic administrative agencies

                eee) Operating companies

            cc) Judicial review or other legal recourse

        b) Requirements of domestic telecommunications law for the use of the international network (to what extent does domestic law influence these requirements?)[12]

            aa) Contents of the requirements

                aaa) Setting of tariffs, accounting

                    (1) International framework (multilateral/bilateral) agreements, including their transformation into domestic law)

                    (2) Domestic law unaffected by international law

                bbb) Technical standards

                    (1) International framework

                    (2) Domestic law

                ccc) Liability (for malfunction, etc.)

            bb) Regulatory powers for setting tariffs and technical standards

                aaa) International organizations

                bbb) Bilateral coordination

                ccc) Domestic legislature

ddd) Domestic administrative agencies

eee) Operating companies

cc) Judicial review or other legal recourse

2. Access of foreign networks to and terms of usage of domestic networks
   a) Are several domestic networks accessible from abroad?
   b) Requirements of domestic telecommunications law[6] for access to domestic network(s)
      aa) Contents of the requirements
         aaa) International regulations (including their transformation into domestic law)
         bbb) Domestic law unaffected by international law
      bb) Regulatory powers
         aaa) International organizations
         bbb) Bilateral coordination
         ccc) Domestic legislature
         ddd) Domestic administrative agencies
         eee) Operating companies
      cc) Judicial review or other legal recourse
   c) Terms of usage of the national networks
      aa) Contents of the terms
         aaa) Tariffs, accounting between networks
            (1) International framework (including transformation into domestic law)
            (2) Domestic law unaffected by international law
         bbb) Technical standards
            (1) International framework (including transformation into domestic law)
            (2) Domestic law unaffected by international law
         ccc) Liability (for errors, malfunction, etc.)
      bb) Power to regulate tariffs and technical standards
         aaa) International organizations
         bbb) Bilateral coordination
         ccc) Domestic legislature
         ddd) Domestic administrative agencies
         eee) Operating companies
      cc) Judicial review or other legal recourse

B. Legal regulation of the terminal and network equipment markets
   I. Demand side (procurement)
      1. Impact of the regulation of telephone services on the terminal and network equipment market
         a) Who procures the equipment?
           aa) To what extent does the domestic telecommunications law allow the network owners/operators and the users to purchase equipment according to their own choice?
           bb) Competitive situation of network owners/operators in purchasing network and terminal equipment
         b) Conditions of the procurement of equipment
           aa) Power to set the conditions
              aaa) International framework
              bbb) Domestic legislature and administrative agencies
              ccc) Operating companies
           bb) Contents of the conditions
              aaa) Technical standards and research/development of equipment
              bbb) Pricing, contractual terms
              ccc) Who maintains the equipment; under what conditions?
              ddd) Criteria for choice among several suppliers
      2. Impact of further regulations (besides telecommunications law) on the terminal and network equipment markets
         a) Impact of the regulation of foreign trade on the domestic procurement of terminal and network equipment
           aa) General rules for foreign trade in goods
           bb) Particular rules for foreign trade in terminal and network equipment
         b) Impact of other regulations (e.g., antitrust law; general regulation of economic activities)

  II. Supply side
      1. Effect of demand-side situation on the access to the market of network and terminal equipment for suppliers
      2. Impact of economic dependencies and other relations between demand and supply sides on the market for network and terminal equipment

1. This part calls for a survey of the regulations. Details should be given at parts II and III.
2. It should also be described to what extent the relevant institutions have actually exercised their regulatory powers.
3. The notion »public networks« means common carriers that offer their telephone services to all interested parties. The notion includes operators being owners of the networks as well as companies that offer telephone services by means of leased lines.
4. The »users« of public networks may be:
   - customers, who use telephone services for their own needs
   - lessees, who offer telephone services to third parties by means of leased lines
5. In the following parts, the international regulations and their transformation into domestic law should also be considered even if this may not be particularly mentioned in the outline.
6. General regulations other than telecommunications law should also be considered (e.g., antitrust law)
7. As far as private networks are operated by means of lines leased from common carriers, the conditions for access and usage, as stated at Part II.1.a) dd), should be referred to.
8. The different kinds of telephone networks have to be taken into account (see Part II.1.a)–c) above).
9. In this part, regulations regarding terminal equipment should only be dealt with, insofar as the admission of the equipment to the network is concerned. The impact of these regulations on the market for terminal equipment is to be treated in Part B of the outline.
10. The notion »international network« embraces all networks used for transborder telephone services except domestic networks.
11. »Requirements of access« means the criteria for determining which domestic carrier has access to foreign networks.
12. The conditions for access to and usage of networks used for transborder services can only be described comprehensively if the respective foreign telecommunications law is taken into account. This would go beyond the scope of a purely national report. However, information on bilateral relations should be added if available.

Part 2: Remote data processing (also: Videotex and remote sensing)

A. Legal regulation of transborder data processing

   I. General legal rules that may be applicable to transborder data processing

      1. Export of data
         a) General laws for the protection of national security and public safety (e.g., protection of secrets related to national security)
         b) Rules for the protection of domestic economic interests (e.g., regulations imposing tariffs on exports of data, disquettes, cassettes, hardware and software)
         c) General laws for the protection of private and individual interests
         d) Privacy protection

      2) Import of data
         a) General laws for the protection of national security and public safety
         b) Rules for the protection of domestic economic interests (e.g., regulations imposing tariffs on the import of data, disquettes, cassettes, hard- and software)
         c) General laws for the protection of private and individual interests
         d) Privacy protection

   II. Regulations relating to transborder data processing as a service
      1. Import of data processing services
         a) Commercial data processing services (data processing services offered to third parties that are not members of closed-user-group networks)
            aa) Principles of international business transactions law of the reporting country for transborder business in services in general (especially import regulations)
            bb) Particular rules for data processing services

```
            aaa) Data processing
            bbb) Data storage and retrieval
      b)  Intra-company communication
          aa) Data processing
          bb) Data storage and retrieval
      c)  Closed-user-group networks
          aa) Data processing
          bb) Data storage and retrieval
   2.  Export of data processing services
      a)  Commercial data processing services (data processing services
          offered to third parties that are not members of closed-
          user-group networks)
            aa) Principles of international business transactions law of the
                reporting country for transborder business in services in
                general (especially export regulations)
            bb) Particular rules for data processing services
                aaa) Data processing
                bbb) Data storage and retrieval
      b)  Intra-company communication
          aa) Data processing
          bb) Data storage and retrieval
      c)  Closed-user-group networks
          aa) Data processing
          bb) Data storage and retrieval


III. Regulations applicable specifically to transborder data processing
     survey of international law

   1.  Basic legal principles of domestic telecommunications law for the
       transborder transmission of data[1]
          a)  Transformation of legal requirements set up by interna-
              tional law into domestic law and practice
                aa)  Survey of the relevant international law
                     aaa) Multilateral agreements (e.g., ITU, regional
                          organizations)
                     bbb) Bilateral agreements
                bb)  Scope of the issues of telecommunications reserved
                     for domestic regulation
                cc)  Domestic regulatory power to transform interna-
                     tional requirements into domestic law and practice
```

aaa) Power to issue regulations affecting the domestic sphere and regulations issued[2]
(1)   Legislature
(2)   Administrative agencies
(3)   Operating companies providing data
transmission services
bbb) Power to issue regulations affecting the international or foreign sphere
(1)   Legislature
(2)   Administrative agencies
(3)   Operating companies providing data
transmission services
dd) Content of the international rules as transformed
into domestic law (including application and construction of the rules)
b) Domestic law unaffected by international law
aa)   Regulating Power
aaa) Legislature
bbb) Administrative agencies
ccc) Operating companies
bb)   Survey of the contents of the domestic law
(including application and construction)

2.   Rules of domestic law regulating the relations between domestic
operating companies providing international data transmission
services and domestic users of those services
a)   Use of data transmission services
aa) Public networks (common carriers)[3]
aaa) Who in fact operates public networks?
bbb) Legal requirements for installation and operation of
public networks
(1)   Content of requirements
(2)   Jurisdiction (for making the regulations and
granting licenses, etc.)
(3)   Judicial review or other legal recourse against
regulatory decisions
ccc) What services legally may be offered via the public
network?
(1)   Transmission services alone
(2)   Enhanced services (i.e., transmission *and* data

processing services)

ddd) Requirements for access to and use of public networks[4,5]
  (1) Jurisdiction to regulate access and use of networks – who actually regulates?
  (2) Who has access to the networks?[6]
    (2.1) Users (ultimate consumers) of data processing services
    (2.2) Offerors of data processing services (who offer data processing services to other parties.
    (2.3) Lessees of networks, who offer either transmission services alone or enhanced services
  (2) Setting of tariffs
    (1.1) Regulatory jurisdiction (or market pricing)
    (2.3) Principles of setting tariffs
  (3) Liability for errors in data processing
  (4) Technical standards (especially for terminal equipment and its usage)
    (4.1) Source of regulation: international or national; governmental or private
    (4.2) Contents
  (5) Judicial review or other legal recourse

bb) Private networks

aaa) Who operates private networks?

bbb) Legal requirements for installation and operation of private networks[6]
  (1) Regulatory power[7]
  (2) Judicial review or other legal recourse
  (3) Contents of requirements[7]

ccc) Which services are offered through private networks?
  (1) Data transmission for the network operator only
  (2) Data transmission also for third parties

ddd) Are private network operators allowed to sublet the networks? If so, under which conditions is a sublease allowed?

cc) Networks operated by closed user groups[6]
    aaa) Who operates closed-user-group networks (e.g., Swift, Sita)?
    bbb) Legal requirements for installation and operation of closed-user-group networks[6]
      (1) Contents of requirements[7]
      (2) Regulatory power[7]
      (3) Judicial review and other legal recourse
    ccc) What services are offered?
      (1) Data transmission for the network operating company only
      (2) Data transmission also for third parties
    ddd) Conditions for access to and usage of the networks
      (1) Who can become a member of the »user group« and thus gain access to the network?
      (2) Setting of tariffs
      (2.1) Principles
      (2.2) Who determines the tariffs?
      (3) Liability for errors in data processing
      (4) Technical standards
      (5) Judicial review or other legal recourse
      (6) Government supervision of private networks
b) Admission of terminal equipment[8,9]
  aa) Who regulates the admission of terminal equipment to the network?
    aaa) Public authorities
    bbb) Operating companies
  bb) What terminal equipment is part of the network according to domestic telecommunications law and is therefore subject to the respective regulatory powers?
  cc) Criteria for admission (e.g., technical standards for compatibility; non-discriminatory competition for foreign suppliers of terminal equipment)
  dd) Judicial review or other legal recourse
3. Rules regulating the relations between domestic and international or foreign network operators
a) Access to and modes of usage of international networks[10,11] by domestic carriers
  aa) Requirements of domestic telecommunications law for access to international networks[12]

316

        aaa) Contents of requirements
           (1)   International preconditions (multilateral or bi-
                 lateral agreements)
           (2)   domestic telecommunications law
        bbb) Regulatory powers
           (1)   International organizations
           (2)   Bilateral agreements
           (3)   Domestic legislation
           (4)   Domestic administrative agencies
           (5)   Operating companies
    bb) Requirements of domestic telecommunications law for
        the use of international networks (to what extent are
        these conditions influenced by domestic law?)[14]
        aaa) Contents of conditions
           (1)   Tariffs, accounting
               (1.1) The international framework (bilateral
                     and multilateral agreements and their
                     transformation into domestic rules)
               (1.2) Domestic law unaffected by international
                     law
           (2)   Technical standards
               (2.1) International framework
               (2.2) Domestic Law
           (3)   Liability for errors in data transmission
        bbb) Regulatory powers for setting tariffs and technical
           standards
           (1)   International institutions
           (2)   Bilateral agreements
           (3)   Domestic legislation
           (4)   Domestic administrative agencies
           (5)   Operating companies
    ccc) Judicial review and other legal recourse
b) Access to and modes of usage of domestic networks by
    foreign network operators
    aa) How many domestic networks are accessible from
        abroad?
    bb) Requirements set by domestic telecommunications law[6]
        for access to domestic networks
        aaa) Contents of requirements
           (1)   International framework

        (2)   Domestic law
      bbb) Regulatory powers
        (1)   International organizations
        (2)   Bilateral agreements
        (3)   Domestic legislation
        (4)   Domestic administrative agencies
        (5)   Operating companies
      ccc) Judicial review or other legal recourse
  cc) Conditions for the use of domestic networks
    aaa) Contents of conditions
      (1)   Tariffs, accounting between domestic and international networks
        (1.1) International framework and transformation into domestic law
        (1.2) Domestic law
      (2)   Technical standards
        (2.1) International framework and transformation into domestic law
        (2.2) Domestic law
      (3)   Liability for errors in data transmission
    bbb) Regulatory powers over tariffs and technical standards
      (1)   International institutions
      (2)   Bilateral agreements
      (3)   Domestic legislation
      (4)   Domestic administrative agencies
      (5)   Operating companies
    ccc) Judicial review or other legal recourse

B. Regulation of the markets for network and terminal equipment

  I. Demand side

    1. Impacts of the regulation of data transmission services on the markets for network and terminal equipment
      a) Demand
        aa) To what extent does the domestic telecommunications law allow the operating companies or the users to purchase network and terminal equipment according to their own choice?

        bb) Competition among the network operators in purchasing network and terminal equipment
   b) Conditions of procurement of network and terminal equipment
        aa) Regulatory powers to set conditions
           aaa) International framework
           bbb) Domestic legislature and administrative agencies
           ccc) Conditions set by operating companies themselves
        bb) Contents of the conditions
           aaa) Technical standards and development of equipment
           bbb) Pricing, contractual conditions
           ccc) Maintenance of equipment; conditions
           ddd) Criteria for choice among several suppliers

2. Impact of other regulations (besides the rules for data transmission services) on the market for network and terminal equipment
   a) Effects of the rules regulating international business transactions upon the market for network and terminal equipment
        aa) General provisions for the trade in goods
        bb) Particular rules for network and terminal equipment within the law relating to international business transactions
   b) Impact of other regulations, e.g., antitrust law, especially regulations against misuse of demand power; general regulation of economic activities

II. Supply side

1. Effect of the demand-side situation on access to the market for network and terminal equipment

2. Impacts of economic dependencies and other relations between the supply and demand sides on competition in the market for network and terminal equipment

1. This part of the outline calls for a survey of the regulations. Details should be given at parts III 2 and 3.
2. The constitutional framework of the legislative activities as well as the content of the provisions should be explained.
3. »Public networks« means common carriers, which offer their data transmission services to any interested parties. »Operating companies« includes the owners of the networks and also companies that use leased lines to offer data transmission services.
4. »Users« of public networks may be:
   – customers, who use the data transmission services for the remote processing for their own needs
   – lessees, who use leased lines to offer third parties remote data processing capacities.
5. Also the international regulations and their transformation into domestic law are to be considered, even if this may not be particularly mentioned in the outline.
6. Also legal rules other than telecommunications law should be taken into account here (e.g., antitrust law)
7. If the private networks are operated with lines leased from common carriers, the conditions for access and usage of the networks are to be treated, as stated at part III 2a, aa, ddd, dd above.
8. At this point, the different kinds of data transmission methods have to be taken into account (see part III 2a above)
9. Regulations relating to terminal equipment should be dealt with here only insofar as the admission of the equipment to the network is concerned.
   The impact of these regulations on the market for terminal equipment is to be treated in part B of the outline
10. Account should be taken of whether the regulation of access to international networks distinguishes
    a) between different kinds of data to be transmitted or different kinds of data transmission services
    b) between »pure« data transmission services and enhanced services.
11. If special rules exist for the transit of data on the way to third countries, they should be mentioned separately.
12. The notion of »international networks« encompasses all networks that are used for transborder data transmissions, except domestic networks.
13. »Requirements of access« means the criteria for determining which

domestic carrier has access to foreign networks.

14. The conditions under which networks for transborder data transmissions may be accessed and used can only be covered comprehensively if the respective foreign telecommunications law is taken into account. Although this goes beyond the scope of a national report, information on bilateral relations should be added if available.

Part 3: Audiovisual media programmes

A. Regulation of the flow of media programmes from abroad to the reporting state (RS)
   (Admission of programmes to the domestic territory; principles and conditions of access)

   I. Legal relations between foreign states and programme and transmitting companies on the one hand and the reporting state on the other

      1. The international framework and its transformation into national law
   (Extent of international obligations of RS to give access to its territory for foreign programmes)
         a) Multilateral agreements and international organizations subscribed to by RS
            aa) ITU convention and rules arising from it
               aaa) Relation of RS to ITU
               bbb) Audiovisual broadcast programmes
                  (1) Jamming
                  (2) Prohibition of reception
                  (3) Technical standards and import regulations for receiver equipment
                  (4) Different treatment according to origin and/or domicile of foreign programme/transmitting company
               ccc) Direct-Broadcast Satellites (DBS)
                  (1) Jamming
                  (2) Prohibition of reception
                  (3) Technical standards and import regulations for receiver equipment
                  (4) Different treatment according to origin and/or domicile of foreign programme/ transmitter company
                  (5) Different treatment of intended/unintended overspill
               ddd) Cable TV (CATV)
                  (1) Ability of foreign cable operators to link their

systems with domestic cable networks
- (1.1) General conditions of access
- (1.2) Setting of tariffs
- (1.3) Technical standards
- (1.4) Programme standards
- (2) Access to networks for foreign programmes
  - (1.1) General conditions of access
  - (1.2) Setting of tariffs
  - (1.3) Technical standards
  - (1.4) Programme standards
- bb) Transformation of ITU rules into national law (for broadcast, DBS and CATV programmes)
  - aaa) Power to transform ITU rules into national law
  - bbb) Form and extent of transformation
  - ccc) Jurisdiction for application of transformed rules to foreign programmes of companies
  - ddd) Practice of application
  - eee) Judicial review or other legal recourse against regulatory decisions
- cc) Human Rights Conventions and rules arising from them
  - aaa) Extent of adoption by RS
  - bbb) Audiovisual broadcast programmes
    - (1) Jamming
    - (2) Prohibition of reception
    - (3) Technical standards and import regulations for receiver equipment
    - (4) Preferential treatment of states of programme companies
  - ccc) Direct-Broadcast Satellites
    - – subdivided as above bbb)
  - ddd) Cable television
    - – subdivided as above bbb)
- dd) Transformation of Human Rights Convention into national law (for broadcast, DBS and CATV)
  - aaa) Power for transformation of Human Rights Conventions into international law
  - bbb) Form and extent of transformation
  - ccc) Jurisdiction for application of transformed

rules to foreign programmes of companies
ddd) Practice of application
eee) Judical review or other legal recourse against regulatory decisions
ee) Other multilateral agreements subscribed to by RS
aaa) Audiovisual broadcast programmes
bbb) Direct-Broadcast Satellites
ccc) Cable Television (CATV)
ff) Transformation of other multilateral agreements into national law (broadcast, DBS and CATV)
– subdivided as above dd) –
b) Bilateral agreements
aaa) Scope left for bilateral agreements under ITU rules
(1) Audiovisual broadcast programmes
(2) Direct-Broadcast Satellites
(3) Cable television (CATV)
bbb) Noteworthy bilateral agreements to which RS subscribes
ccc) Special rules provided by bilateral agreements to which RS subscribes
(1) Audiovisual broadcast programmes
(1.1) Jamming
(1.2) Technical standards and import regulations for receiver equipment
(1.3) Preferential treatment for certain states/programme companies
(1.4) Bilateral monopolies
(2) Direct-Broadcast Satellites
– subdivided as above (1)
(3) Cable television
– subdivided as above (1)
c) Summary: Scope of action left to reporting state under international law or international law as transformed into national law for regulation of access of audiovisual broadcast programmes to its territory.

2. National law independent of international framework (Regulations generally governing the emission of audiovisual broadcast, satellite and cable programmes)
a) Structure of the domestic media and their regulation

aa) Constitutional bases of the national media organization
aaa) Newspapers, magazines and other print media
bbb) Audiovisual broadcast programmes
ccc) Direct-Broadcast Satellites
ddd) Cable television
bb) Power to regulate, legal technique or regulation
– subdivided as above aa)
cc) Essentials of the national media regulation
– subdivided as above aa)
b) General laws applicable to media programmes (classified according to legal spheres or objects of legal protection, e.g.:
– General laws
– Penal laws
– Law against obscenity
– Law of advertising
– Antitrust law
– Other telecommunications laws)
c) Specific applicability of national law, actually or potentially, to incoming foreign programmes
aa) Audiovisual broadcast programmes
bb) Direct-Broadcast Satellites
cc) Cable television

II. Legal relations between reporting state and receivers (Regulations governing the *reception* of broadcast/cable transmitted programmes and legal recourse of receivers to enforce rights of reception)

1. The international framework and its transformation into national law
   a) Multilateral agreements
   aa) ITU convention and rules arising from it
   aaa) Audiovisual broadcast programmes
   (1) Prohibition of reception
   (2) Technical standards and import/operating regulations for receiver equipment
   (3) Tariffs for reception
   bbb) Direct-Broadcast Satellites
   – subdivided as above aaa)

         ccc) Cable television
             (1)   Principles of access to networks
             (2)   Technical standards and import/operating re-
                   gulations for receiver equipment
             (3)   Tariffs for access
     bb) Human rights convention and rules arising from them
         aaa) Audiovisual broadcast programmes
             (1)   Prohibition of reception
             (2)   Technical standards and import regulations for
                   receiver equipment
             (3)   Tariffs for reception
         bbb) Direct-Broadcast Satellites
             – subdivided as above aaa)
         ccc) Cable television
             – subdivided as above aaa)
  b) Bilateral agreements
     aa) Frame for bilateral agreements under multilateral rules
         aaa) Audiovisual broadcast programmes
         bbb) Direct-Broadcast Satellites
         ccc) Cable television
     bb) Rules provided by bilateral programmes
         aaa) Audiovisual broadcast programmes
             (1)   Technical standards and import regulations for
                   receiver equipment
             (2)   Tariffs
         bbb) Direct-Broadcast Satellites
             – subdivided as above aaa)
         ccc) Cable television
             – subdivided as above aaa)
  c) Transformation of international agreements on receiver's
      rights into national law (for broadcast, DBS and CATV
      programmes)
     aa) Power for transformation of rules into national law
     bb) Form and content of transformation
     cc) Jurisdiction for application of transformed rules
     dd) Practice of application
     ee) Judicial review or other legal recourse against regulatory
         decisions
  d) Summary: Scope of action left to reporting state under
      international law for regulation of relations between state

326

and receivers of broadcast/cable-transmitted programmes from abroad

2. National law independent of international framework (Regulations governing the *reception* of broadcast/cable transmitted programmes for reasons of public interest)
   a) Constitutional framework of audivisual media reception (Civil rights of receivers and their judicial review)
      aa) Audiovisual broadcast programmes
      bb) Direct-Broadcast Satellites
      cc) Cable television
   b) Power to regulate, legal technique of regulation
      – subdivided as above a)
   c) Content of regulations (Audiovisual broadcast, DBS and CATV)
      aa) Prohibition of reception/principles of access to networks
      bb) Technical standards, manufacturing and operating inter-dictions for receiver equipment
      cc) Reception tariffs

III. Legal relations between media companies and individuals, including personal claims against companies (Audiovisual broadcast, DBS and CATV)

1. International agreements and their transformation into national law
   a) Protection of privacy law; protection of honour; right to have a counter-statement published
   b) Copyright law
   c) Illicit advertising (individual claims)

2. Conflict law of the reporting state
   – subdivided as above 1.

3. National rules providing individual claims against programme companies and thus potential barriers to free transborder flow of media programmes
   – subdivided as above 1.

B. Establishment and activities of foreign programme companies/programme transmitting companies *on the territory of the RS*

I. International framework

   1. Establishment and operation of transmitter stations and cable networks
     a) Audiovisual broadcast programmes
     b) Direct-Broadcast Satellites (including participation in national satellite operating companies, operations of national satellite systems)
     c) Cable television (establishment and operation of cable networks)

   2. Establishment and activities of programme companies
     a) Multilateral agreements (e.g., EEC-treaty)
     aaa) Audiovisual broadcast programmes
     bbb) Direct-Broadcast Satellites
     ccc) Cable television
     b) Bilateral agreements (e.g., AFN, RFE)
     – subdivided as above a)

II. National framework
– subdivided as above I.

C. Regulation of the flow of media programmes transmitted from reporting state to other countries (legal relations between RS and programme companies transmitting to other countries)

  I. International framework and its transformation into national law

   1. ITU convention and rules arising from it
     a) Audiovisual broadcast programmes
     (rights of RS to transmit abroad)
     b) Direct-Broadcast Satellites
     (Orbital positions of RS)
     c) Cable television
     Access of domestic programmes to foreign cable systems)

   2. Other multilateral agreements
     – subdivided as above 1.

   3. Bilateral agreements
     – subdivided as above 1.

II. National law independent of international framework

1. Regulations governing the establishment and operation of transmitting facilities
    a) Constitutional framework
       aa) Audiovisual broadcast programmes
       bb) Direct-Broadcast Satellites
       cc) Cable networks
    b) Power to regulate, legal technique of regulation
       – subdivided as above a)
    c) Content of regulations
       aa) Principles of authorization
           aaa) Audiovisual broadcast programmes
           bbb) Direct-Broadcast Satellites
           ccc) Cable television
       bb) Rules governing the content of programmes
           – subdivided as above aa)
       cc) Other conditions of authorization, including tariffs
           – subdivided as above aa)

2. Regulations governing the production of programmes for abroad
    – subdivided as above 1.

Bibliography

Books

Adam Smith Institute: Omega Report – Communications Policy, 1984
Aitken, Jonathan: Officially Secret, 1971
Bakewell, Joan/Garnham, Nicholas: The New Priesthood – British Television Today, 1970
BBC External Services Publicity Unit: Voice for the World. The Work of the BBC External Services, 1982
Black, Peter: The Mirror in the Corner – People's Television, 1972
Briggs, Asa: The History of Broadcasting in the United Kingdom:
 – Vol. I: The Birth of Broadcasting, 1961
 – Vol. II: The Golden Age of Wireless, 1965
 – Vol. III: The War of Words, 1970
 – Vol. IV: Sound and Vision, 1979
 – Governing the BBC, 1979
British Broadcasting Corporation: Annual Review of BBC – Broadcasting Research Findings, No. 8, 1981/82, 1983
 – Annual Report and Handbook 1987, 1986
 – Annual Report and Handbook 1984, 1983
Bruce, Robert R./Cunard, Jeffrey P./Director, Mark D.: Country Report: United Kingdom, in: International Institute of Communications: Report of the Study of Telecommunications Structures. From Telecommunications to Electronic Services. A Global Spectrum of Definitions, Boundary Lines and Structures. Vol. 2, 1985
Coase, R.H.: British Broadcasting. A Study in Monopoly, 1950
Codding, George A. Jr./Rutkowski, Anthony M.: The International Telecommunication Union in a Changing World, 1982
Comedia Publishing Group/Local Radio Workshop: Capital – Local Radio & Private Profit, 1983
Cotterell, Leslie E.: Performance, 2nd ed., 1984
Council of Europe: Swindon Viewpoint – A Community Television Service, CCC/DC (76) 98, 1977
 – Directorate of Human Rights: Human Rights of Aliens in Europe, 1985
Dalfen, Charles M.: Principles Governing Direct Satellite Broadcasting, in: Manual on Space Law, Vol. I, 1979
Dickinson, Margaret/Street, Sarah: Cinema and State – The Film Industry and the British Government 1927-1984, 1985
Dietz, Adolf: Copyright Law in the European Community, 1978
van Dijk, P./van Hoof, G.J.H.: Theory and Practice of the European Convention on Human Rights, 1984
Drzemczewski, Andrew: European Human Rights Convention in Domestic Law, 1983
Engel, Christoph: The Position of Public Monopolies on Broadcasting Under the European Convention on Human Rights, in: Mestmäcker, Ernst-Joachim (ed.): The Law and Economics of Transborder Telecommunications: A Symposium, 1987
Frank, Götz, Völkerrechtliche Probleme des Satellitenrundfunks, in: Hans-Bredow-Institut: Internationales Handbuch für Rundfunk und Fernsehen 1986/87, 1986
Garnham, Nicholas: Structures of Television, rev. ed. 1978, reprinted 1980
Glasgow University Media Group:
 – Vol. I: Bad News, 1976
 – Vol. II: More Bad News, 1980

Grabitz, Eberhard (ed.): Kommentar zum EWG-Vertrag, May 1986

Hans-Bredow-Institut: Internationales Handbuch für Rundfunk und Fernsehen 1986/87, 1986

Harrison, Martin: TV News: Whose Bias?, 1985

Hennessy, Peter: Public Watchdogs and Executive Poodles, in: May, Annabelle/Rowan, Katheryn (ed.): Inside Information: British Government and the Media, 1982

Heuermann, Arnulf/Neumann, Karl-Heinz: Die Liberalisierung des britischen Telekommunikationsmarktes, 1985

Hewitt, Patricia: The Abuse of Power – Civil Liberties in the United Kingdom, 1982

Heyn, Jürgen: Partizipation und Lokalkommunikation in Großbritannien. Video, Fernsehen, Hörfunk und das Problem der Demokratisierung kommunaler Kommunikation, 1979

Hoffmann-Remy, Ulrich: Die Möglichkeiten der Grundrechtseinschränkung nach den Art. 8-11 Abs. 2 der Europäischen Menschenrechtskonvention, 49 Schriften zum Völkerrecht, 1976

Hollins, Timothy: Beyond Broadcasting: Into the Cable Age, 1984

Holloway, Kate: Modern Trends in Treaty Law, 1967

Hondius, Frits W.: International Control of Broadcasting Programs in Western Europe, in: McWhinney, Edward: The International Law of Communications, 1971

Hood, Stuart: A Survey of Television, 1967

Hughes, Patrick: British Broadcasting: Programmes and Power, 1981

Jasentuliyana, Nandasiri/Lee, Roy S.K. (ed.): Manual on Space Law, Vol. I-II, 1979

Jonscher, Charles: Telecommunications Liberalization in the United Kingdom, in: Snow, Marcellus S.: Telecommunications Regulation and Deregulation in Industrialized Democracies, 1986

Lambert, Stephen: Channel Four, 1982

Lewis, Peter M.: Community Television and Cable in Britain, 1978

Lewis, Philip (ed.): Gatley on Libel and Slander, 8th ed., 1981

Lincoln, Anthony: Landesbericht Großbritannien, in: Bullinger, Martin/Kübler, Friedrich (ed.): Rundfunkorganisation und Kommunikationsfreiheit, 1979

MacCabe, Colin/Stewart, Olivia (ed.): The BBC and Public Service Broadcasting, 1986

MacMillan, P.R.: Censorship and Public Morality, 1983

Mahle, Walter A.: Großbritannien – Ein Modell für die Bundesrepublik?, Arbeitsgemeinschaft für Kommunikationsforschung e.V. (ed.): Kommerzielles Fernsehen in der Medienkonkurrenz, Vol. I, 1984

Mansell, Gerard: Let Truth be Told – 50 Years of BBC External Broadcasting, 1982

McDonnell, James: Broadcasting Policy and the Challenge of Information Technology: The Case of British Cable Television, in: Mosco, Vincent (ed.): Policy Research in Telecommunications, 1984

Merkin, Robert/Williams, Karen: Competition Law: Antitrust Policy in the U.K. and the EEC, 1984

Mestmäcker, Ernst-Joachim: Europäisches Wettbewerbsrecht, 1974

– Medienkonzentration und Meinungsvielfalt, 1978

Mestmäcker, Ernst-Joachim/Schulze, Erich: Kommentar zum deutschen Urheberrecht, 1976 ff.

Michael, James: The Politics of Secrecy – Confidential Government and the Public Right to Know

Moorfoot, Rex: Television in the Eighties – The Total Equation, 1982

Munro, Colin R.: Television, Censorship and the Law, 1979

Nowotny, Burkhard: Rundfunk bürgernah – Regionalisierung, lokale Sender und Privatfunk in Großbritannien, 1982

O'Higgins, Paul: Cases and Materials on Civil Liberties, 1980

Paulu, Burton: Television and Radio in the United Kingdom, 1981

Phelps, Guy: Film Censorship, 1975

Quicke, Andrew: Tomorrow's Television – An Examination of British Broadcasting Past, Present and Future, 1976

Reiter, Hans-Peter: Die Struktur des britischen Rundfunks – Folgerungen für die Medienlandschaft der Bundesrepublik Deutschland, 1986

Robertson, Geoffrey/Nicol, Andrew G.L.: Media Law – The Rights of Journalists and Broadcasters, 1984

332

Roš, Mirko: Die unmittelbare Anwendbarkeit der europäischen Menschenrechtskonvention. Ein Beitrag zur Lehre der self-executing treaties. Schweizer Studien zum internationalen Recht, Vol. 38, 1984

Ross, Gordon: Television Jubilee – The Story of 25 Years of BBC Television, 1961

Schlesinger, Philip: Putting ›reality‹ together – BBC news, 1978

Schmid, Bernhard: Rang und Geltung der Europäischen Konvention zum Schutze der Menschenrechte und Grundfreiheiten vom 3. November 1950 in den Vertragsstaaten, 1984

Schulze, Erich: Rechtsprechung zum Urheberrecht; Entscheidungssammlung mit Anmerkungen, Vol. 2, 1987

Sendall, Bernard: Independent Television in Britain, Vol. 1: Origin and Foundation, 1946-62, 1982

Shulman, Milton: The Least Worst Television in the World, 1973

Sieghart, Paul: The International Law of Human Rights, 1983

Sigel, Beat: Über die Grundrechte, insbesondere die Pressefreiheit, in der Schweiz und in Großbritannien, Züricher Studien zum öffentlichen Recht, 1981

Silbermann, Alphons/Zahn, Ernest: Die Konzentration der Massenmedien und ihre Wirkungen, 1970

Silvey, Robert: Who's Listening? The Story of the BBC Audience Research, 1974

Simson, Werner von: Towards a Bill of Rights in Great Britain, in: Jürgen Schwarze/Wolfgang Graf Vitzhum (ed.): Grundrechtsschutz im nationalen und internationalen Recht, Werner von Simson zum 75. Geburtstag, 1983

Smith, Delbert D.: International Telecommunication Control, 1969

STAMM 1984: Presse- und Medienhandbuch, 37th ed., 1984

Street, Harry: Freedom, the Individual and the Law, 5th ed., 1982

Supperstone, Michael: Brownlie's Law of Public Order and National Security, 2nd ed., 1981

Sutherland, John: Offensive Literature – Decensorship in Britain 1960-1982, 1982

The Europe Yearbook 1985, A World Survey, Vol. I, 1985

The British Year Book of International Law 1984, 1985

Thomas, Howard: The Truth About Television, 1962

Tunstall, Jeremy: The Media in Britain, 1983

Veljanovski, C.G./Bishop, W.D.: Choice by Cable – The Economics of a New Era in Television, 1983

Wedell, E.G.: Broadcasting and Public Policy, 1968

Wilberforce, Lord: Die bürgerlichen Grundrechte des Einzelnen, Speech held before the Juristische Studiengesellschaft in Karlsruhe, 1966

Wintour, Charles: Pressures on the Press, 1972

Wyndham Goldie, Grace: Facing the Nation – Television and Politics 1936-1976, 1977

Yardley, D.C.M.: Introduction to British Constitutional Law, 6th ed., 1984

Law Journal Articles

Barendt, Eric: Freedom of Speech and Broadcasting, 8 Journal of Media Law & Practice, 1987, 91 ff.

Cameron, Peter: Censorship and the Video Recordings Act, 7 Journal of Media Law & Practice, 1986, 93 ff.

Cooke, John: Contempt and the Media, 7 Journal of Media Law & Practice, 1986, 2 ff.

Douzinas, Costas/McVeigh, Shaun/Warrington, Ronnie: It's all Greek to Me: Libel Law and the Freedom of the Press, 137 New Law Journal, 1987, 609 ff.

Duffy: English Law and the European Convention on Human Rights, 29 International and Comparative Law Quaterly, 1980, 585 ff.

Engel, Christoph: Das Völkerrecht des Telekommunikationsvorgangs, 49 RabelsZ, 1985, 90 ff.

Ford, Michael: Bringing the World to Your Door. The Role of British Telecom, 14 Intermedia No. 2, 1986, 40 ff.

Frazer, Tim: Unchanging Times: The Monopolies and Mergers Commission Report on the BBC and ITP, 7 European Competition Law Review, 1986, 96 ff.

Gibbons, Michael/Hartley, Jill/Evans, Janet/Metcalfe, Stan/ Simnett, Jonathan: Technology and Policy in Cable TV Development in the UK, 8 Telecommunications Policy, 1984, 223 ff.

Grant, Warren L.: In the Public Interest? The Disclosure of Confidential Information, 6 Journal of Media Law & Practice, 1985, 178 ff.

Hardman, David: Into the Future with EUTELSAT, 14 Intermedia No. 4/5, 1986, 52 ff.

Johnson, Peter: Competition, Copyright and the Public Interest, 7 Business Law Review 1986, 6 f.

Mestmäcker, Ernst-Joachim: Copyright in Community Law, 10 Journal of World Trade Law, 1976, Special Supplement No. 3

Millett, Timothy: Free Movement of Goods and Public Morality, 137 New Law Journal, 1987, 39 ff.

Mytton, Graham: Audience Research for International Broadcasting, 14 Intermedia No. 2, 1986, 35 ff.

N.A.: The Video Recordings Bill, 5 Journal of Media Law & Practice, 1984, 74 ff.

– TV Censorship – The IBA's Decision to ban MI5's Official Secrets, 6 Journal of Media Law and Practice, 1985, 205 f.

Paterson, Owen: The British Renaissance: An Assessment of Satellite Developments in the U.K., Satellite Communications (Jan. 1983), reprinted in: The Third Biennial Communications Law Symposium. International Satellite Television. Resource Manual, 1983, 80 ff.

Pelton, Joseph N.: INTELSAT: Global Telecommunications for the 21st Century, 14 Intermedia No. 4/5, 1986, 52 ff.

Robertson, Geoffrey: What Should the IBA Do?, 6 Journal of Media Law & Practice, 1985, 269 ff.

Schnurr, Lewis E.: Conduit – Content Convergence: Its Causes and Effects, 53 Telecommunication Journal IX, 1986, 537 ff.

Schwartz, Ivo E.: Broadcasting Without Frontiers in the European Community, 6 Journal of Media Law and Practice, 1985, 26 ff.

White, Harold M. Jr./Lauria, Rita: International Space Law and Direct Broadcast Satellites, 3 Space Communication and Broadcasting, 1985, 321 ff.

Williamson, John A.: Cable and DBS Industries in a State of Disarray, Telephony, May 27, 1985, 16 ff.

Government and Other Official Reports

British Standards Institution: Annual Report 1983-84, 1984

Broadcasting Committee: Report, Cmnd. 1951, 1923

– Report, Cmnd. 1753, 1962

Broadcasting Complaints Commission: Report 1987, 1987

Cabinet Office/Information Technology Advisory Panel: Report on Cable Systems, 1982

Defence Committee: First Report, Session 1982-83, The Handling of Press and Public Information During the Falklands Conflict, Vol. I, Report and Minutes of Proceedings, H.C. 17-I, 1982

Department of Trade and Industry: The Recording and Rental of Audio and Video Copyright Material, Cmnd. 9445, 1985

– United Kingdom Table of Radio Frequency Allocations, 1985

– Deregulation of the Radio Spectrum in the UK (study by CSP International), 1987

– Radio Regulatory Division: Annual Report 1985/86

– The Development of UK Communications Systems. Discussion Document, April 9, 1987

Greater London Council: Cabling in London: Report by the Economic Policy Group, 1982

Home Office: Report of the Committee on the Future of Broadcasting, Cmnd. 6753, 1977

– Broadcasting, Cmnd. 7294, 1978

– Report of the Committee on Obscenity and Film Censorship, Cmnd. 7772, 1979 (reprinted 1981)

– Direct Broadcasting by Satellite, 1981

– Report on the Inquiry into Cable Expansion and Broadcasting Policy, Cmnd. 8679, 1982

- Report of the Committee on Financing the BBC, Cmnd. 9824, 1986
- Radio: Choices and Opportunities, Cmnd. 92, 1987
- Subscription Television, Final Report (study by Booz Allen and Hamilton International Ltd.), 1987

Home Office/Department of Industry: The Development of Cable Systems and Services, Cmnd. 8866, 1983

House of Commons Defense Committee: 3rd Report, 1979-80, The D-Notice System, HC 773.

Interception of Communications Act, 1985, Chapter 56: Report of the Commission for 1986, Cmnd. 108, 1987

Kommission der Europäischen Gemeinschaften: Zwischenbericht über Realität und Tendenzen des Fernsehens in Europa: Perspektiven und Optionen, Kom (83) 229 endg., 1983

Monopolies and Mergers Commission: Films – A Report on the Supply of Films for Exhibition in Cinemas, Cmnd. 8858, 1983
- The British Broadcasting Corporation and Independent Television Publications Ltd. A report on the policies and practices of the British Broadcasting Corporation and Independent Television Publications Limited of limiting the publication by others of advance programme information and of not granting licences which would allow others to publish such information beyond certain specified periods, Cmnd. 9614, 1985

Office of Fair Trading: A Report by the Director General of Fair Trading on an Investigation Under Section 3 of the Competition Act 1980, Thames Television Ltd., 1984

Report of the Independent Review of the Radio Spectrum (30-960 MHz), Cmnd. 9000, 1983

Royal Commission on the Press: Final Report 1977, Cmnd. 6810, 1977
- Final Report, Appendices, Cmnd. 6810-1, 1977

Other Sources

British Board of Film Classification: Annual Report and Accounts for 1985, 1986

British Broadcasting Corporation: Choices and Opportunities: The BBC's Response to the Radio Green Paper, 1987

Cable Authority: Guidance to Franchise Applicants, March 1985
- Licensing of Cable Diffusion Services – Notes for the Guidance of Prospective Licensees, May 1985
- Cable Programme Services: Inclusion of Feature Films, November 1985
- Annual Report and Accounts, 1986
- Annual Report and Accounts 1986-87, 1987

Channel Four Television Company Limited: Report and Accounts for the Year Ended 31st March 1987, 1987

Home Office: Cable – Interim Licensing of Pilot Projects: Guidance Note, July 1983

Howard, George: The BBC, Educational Broadcasting and the Future, Speech given at Leeds Polytechnic, March 3, 1981 (published by the BBC)

Independent Broadcasting Authority: Agreement for Appointment of Television Programme Contractor (Ulster Television Limited), Dec. 31st, 1981
- Enhanced C-Mac – Satellite Television with the Future in Mind, 1983
- Agreement for Appointment of Programme Contractor for Local Sound Broadcasts, Proof June 1984
- Annual Report & Accounts 1984-85, 1985
- Independent Television and Radio – A Pocket Guide, 1985
- Television Programme Guidelines, April 1985
- Notes for Reference – British and Overseas Acquired Material on Independent Television, August 1985
- IBA Evidence to the Committee on Financing the BBC, 1985
- Guidance Notes for Organizations Interested in the Provision of DBS Services, Press Release, Sept. 3, 1985

- Annual Report & Accounts 1985-86, 1986
- The IBA's View – The Future of UK Independent Radio, June 1987

Independent Television Companies Association: Financing Broadcasting, 1985

OFTEL: A Guide to the Office of Telecommunications, 1985
- DIEL – The Advisory Committee on Telecommunications for Disabled and Elderly People, October 1985
- BACT – The Advisory Committee on Telecommunications for Small Businesses, December 1986
- PTO Contract Terms and Conditions – A Consultative Document, 1987

Post Office: Telecommunications – Evidence to the Government Enquiry into the Future of Broadcasting, 1974

Press Council: Guidance on Procedure for Complainants, Press Council Leaflet 109, 1984
- The Press and the People, 33rd Annual Report, 1986